I TATTI STUDIES IN
ITALIAN RENAISSANCE HISTORY

Published in collaboration with I Tatti
The Harvard University Center for Italian Renaissance Studies
Florence, Italy

GENERAL EDITOR
Nicholas Terpstra

LOVE AND SEX IN THE TIME OF PLAGUE

A Decameron Renaissance

GUIDO RUGGIERO

Harvard University Press

Cambridge, Massachusetts

London, England

2021

First printing

Library of Congress Cataloging-in-Publication Data

Names: Ruggiero, Guido, 1944– author.
Title: Love and sex in the time of plague : a Decameron renaissance /
    Guido Ruggiero.
Other titles: I Tatti studies in Italian Renaissance history.
Description: Cambridge, Massachusetts : Harvard University Press, 2021. |
    Series: I Tatti studies in Italian renaissance history | Includes
    bibliographical references and index.
Identifiers: LCCN 2020047004 | ISBN 9780674257825 (cloth)
Subjects: LCSH: Boccaccio, Giovanni, 1313–1375. Decamerone—Criticism and
    interpretation. | Love in literature. | Sex in literature. |
    Renaissance.
Classification: LCC PQ4293.L72 R84 2021 | DDC 853/.1—dc23
LC record available at https://lccn.loc.gov/2020047004

For a fictional savior and a real one:
Alibech and Laura

CONTENTS

LOVE AND SEX
IN THE TIME OF PLAGUE

Listening to the *Decameron*

An Introduction

*T*he year 1348 shocked the world, or at least the world as viewed from the West; for it was the year that an apparently new plague that would become known as the Black Death struck Europe, carrying off from one-half to two-thirds of its population. Indeed, it is still remembered today as one of the greatest disasters of history. But, at the time, it seemed to confirm widely shared apocalyptic visions that the end of time was nigh. And with good reason, for the tremendous dying off had left the survivors wandering in the suddenly empty streets of once thriving towns and in the countryside contemplating abandoned fields and villages with fear about what further calamities an angry and punishing God had in store for a sinning humanity.

Giovanni Boccaccio claimed that in response to that deeply disturbing disaster he wrote the *Decameron,* one of the greatest and best-known works of Western literature. Although he had begun collecting and rewriting the one hundred tales that make up the heart of his masterpiece before the plague struck and continued revising them afterward, he maintained that he had decided to write it in order to help his fellow Florentines weather the emotional stress of the staggering loss and devastation of the Black Death. His tales, he promised, would provide a pleasant diversion from the cruel reality of those empty streets and vacant palaces that literally haunted their once flourishing city and his imagination.

Significantly, one of the themes of those stories that he asserted would be most useful in doing so was love: a crucial emotion, key to recovering normal family life and community after that destruction. But he promised that love could offer something more valuable yet—for it was an emotion that he noted was especially important for uplifting the spirit of the women who had suffered so much, both from the plague and from the unhappy arranged and loveless marriages and unjustly restricted life they led. In sum, Boccaccio declared that the healing power of love in the time of the plague was his motive for retelling the tales of the *Decameron* and an ideal antidote for the material and emotional disaster that had struck his world.

Yet where Boccaccio saw love, he also saw sex. For the two were deeply intertwined in the culture and life of the day for him and his compatriots. And love both ideally and regularly led to shared sexual pleasures, at least in the tales of the *Decameron*. The reverse, unsurprisingly, was not always the case. Sex did not necessary lead to or even involve love, and therein lay a series of problems moral, practical, and emotional. Problems that at first might seem to have been quite similar to problems faced today, but Boccaccio's second half of the fourteenth century was not the modern world, and the way those problems were lived and felt at the time opens up revealing vistas on a complex of values and emotions that were often decidedly different. And this was the case even if they were in many ways foundational for our own values and emotions.

To return to a metaphor that I have used before, that world of love and sex at the time of the plague in Italy was rather like the world that Alice encountered when she went through the looking glass in *Alice in Wonderland*. People, things, and practices seemed familiar, but, tellingly, nothing worked there in quite the same way as it did before she entered her disorienting wonderland. Our own wonderland of Boccaccio's *Decameron* reads in much the same way, for at the same time that it often seems not quite right and disorienting, as we explore it in this book, its historical settings and textures offer fascinating comments

and critiques both positive and negative on sex and love in the time of
the plague and perhaps today as well as we respond to the dislocations
and traumas of a modern pandemic.

In Florence in Boccaccio's day, for example, it was recognized
and feared that the passions and practices associated with love and
courting slid all too easily into the pleasures and myriad dangers of
sexual intercourse, formally labeled illicit. Adultery and youthful premarital sex, in fact, were the assumed ideal locus of love, at least in the
literary traditions of courtly love, the *dolce stil nuovo,* and the poetry of
noted and much-imitated writers like Dante and Petrarch. In contrast,
love in marriage, both in literature and practice, was a relatively unlikely proposition. For, while courting provided an important measure
of status and setting for social interaction, the emotional love that was
seen as developing in that context was viewed as too driven by youthful
passions and too quickly passing to be used as the base for the carefully
planned family alliances that were held to be at the heart of successful
marriages—marriages that served greater family goals and provided the
stable disciplinary base for an ordered society, socially and sexually.

Love was simply too quick, too fleeting, and too irrational an emotion to forge a long-term relationship like marriage. And, in turn, marriage, as a binding relationship entailing a series of obligations, was
literally too constraining and unfree to allow one to follow one's desires and freely choose a lover, while true love was nothing if not free.
In many ways, it was that freedom to love that made it an emotion both
attractive and dangerous—deeply dangerous and often far distant from
the modern world of Valentine cards or saccharine love stories. Yet,
as we shall see, Boccaccio's tales suggestively break free from this vision of the correct order of things. And anticipating that thesis of this
book, they broke free to attempt to "civilize" the emotions associated
with love and sex, to make them less dangerous for the newly reordered
urban civil society that was to be rebuilt following the devastation of
the plague.

Having said that, however, this is not really a book about Boccaccio
or why he wrote the *Decameron.* For, well beyond considering Boccaccio's intent in writing it and his vision of love and sex, it is a reading of
that fascinating and still evocative work, attempting to imagine how
that masterpiece was heard in its day and how it might be heard anew

today from a historical perspective.[1] Much like a great symphony—a human symphony of the first Rinascimento[2]—the *Decameron* is even more telling for me, this study, and Boccaccio's contemporaries, because it offers a rich entry into how they heard its many riffs on love: now laughing, now tragic; sometimes humble, often aristocratic; frequently realistic, and from time to time playfully whimsical. As a result, my goal in retelling these tales in their historical setting marries the interests of the literary critic in reopening (and ideally reevoking) the excitement of great tales and of the historian in rediscovering the historical texture of suggestive texts to offer hopefully new insights and textual pleasures.

For the *Decameron,* with its one hundred tales told over ten days by Boccaccio's fictional group of young aristocrats, sang of the life of a city, Florence, that was rapidly developing into one of the most important and richest economically and culturally in what would become Europe. And thus it was encountered there and elsewhere in the urban world of northern Italy, I would suggest, with a shock of recognition that the life of which it sang had not only changed profoundly but was continuing to change rapidly in the wake of the plague. Merchants, bankers, lawyers, secular scholars, and the humbler artisans of their world had come to matter—the *popolo* (literally the people) as they styled themselves. In turn, the old landed nobility and their ways no longer were the stuff of the tales that mattered there, except perhaps as lessons on an outdated past—lessons to which the *Decameron* regularly returned.[3]

The Shared Culture of the *Decameron*

In this book, then, I reread a great and much-discussed text melding both the innovations of literary criticism and recent historical work based largely on archival research to imagine how the symphony of life that is the *Decameron* was heard (and read) by contemporaries and what that says about love and sexual relations as they were imagined, lived, and felt in the shared culture of the day. Evidently, reconstructing that cultural world is no easy matter. Fortunately, however, massive scholarship on the period over the last two generations has provided a great deal of information on the history of the period in Florence and its cultural world, along with that of the cities of northern Italy.[4] Integrating this in the readings that follow hopefully will add new depth and new perspectives. In turn, unlike more traditional literary studies, this book is less concerned with the literary antecedents of the *Decameron*— extensively studied by others[5]—which allows it to focus on how its tales were heard, read, and imagined at the time of the plague.

And while more traditional political and military history plays a role in the analysis that follows, a critical role at times, it is the culture of the day and the way everyday people lived life and imagined it that is central for hearing the *Decameron* as it played in its day. Essentially, then, this is a historical study of the shared culture of the day from the perspective of the *Decameron* and in turn the *Decameron* itself from that perspective; in a way, then, it is a microhistory of that culture built upon a literary text. This way of considering the culture of the day obviously has its limits, but if we conceive of it as a generally shared series of discourses on the way the world and society worked and had meaning at the time, it is a useful, and I would argue a necessary, conceptual tool for understanding how a text was received—in this case, how the *Decameron*'s tales were received, lived, and felt in their day.[6]

Of course, fine-tuning is necessary because, as a series of shared discourses, it was not monolithic or strictly structured but rather fluid and rife with contradiction and conflict. Thus one needs to consider how a text would work in that culture and how its themes might play when they clashed at times with aspects of culture that were not widely shared or how various groups of readers might respond to aspects of that primary culture differently in particular moments and contexts. Thus, for example, while arranged marriage rather than marriage for love might be accepted as the norm in the shared culture of the day at virtually all social levels, exceptions might well ring true. And they are, in fact, a motif that the *Decameron* returns to repeatedly. Or again, adultery was generally frowned on and officially a crime in the shared culture of the fourteenth century, striking as it did a troubling note for husbands, patriarchs, and, too often overlooked, for wives as well. Yet, at the same time, often both literary tradition and the *Decameron* portrayed such illicit passions as the epitome of uplifting desire when true love was involved. But it is exactly in dealing with such lacks of a neat fit between the shared culture of the day and what a text like the *Decameron* has to say that we find the most revealing historical and literary discoveries.

Trying to discover what Boccaccio intended to say in a work as diverse as the *Decameron* is equally problematic, for, as literary critics have been pointing out for some time now, the author is dead. Luckily, I would suggest in Boccaccio's case, for he has been thoughtfully and with great skill manhandled (and woman-handled as well) across the last century and into this one by creative readings. As a misogynist, a would-be aristocrat, a strict moralist with a negative vision of his peers and his day (and worse), a once apparently laughing lover of women and his world has been brought low, with impressive scholarship and convincing acumen. In fact, the wide range of interpretations of the man and what he intended his most famous work to say seem clearly a direct result of the impossibility of knowing the mind of an author dead almost seven hundred years or anticipating that he would be consistent in his retelling of one hundred tales using the voices of ten different narrators or that he had any interest in being consistent. And, I would add, it is also a reminder of the ways in which an extremely rich and multivocal text lives on in different cultures and societies with changing meanings and a life of its own—a tribute to the creativity of critics, authors, and texts themselves.[7]

In the end, then, I should confess right from the start that while I make no claims to offer the final correct judgment, I tend to think of Boccaccio, at least when he was writing the *Decameron,* more as a man who thought of himself as a smiling lover of women and humanity with all its foibles and sins. No feminist, clearly, he seems to have portrayed his women characters often with unusual attention and sympathy, *albeit with significant exceptions,* and obviously without being able to escape many of the stereotypes of his day. Still, the women of his *Decameron* often seem to have escaped the status of the stereotypic love objects of his earlier rather courtly writing influenced by the *dolce stil nuovo* and conventions of courtly love, even if the frame tale that surrounds the tales themselves still evokes those conventions. It seems, however, that his vision continued to evolve after the *Decameron,* for, as he grew older (perhaps under the influence of his friendship with Petrarch and the heavily classical turn of Florentine and Italian high culture in his later years), it appears that he became much more traditional and closed in his thinking about women, love, and life in general.

Nonetheless, with no lack of reservations, in this study I would like to try to resurrect this Boccaccio from his death as an author in two ways: first, as Boccaccio-writer (and rewriter) and then as Boccaccio-lover-character in his own work. One of the most interesting and revealing things about the novella tradition in which Boccaccio wrote the *Decameron* is that it tended to require stories that emphasized action and deeds over reflection or close consideration of emotional states or decision making—there are no Hamlets or Montaignes in the genre. Thus, when the action stops or characters explain their action with detail that breaks the flow of the narrative, an argument can be made that Boccaccio-writer is speaking to his audience—often explaining something that needs to be explained because it is not necessarily obvious or a shared way of seeing what is going on in the tale. In essence, the reader often is being offered Boccaccio-author/writer's particular position in the ongoing discourses of the shared culture of his day.

Adultery, for example, regularly requires this treatment in the *Decameron,* although it is so frequently considered that the discussion can become quite formulaic—dull husbands, overaged husbands, nonfunctioning husbands, and foolishly pious husbands flash by almost too quickly. But they still serve their purpose (at least one of their purposes): to make the formally illicit and troubling sin of adultery acceptable and adulterers attractive rather than threatening characters. As we shall see, violence, especially against women, also entails more detailed breaks in the action to explain and defend the actions of characters. At a deeper level, with a historical understanding of what the shared culture of the day would accept as correct, attractive, or even simply understandable, when the action deviates from those invisible but very real boundaries in what can be said or told, the way the action develops again provides strong indications of the writer's intent. Powerful men breaking down in tears (a negative display of emotion that was viewed as highly untoward at the time) or young women not breaking down in tears in the face of tragedy (a highly unexpected lack of emotion in a woman) both fly by quickly for a modern reader. But they are responses that speak worlds to contemporary readers about how the author is portraying a character and what he is saying about him or her. Such structuring of the action of a tale by Boccaccio-author gives us frequent insight into what he is trying to lead his contemporaries to hear in that particular tale at that particular moment, and, thus, it allows us to hypothesize what he was thinking in that context as well, even if I would

argue that he is quite capable of arguing other and at times contradictory positions in other tales.

Boccaccio, however, is a writer who from time to time also stops
his narrative and seems anxious to tell us what he thinks, especially
about love and sexual desire. Obviously, such apparently honest moments of self-revelation must be treated with caution. Still, they are revealing for what we might label Boccaccio-character—the self-portrayal
that Boccaccio provides for his reader as regularly an older man with
graying hair (actually, he notes that it is white) who remains a true lover
of women, appreciating them and their beauty but also desiring them
himself. Indeed, in Boccaccio-character, love and sexual desire slide together again in suggestive ways, much as they do in the tales themselves.
And it is clear that he defends this and Boccaccio-character as positive
and as the normal, correct order of things and appears to assume that
this presents him as an attractive character. Clearly, it would be unwise
to presume that Boccaccio-character and Boccaccio-writer are one and
the same, but each in their own way add much to how we understand
what Boccaccio was saying about love and sex in the *Decameron*.

Turning to the *Decameron* itself, for all its humor and playfulness, as
we have seen, its symphony of life starts out on a dirge-like note of death;
for, in 1348, the year it was supposedly composed, as noted earlier, the
world seemed clearly to be coming to an end. And finally at that. For the
deeply religious world of the day had long been threatened by the various
godly destructions promised by the Bible, church fathers, numerous medieval theologians and prophets, and fire-breathing preachers. But what
made that dark cloud of fear that had long hung over the Christian world
have greater weight at the time was the way a series of signs of the end of
time seemed to have been piling up in recent days with menace. Indeed, the
world had changed so drastically and disconcertingly in the burgeoning
cities of Italy in the thirteenth and first half of the fourteenth century that
such promises of imminent destruction and apocalypse had progressively
gained greater purchase, with competing prophets and heretical orders,
not to mention popes and other mainstream church leaders, heralding
the last days, even if there was considerable debate about what those last
days would be like and how imminent they might be.

In that environment, what seemed to be the ultimate warning, heralding the end, was the first wave of the plague that year, 1348, which,

according to modern estimates, wiped out in a few devastating months at least half the population of Europe and may well have reduced the population of Florence from over 100,000 souls to fewer than 40,000. Forty thousand survivors wandering among the empty homes and palaces of the city and the mass graves where family, friends, and neighbors had been hurriedly interred with no time for customary ceremony or grieving. To many, the world seemed to be in the hands of the cruel and vengeful God of the Old Testament, punishing humanity once again as He had done with the destruction of Sodom and Gomorrah and, before that, the Flood. And this seemed to promise that the worst was yet to come, and soon.

The two most popular threatening futures at the time focused on the apparently more well-known vision of the return of Christ and His Last Judgment—a frightening prospect that nonetheless offered the hope of eternal pleasures for the saved and the end of a corrupt and sinning world. Less familiar today, but perhaps having more purchase at the time in Florence and the cities of northern Italy, was not the complete end of time but the end of one time and the beginning of a new one when Christ and His Church would be replaced by the rule of the last person of the Trinity, the Holy Spirit. This vision held that the Trinitarian nature of the Christian God meant that human history would progress through three radically different ages or dispensations dominated progressively by each facet of the deity that would bring humanity ever closer to God and the final Last Judgment.

The first age had been that of God the Father, a wrathful God whose rule was laid out in the Old Testament. That age had ended with the coming of His Son, Christ, who, with his self-sacrifice and loving death on the Cross, inaugurated a new and dramatically different dispensation: an age of love between God and humanity, ruled over by the Christian Church and the New Testament. Everything was overthrown in that profound revolution—humanity moved from being damned by a wrathful God to being saved by a loving God; indeed, it seemed as if God Himself had changed, His most basic relationship with humanity moving from wrath to love. Could we say that even God's emotions had changed and as a result changed the essential reality of His created world? A strange idea easily refuted by theologians, but in a way the transcendental history of Christianity might be, and for some, was imagined as turning on the great timeline of even God's changing emotional relationship with humanity and the impact of Christ's love on the very nature of His creation. And, in a way, this could even be imagined as having a sexual dimension with Mary as God's mate (and mother) impregnated by the Holy Spirit to give birth to Christ and a new dispensation—a moment that, in fact, fascinated Renaissance artists with their ubiquitous imaginative representations of that moment when Mary became the future virgin mother of God as Man.

Be that as it may, the next and last age, it was believed, would come after a period of turmoil, like that which Italy seemed to be undergoing. Christ and His Church would be destroyed, and a new, last age would begin under the control of the last person of the Trinity, the Holy Spirit. There was disagreement about exactly what that last age would be like, but there was a general agreement that it would be dramatically different. Most importantly, humanity would have a more directly spiritual and loving relationship with God—love, again, was key. And that love would drive a direct spiritual connection with the Holy Spirit where the discipline of the Church would be no longer necessary. Many argued that property would disappear, and perhaps even human bodies, to make it possible to live a loving life of pure spirituality, unlinked from carnal sexual desire. But the contested details of that last age need not detain us for the moment, although, as we shall see, they do play a role in the *Decameron*. Suffice it to say for now that the dramatic mortality of the plague seemed rife with threat and, at the same time, promise, at least for those many who believed that it heralded a new, last age or alternately the Last Judgment itself.

Given the tremendous mortality and the perceived disruptions of the very social fabric of the day, however, many contemporaries focused on fear and threat rather than promise. And the opening of the *Decameron* plays those notes with deep apprehension. Listen to these famous lines: "Thus I say that there had already passed 1348 years from the fruit-bearing (*fruttifero*) incarnation of the Son of God when in the illustrious city of Florence, more beautiful than any other Italian city there struck the deadly plague: which either because of celestial forces or because of our evil deeds in order to correct us a *justly irate God struck down humanity*."[8] In the face of this mortality that indiscriminately struck down rich and poor, young and old, pious and the worse sinner, "reverence for the laws, whether divine or human, virtually disappeared as those responsible for them were like others dead or lying sick without their lieutenants. . . . Thus each person was left free to behave as they pleased."[9] Law, government, and the very social order that stood behind and upheld civil society seemed to have been destroyed, much as promised by those expecting a new last age of the Holy Spirit.

The dirge continued with yet darker notes as Boccaccio describes how many tried to flee "the wrath of God punishing the evil ways of humanity," fleeing "their city, their homes, their places and their relatives" but to little avail as the plague struck everywhere and everyone.[10] There was no escaping the cataclysm. Still worse was the total breakdown of the social order of the city: "Ignoring the fact that fellow citizens abandoned each other and virtually no neighbor came to the aid of their neighbor and relatives rarely or never visited their relatives. . . . [what was worse] was that men and women were so stricken by fear that brothers abandoned their brothers and uncles their nephews and sisters their brothers and often wives their husbands, and the worst thing of all is almost unbelievable, the fathers and mothers their own children."[11] Death and the dissolution of the moral, social, and civic order that made Florence and Christian society possible, especially its familial base, seemed indeed to herald the end of an age and yet at the same time perhaps promise a new age of love. Strange days indeed. Strange days that we have largely forgotten, even as the *Decameron* is haunted by them and has the power to make them live again for the reader who listens.[12]

The *Decameron* and Its Frame Story

These, then, were the opening dark notes of the *Decameron*, part of a frame story that Boccaccio used to situate the one hundred tales (*novelle*) that make up the heart of his masterpiece. This frame story, in a form of metafiction narrated by Boccaccio-author,[13] after providing a striking account of the devastation of the plague (which we have merely sampled), segues into an account of how an idealized group of youths met in a Florentine church, Santa Maria Novella, as the plague was winding down. Seven young women from upper-class families there, discussing the devastation of the plague and how to deal with its terror and disruption,

came to the conclusion that it might be best to abandon the city and retire to the nearby countryside to try to live a more pleasurable and carefree life less overwhelmed by mourning and fear. As they were considering this, and worrying about its propriety, they spied three young men
entering the church who were friends and apparently more than that for
a couple of the women. Eventually, after concerns about protecting repu-
tations and morality were worked through, the group decided it was wise
and morally unobjectionable to retire together (as a *brigata*) to the hills
above Florence to escape the devastation of the plague.

In fact, Boccaccio-author assures his listeners, and will do so periodically throughout the frame story, that this group would maintain
traditional moral standards and do nothing that would be considered
incorrect in their rural retreat—the promised setting of the frame, then,
is to be morally correct and chaste, at least in appearance. Yet the banter
of the *brigata* leaves room for doubts, adding to the fascination and con-
troversy of the frame story, and, at the same time, suggesting that even
in that ideal world of love and courtship, sex was expected to follow on
the heels of true love. Indeed, Boccaccio seems to fuel such speculations
by claiming to observe the necessities of honor by not giving the real
names of the group to protect their reputation from those who might
suspect misbehavior. Rather, he gives each member a pseudonym that
he suggests has deeper meaning, cleverly augmenting the uncertainty
about these characters and how the frame story should be read—an uncertainty that has become a virtual industry for critics.

Without entering into those discussions for the moment, he names
the seven women: Pampinea, Fiammetta, Filomena, Emilia, Lauretta,
Neifile, and Elissa; and the three men: Panfilo, Filostrato, and Dioneo.
Many of these names had been used in his earlier works on love and / or
had associations with Greek words that have further fueled speculation
about the storytellers and their motives for telling specific stories. And
while these debates are interesting, they are somewhat less significant
for our interest in analyzing how the tales they told would have been
heard and understood at the time. Thus, although from time to time
we will consider the implied motives of the storytellers, on the whole
those issues are of less concern in what follows.

So the *brigata* retire to the hills above Florence to a villa setting
that the frame story sets out carefully in all its aristocratic and rural

splendor with helpful servants, gracious gardens, and a peaceful lush atmosphere that breathes escape, tranquility, and safety from the ravages that continue below in the city. In sum, in the frame story, a disturbing and troubling world beset by plague has turned safely elegant, aristocratic, and idyllic, apparently a rural utopian-like fantasy realm of peace and play far distant from the apocalyptic reality of their city.

But it is less rural than it might at first appear, and in a way it seems more like a return to the highest ideals of the old preplague urban order played out in a fantasy of a perfect countryside. Ordered, elegant, and eminently civil, there are no farmers, villains, or rural characters in sight, not even a pastoral shepherd or a peasant girl with a water jug on her head. Instead, we are in elegant rooms or gracefully ordered roomlike gardens, carefully organized (amazingly mosquito-free, if one knows the hills above Florence), where nature is tamed and civilized in the sense of remade into the ideal of urban civility in a fantasy rural setting.

Once the *brigata* has settled in and tasted the comfort and order of the place—once again its urban civility—they gather together to discuss what they should do to pass their time in an honest and pleasant way. Very much in the context of the aristocratic ideals of the day, they lean toward playing games that test their cleverness and manners and eventually settle on a storytelling contest, where every day each person will tell a tale or novella that they find particularly interesting or diverting. As the name "novella" implies, these tales at their best related something novel or new or that induced wonder or curiosity to fascinate listeners (and readers) and revealed the superiority of their particular narrator. To level the playing field, each day after the first, a king or queen selected in turn from the *brigata* sets the theme for the tales to be told, thus requiring that each narrator present a similar tale each day with the same constraints on the subject.

Significantly, after the first day, the character Dioneo asks for and is given license to not have to follow the day's theme and also to speak last. As a result, his personality, as a rather irreverent character who seems to be always pushing the limits of the group in terms of morality, especially sexual, is quickly established along with his often blasphemous sense of humor. Essentially, he has the group's permission to press and question their values and those of the tales' listeners as well, which makes his tales often the most challenging, boundary testing, and imaginative and allows a more irreverent reality to leak into the frame story and the tales as well.

So the tales were related in a playful competition, a competition that no one officially won in the end, aside from perhaps Boccaccio and his readers over the centuries. For although most of the tales were actually older stories that he recrafted and placed in the mouths of his narrators, regularly with significant variations both in tone and content, they presented a very different world from that of the frame story. Thus, while the frame involved unusually refined and mannered upper-class youths in a utopian setting that masked the realities of the plague that raged in the real world beyond their fantasy retreat, the tales of the *brigata* sang of their contemporary urban world as well as earlier times that always seemed to reflect back on their day—in sum, they played the notes of a symphony of life (and love and sex) as it was lived and understood in mid-fourteenth-century Florence at the time of the plague.

And that world, as noted earlier, was one of such rapid and ongoing change that the plague could be and was seen as a sign of the end of an age or perhaps even the end of time itself. Such spiritual forebodings had gained additional purchase and weight because the social, political, and economic changes of the last century had radically transformed Florence and the north of Italy well before the plague struck. Its burgeoning cities, flourishing economies, exploding governments and bureaucracies, social upheavals, and rapidly evolving urban culture had deeply undermined traditional ways of understanding the world and life and, in turn, love and sex and the emotions associated with both. In many deeply significant ways, this land littered with rich cities and new non-noble elites had become strikingly different from the rest of the West—excitingly and troublingly different. And Boccaccio's Florence was at the forefront of those changes, for better and worse.

The Historical World of the *Decameron*

To quickly reprise a story too complex and too vast to cover in detail in this introduction,[14] Florence was a relative latecomer to the rapid and disorienting growth of the cities in the north of Italy in the High Middle Ages. But, in the thirteenth century, it took advantage of the ongoing battles between popes and emperors to ally with the papacy and to become the leading bankers of the Church. In that capacity, Florence developed a Western European network of commercial and financial contacts that allowed the city to not only win great wealth handling papal revenues (siphoning off significant profits in the process) but also to set up a commercial empire that spanned Europe, producing and selling luxury cloth, one of the primary motors of its economy. As a result, Florence, which had once been a quiet backwater on a curve of the hardly navigable Arno River, had literally exploded across the thirteenth century, with its population jumping from about 40,000 souls early in that century to close to 100,000 in 1300. And, in the process, it was rapidly becoming one of the richest and most powerful cities not just in Italy but in the West.

Although Florence's growth was more rapid than that of most of the other cities of northern Italy, it shared with the most prosperous a much more vital and diverse economic base than that found elsewhere in Europe. In those Italian cities, trade, primarily driven by luxury goods like high-quality cloth, along with spices imported from the East; banking, primarily driven by papal banking and new methods of extending credit that avoided or ignored the Church's prohibition on usury; and relatively efficient urban governments that promoted both made them powerful engines of wealth production. In this they were decidedly different from the few larger cities of northern Europe that existed primarily as administrative centers for the Church or kings and princes.

The much more articulated and invasive governments of these Italian urban centers, in turn, aggressively attempted to regulate a local economy and the artisan guilds that produced the luxury products that they traded and much of the basic material needs of an increasingly large and demanding urban population. At the same time, they also developed a broader European reach to attempt to control larger markets and win profits well beyond the north of Italy. In addition, more assertive exploitation of rural labor and rural agricultural production helped make it possible to sustain a greater concentration of the population in urban centers. The result of all this was that relatively rapidly these cities of northern Italy began to collect a portion of the wealth from not just their hinterlands or the larger territories they conquered or subdued but also from much of the rest of the West. In a way, speaking very broadly, much as in the eighteenth century Paris drew a significant portion of the wealth of Europe into one city, and London in the nineteenth century pooled the wealth of its world-spanning empire to do the same, the cities of northern Italy drew the wealth of the Mediterranean and a developing Europe to support their impressive growth and rapid social and cultural change.

Perhaps the most significant consequence of this, beyond the great riches that flowed into the most successful cities of Italy, was the way these large cities and their complex economies changed dramatically the social world of their day. For while nobles and clerics remained the leaders in the rest of Europe, with kings and princes at once both challenging their dominance and relying on it, in most of the cities of northern Italy, nobles had lost power to the urban populace who had taken control of government, usually violently, and in the process had hamstrung them with restrictions or simply outlawed them in city after city from the mid-thirteenth century. In Florence, in fact, being labeled a noble or a magnate (a name legally associated there with the old nobility, although not all magnates were actually nobles) was seen as highly negative and indeed a serious legal and economic handicap, as we shall see reflected in the *Decameron*.

Tellingly, when nobles are presented more positively in its tales, usually they are not Italian or are presented in some safely distant past. In sum, noble status was a questionable attribute in the streets of Florence, and the cities of northern Italy more generally, and for those there who heard the *Decameron*'s tales. But, of course, in the complex and contested ways of such epochal social changes, that was not always or everywhere the case. And, significantly, in most of the rest of Europe, even as nobles had their detractors, the nobility continued to command power and respect as those who were on top of society and belonged there by natural right in the God-given order of things. In theory, in the cities of northern Italy, however, the new leaders of the society, the economy, and the government who replaced the old nobility were the people themselves, usually called, as noted earlier, *il popolo*, the people.

Il popolo was a heterogeneous group comprised of most of the adult male population that lived and worked in the city. The marginal poor, new immigrants, and often old nobles were excluded. Politically, women and children were excluded as well. What this meant in most cities was that most members of the *popolo* were guild members. These guildsmen were not just artisans, however, as most professions, including bankers, merchants, lawyers, and luxury cloth producers, were organized into guilds. In theory at least, guilds controlled the production and sale of goods, the workers at all levels of the city, as well as the government and much of the ordering of civic life. But, of course, guilds and a *popolo* that included everyone from bankers to bakers and butchers was too variegated a group to rule effectively or to identify who really mattered economically and socially in this much more diverse and socially articulated society.

In reality, in that very diversity lay one of the most pressing uncertainties of late thirteenth- and fourteenth-century life in Florence and elsewhere in the urban centers of Italy. When the traditional nobility had ruled and controlled most wealth, it was relatively clear who was important and who deserved their position on top of society. And that position was supported by a host of cultural and traditional values both social and religious. Driving out the old nobility in the context of the increasingly complex social and economic world of the day put all that up for grabs. Traditional values and cultural norms crumbled before new economic and social realities, and the tales of the *Decameron* were being told right in the midst of the sorting out of this complex and highly contested transition, a transition aided and aggravated by the devastation of the plague.

The questions that turned around who was on top of society, who deserved to be there, and why they deserved to be there, indeed, following the plague were if anything rendered more problematic in cities like Florence. In fact, they were often contested violently in the streets as well as in governmental councils and prescriptive literature. Perhaps less recognized by scholars, the answers provided to such questions (and the way those answers were incorporated into new cultural values that were carefully conceptualized as not new but safely traditional and old) were central themes of the shared culture of the day. As we will see, the deeper issues opened by many of the tales in the *Decameron* regularly turn on such issues, relatively obvious at the time, that today need to be carefully teased out of the text in order for their troubled and troubling themes to be heard and appreciated.

And, significantly, that is why its stories cannot be considered historically as reflecting a medieval world or the values, social and cultural, of the rest of Europe. Indeed, in the *Decameron,* we are in a new
world, albeit claiming to be old and not new at all: the Italian Renaissance or Rinascimento, a world deeply different in many ways socially,
economically, and culturally from the rest of the medieval West. For the
moment, however, suffice it to say that in Florence, as in many other
cities of northern Italy across the fourteenth century, the *popolo* was
breaking down into competing social and economic groups. In a way,
with the advantage of hindsight, this might be seen as having been unavoidable, as one of the critical factors in uniting a very disparate *popolo*
in the thirteenth century was the battle to overcome the traditional nobility. Once that was accomplished (in most cities by the end of the century), the different needs and values of the various groups that made up
the *popolo* came to the fore. Simply put, a banker had limited common
ground to build an alliance upon with a butcher or a baker beyond op-
posing noble claims to dominate their cities.

Thus, although the labels would be different in different cities, and
even within cities, the *popolo* tended to break down into groups that
shared more in common economically and socially: most significantly
the *popolo grosso* or *grasso* (the important people, the big people, or the fat
[*grasso*] people) and the *popolo minuto* (the little people). Those members
of the *popolo* seen as the economically powerful in cities like Florence—
bankers, merchants, big luxury cloth producers for the international
market—tended to be accepted as members of the *popolo grosso,* while
humbler artisans like butchers, bakers, cobblers, and even painters were
seen as members of the *popolo minuto.* Over and over again in the *Decameron,* we will encounter these social divisions and what they mean for
the different ways characters are presented as behaving, thinking, and
feeling.

And not only that, but also for portraying how those on top of society *ought to* behave, understand, and feel. For, in a deeply Christian society, still suspicious of great wealth and the sins that often accompany
it, such as greed, envy, and profiting at the expense of fellow Christians,
wealth alone was a dangerous measure of status and personal or family
worth. In fact, in distinguishing who really mattered and deserved to
be on top of society, highly contested cultural markers were created,

defended, and came to play crucial roles that went well beyond wealth. Perhaps the most important was one of the most crucial also for the tales of the *Decameron* and their characters: *virtù*.

"*Virtù*" was a term with a pedigree stretching back at least to the ancient world and had long been associated with the range of behaviors that not just identified but made one person better than another. In the Middle Ages, simplifying greatly, these behaviors had been associated with noble and knightly values, such as courage in battle, the violent directness of a warrior, the honesty of a man who was defined by his words and a code of honor, the open-handedness of a person for whom personal relationships were more important than wealth, and all this ideally was displayed by a refined, mannerly person. Of course, these were ideals, and in the rough and ready world of the Middle Ages, few lived up to such high standards, and more quotidian values were layered over these ideals in ways that might seem with the advantage of hindsight to contradict them. But as an ideal, and in practice, this vision of *virtù* supported the virtually unquestioned superiority of the nobility, even if often it entailed much less attractive behaviors, such as high-handed ways, quick violence against those deemed as less important, and an emphasis on honor and family that easily translated into vendetta and disruption, as the *Decameron* notes negatively from time to time.

In a manner sometimes overlooked, many of these attributes were actually utilitarian in a largely rural society with a limited economy and minimal government. The emphasis on violence, power, and personal relationships dominated by honor allowed the nobility to impose on society an order that in many ways was adequate to their needs, especially as they were aided in this by Christian ideals that supported their position on top of the social hierarchy and that advocated peacefulness and acceptance of the status quo. The problem, however, was that such values, especially with their emphasis on violence and the violent defense of honor and noble status, once seen as the essence of *virtù*, in the complex burgeoning cities of northern Italy came to be seen as problematic early on in the Rinascimento.

That urban world, its rapidly developing economy, and its diverse social makeup required a less violent environment where government attempted to maintain the order necessary to amass a large, variegated, and productive population. Moreover, by replacing private violence driven by honor and a traditional social hierarchy with law, courts, and its own violence labeled justice, governments promised a more secure urban peace and to promote an environment where business and the economy could flourish without the prepotencies of the old nobility interfering. Although this program was seldom as successful as claimed at the time, one of its first priorities in the thirteenth and early fourteenth century had been to drive out or at least neutralize the traditional nobility in the name of providing peace and justice for denizens of the city.

And *virtù* was a highly important cultural fellow traveler of this program and its promised order, as the *Decameron* reveals repeatedly in a myriad of different ways and moments. For as the economy, society, and government changed and developed, so too did *virtù*. Perhaps most significantly, the violence that was so central in the earlier vision of *virtù* in virtually all its forms was largely eliminated from the mix of what made one person better than another. It was replaced by an emphasis on reason over emotion, self-control, and a careful calculating approach to life that allowed one to control the present and, tellingly, the future as well. On the whole, strong emotions were to be avoided and a rational approach that fit well with the new economic and social world of the day was stressed. In sum, a traditional term labeling a traditional set of values slowly morphed into something quite new that fit well with the new needs of the urban world of the day and its new leaders. But, tellingly, it did so, and became in turn traditional, by transforming as it maintained the time-honored term that identified what made one person better than another: *"virtù."* And, in the process, the behaviors of the old nobility became not just counterproductive in the urban world of the day but incorrect and literally disqualifying for garnering power, respect, status, or, ultimately, *virtù*.[15]

As a label with such great power in a period of rapid and profound change, exactly what *virtù* meant and required was an issue that, not surprisingly, engendered considerable debate. And in the complex social world of the Rinascimento, what it meant for people of different social levels was also a relatively new and highly contested issue. In the Middle Ages, when in broad outline *virtù* marked out a violent, masculine warrior elite, it appears the term was seldom applied to the lower classes or women, unless it was being used in a spiritual sense, referring to those who were superior as Christians rather than socially or economically. In the urban world of fourteenth-century Florence, however, both denizens of the lower classes and women could exhibit *virtù*. In each case, however, what that label implied was different and adhered to newer values associated with the ideals intertwined with, on the one hand, new social distinctions and, on the other, with changing understandings of what we label "gender" today. Thus, in the *Decameron,* we will encounter adulterous lower-class women who exhibit behavior labeled *"virtù"* as well as *virtù*-ous peasants, artisans, and even rogue clerics— something that in the Middle Ages would have been largely unthinkable, and unthinkable in much of the rest of Europe in the fourteenth century as well, thus, in a way, making the *Decameron* much more transgressive there than in the urban world of Renaissance Italy.

As such distinctions were highly contested and still in flux, in fact, the *Decameron* is an invaluable source for those interested in how this crucial term, *"virtù"* (virtually a form of social DNA for the early Rinascimento), was developing at the time. One area that was especially problematic and where the *Decameron* may have been somewhat anomalous in its day was in the emphasis placed in many of its tales on the mannerly behavior required to exhibit true *virtù,* at least for the upper classes. As we will see, at times members of what would have been labeled then the *popolo grosso,* and hence on top of society, in the *Decameron* are demoted from that social position because they lack the good manners that *virtù* clearly requires there. And, at the same time, a number of characters who fall short of the economic wealth required to be counted as members of the *popolo grosso* seem to gain higher status because they display refined manners, albeit usually along with a significant number of the other attributes associated with *virtù*. Indeed, at times, as we shall see, these distinctions require Boccaccio-author to stop the flow of events in a tale to win over the sympathy of contemporaries to such evaluations that apparently would not have garnered immediate support.

It has been often suggested that this emphasis on mannerly behavior reflects Boccaccio's experience in the courtly and mannerly world of Naples, where he worked as a young banker and was evidently much impressed by the courtly life of the city and its nobility. Clearly, his earlier writings owe much to his fascination with that world and its courtly values. And Naples and its courtly world are still prominent in the *Decameron,* but it should be noted, as the tales themselves often suggest, that a command of refined manners and mannerly behavior were also presented as Florentine, a telling means of separating the often reasoned and clever but unmannered behavior of artisans and the lower classes of that city from the reasoned and clever behavior of those more truly deserving upper-class status.

In the close and intimate urban world of Florence, it would have been difficult to sustain the position that there were not lower-class denizens of the city who displayed most of the attributes of *virtù,* but mannered, virtually courtly behavior was a measure that few could attain, and when they attempted to do so, as the tale of Calandrino's attempt at refined love discussed in the first chapter underlines, they could be expected to fail miserably. Thus, a vision of *virtù* that included refined behavior and manners separated out the true gentleman or gentlewoman from the rest in Florence and identified him or her as superior—in the *Decameron* at least. And, at the same time, it helped to win readers' smiling sympathy for the dangerous *virtù* of lower-class characters and women and to defuse the threat that otherwise such behavior might have seemed to imply for a newly solidifying vision of a quite different ideal social hierarchy and elite from that which dominated the rest of Europe. Lacking in manners and refined behavior, clever lower-class people would safely remain lower class, while the old nobility lost place to a new *popolo grosso.*

Hand in hand with manners went an aspect of *virtù* that might seem to contradict its whole rational underpinning: the often positive nature of emotions that accompanied love and sexual desire. For although such powerful and often violent emotions frequently seemed to overwhelm reason and were recognized as creating many problems, they also regularly were portrayed as driven by and displaying true *virtù* at its best. Thus, throughout the *Decameron,* along with *virtù* and cultivated manners, love and being a refined lover marked out one as a superior and refined person richly imbued with *virtù* and deserving to be on top of society. And, in turn, failing to be a refined lover could mark out a character as lacking *virtù* and not a gentleman or gentlewoman, no matter how wealthy or important they might be. Indeed, how this rather strange mix of reason and emotion, measured manners and unmeasured passion, self-control and loss of same in love went together is one of the driving forces in the tales, almost as if the apparent paradoxes implied in this contradictory mix propel the stories back again and again to the troubling conflicts involved—moments whose tensions seemed to be deeply enmeshed in the emotions that surrounded love. And, as will become clear in what follows, a man or a woman who did not know how to be a refined, mannered lover clearly could not be a gentleman or gentlewoman and exhibit true *virtù* in the *Decameron* for all the apparent illogic that that implied. Indeed, it is worth suggesting that not only did its tales reflect a social vision of love and lovers that many contemporaries supported, by presenting lovers as *virtù*-ous and in a positive light, it also argued for the acceptance of such critical, but conflicted, social judgments.

This concern with the changing behaviors that confirmed *virtù* opens up another complex issue that will be central to our analysis, the question of how behaviors, especially those involving love and sex, contributed to and revealed a sense of identity at the time. Actually, this is an issue that has been a matter of intense scholarly debate over the last few decades, as a number of scholars following in the footsteps of Foucault have accepted the idea that there was no sense of sexual identity in the premodern world. They have argued powerfully that such ways of understanding identity only developed in the nineteenth century in the context of the development of social science disciplines that created the modern discourse of sexual identity and identity more generally. These disciplines, in the context of a larger move to find an internal sense of identity, largely unknown in the premodern world, created the modern sense of self dominated by a powerful inner concept of a personal, individual identity with all that that implied.

Without attempting here to retrace the contours of this intense and rich debate, following in the footsteps of Stephen Greenblatt's seminal work on early modern identity formation, *Renaissance Self-Fashioning*,[16] I have argued in several works over the last fifteen years a modified position on the issue that while admitting that there was little sense of an internal sexual identity in the modern sense, there was a clearly Rinascimento sense that shines through in contemporary archival and literary texts across the board. Thus, I suggested that "sexual identity and identity more broadly . . . were what might be called 'consensus realities': imagined realities, but no less real for that, which were shared with the groups with which an individual lived and interacted, groups such as family, neighbors, friends, social peers, fellow workers, fellow confraternity members, and broader communities and solidarities. These consensus realities, as they were shared understandings [and negotiated ones as well] were not necessarily tightly structured; nor were they the same from group to group."[17] But they were highly significant for the way individuals negotiated a much more social sense of identity in the intimate cityscapes of their day, as an attentive reading of the *Decameron* repeatedly reveals.

In such a work, where the identification of a character is central for the narration of the stories told, the question of how identity is read and heard by contemporaries becomes critical for analysis. As we shall see in the discussion of the characters Nastagio degli Onesti in Chapter 2, Ghismonda and Lisabetta in Chapter 3, or Gualtieri in Chapter 5, how a contemporary would have understood their identities in the context of consensus realities becomes central in understanding the implications of their behaviors and the way their tales are told. In the imaginative economy of the *Decameron,* this was especially important, for in this process of social evaluation there was a profound potential for disciplining behavior and organizing the life of the small urban societies of the day—a process so central that the tales return to it over and over again to explain behavior. And thus, significantly, they have the potential to reveal at a deeper and more functional level how the emotions associated with love and sex were evaluated at the time, the level of consensus realities that if unrecognized has the potential to limit our ability to understand the tales themselves and, in turn, when evaluated has the ability to reveal much about love and sex at the time, as we shall see.

Love and Sexual Desire and Their Associated Emotions in the *Decameron*

Less clear is exactly what love or sexual desire were seen as being in the *Decameron* or more generally in the early Rinascimento. Actually, even today we have a decided lack of clarity about both. And the current debates among neuroscientists, cognitive scientists, psychologists, and

historians of emotions (and lovers for that matter) have merely made
the matter less clear it seems, even if perhaps eventually cognitive scientists or neuroscientists will answer all questions and we will be satisfied
with a science of emotions that makes the apparently unreasonable reasonable.[18] William Reddy, in his path-breaking works on love, has re-
viewed with care the scientific literature on love and sex and the emotions associated with both, arguing that like all emotions they have a
significant cognitive and ultimately cultural quality that not only has a
historical dimension but that calls for historical study. Thus, he concludes, "There is, therefore, nothing in the latest neuroscience research
on sexual desire, sexual arousal, or romantic love that permits one to
conclude that these states are caused or orchestrated by hard-wired
brain systems. Instead, the most sophisticated methods presently available yield results that are compatible with the idea of a substantial role
for cultural determinants in the occurrence of and experience of such
states."[19]

But, in the end, for the discussion of love and sexual desire and the
emotions that were seen as swirling around both as they were imagined in the *Decameron*—the focus of this book—what is most important
is how they were portrayed in its tales and the way in which those de-
pictions interacted with and reflected the understanding and living of
love and sexual desire in Florence and the cities of northern Italy in the
Rinascimento. To briefly introduce the issues involved, it seems clear at
least that love was viewed as a powerful and complex emotion or perhaps
more accurately as invoking a group of more basic emotions. Moreover,
as we shall see in the tales, all love, even the most spiritual "true" love,
was assumed to be accompanied by sexual desire and the more basic
emotions that accompanied it. It is important to note, however, that
the emotions that are associated with desire when love and sex are correctly conjoined tend to be viewed in a positive sense and should not be
confused with lust *(foia)* and other less savory emotions, which usually
implied negative forms of sexual desire often associated with the lower
classes, unsavory relationships, or simply negative obsessions. This close
association of love and sexual desire thus highlights the fact that neither
love nor sexual desire seem to have been seen as one isolated emotion.[20]
At the same time that each was deeply interrelated, they served as powerful blanket concepts that included a range of feelings associated with

a number of different forms of desire and attachment. These feelings could involve feelings of pleasure or pain, hope or despair, attraction or repulsion, rage or calm, disdain or acceptance, honor or shame, but with a special place reserved for a deeper passion: a deeper passion at once both spiritual and sexual, driven by a powerful, overwhelming desire that seems to have been identified as true love.

It appears that, beyond the *Decameron,* in the life of the day, this mix of feelings associated with love, usually associated with the relationship between a man and a woman but not necessarily so (and perhaps not traditionally so), was undergoing what might be labeled a "civilizing" process in the early Rinascimento. And this was definitely the case in the *Decameron.* "Civilizing" not in the modern often pejorative sense of the term but in a contemporary Rinascimento sense, where "civilizing" implied making a person a successful, *virtù*-ous participant in the civil / civic urban-centered world of the day—in essence, civil.[21] Once again, as discussed above, life in the city, civic life, increasingly required civil behavior: the peaceful, mannerly life that promised order and a certain self-control and disciplined behavior. Love, with its threat of uncontrolled emotions, violent passions, and sexual desires, quite literally needed to be civilized *in that sense* in order to become a safe and positive emotion. And without those necessary civil dimensions, its dangers were very much a concern of those hearing the *Decameron*'s tales of love and, in turn, the tales themselves.

In fact, for the noble class of the Middle Ages, love without such restraints had been a potentially very dangerous emotion, as a number of the tales that are set in an earlier day emphasize. Violence, murder, and bloody crimes often went hand in hand with the group of feelings that gathered around love and its accompanying sexual desire. And that may well be because, in fact, or at least in perception, love was seen as an emotion too strong to be contained and constrained even in marriage, which was ideally based more on a peaceful alliance between families rather than the dangerous passions that love could explode suddenly between a couple. Marriage, from this perspective, was ideally and traditionally more a yoke to bind two people and their families together for a productive and secure life than a deeply passionate and / or spiritual relationship.

As a result, as noted earlier, true love was often viewed as possible only outside of marriage *and thus adulterous or premarital* with all the dangerous irregularities that each implied. Indeed, the echoes of such illicit and violent loves and their associated sexual expressions pullulate in the tales of the *Decameron*. But there is, at the same time, a not so subtle shift in the treatment of what was viewed as true love there: for, over and over again, the positively portrayed outcome of such dangerous love is a conclusion that turns away from adultery or pre-marital sex as the norm for true love between truly *virtù*-ous lovers, replacing it with an ideal of a marriage that promises safe—we might say again civilized—sexual pleasure and companionship based on a deeply felt true love against all odds and against all opposition. This radical break with a more traditional view of an ideal of love existing only in adulterous relationships free from the constraints of marriage is often undervalued or even overlooked by modern readers of the *Decameron*, perhaps because of our contemporary assumptions about the way love, marriage, and sex go together as the normal order of things.[22] Crucially, however, such an idea in the fourteenth century was anything but normal and indeed usually seen as quite dangerous for family goals, social order, and disciplining young emotions.

Significantly, then, deeply felt love, as a powerful emotion that threatened to disrupt the civil order of society, in the *Decameron* was regularly reincorporated in its tales into the new social order of the day via marriage—presented as literally civilizing both love and sex. Marriage, in this radical vision, took dangerous passions and safely contained them within a traditional institution that guaranteed family and lineage. Few at the time would have seen this ideal as particularly practical or likely, as most would have doubted that strong passions like love or sexual desire were so easily reined in by marriage, especially when lovers were young and even true love was often seen as fleeting and whimsical.

Nonetheless, the *Decameron* presents the case for true love and its accompanying sexual pleasures as the base for successful marriages, returning repeatedly to the unhappy and dangerous outcomes of traditional arranged marriages often involving unloving, unhappy couples of widely different ages and desires. And, over and over again, these negative examples of loveless and pleasureless marriages and the negative emotional life they offered are contrasted with the happy ending of true love in well-founded marriages where loving couples, having decided to marry, live happily ever after. Although it might be pointed out with a certain irony that few tales continue to describe the life of those married lovers living happily ever after, suggesting perhaps that that improbable conclusion for the Rinascimento was hard to demonstrate even in the happiest of the *Decameron*'s tales.

That said, however, we do have significant archival evidence that the radical ideal of marriage for love and sexual pleasure was actually followed by some at the time in Florence and in the other cities of northern Italy and that it often entailed violence, both in terms of violent resistance by families interested in maintaining more traditional familial goals for marriage and violence by the lovers themselves or their supporters attempting to overcome those traditional goals to marry instead for love. Thus, returning to the tales of the *Decameron*, despite their emphasis on the ideal of peaceful and civilized marriages based on love, they also at times portray contemporary forms of violence associated with love, especially what was deemed true love, to win marriage. Moreover, this violence was usually presented positively, suggestively, in contexts much like those found in contemporary judicial documents. In fact, Boccaccio-author periodically describes in detail such love-driven violence with Dantean relish (often troubling to modern readers) and as virtually a heroic requirement proving true love, thus leaving us with a civilizing and peaceful institution frequently founded on violence and the disruption of the social order that it was supposed to support and civilize.

If this all seems complicated and even at times contradictory, that is, of course, because it was. The many transitions that the cities of northern Italy were undergoing economically, socially, and culturally were nothing if not complicated, and the responses were seldom as neatly symmetrical and logical as social theorists, critics, or historians might desire or like to imagine. Rather, they were complex and rich with contradictions, much like the tales of the *Decameron*, and perhaps, we might point out, like the normal disorder and messiness of everyday life and contradictory values found in most societies. In those contradictions we can see the complexity and force of love and sexual desire and the feelings associated with both in the Rinascimento that at times still seem familiar today but often range far afield and involve much stronger and more dangerous feelings and emotions. For I would suggest that an often overlooked aspect of the way the modern world has developed is the way love, desire, and feelings in general have been pared down and controlled internally and externally to lose much of their power, force, and at times dangerous potential for violence.

In this I am not claiming a linear process of the civilization of manners but rather an ongoing complex process of adapting emotions to different societies and cultures and their shifting relationships with the expression of feelings and passions—a history just beginning to be explored. And from time to time today in our supposedly more civilized and controlled society, when those feelings break through our carefully honed filters of self-control and culture, we are astounded and deeply troubled by the things that love and desire and the emotions associated with them can play a role in triggering. In the *Decameron*, we jump to a different world and culture, where different controls are being put in place, driven by decidedly different social and cultural forces. A world and a culture where love, sexual desire, and their associated feelings were imagined in ways often strange to the modern eye and seen at the time as involving dangerous clusters of passions far distant from the modern.

This book, then, aims to reopen the *Decameron* and its symphony of life, a symphony of Rinascimento love and sexual desire and their associated feelings and passions, in sum, love and sex—when they were imagined as congeries of emotions dangerous, dark, seductive, and yet crucially alive with the melodies of life itself in the time of the plague.

1

Laughter

Imagining Love, Lust, and Virtù
in the Rinascimento

Where the Reader Falls in Love in the Rinascimento
and Suffers Therefrom

Imagine . . .

Imagine yourself as a no-longer-young Florentine painter in the fourteenth century, painting frescoes with two of your comrades, Bruno and Buffalmacco, in the country villa of a powerful member of the Florentine *popolo grosso*—the big people or the people that really mattered in local parlance.[1] It is an excellent commission for a humble artisan, and you are happy for the opportunity to make some money and perhaps even show your budding mastery of perspective, which is making fellow artisans like Giotto seem more than mere wall painters. One morning, as you are taking a break to drink at the well, you encounter a beautiful young woman, lightly clad, washing her hands. Her body and beauty immediately kindle in you desire, an emotion that you decide is love.

It never crosses your mind to consider it lust, because she seems much too refined for mere lust and thus evokes, in turn, a more refined emotion than the more straightforward type of craving that you feel at times for women who are your peers. In fact, you realize that what you are feeling is a highly refined emotion that calls for refined upper-class manners and that has the potential to ennoble your petty everyday life and make it rich, beautiful, and meaningful. In sum, you are experiencing that transforming and powerful Rinascimento emotion that you know as love and in its perhaps most typical and devastating form, an overwhelming love at first sight. Suggestively and crucially, you are thinking and not just feeling this emotion and distinguishing it from a wide range of possible other ways of understanding the group of feelings you associate with love.

So you greet her warmly and with your best manners. And, much to your surprise, she replies, giving you a curious look as if she is interested in even you, a lower-class man, notwithstanding your years and lack of status. Perhaps she recognizes that you are more than the mere artisan that others see you as—seeing in you a talent or *virtù*[2] that sets you apart and above your peers and makes you worthy of her attention. Thus she seems even more a discerning and cultivated lady worthy of a higher form of love, an emotion certainly not to be confused with a form of desire widely seen as demeaning and negative such as lust.

Still, you cannot resist staring, but at her eyes—the springs of love—not her lightly clad body, the source of lustful temptations. You are at a loss for words, overcome by the powerful group of feelings that such love commands. She acknowledges your discomfort with a roll of her eyes and a "few little sighs," and you are deeply wounded by love's arrows, which presumably have pierced your heart as contemporary poetry and art require. Returning to work, the emotions associated with love give you no peace, and you are overcome by sighs of your own. In fact, you are so changed that your fellow painter, Bruno, asks, "What the devil is the matter, partner," and you confess that you have fallen head-over-heels in love.

Clearly concerned about the potential dangers of your powerful passion and the dangerous thoughts it might engender about sexual pleasures to be shared, Bruno warns you that your love is probably Niccolosa, the wife of the son of the gentleman who owns the villa, confirming your supposition that you have fallen in love with someone well above your station in life. True love, however, often calls on one to reach above one's station, and social distance is merely one more obstacle among the many that true lovers must regularly overcome to enjoy the gratification of their love. Bruno promises to help you win your love and advises proceeding carefully to keep it secret from both her husband and your wife, Tessa, a jealous woman, who is definitely not and never was your true love. At best she is merely a partner in life imposed upon you by family and necessity. With her, sex is not a shared pleasure but rather a shared duty, the marital debt required in a good Christian marriage.[3] Actually, there is nothing unusual in this, as the arranged nature of marriage means that such matches are rarely based on love, even at the level of humble artisans. In turn, that means that most true love involves either adultery or premarital affairs, making the love you feel illicit and a potentially dangerous emotion.[4]

Returning to your new and true love, however, with Bruno's help you decide to demonstrate what a refined lover you are, fully worthy of her by measuring up to the high standards set by contemporary love poets like fellow Tuscan Petrarch (Francesco Petrarca), whose love poems were being sung in the streets, or the earlier popular poet of the dolce stil nuovo, Dante Alighieri, whose writings in Tuscan dialect had a wide following. On Bruno's friendly advice, you court your love by sending her words of love and poetry you have written for her using him as your intermediary—again a common strategy of lovers anxious to keep their illicit affairs secret.

Moreover, he suggests that you bring your rebec to the villa and serenade all with songs of love in the hopes that she will hear you and find you a yet more perfect and irresistible lover. You also send her presents that press your finances. This too is required to cut the figure of a noble lover. And she returns little presents of her own that confirm her interest in you and your exceptional qualities as a lover. As a result, your feet become like quicksilver, and, like many a lover, you cannot stand still or focus on anything besides your growing love as you dash here and there at the villa in the hopes of catching another glimpse of her.

In your chance encounters, she continues to reward you with smiles and encouraging looks. Things stall at that stage of rather timid but deeply felt courtship, however, as is often the case, given the dangers of illicit and adulterous love when it leads on to the sexual pleasures that it virtually demands. Thus, although she seems to share your passion and desire, there appears to be no way to be alone with her to enjoy the fruits of your shared love and the hopefully pure sexual satisfaction that should reward such refined desires and courtship. For, of course, as a sophisticated lover, you understand that shared pleasure, not possession or mere lustful coupling, is what you really should desire. Finally, however, Bruno suggests that it is time to move on to more forceful action, for she clearly loves you but, as a woman, seems typically reluctant to risk her reputation to act more concretely on that emotion.

Thus, at considerable cost, he prepares a *carta di voler bene*—a magical paper or parchment widely used by lovers to bind and control the love of their beloved.[5] He promises that when you touch her with it, she will be unable to resist the love she feels and will follow you wherever you go without question and accept your every advance. Perhaps such power to command is questionable for a lover. But your love, like that of many, recognizes no limits in seeking its fulfillment. And magic, well used, is a common tool in bringing love to a happy sexual conclusion, especially for lovers blocked by fear or minor moral scruples over what is in the end simply a "natural" desire.

One day, then, when everything is ready, you encounter your love in the courtyard again. As planned, you touch her with the *carta*. And it works! She follows you submissively into the barn. Then, as you close the doors behind you, she, overcome by love and the sexual desire that accompanies it, no longer constrained by worries about her reputation, and, thanks to the *carta,* throws you into the hay and jumps on top of you, declaring her love. Love and sex. Perhaps not quite as refined as you imagined, but when pure love finally reaches its natural goal, pure passion, a little extra enthusiasm is not to be faulted, especially as this is a fine lady throwing herself upon you because she can no longer contain the strong emotions of the love that she feels for you. Delaying the shared pleasure to come, she tarries for a moment to look into your eyes with love from astride your body—seeing there again love not lust.

Yes, this looks like it is going to be the best day of your life. But, in history as in life, it is virtually a truism that looks are often deceiving, especially when love and sex are involved. And rather than the best day of your life, this one is about to become one of the worst. For, as you attempt to kiss her sweet lips, a heavenly pleasure you have been waiting much too long to enjoy, your wife, Tessa, in a fury, bursts through the door of the barn and your love flees along with her poetic gaze. Immediately, Tessa, like a wild animal, is on you, digging her nails into your face and hammering you with blows—the reality of your married life has returned to destroy your pure adulterous love and your anticipated refined, noble sexual pleasures. To make matters worse, your comrades, even Bruno, suddenly appear and roar with laughter at the hiding you are taking.

Refined love's anticipated pleasures have turned into mocking laughter and violence—admittedly also not an unusual experience in the Rinascimento. But the question that must be on your mind, as your body is being pummeled, is what is happening? Well, first off, I must confess that you have been lured into a fourteenth-century novella and, if it makes you feel any better, you are the Florentine hero, or perhaps it would be more honest to make a clean breast of it and admit that you are its hapless victim, Calandrino. In fact, Florentines were famous for the type of joke you are caught up in, referred to as a *beffa* or at times a *burla,* a joke that ideally cleverly victimized the foolish or those whose behavior invited public ridicule as a form of social demeaning humor and discipline.[6] Still, at least you are in a supposedly funny tale in a famous collection of stories, the *Decameron,* told by the most renowned storyteller of that century in Italy and probably in Europe, Giovanni Boccaccio.[7] As discussed earlier, Boccaccio's masterpiece is a collection of one hundred tales placed in a frame story where ten upper-class youths fleeing the plague in 1348 retire to the hills above Florence to retell stories in an effort to escape the sorrow and depression created by that great disaster that carried off perhaps as much as two-thirds of the population of Europe. And love and sex were often the subjects of their tales.

Where, Yet Again, the Question "What Is Love?" Is Asked

But this is the moment perhaps to re-ask an over-asked question: What was this thing called love that you have suffered? Of course, today love and lust are rather like pornography. Most people believe they know them when they encounter them but would be hard-pressed to define either. And although historians have weighed in on the subject of love frequently and with impressive acumen, there still remains considerable debate about what the term meant in the Rinascimento or means today for that matter. Yet, one may take heart from a statistic published recently by Google that ranked the questions most asked of their search engine. They reported that by far the number one was "What is love?"[8] So historians are not alone in their uncertainty. And if one places that query in a more cutting-edge historical perspective, it becomes more difficult yet for, as most are aware, with the cultural turn of the last generation, a number of literary critics and historians have come to the realization that what we once assumed was a straightforward emotion is to a greater or lesser degree, depending on theoretical loyalties, a historical construct built from a bundle of emotions, perceptions, thoughts, and social and cultural ways of encountering others and life itself.[9] As a result, looking at love (or lust) in a period as distant as the Rinascimento might well seem a hopeless task.

Still, I would suggest that your love as Calandrino, like most love at the time, was a complex bundle of often contradictory feelings and thoughts, at once ennobling and debasing, attracting and distracting, wise and foolish, liberating and binding, happy and tragic, constructive and destructive, all frequently skating dangerously on the edge of the wild, mad, and violent—a mix that contemporaries saw as uniquely powerful, engaging, and dangerous, often far from the modern saccharine conceits of Valentine cards or our seemingly endless modern repetitions of Petrarchian topoi.

This is not the place to consider the fascinating question of how this strange and often contradictory mix of emotions came together in the Rinascimento or how the mix and emphasis on various aspects of it changed over time to become what we label with perhaps unwarranted pride "modern" or even "postmodern"; rather, what I would like to do is look more closely at a few of the more contemporary variations on the range of passions associated with love and lust presented in Boccaccio's *Decameron*, reviewing them with an archival historian's not-so-innocent eyes. In turn, I am interested in how Boccaccio restructured and reorganized the tales he retold to present a rather original vision of the ideal way love and sex should go together, a vision whose radical nature at the time is often overlooked today, because in many ways it has become the norm in modern Western society, at least until recently. In sum, questions that are ultimately historical. Hopefully, however, in attempting to answer such questions, this book will open new perspectives on both the intriguing tales of the *Decameron* and on the complex and turbulent social and cultural history of its day and perhaps even occasionally on our own complex and turbulent time with a pandemic of our own.

But, to return to your fate as Calandrino-the-lover, black and blue and being dragged off by Tessa, I suppose you might still be asking for an explanation about what was so funny. To begin to understand, however, first you will have to shed Calandrino's point of view as a lover, because lovers, as the period understood well, for all their reflections on their love, were often incapable of understanding what was happening around them. Love and sexual desire were not imagined as emotions before or without thought; rather, they were emotions where the thoughts that came with them were often distorted and ultimately wrong. In large part, that was because love and desire were understood as passions that warped one's thoughts and senses and overwhelmed with strong feelings one's ability to judge events.

An anonymous sixteenth-century playwright expressed it well in the introduction to a comedy that highlighted the strong powers of love and sexual desire, *La Veniexiana*, noting, "The ancients innocently imagined Cupid, the son of Venus, as a blind, winged child, armed with a quiver of arrows, thus expressing the nature of love: blindly irrational, flying to the core of every man and so completely confounding his intellect that he becomes a child once again and returns to his pristine state of foolishness." Foolish, childlike, confounded, yet a lover like Calandrino was still thinking through his feelings and desires, even if thinking irrationally. Continuing, the author explains, "This is in fact due to the senses, which, overwhelmed by an attraction to something, represent it as being different from what it actually is, making it seem either better or worse. Thus, with judgment blinded, desire forces every sense to fall into line."[10] In the end, then, you as Calandrino with misleading input, we might say, from your senses saw true love and pure passion for a noble wife, and then, following on your misjudgment, you acted on it with *apparent* reason and the *apparent* help of your *apparent* friend Bruno. But at every step you were wrong, led astray by love and false appearances.

Still, that was only at a surface level, for what made the *beffa* that victimized you particularly attractive and funny was that it played upon a very fourteenth-century sense of ways of thinking and acting that separated fools from the wise and the best from the rest—a set of

behaviors that, as noted earlier, was labeled at the time *"virtù."* Once
upon a time in a more militaristic society, *virtù* tended to be associated
with the masculine, direct ways of a warrior nobility who dominated
society and their vision of what placed them deservedly on top of the
social order. Thus, at its most straightforward and simple, it was seen
as involving a series of "positive" attributes with a strong militaristic
lean that included direct, often violent, action and words, honest direct
manners and ways. And, crucially, blood, especially the blood spilled
in war and more metaphorically bloodline. Both determined who belonged on top of society. In Italy, however, as urban centers, commerce,
and an entrepreneurial culture came to dominate the economic and
social life of the peninsula in the twelfth and thirteenth centuries, the
positive attributes associated with *virtù* shifted away from an emphasis
on blood and direct and often violent action to emphasize reason
(sliding into cunning, *furbizia*), moderation, and behavior that was seen
as more controlled and controlling. Bloodshed and bloodline lost much
of their force to newer ideals of *virtù* that emphasized emotional control
and passions moderated by reason.[11]

With this emphasis on reason and emotional control, however, the
vision of love and sexual desire that our later anonymous playwright
and many writers at the time saw as distorting reason, and at times virtually overwhelming it, seemed to not be particularly suited to a life
of *virtù*, as your own experience as Calandrino reveals troublingly. For,
from this perspective, you were the perfect butt of Bruno's *beffa* because
as you imagined your love, you too were misled by your uncontrolled
emotions; thus, acting without *virtù*, you felt that you were young again,
attractive and refined, understood what was going on, and were a lover
worthy of an upper-class mistress. Actually, however, blinded by your
love-induced emotions, you lacked the *virtù* that the best of your peers
shared in the fourteenth century and thus deserved to be the victim of
a disciplining and clever joke and, of course, the laughter of your comrades and the readers of your tale.

The often contradictory implications of *virtù* for love and sexual
desire, however, struck deeper chords in the imagination of the Rinascimento. For especially active male lovers at the time were regularly
depicted in literary and archival accounts as feminine. This appears
strange from a modern perspective where aggressive male seducers are

often viewed as hypermasculine, driven by ego problems, overactive hormones, or more psychological explanations. But the Rinascimento, thinking of love's problems in terms of *virtù* and the lack of emotional control and irrationality that love and desire could induce, knew that such men were actually feminine.[12] Adult men, real men, controlled their emotions with reason to be *virtù*-ous, unlike women, who were dangerously passionate creatures and had great trouble controlling the feelings associated with love or sexual desire or even thinking clearly about them. This was one reason why women had to be married in their early teens, as soon after puberty as possible—just as they were seen as being in particular danger to falling victim to such new and dangerously uncontrollable emotions.

Moreover, this was why their marriages had to be arranged by mature and sober patriarchs, unmoved by unsettling emotions like love or other more troubling youthful feminine desires. The marriages that fathers arranged were reasonable and driven by *virtù*, not something as blind and unstable as love or desire or, heaven forbid, simple lust. But a corollary to this vision was that men who were overly active lovers also lacked *virtù*, for evidently their minds and reason were overcome by similar emotions to those that endangered young women in love. As a result, for the Rinascimento, such men were not hypermasculine but rather feminine like women, who exhibited the same lack of control and *virtù*—just as you did as Calandrino.

How Cimone Finds *Virtù*, Becomes Civilized and a True Lover

Yet, what is one to make, then, of the paeans to love in the Rinascimento and in the *Decameron*? Is love merely a loss of control that overthrows *virtù* and opens one to cruel *beffe* and worse? The answer for contemporaries, as Boccaccio's tales show well, is a classic: yes and no. Love and its accompanying desire can overwhelm *virtù*, as happened to you as Calandrino, but with seeming paradox, it can have exactly the opposite effect. For love in the Rinascimento was not understood as a pure emotion, if there ever was such a thing, but rather, as suggested earlier, it was seen as involving a complex intermixing of reason and a range of feelings that swung from pure desire to the most troubling forms of dark passion. Perhaps the best example of this is to be found in the first tale told on the fifth day of storytelling in the *Decameron* and thus exactly at its heart.[13] The day of tales is dedicated to the adventures of lovers who overcome many obstacles to obtain in the end their desires and frequently the sexual pleasures that love requires. And this tale relates the virtually miraculous success of a simple-minded youth from Cyprus called Cimone, who, falling in love, overcomes all attempts by fickle fortune to block his true love.

Panfilo, who tells the tale to the *brigata*, begins it by informing his listeners that this young man's father, "a very noble man, called Aristippus, richer in worldly things than any of his compatriots,"[14] was nonetheless crushed by the fact that "one of his children, who surpassed all the other youths in terms of appearance and physique, but was virtually a fool *(quasi matto)*."[15] In fact, this Cimone was so simple-minded and lacking in *"virtù,"* the tale explains, that he was incapable of "civil life" in the urban world of the day and lived virtually at the level of an animal. As a result, both his family and neighbors had essentially given up on him and had taken to calling him Cimone, a name that in local parlance meant that he was virtually an ignorant beast without the *virtù*, the manners, or the intelligence to be a meaningful or even a participating member of civil society. Indeed, as the tale relates, "he was never able to get into his head letters or good manners and . . . [thus he went about] with . . . manners more similar to a beast than a man."[16] In essence, Cimone was even more lacking in *virtù* than Calandrino, for Cimone never had that *virtù* that Calandrino momentarily lost when he was led astray by love; although it should be noted that Calandrino's tales often focus on his lack of *virtù* and ensuing pratfalls.

With apparent paradox, however, eventually love would have the exact opposite effect on Cimone. Rather than causing him to further lose his reason and *virtù*, it actually miraculously led him to discover and embrace both. Sent to live in the country largely because his case was deemed hopeless—in other words, safely distant from the urban world of his day, where civil life and *virtù* were required and ruled[17]— he lived there the simple life of a peasant. One spring day (the traditional season of births and rebirths), however, he found himself wandering through a beautiful forest and, "guided by his *fortuna*," he came upon a clearing with a "very beautiful and cool fountain."[18] Much like Calandrino's discovery of his love at the fountain of the villa he was

painting, Cimone found "lying asleep by the fountain . . . a very beautiful young girl, with a dress that was so transparent that virtually
nothing of her exquisite body was hidden."[19]

Given his beast-like nature, one might assume that this sight would
have given rise to feelings of lust—an assumption that the text seems to
invite, focusing as it does on the young woman's virtual nakedness with
a voyeuristic gaze. Yet, the uncouth and unmannered Cimone has a tellingly different response to this vision discovered as he wandered lost in
the wilderness. For, much like Dante, similarly lost in a dark wood as
his *Divine Comedy* opens, his life was about to change from a tragedy to
a comedy, albeit a more human one, but also driven by love in the end.
In Cimone's case, however, it was not just the wilderness of exile from
civic life (in Dante's case Florence, in Cimone's Cyprus), or their own internal wildernesses, but also the wilderness of his beast-like lack of wit
and *virtù* that made him incapable of living the civil life of his urban society. Yet, rather than responding as a beast, gazing on the beauties revealed to him, "Cimone stopped short, and leaning on his stick, began
to stare at her without saying a thing, overcome by admiration, as if he
had never before seen the form of a woman."[20]

And miraculously "in his uncouth breast, which despite endless
teaching had remained stubbornly closed to every vestige of civil pleasures *(cittadinesco piacere),* he felt the stirrings of a thought which told his
gross, stolid mind that this girl was the loveliest thing that anyone had
ever seen."[21] Reflecting on her beautiful form, her sexual beauty, Cimone
was literally un-dumbfounded. He was profoundly transformed by that
sudden and explosive Rinascimento version of love—love, once again, at
first sight. But it was a love that once more critically involved both emotion and reflection, thought as well as feeling. In a way that virtually
seemed to echo the *dolce stil nuovo* love poetry of an earlier generation or
the Platonic theory of the ascent from beautiful things and love of individuals to the love of true beauty, on to knowledge itself, and the divine,
Cimone's suddenly kindled thoughts ranged over her physical beauty
with love, "and in the end he had so many thoughts that he realized that
divine things were more worthy of reverence than the earthly."[22] From a
simple beast, he had become a true man and a philosopher at that.

Significantly, when the young woman, Efigenia, awoke, Cimone
approached her in a controlled and civil manner with no sign of lust.

And although she was aware of, and somewhat concerned about, his uncouth reputation, perhaps sensing a change in his manner, she allowed him to walk home with her.[23] Again he exhibited no signs of his former beastly or uncivil behavior. And immediately after leaving her, Cimone rushed to his father and insisted that he be allowed to return to the city and leave the countryside for good, nicely symbolizing his decision to become finally a member of civil society—the Rinascimento equivalent of becoming civilized. There he began to take care in his dress and "to go about with young men of quality and learn the manners required of a gentleman, especially of those in love. [Thus], quickly to everyone's amazement, he not only acquired the basic learning [required of a gentleman], but became a very impressive philosopher."[24] In sum, he became "the most elegant and mannered youth in Cyprus with a wider range of *virtù* than any other."[25]

This miraculous transformation turned on something very unlikely from a Rinascimento perspective: *virtù* and *fortuna* working together. Normally these two powerful forces were seen as in conflict. And actually that conflict—a major conundrum of the period—turned on the way that the goddess Fortuna seemed capable of overturning the best-laid plans based on *virtù:* a worry that haunted Machiavelli's writing a century and a half later as well as that of many other earlier defenders of the power of *virtù,* including Boccaccio. The key to this unlikely cooperation was love itself—obviously yet another word of unique power for the imagination of the day and ruled over by yet another powerful god, Amore. For it is in the presence of Cimone's love (and it was crucially a true love and desire, not mere lust)[26] that Fortuna first relented in her cruel treatment of the youth and then joined in to help him overcome the trials that stood in the way of his success in winning his love.

In fact, the tale offers a short but telling disquisition on the contemporary vision of the conflict between Fortuna and Amore that concisely explained Cimone's original beastly nature and coarse, unmannerly ways totally lacking in *virtù* and, in turn, his miraculous transformation: "It is clear that . . . invidious Fortuna had bound in a tiny corner of his [Cimone's] heart with the strongest of ties that great *virtù* placed in his noble (*valorosa*) soul by heaven. These bounds were . . . broken and overthrown by Love, given that He (Amore) was so much more powerful than Her (Fortuna)."[27] Exceptional power indeed. But once love overcame Fortuna, she was also capable of giving into another of her often recognized feminine whimsical ways, becoming the female goddess who favors young lovers and the sexual desires of young men in love.

In a way, the illogic of this transition may not have troubled Boccaccio's contemporaries as much as it troubles some modern critics, because the essence of Fortuna was her feminine and illogical nature. Thus, the same goddess who opposed *virtù* repeatedly and placed a series of obstacles in the path of even Cimone's love and desires could be seen as having a weakness for young men and lovers at the same time; indeed, in Cimone's case, as in many others, she could and did favor him, even as she frequently opposed him.[28] As was often true in the *Decameron*, and in life more generally, the feminine whimsy of Fortuna was seen as both hindering young love by throwing one obstacle after another in its path and supporting it with seemingly miraculous turns of fate. And, in a way, in that illogic, the dynamic of the strong emotions and the complex twists of young lovers and their stories were at least partially explained and indeed lived.

As a result, Cimone overcame with his newly released *virtù* and a favorable Fortuna the many obstacles that Fortuna herself placed in the way of his love, becoming at once a heroic, passionate lover and finally a *virtù*-ous man worthy and capable of living successfully in the civil society of the urban world of his day—unlike poor Calandrino, who merely imagined he was doing so, a victim of his misleading emotions. In the end, then, he won Efigenia's love, marrying her to live happily ever after, as such true love stories tend to end in the *Decameron*. But the key to that happy ending was the alliance of Amore and *virtù*, along with the whimsical aid of Fortuna in support of a young lover driven by a true love that had transformed him from a dumb animal into a civilized citizen of his urban society. Examples could be easily multiplied in Boccaccio's tales. Love as an uncontrolled passion more driven by lust than Amore and lacking the power of *virtù* often resulted in disaster or base humor or both, as in the case of Calandrino. True love and its accompanying sexual desire, in contrast, for all its dangers and wild passions, in conjunction with *virtù* had the power to work miracles and bring out the best in lovers. And perhaps the largest miracle of all was that they not only could overcome Fortuna, they often won her whimsical favor in support of their pleasures and happy endings.

Where Calandrino's Inadequacies as a Lover Are Explained at Least in Part

Returning to Calandrino's love, however, his passions open a telling perspective on another aspect of love and sex in the Rinascimento—the way they seemed to reflect and reinforce the social hierarchy of its day. Boccaccio's slightly older contemporary, correspondent, and friend Petrarch, undoubtedly the most famous love poet of the age, exemplifies the social dynamic of love well. His vision of love has been exhaustively analyzed, with most modern critics agreeing that his poetry often speaks more about Petrarch himself than about Laura, the object of his love. In fact, much the same could be said about his older compatriot, Dante. Both writers stressed the way their love ennobled them as lovers—in essence, placing them on the top of the social hierarchy of their urban world. In a way, rather like Cimone, their loving and desire released the *virtù* locked away in a corner of their souls by the social conflict, competition for status, and violence of contemporary urban life and ennobled them. With a love that emphasized its superior spiritual dimensions without denying its carnal dimensions (especially for Petrarch), they became refined and mannered with inspired judgments of physical beauty, truth, and goodness that set them above the common herd.

In an urban world where, as discussed earlier, the traditional measures of nobility and status—blood, family, and military prowess—no longer obtained, and new measures of social placement were being sought, the ennobling force of love made it especially attractive. Refined lovers, demonstrating in their love an ennobling *virtù*, could and did claim the aristocratic status that was no longer guaranteed by rural estates, bloodline, or military skill. Dante, the son of a spice merchant, or Petrarch, the son of a lawyer and bureaucrat, as lovers became superior beings in the much more complex and socially contested urban order of their day and were, in fact, in both cases recognized as such thanks in no small measure to their love poetry.

Of course, the ennobling quality of love had a long medieval tradition and is often cited as part of a broader attempt to soften the violent tenor of a life and society then dominated by a military nobility. But what was new in thirteenth- and fourteenth-century Italy and its urban world was that love had become a weapon in the intense social conflicts of the day, just as the old nobility was losing its unquestioned right to be at the top of the social hierarchy. Boccaccio, definitely influenced by this use of love as well as by his friend Petrarch and his deep appreciation of Dante, in his early writing at least, also tended to represent true love and its accompanying desires as ennobling emotions in works such as his *Filostrato, Teseida delle nozze d'Emilia, Elegia di Madonna Fiammetta, Ameto,* and *Amorosa Visione,* and thus not surprisingly in the *Decameron* both in the tales themselves and in its frame story.[29]

One thing that added to the power of this way of seeing love was the long-accepted truism that true love and desire were not common or for the common herd. The passions that the lower classes shared were common like them, and, rather than true love and desire, they turned on its negative counterpart, lust. In fact, Calandrino's fantasies of love were humorously portrayed as falling far short of the mark and played a central role in powering the *beffa* that victimized him and justified it. In virtually every instance, what he imagined as revealing what a mannered and superior lover he was demonstrated exactly the opposite and reassured Boccaccio's aristocratic *brigata* and readers that artisans like him were not capable of refined love. Only the upper classes had the cultivated manners and subtlety of vision to transform their desires, especially the baser sexual passions like lust, into transcending spiritual love and refined sexual desire. With a refined and discerning vision, their *virtù* purified their passions into an ennobling spiritual quest for the higher goods of truth and beauty even in sex, allowing them to avoid the worse dangers of uncontrolled emotions.

That was merely an ideal, of course. Yet, as an ideal, it carried a significant weight, for true lovers were far superior to those simply indulging their common passions. One major problem with this ideal and its weight for the Rinascimento imagination, however, was the question of who really should be seen as belonging to the upper classes at a time when the old measures of status no longer clearly marked out the social elite. This was an especially weighty concern, as it was a period when, as discussed earlier, the *popolo* who had claimed power in city after city in Italy at the turn of the fourteenth century in the name of all the people was breaking up into groups competing for just that status. In this context, across that century, eventually a group made up of the leading entrepreneurial families of the *popolo*, augmented by lawyers, doctors, and the odd noble who had joined in the urban economy of the day or married into families that had done so, triumphed in the cities of Italy—the *popolo grosso*, as they were often labeled at the time.[30] And one of the most important things that set them apart and above was normally seen as displaying and living by that newer vision of *virtù* outlined above that featured reason, moderation, and control of emotions along with a more traditional dash of manners and civil and social graces including love.

Love, then, played a meaningful role in social distinctions, but once again its role was complex, largely because what exactly constituted *virtù* and how it related to love was not straightforward. Indeed, it was multifaceted and often highly contested. Like many labeling words of power, then, not all agreed on the exact mix of attributes that *virtù* entailed in the hotly contested social world of the fourteenth century. Some with a more aristocratic leaning placed more emphasis on manners and social graces, and, in that framework, love was more important in displaying *virtù*, while others placed more weight on moderation, control of emotions, and reason sliding into cunning and *furbizia* (that special kind of Rinascimento cunning that was attractive, even if it was not quite moral or just). As might well be expected, in a period of transition where social judgments were disputed and uncertain, while the tales of the *Decameron* return frequently to the importance of *virtù* in marking out whom the best people in society should be and ultimately were, from time to time they seem ambiguous about just what *virtù* entailed and who actually demonstrated it. And, significantly, once again this ambiguity often emerges when the storytellers turn to tales of love and desire.

Where Pampinea Tells Two Apparently Contradictory Tales on the Social Pitfalls of Loving, Marrying, and Pleasure

Two contrasting stories both told by the same narrator, Pampinea, illustrate this well: the third story of the third day, which turns on an aristocratic woman's rejection of her *popolo grosso* husband as a worthy lover for someone of her status, and the third tale of the second day, which highlights an English princess's recognition of a young man from the *popolo grosso* as a perfect lover and sexual partner even for someone of her high rank. In Pampinea's third day tale, she is faced with a difficult proposition that comes up often in the *Decameron:* how to make her audience accept a young upper-class wife as a palatable character, given that she wishes to commit adultery at the expense of her well-to-do and hard-working husband. Eventually, she wins her audience's sympathy with a clever plot that demonstrates both her character's *furbizia* (cunning) and *virtù* along with the foolishness of a sanctimonious friar who she enlists to unwittingly set up her affair. Actually, that plot is so clever and her *virtù*-ous playing of the gullible friar so delicious that by the end readers are ready to forgive all the sexual dishonesty involved in her display of *virtù*.[31]

But Boccaccio sets the stage for this using a quicker strategy early in the tale to gain sympathy for the character. Noting that she is a Florentine in a city known for its fraud and cunning, his narrator, Pampinea, describes her character, without revealing her name, as a *"gentil donna* adorned with both beauty and manners and with as lofty a soul and as subtle an intelligence as nature had given to any woman of her time."[32] The excuse for not naming her is that some people might take offense at her clever plot and her adultery, even if in the end the whole affair would be more justly "overlooked with a laugh."[33] In other words, she is a refined upper-class woman who deserves a lover of similar quality, especially because her adultery was not all that serious a matter, as it was motivated by a desire for a more refined and noble love.

Her husband, who may well not have agreed with that proposition if he were not a mere literary character, is portrayed as being incapable of offering that kind of cultivated love and sex that she deserves, even if he is wealthy and clearly qualifies economically as a member of the Florentine *popolo grosso*. Pampinea clarifies these subtle distinctions as the tale begins:

> This lady of gentle birth *(alto legnaggio)* finding herself married to a master woolen cloth producer *(artefice lanaiuolo)*, although he was very rich, [she] could not restrain her deep

contempt [for him], because she believed that no man of low
condition, however rich he might be was worthy of a *gentil
donna* [like her]. And seeing that for all his wealth all he was
capable of was distinguishing wool from cotton, overseeing
the setting up of a loom, or debating types of yarn with a
spinstress, she decided to avoid his embraces as much as she
possibly could and instead satisfy herself with someone
more worthy than a master woolen cloth producer *(lanai-
uolo)*. Thus she fell in love with a most gracious man in his
middle years.[34]

This negative valuation of a boorish husband, while it offers a quick
excuse for the adultery that is to follow, offers as well a perfect snapshot
of the social tensions and animosities that troubled Florence and much
of the urban world of northern Italy at the time.

For it reflects the perspective of a woman who sees herself as coming
from an old and distinguished family line, whose position on top of the
social hierarchy should be unquestioned, from her perspective at least.
Yet, it is significant that she is not referred to as a noble but rather as a
gentil donna, for the old Florentine nobility had long been eliminated
(at least officially) from the social and political world of Florence by
the mid-fourteenth century. Nonetheless, she considered her own social
status on top of society secure because of her family line, something
that she was unwilling to grant her rich and powerful upstart husband.
Instead she paints him as a base artisan, and a boring one at that, with
his inability to discuss anything beyond business and his craft with artisans even more base than he and, worse yet, even his women laborers.

Still, it was just his business and craft, the woolen industry (along
with banking) that had rapidly transformed Florence from a rather
sleepy, also-ran, little city in a not particularly promising corner of Tuscany into a major international power and one of the richest cities in
Europe in a little more than a century following the middle of the thirteenth century. And significantly, artisan entrepreneurs like her husband
were among the most important leaders of the *popolo grosso* and coming
to politically and socially dominate Florence. Actually, contemporaries
probably would have assumed immediately that the reason her family
had married her to this man she disdained was because they recognized

(or feared) that he and others like him had arrived and were successfully replacing them on top of society.[35] In sum, our anonymous wife rejects her *popolo grosso* husband because he is not refined, mannered, or cultured enough to be her lover. He literally lacks the *virtù* to offer her true love or the refined pleasures of the sex that went with it. But, of course, he did not lack *virtù* from his own perspective or that of many of his fellow leaders of Florence, who embraced the term with more of an emphasis on the very reason, moderation, planning, and cunning that they saw as making them rich and successful and setting them on top of society.

And, tellingly, the tales of the *Decameron* are quite capable of switching to this perspective and rejecting this *gentil donna*'s logic, actually with the same narrator, Pampinea, presenting the other side of the coin in the third tale of day two. Once again, Fortuna and *virtù* are the protagonists in a story of love. Fortuna actually starts out as the culprit, aided by what might be read as a decided lack of *popolo grosso virtù*, for the tale relates that in a not-too-distant past in Florence, three young brothers—the oldest was not yet eighteen—sons of a rich noble knight *(cavaliere)* found themselves so rich at their father's death that they felt they could indulge their every youthful whim. As a result, they spent their days living down to the stereotypical un-*virtù*-ous and wasteful ways of the old nobility at least as perceived at the time: "without anything governing their behavior beyond their own pleasure . . . they began to spend [their inherited wealth] retaining a plethora of servants, keeping numerous thoroughbred horses, hounds, and hawks, holding court regularly, giving presents and arming themselves [as nobles]."[36]

The upshot was exactly the fate that both Fortuna and a Florentine vision of *virtù* promised for such out-of-date behavior. Quickly, they found themselves on the verge of bankruptcy. But with a logic that would have made perfect sense to the *popolo grosso* of a banking city like fourteenth-century Florence, they sold the last of their possessions in the city and went off to England, where they began to lend money to the nobility there. Soon, thanks to their *virtù* as usurers and a frugal lifestyle more in line with Florentine *popolo grosso* values, they took full advantage of the unwary and outdated English nobility, recouped their fortunes, and returned to Florence rich and powerful again.

To keep the money coming in from England, they sent a young nephew of theirs, Alessandro, to London to continue lending money.

In Florence, however, they could not resist returning to their old spend-thrift and noble ways, forgetting quickly the *popolo grosso virtù* that had allowed them to remake their fortune at the expense of the presumably equally spendthrift English nobility. Alessandro kept them in cash for a while, but soon political problems in England created problems for business there. And the brothers back in Florence, without the constant infusion of cash from their nephew, found themselves once again in dire straits. So dire, in fact, that they were thrown into debtor's prison, "leaving their wives and little children to wander through the country-side . . . dressed most poorly."[37] Even the industrious Alessandro came on hard times, finding his business in England failing as his loans to nobles backed up by their estates came a cropper of the confiscation of those estates and disruptions there. To make matters worse, all the tur-moil, plus his usurious activities and his claims on the local nobility, did not put him in the best light with his debtors there; thus, he real-ized that it was time to seek a change of climate and return to the rela-tive safety of Florence.

So, he set off to return home. And as luck would have it—a more smiling Fortuna favoring, as was her wont, a handsome, mannerly young man—he encountered on his journey a caravan taking a young abbot to Rome to visit the pope. Fortuna was soon joined by *virtù* and obviously in a story about love, Amore and sexual pleasure could not be far behind. The abbot, noticing Alessandro and his good looks and mannerly ways (his *"virtù"*), took up a conversation with him. Hearing "his fine, logical way of speaking and more particularly considering his manners, he judged him to be a gentleman *(gentile uomo)* despite the lowly nature of his occupation; thus he became even more taken by him."[38] As a result, they passed the time of their journey enjoying each other's company with the abbot becoming ever more attracted to Alessandro. That is until one night things came to a head with a devel-opment that at first readers then and now might have interpreted as driven by a love, not atypical of the time, between male youths, which Pampinea labels "dishonest."[39]

It seems that that night, with the travelers lodging in a small inn, the host suggested that Alessandro might share the abbot's room, not having another place to give him to sleep. Alessandro was reluctant to impose on his newfound friend and travelling companion. But actually,

sharing rooms and even beds in inns was not an uncommon experience for fourteenth-century travelers; thus, finally, he agreed to share
the room with the abbot, who was already in bed and apparently asleep.
As often occurs in such tales, however, he was not. Moreover, he had
overheard the conversation between the host and Alessandro and was
overjoyed with its outcome. For, when Alessandro entered the room,
"the abbot, who was not asleep, was actually deeply reflecting upon his
newly aroused desires."[40] Had sexual desire or even lust entered this tale
of masculine friendship across major social divides—a desire of the theoretically most troubling sodomitical variety? Deeds quickly seemed to
confirm such assumptions. For, as soon as the inn quieted down, the
young abbot "with a humble voice called Alessandro and asked him to
join him in the bed," and he, after many objections, "undressed and
lay down beside him."[41] Once he climbed into bed next to the abbot,
the cleric "began to caress him just like courting youths *(giovani)* touch
their lovers *(amanti)* which caused Alessandro to worry . . . that the
youth was moved by an impure love *(disonesto amor)*."[42]

The abbot, however, quickly laid to rest all such misplaced fears.
With a smile, "he" tore open his shirt and said to Alessandro (but actually to us all), "Drive those foolish thoughts from your head, Alessandro. Put your hand here, and you will discover what I am hiding."[43]
What Alessandro discovered were "two firm and delicate little breasts."[44]
In sum, that he was she. The abbot was actually a young woman cross-
dressed as a man. Alessandro responded as a young man should in such
tales, taking her in his arms and attempting to kiss her. But she stopped
him and explained that she was a virgin on her way to the pope to secure
his approval of her marriage. And calling upon love and fortune, driven
by *virtù*, she explained, "I don't know whether it is your good fortune
or my past problems, but from the first moment I saw you, I burned
with a love deeper than any woman has ever felt for any man. And thus
I decided that I want you more than any other as my husband."[45] Alessandro's superior manners and behavior, despite his questionable occupation as a Florentine banker (and worse yet a usurer), had won this obviously noble woman's love. Driven by love and its accompanying sexual
desires, but restrained by reason and the modesty required of a young
virgin, she suggested that they marry immediately. And although the
tale makes no claim for Alessandro's suddenly falling in love with the

young abbot, even seeming to suggest that his motives for accepting her offer were perhaps more mercantile and typical of the Florentine *popolo grosso*—"given the size of her retinue he realized that she was rich and noble, and that she was very beautiful as he could see"[46]—he readily accepted her offer of marriage.

In turn, wasting no time, once he accepted, "she sat up on the edge of the bed where there was a picture of Our Lord, gave him a wedding ring, and they wed. Then they fell into each other's arms, and for what remained of the night with the greatest mutual pleasure they enjoyed themselves."[47] Fortune, love, and *virtù* working together happily crossed social divisions, resulting in mutual sexual pleasure. And as the tale eventually revealed, they did so in the most radical manner, for the young abbot was actually the daughter of the king of England, fleeing a marriage that her father was trying to arrange with the king of Scotland for political reasons. Unwilling to be a pawn in his political schemes and sacrificed in a loveless marriage to a much older man, she had fled to seek a match where a truer passion and pleasure could be found. In Alessandro she had discovered, thanks to Fortuna and his display of *virtù* in his mannered ways and conversation, exactly the love match and marital pleasures that she sought.

From a Florentine perspective at least, Alessandro, although he belonged to an old noble family, actually lived as, and made his living as, a member of the higher echelons of the Florentine *popolo grosso* and as such had the *virtù* to be an attractive lover even for an English princess. (One wonders what the English would have made of this vision.) And, significantly, for once in the *Decameron*, the details of living happily ever after in marriage are detailed, as the young man goes on to demonstrate the larger success that his *virtù* seemed to promise his princess. For, in the end, he returned to England with the pope's approval for his marriage; won over his father-in-law, the king of England; became a major baron; helped bring peace to the kingdom; and some even claimed eventually conquered Scotland to become its king.[48] Not so much *amor vincit omnia* as *virtù vincit omnia* with a useful dash of a Fortuna smiling on a young man.

What made the difference between Pampinea's two stories for her listeners was the different emphasis on how *virtù* could operate in a Florentine social context. Her wool-working entrepreneur, while clearly a

significant member of the *popolo grosso* of Florence, is distinguished in
the tale by those aspects of *virtù* that helped make him rich and powerful and that were widely respected. But he had focused on those attributes so exclusively that he opened himself to criticism from those
who stressed graceful manners and love as important markers of social
status. They envisioned a more mannerly and refined *popolo grosso* on
top of society fully capable of the gentlemanly behavior demonstrated
by Alessandro—a vision that would eventually win out in Italy with a
more aristocratic elite attempting to distinguish themselves from the
rest of the *popolo* and even the *popolo grosso*. In the fifteenth century in
Florence, for example, ex-usurers and bankers like the Medici would become princes with their quiet glories and progressively less quiet ones as
well—and in the sixteenth century, they would actually marry into the
royal families of Europe much as Pampinea's tale anticipated.

How Lust Resulted in the Downfall of the Angel Gabriel and Master Simone's Surprising Success as the Count of the Cesspool

In contrast, while love, when melded with *virtù*, could demonstrate, and
even at times create status, sexual desire without true refined love, especially when perceived negatively as lust, never allowed a move up the
social scale, even when combined with *virtù* and *fortuna*. Tales like that
of the clever friar, who cunningly convinced a vain Venetian noblewoman that the angel Gabriel was in love with her heavenly beauty and
wished to use his humble human body in order to express the passionate love the angel felt, demonstrate this to readers with a dark
humor (IV, 2). The friar in this tale carried off his scam by convincing a
stereotypically foolish Venetian woman, who needed little convincing,
that she was so beautiful that the angel Gabriel had fallen madly in love
with her. That, however, created one significant problem for the angel,
as, being a spiritual being, he lacked a physical body to consummate his
desire. To overcome that serious problem for a love-driven spirit, the
devious friar explained to his victim that he had offered Gabriel the use
of his body on loan, as it were, to enjoy his passion for her in exchange
for being allowed to enjoy paradise while the angel was otherwise occupied. As a result, the friar, angel-like, flew high several times with his

virtù-ous ploy, enjoying his foolish prey as an angel come down to earth to love and sexually serve the most beautiful noblewoman of Venice.

In the end, however, these high-flying pleasures were brought low. First, when attempting to escape her brothers who arrived to investigate the rumors that were circulating about their sister's heavenly affair, the friar launched himself from her window, literally attempting to take flight—and instead plummeted into the canal beneath her window, lacking Gabriel's more normal and less sexual flying capabilities. And, a second time, he was literally brought to ground when the man who rescued him covered him with honey and dressed him up as a boar, ostensibly to help him escape. Things quickly went from bad to worse, however. As the friar was harried by the flies and gnats that the honey attracted, his "savior" led him to Saint Mark's Square, where he was exposed to the public gathered there as the angel who had come down from heaven to service the women of Venice. What followed was a ritual debasing that echoed a yearly Venetian festive slaughtering of a bull and twelve pigs by the artisans of the city in the square from which he was saved, only much the worse for wear, by his fellow friars.[49] Lust, masquerading as heavenly, and a cunning *virtù* had taken him from flying high as the angel Gabriel—the airy heights of the Christian and sexual world of the day—to public humiliation and being pelted with filth in Saint Mark's Square, a dramatic physical, moral, and social fall. True love could elevate, false could, and did at times, especially in moral tales, bring one low.

But perhaps the best tale that illustrates the way giving in to lustful sexual desires and their dangerous passions could undercut status and demean both figuratively and literally features once more Calandrino's buddies and victimizers, Bruno and Buffalmacco. In the ninth tale of the eighth day, the two decide to chastise with a clever and disciplining *beffa* a certain Master Simone, a physician who was well known in Florence as being more endowed with riches than intelligence or *virtù*. Actually, the narrator, Lauretta, begins the tale with a short disquisition on the foolish behavior of those who go off to study law or medicine at the University of Bologna and return to Florence full of airs and pretensions. In Florence, as in much of the rest of the peninsula, a university degree and being a lawyer or a doctor usually qualified one as a member of the *popolo grosso,* and Simone's reported wealth only underlined that status.[50] But foolishness and the foolishness engendered by lust could seriously undermine even that status, just as being a refined lover demonstrating *virtù* could confirm it.

Simone, it seems, lived near Bruno and Buffalmacco in Florence. And although, as the story makes clear, the two artisan painters were far below him on the social scale and actually quite poor, observing them, Simone was impressed by the way they always seemed to be so happy and appeared to live well beyond their means. Given their predilection for clever schemes at the expense of others that always seemed to bring them money or other rewards—a virtual *topos* in the other *Decameron* stories that feature them—it might be hypothesized that the real reason for this was their *virtù*-ous and profitable trickery. Be that as it may, however, Simone "convinced himself, having heard that they were very clever [*astuti*], that they must be drawing large profits from some other source that no one else knew about."[51] So, Simone decided to make friends with them and eventually gained the confidence of Bruno after wining and dining him for a while.

When finally he asked Bruno directly how he and his friend managed to live so well, the painter, recognizing his "crass stupidity," with clever *virtù* offered exactly the bait that he knew would hook his mark: "Master (Simone), there are few people to whom I would reveal how we do this, but as you are a friend and I know you won't tell anyone . . . we simply go the course and in this way we get all the pleasures and necessities of life without doing harm to anyone; and from this comes our happiness which you have noticed."[52] Simone quickly focused on the obscure phrase "going the course" and eventually got Bruno to explain what it meant. He confided that recently the famous necromancer Michael Scott had visited Florence. When he departed, however, he left behind two of his disciples, who organized a secret sect dedicated to magically "going the course," which Bruno and Buffalmacco had joined. At regular meetings of the group members, all their wishes were magically fulfilled, replete with wonderful dishes, beautiful music, and "above and beyond all these other pleasures, there are the beautiful women who as soon as a man wishes are brought to us there from every corner of the earth."[53]

Bruno then lists the exotic princesses and queens who are at their beck and call and doubles the dose, bragging, "but it seems to me that we are better off than the others, Buffalmacco and me ... when one considers that we enjoy the love of two such queens as these [Buffalmacco's mistress is the queen of France and Bruno's the queen of England], not to mention the fact that when we want one or two thousand florins from them, we don't get them."[54] Although Bruno humorously denies that they actually got the florins they ask for, again playing on the foolishness of Simone, the doctor apparently is so taken by the idea of getting florins along with sex that he is more determined than ever to "go the course." His lust is fired both in terms of the florins he believes mistakenly are to be had and in terms of commanding the sexual services of the most noble and beautiful women in the world; thus, he immediately began to beg Bruno to let him join the group. Significantly, it is made clear that Simone was not interested in ennobling love or shared sexual pleasure. Indeed, it never entered the discussion. Money and his own self-centered sexual pleasure were what he passionately desired, in many ways perhaps the two greatest lusts of the day. And Bruno seemed to be able to command them magically.

Of course, this then kicked in a series of Bruno and Buffalmacco's typical scams to relieve Simone of as much wealth as possible. Driven by his lust, he was a victim easily plucked. To increase his eagerness, they made a point of the social advantage that went with sexually enjoying the woman that would be his mistress. For they promised that, if he joined their group, his mistress would be none other than "the Countess of Civillari, the most beautiful piece *(cosa)* that one can find among all the ass-cultivators of humanity."[55] After they described this great catch in more detail with clever wordplay that revealed to readers that the countess was not quite what Simone imagined, even if lost in his lust, he was more than ever convinced that he was ready to go the course. But eventually the plotters had to deliver, and as this was a story about how *beffe* correct misplaced desires and unwarranted claims of social and intellectual superiority, it had to conclude with a *virtù*-osity that made the doctor rue his unbridled lust and that replaced him firmly in his deserved place in society.

Cleverly, then, the pair informed him that, thanks to their efforts on his behalf, he had been elected a member of their company. And that very night they promised that he would be carried to their meeting and enjoy his countess, who planned to make him what he assumed was a Knight of the Bath but was actually a bathed knight (*cavaliere bagnato*) and tellingly so.[56] They warned him, however, that there was just one little problem. They were worried because, in order to get to the meeting, he had to be picked up in the graveyard of the church of Santa Maria Novella by a rather fearful figure that might scare a man of lesser courage. Simone was to wait there dressed in his best robes for "a black beast with horns . . . which though not very large . . . will attempt to frighten you." When it saw that he was not afraid, they promised him, "it will come slowly toward you, and as soon as it has drawn near . . . you must . . . without invoking God or any of the Saints, leap on its back."[57] Simone reassured them that they had nothing to be worried about as far as his courage was concerned, regaling his friends with tales of his "courageous" sexual assaults on women in Bologna, demonstrating, if there was any need, that he was no lover and his total lack of *virtù* in his lusts to the last.

The stage was set for the final act. That evening, as master Simone waited in the graveyard in his best academic gowns suitable for enjoying his noble "piece," Buffalmacco, who was a large burly man, dressed himself up in a bear costume and donned a carnival mask with a devil's face and horns to become quite an impressive demon. He then entered the piazza of Santa Maria Novella, where the doctor was waiting, and began dancing and jumping all over the square, "hissing, screaming, and shrieking like one possessed. . . . When the doctor saw and heard all this, his every hair stood on end and he began to tremble all over, as if *he was more afraid than a woman*."[58] Once again, strong passions had rendered a man feminine and a victim of his emotion, but in this case it was fear not love. Still, he managed to strike up the courage to climb on the demon's back as he had been instructed. In his panic, however, he forgot that he was not supposed to irritate the demon by invoking God or any of the saints. Thus, he whispered to himself as he was climbing on the creature's back, "God save me."[59]

And that was the last step on the way to his final downfall, for the demon Buffalmacco, hearing that frightened appeal, which he and Bruno had anticipated Simone would make sooner or later, silently took him to what the foolish doctor believed was to be his promised domains, if not his promised mistress. For he thought he had been promised that he would become a Knight of the Bath; and the tale's narrator explained, "At that time there were some ditches in those parts

into which laborers used to pour the offerings of the Countess of Civillari [the cesspools] to enrich their lands."[60] Not to put too fine a point
on it, there Buffalmacco heaved him into the shit, ostensibly for having
appealed to God in his fear. In the end, the doctor with all his riches,
his degree from Bologna, and his academic robes was dumped into a
cesspool—a rather different bath to be the knight of, and one that confirmed his status (much like that of the flying friar posing as the angel
Gabriel) as being anything but a refined lover.[61] Lustful desire, sexual,
social, and monetary, without any sign of *virtù,* had revealed him to be
not a noble or even a noble lover but rather the Lord of the Cesspools
thanks to a clever *beffa*—and with poetic justice left him bathed in shit.
In sum, as true love ennobled, mere lust brought even a well-established,
but greedily foolish, member of the upper classes low.

Where the Reader's Failure as Calandrino the Lover Is Explained with a Smile

At the level of artisans like Calandrino, then, lower down the perceived
social scale, love rarely was available as a way to claim a higher status.
Only exceptional *virtù* could allow a leap from artisan status to become
a refined elite lover, and when that occasionally happened it demonstrated its tremendous power. In fact, in Calandrino's tale of his imagined noble love, the story evoked laughter by ironically mocking the way
his attempts at *virtù*-ous, refined love fell far short of the mark, as was
assumed to be more normally the case. His struggles to sound like a refined lover with a sophisticated mastery of the language of love regularly came across as base and coarse. For example, when Bruno offered
to press his case with his new love and asks him what loving words he
wants him to convey to her, he offers, "Wow! You should tell her first
right away that I wish her a thousand bushels of the most best to im-
pregnate her and let her know that I am her super-servant, if she wants
anything—do you understand?"[62] Needless to say, this was hardly Petrarch or a speech that would convince anyone that Calandrino had
been ennobled by his love or any *virtù* that might accompany it, in
telling contrast to Cimone's transforming love.

Bruno, as his adviser, also alerts him to the fact that he has to play
his cards carefully to keep the budding affair secret, and Calandrino

assures him that he knows how to play the role of a discrete adulterous lover. Yet, when dinnertime came and the company gathered in the courtyard with his love and her supposed husband, he "began to look at Niccolosa and do the strangest *(i piú nuovi)* things ever seen, of a manner and so obvious, that even a blind man would have realized [what he was supposedly keeping secret]."[63] Again, his display of his lack of *virtù* in his courtship offered contemporary readers of the tale both laughter and reassurance that his desire has not ennobled him in any way.

Moreover, his songs and his playing of his humble rebec,[64] although enjoyed by his "comrades," marked him out as lower class as well; no gentleman lover would have been caught dead playing such an instrument unless he was impersonating a pastoral, rustic lover. But Calandrino was not impersonating one; he was unwittingly demonstrating that he was one. Even his falling back on love magic suggested that he was not a true lover and had little understanding of how to actually be one. And, of course, the object of his love was not the refined upper-class wife he foolishly believed her to be but merely a clever prostitute in on the *beffa* at his expense and enjoying her role leading him on. Needless to say, as a lower-class artisan, he did not even have the eye or the judgment to tell the difference. In sum, the way he attempted to reach beyond his station in life using love simply did not work. And it would never have worked. A lower-class artisan, he lowered love and sexual desire to his level, even as he dreamed of reaching up to enjoy its refined pleasures and being ennobled by it himself.

In fact, in the face of that cruel realization, it might well be conjectured that this and the other Calandrino tales that bring laughter to the last days of the *Decameron* tell a less humorous story from a social perspective. For, as we shall see, the tales of the *Decameron* show repeatedly the power of *virtù* to garner positive results for lower-class characters, and indeed even women. This had the potential, however, to be a troubling proposition in a society where social mobility and new men were challenging traditional social verities, and a newer social elite, the *popolo grosso,* was fighting to confirm its place on top of society. Crucially, from this perspective, the tales make clear that there was the *virtù* of the upper classes and the *popolo grosso,* who would become progressively more aristocratic, and then there was the rather different *virtù* of those lower down the social scale, especially distinguished by its lack of manners and refinement. In exceptional cases, as we shall see, someone at the bottom of the social scale could surprisingly master the *virtù* of the elites with virtually miraculous results that proved more the strength of *virtù* than the potential for members of the lower class to be able to move up the social scale at least from the perspective of Boccaccio and the *Decameron*. Beyond such unlikely miracles, the cleverest denizens of the lower classes, men like Bruno and Buffalmacco, displayed great *virtù*, as their many successful *beffe* and scams demonstrated. But they lacked the refined manners, graces, and social skills that made one a lover and a true member of the highest social levels. No contemporary would have ever labeled them gentlemen. And their tales portray them as happy with that and uninterested in elite graces or refinements, never questioning their social place, at least in the imaginary of the *Decameron*'s laughing tales.

Calandrino, in his many moments as the victim of his comrades' clever *beffe*, demonstrated repeatedly and reassuringly that most artisans were incapable of matching the more refined *virtù* of their social superiors.[65] In fact, over and over again, the tales portray lower-class love as closer to lust and give such passions a bawdier and lower tone. In doing this, however, even such tales and such sexual desires are rarely condemned unless they involve mistreating undeserving victims. And I would suggest that this creates a problem for critics who want to interpret the *Decameron* as ultimately moralistic or ironic in its treatment of sex, sexual pleasures, and the passions that accompany them. In fact, Boccaccio usually carefully constructs the tales to motivate lower-class desire and even lust positively, as at worst small "natural sins" or very human desires—fashioning them, then, as largely enjoyable and unthreatening for a contemporary audience.

Laughter is often seen as the greatest antidote to fear; and laughing at Calandrino and his lower-class antics and humiliation in the *Decameron* help make the other tales that stress the success that *virtù* could bring even to humble characters considerably less threatening. In turn, with stories like that of the pretentious and lustful doctor Simone becoming the Lord of the Cesspools or the boring but unlovable rich wool weaver betrayed by his wife and her clever, refined adultery, the tales also warned that status could be lost if one did not live up to the higher standards that upper-class *virtù*, true love, and refined sexual desires required, even as those standards might be contested. Yet, on those rare occasions worthy of a novella, when those words of power, *virtù*, Fortuna, and Amore all cooperated, they were so potent that they could turn even the beastly Cimone into the ideal citizen of the *Decameron*'s imagined Rinascimento city and world.

For Calandrino, however, there was no hope. Thus Boccaccio's fellow Florentines among the *popolo grosso* could find in the often laughing tales of his victimization an attractive vision of how their superior *virtù* in love set them apart from and above the common herd of the *popolo*, a vision that many shared. And whether they did or did not, as they and other denizens of the cities of Italy became more aristocratic across the fifteenth century, the vision of upper-class *virtù* in many ways increasingly imagined a similarly refined vision of *virtù*, where pure love triumphed over mere lust at least ideally. In that world, as in many *Decameron* tales, pure love and refined passion marked out the best from the rest, and the rest were left with the supposedly simpler pleasures of lustful desire and a smile or even laughter.

2

Violence

Scorn, Retribution, and Civilized Courtship

Where Three Hearts Are Ripped Out in the Name of Love and Its Violent Emotions

Although Calandrino's imagined ennobling love and, if anything, even more imagined refined sexual desire evoked wholehearted laughter from the *brigata* of young aristocratic Florentine listeners, when one reflects on his beating and disgrace or the even more violent and humiliating experiences of Master Simone, ultimately the Lord of the Cesspool, one is struck by the cruelty and violence of the demeaning *beffe* they suffered. And, in turn, if one looks at the heroic and *virtù*-ous (if clearly not virtuous) deeds that the newly civil-ized Cimone used to win his marriage to the woman he loved, one is struck with the violence involved and how crucial it was in proving and securing his love. Clearly, violence and its emotions were closely associated with love and sexual desire in the *Decameron* and, I would suggest, in the Rinascimento as well.

In many ways, this does not seem surprising today when violent crimes associated with love and sex, especially with women as their victim, seem to be on the increase or at the very least seem to have justifiably captured the public's attention and concern. But violence, like humor, I would argue, often has very specific cultural resonances; indeed, it tends to literally vibrate with the tensions and conflicts of its day and milieu. And as is the case with humor and jokes, it is frequently not that easy to understand what an act of violence means or meant in a different time, place, and culture. As argued briefly in the first chapter, Cimone's violence, so troubling today, would more likely have been seen at the time as a quite traditional way of gaining the hand of a woman whose family wished to block marriage, in that case with his beloved Efigenia, as well as a form of heroism in the service of his deeply felt love—virtually as part of a series of dangerous and violent proofs of that *virtù*-ous love and the ultimately honorable sexual desire he consecrated with marriage. In this context, and given that the association of violence, love, and sex is ubiquitous in the *Decameron* (and often responded to by the *brigata* in ways troubling to modern readers), a closer look at the association between them seems in order.

One Friday near Ravenna on the beautiful, virtually paradisi-acal, island of Classe, a young, rich aristocrat, Nastagio degli Onesti, was walking deep in thought about his unhappy failure in courtship and love—and an overwhelming failure it was. One that, in fact, had led him to the brink of suicide and to eventually flee the urban world that had made him recognized as a rich and well-mannered aristocrat in Ravenna. As he walked along, abruptly and disconcertingly, the vi-olence of love and sexual desire overthrew his quiet disquiet, for sud-denly he saw a naked young woman run down by dogs and brutally slain by an enraged knight.

The violence of that murder deeply disturbed Nastagio, and he re-ports it in all its gruesome detail: "like a rabid dog with a blade in hand he [the knight] threw himself at the woman who was on her knees and crying for mercy, being held by the two mastiffs, and with all his force he stabbed her in the breast so violently that it went all the way through her body." But this was just the beginning of a scene of disturbingly graphic violence, for Nastagio continued with his troubling and mor-bidly voyeuristic account, reporting that the blow knocked her to the ground and, as she lay there "crying and screaming: the knight took a knife and cutting her open from behind tore out her heart and with what came with it, threw it all to the dogs, who with great hunger ate it."[1] Hardly a scene that seems to evoke love or refined sexual desire, but both were quite literally at its heart.

Indeed, both the hearts ripped from violently killed lovers and the way violence and love and its concomitant sexual desires went hand in hand in the Rinascimento are virtually topoi of the *Decameron*. When in another disturbing tale Guiglielmo Rossiglione discovered that his best friend Guiglielmo Guardastagno was having an affair with his wife, "the great love *(il grande amore)* that he felt for Guardastagno was transformed into mortal hate."[2] Thus, after luring his ex-friend to a secluded spot, with a group of his followers, he ambushed him. Then, once he had driven a lance through his chest, he dismounted, "took a knife, cut open the breast of Guardastagno, and with his own hands tore out his heart."[3] But with a disquieting poetic cruelty, rather than throwing this heart to the dogs, he had it prepared as a dinner for his wife, serving it to her as a gourmet dish. Then, brutally cutting to the heart of his violent deed for her and the listeners to the tale, after she had eaten it with gusto, he asked her if she had enjoyed the dish. And she replied in her innocent guilt that "she liked it very much."[4]

The contrast with dogs wolfing down a heart, like the animals they were, with an aristocratic woman eating the heart of her lover with pleasure and refined taste (*"gusto"*) merely adds a chilling edge to the cruel violence of her husband. And the contrast between a reasoned cruelty and a merely savage act seems to say a great deal about the more troubling violence associated with reasoned behavior—for in its reasoned and measured cruelty, the deed reflected a particularly troubling form of *virtù*. In that context, cruelly twisting the knife one last time for his formerly beloved wife, he revealed his clever and carefully planned and measured revenge—literally its *virtù*—pointing out coldly to her that the dish she had so enjoyed was the heart of her lover. In the face of his violence, she matched it with her own *virtù* in the name of love, leaping from a nearby window to her death. Violent murder, suicide, and once again a ripped-out heart, suggesting the violence that love and sex could evoke: in this case, a double love, the adulterous love of nobles and the close masculine friendship typified in this tale as "love" between the murderer and his victim as well, all triggered by rage in the face of a friend's and a wife's betrayal.

But perhaps the most troubling heart scene in the *Decameron* is a little less graphic but much more heart-rending because the tale takes the time to carefully transform the illicit lovers into heroes and the man responsible for their death into a victim of his own uncontrolled rage, misplaced sense of honor, and ultimately his own violent love for his daughter. In this tale, when Tancredi, the prince of Salerno, discovers that his daughter Ghismonda has been secretly carrying on an affair with Guiscardo, a mere servant of his, he controls his rage only long enough to act out more completely the violence that his strongly felt emotions seemed to demand. Carefully, and avoiding scandal at first, Tancredi had Guiscardo arrested. Then, after he tearfully berated his daughter for the affair, he secretly had the young man killed. But rather than ripping out the lover's heart himself, a much more civilized prince, he ordered his men to do the brutal deed of cutting out Guiscardo's heart for him.

Civilized cruelty perhaps, but the more troubling brutality was yet to come. The next day, he sent the heart to his daughter in a golden chalice with the message, "Your father sends you this to console you with the thing you loved most, just as you consoled him with that which he loved most."[5] And, once again, his violent love was rewarded with her violence in return, for Ghismonda poured poison over the heart and with noble words drank it down, committing suicide. Thus, in her death, she made herself a heroine of love. The tale makes this perfectly clear by having her, as she lay dying, ask her father to bury her with her love in a public ceremony. Destroyed by his loss, and his suddenly lost beloved daughter, he responded with what might have been seen as his own fatherly love rediscovered, for he allowed the lovers to be reunited in death, buried in a common grave, "with honor." And the tale makes clear that the ceremony was received with general mourning from the people of Salerno, who were deeply moved by the young couple's tragic love and martyrdom. For all that, evidently the violent emotions that love and sex could engender were clearly an explosive mix for lovers, their hearts, and the hearts of society more generally.

Where It Is Asked Who Is the Real Victim of Violence in Nastagio's Love Story and What It Takes to Be a True Lover and Person in the Rinascimento

Clearly, love, sex, and violence were deeply and often tragically associated in the *Decameron*. Yet, upon deeper consideration, these brief tastes of tales of graphic violence might also warn us about the problems of interpreting just what they meant and how they played at the time. For they are so powerful and so troubling today that interpretation becomes almost too easy, and the complexities of the issues involved may be lost in a quite justified modern revulsion in the face of violence so nakedly and graphically depicted. That is almost certainly the case in the tale of Nastagio. Disconcertingly, its narrator, Filomena, opens her account promising that it will please her women compatriots in the brigata "equally for the compassion and the pleasure [it evokes]."[6] Her rationale for this promise is telling, however: "Loveable ladies, just as in us piety / pity (pietà) is to be commended, so it is that cruelty in us is strictly punished / vindicated (vendicata) by divine justice."[7]

Two terms stand out in her explanation. First, "pietà," often translated as simply "pity" but implying in this case a deeper emotion kindled by a form of pious pity evoked by God and divine justice. Second, "vendicata," that divine justice is presented as a form of vendetta or vindication: in essence, implying a divine justice used deservedly against those who do not act when necessary with the required pious pity. Significantly, associating divine justice with vendetta slides us away from most modern considerations of violence and takes us back to a fourteenth-century world where divine justice could have and often did have the deeply familiar quality of vendetta. Dante's extremely violent Inferno in his Divine Comedy comes immediately to mind as the perhaps best-known literary example of divine justice from the century, which also, tellingly, often troubles the modern imagination, even as it was much appreciated by Dante-character as the hero of his Divine Comedy.[8] As the character Dante is guided through Hell by Virgil, both he and his companion thoroughly enjoy the vindictive violence inflicted on the sinners encountered, even ex-friends from this world, and only rarely show sympathy for their suffering. In the few cases where they do, the ground is carefully prepared for that sympathy, whereas, in contrast, more normally violent punishments are presented as just and respected for their justness and for their nicely appropriate brutality.

It has been frequently pointed out that those punishments tend to reflect the kinds of punishments used in governmental displays of violence deployed at the time to punish crime, violent punishments that were presented as positive and deserved.[9] In sum, while Filomena is aware that her story will involve some of the violent emotions associated with love and sexual desire, she is preparing her listeners to see that violence in a positive light. Of course, to be more accurate, Boccaccio is using Filomena as his mouthpiece to present that violence in a positive light. And perhaps in using a woman to do so, as a woman is the victim of that violence, he may be revealing a concern that even his fourteenth-century readers might have felt a certain unease with that violence despite the justification, divine and human, provided in the narration.

Be that as it may, the placing of this tale in Ravenna, as well as on the nearby island of Classe, immediately evoked Dante's *Divine Comedy*. And scholars have convincingly argued that the tale seems to offer a commentary on the tragic tale of the love between Paolo and Francesca told there, although exactly what that commentary might have intended has been grounds for considerable debate.[10] Fortunately for our analysis, however, what that commentary was or even if it was intended as a commentary is less important than the more general echoes of Dante that contemporaries would have heard in this tale and what those echoes would have implied for the way violence and love were associated at the time and the emotions involved. Yet the focus on Dante's sad tale of Paolo and Francesca has contributed to a tendency of critics to overlook a less dramatic and less physically gruesome episode of violence in Filomena's tale that contemporaries would have seen and felt was especially meaningful. For the protagonist of the novella, Nastagio degli Onesti, is portrayed as a victim of violence as well—actually a violence so traumatic that it led him to seriously contemplate suicide, not unlike the self-sacrificing heroines discussed earlier.

The tale makes this clear almost immediately, as Filomena relates that the woman he loved was "a young woman much more noble than he," the daughter of the noble Paolo Traversano, who Nastagio hoped "with his deeds to bring . . . to love him."[11] She, however, did not simply reject his courtship, as perhaps was required by her higher status and desire to protect her reputation for chastity. Indeed, if she had, there probably would have been no tale to tell for Boccaccio's Trecento readers. Rather, despite the fact that he was a very rich young man of good family, labeled, in fact, as one comprised of "very noble and well-mannered men" (*assai nobili e gentili uomini*), and even though his courting deeds were presented as "very great, beautiful and praiseworthy" *(grandissime, belle e laudevole)*, his courtship was rejected. And, crucially, it was rejected scornfully without the gentle or ennobling courtesy that such courtship entailed and his own status required.[12]

Actually, the woman he courted with manners and grace demonstrated such "naked and hard scorn" in return that Filomena took the time to reflect on the reason for her cruel disdain, suggesting that "perhaps because of her singular beauty or her nobility, she became so haughty and disdainful *(altiera e disdegnosa)* that neither he nor anything he liked was pleasing to her."[13] With this violent *disdegno,* even of anything he might simply have liked, her dishonoring rejection of him as a suitor went far beyond a mere declaration that she did not return his love or simply did not wish to be courted—it literally destroyed him as a young, aristocratic lover. Clearly, there was violence in this haughty scorn and rejection, especially when a polite and mannered refusal was what the polite game of courtship called for.[14] Yet, equally clearly, it seems much less violent than ripping out someone's heart and feeding it to the dogs—the cruelty that from our earlier discussion we know will follow shortly in the tale. From a modern perspective, the comparison seems to be between a form of merely psychological violence (disdain / scorn) in contrast with a gruesomely physical form of violence; and that graphically physical attack on a naked and defenseless woman certainly weighs more heavily on the psyche of modern readers. Moreover, the tale itself, as told by Filomena, stresses that physical violence in all its troubling detail.

Yet, for all that, it might be considered that, in the eyes of contemporaries, the gruesome details of the violence inflicted were first, of course, not inflicted on a live woman but a dead one being punished for her sins in Hell (just like Dante's violently suffering sinners). And, thus, it could be viewed as an example of deserved divine justice (and explicitly presented as such in both cases), while the violence that Nastagio suffered was inflicted on a living man for loving and treating well his beloved in the normal and, ideally at least, highly civilized courting life of the youths of Ravenna. In the everyday urban world of fourteenth-century listeners, that might well have weighed more heavily and seemed much more unjust than a modern reader might at first appreciate. For beyond the fact that the former violence was a just divine punishment for a sinner in Hell and the latter the unjust treatment of a living noble lover, a perhaps even more significant factor in the perception this violent disdain evoked turned on the fact that it was much more social, and deeply engrained with significance for the civil society of its day, than a modern interpretation might appreciate.

This, of course, is not to defend the former—totally indefensible from a modern perspective—or the latter, which is often written off as at best a shallow excuse for the cruelty to follow. But, having said that, it is necessary to consider the way contemporaries would have seen the violence that Nastagio suffered—a dishonoring violence so deep and profound that it struck at the very roots of his identity as a person and as a member of his urban world, as his serious contemplation of suicide in the face of that public rejection underlines. In essence, the felt violence of humiliating rejection in love led him to contemplate ending his personal identity via suicide. And, equally telling, as we shall see, he actually seemed to accept this, destroying his social identity by fleeing the social world of his city, Ravenna, to live alone on the nearby island of Classe—in a way, the very heart of his identity had been torn out by his beloved's *disdegno*.

For I want to suggest that a deeper Rinascimento understanding of personal identity was critical for understanding the more profound perils and emotions that clustered around love and desire in the fourteenth century. And that, in turn, deeply colored the way this tale and its multiple levels of violence would have been read at the time and, in fact, the reading of many of the most complex tales of the *Decameron* as well.

In recent works, I have discussed the nature of identity in the Rinascimento and the significant ways it was different from a modern sense of identity. As the cultural turn took off toward the end of the last century, following earlier more philosophical discussions, scholars began to argue that the modern sense of self was the product of modernity itself: from a left perspective, a product of bourgeois capitalism; from a Foucauldian perspective, a product of the discourses of modern disciplines. Both stressed, and in this followed and reinforced more general perceptions, that modern identity was essentially individual, unified, and primarily inner directed and largely a construct of the modern world. Thus it was argued that in the nineteenth and twentieth centuries the operating sense of self—at the heart of the way we conceive of ourselves as an inner-directed individual defending our ontological reality as a person in the economic, social, and political worlds that surround us—came to be perceived for the first time as separate and individual. Simply stated, as a result, we today see ourselves first and foremost as independent beings organizing, defending, and making our own lives, driven by an inner sense of who we really are.

One corollary of this understanding of the modern self was the idea that, before the modern world, no (or, more moderately, very little) sense of an inner true self existed. People saw themselves not as separate inner-directed individuals but rather as mere parts of larger social, economic, familial, and, to a lesser degree, political groups. Thus, one was not Nastagio but Nastagio degli Onesti—one of the noble, but not noble enough in this case, Onesti family. In turn, Nastagio was aristocratic, rich, young, and a man—class / wealth, age, and gender giving him meaningful group identities again. And he was also placed in an important association, as a citizen of the city of Ravenna. We could no doubt continue to place Nastagio in other groups as well, if we were living in Ravenna at the time of his tale, but for the moment it is enough to note that the tale identified him in those terms: noble, rich, young, male, a citizen of Ravenna, and a member of the Onesti family. Even the characterization of him as well-mannered, which seems at first glance more personal, might be more appropriately taken as another sign of upper-class status both socially and culturally, as we saw in the case of Calandrino, who lacked exactly those placing markers of aristocratic identity. Thus, it might be claimed that Nastagio had very little sense of individual, personal identity at all. And, in fact, it has been claimed. In turn, that suggests that he in this story, and other people beyond the imaginative world of literature, had little or no sense of personal identity in the modern sense.

Yet, as will become clear, and as the tale is about to make clear, Nastagio's response to his violent rejection in love was not simply as part of a group. Crucially, it was also as an individual—not a modern one but a Rinascimento one. In fact, his actions in the tale reveal the way Rinascimento identity worked and the very sense and power of such identity at the time. And, more pertinently yet for our discussion, how deeply and dangerously it could be intertwined with love, sex, and honor. For while Rinascimento identity was evidently not modern, I would suggest that there was a significant sense of identity at the time that turned on what I have called "consensus realities." Consensus realities were the imagined, but nonetheless very real and very significant, ways of conceptualizing an individual that were shared by the groups that surrounded one in the small, intimate world of the cities of the Rinascimento and the smaller rural communities that supported the urban life and culture of the day. Often they were not tight in their structure but fluid, functioning more like shared discussions about who a person really was and what might be expected of him or her in terms of behavior, discussions shared within the groups that maintained them and negotiated them with the individual being judged and identified.

The concept of consensus realities, building upon the idea of Renaissance self-fashioning so brilliantly developed by Stephen Greenblatt in his pioneering works on English literature, tries to recognize more fully the agency and individual power at play at the time that often seemed to get lost in the powerful cultural webs that Greenblatt saw as dominating his vision of self-fashioning. The key to the greater sense of agency that consensus realities offers for Rinascimento identity is the hypothesis that these ways of identifying a person were formed and continuously reformed in an ongoing process of negotiation between an individual and the groups with which he or she lived and interacted in daily life, such as the family, the neighborhood, fellow workers, fellow parish members, friends, fellow citizens, and on out in ever-widening circles. In the end, significantly, each group might maintain a quite different consensus reality about who a person actually was, and in each case a person had the ongoing opportunity to negotiate with deeds and words that consensus reality with each group.

For example, as I argued in *Machiavelli in Love,* Machiavelli negotiated quite different identities with his family, his friends, the rulers he tried to win over, and his fellow Florentines. With his family, he was an honorable and supportive family man (an ideal patriarch); with his close friends, he was a humorous (often self-mocking) and very active (if essentially passive) adulterer and lover of courtesans; with rulers, he carefully constructed an image of a thoughtful and perceptive commentator and a military expert as well; and with his fellow Florentines, he was a boldly honest, analytical, and at times quite clever and witty writer. Notably, these various identities were fluid and were not unified nor were they intended to be. Rather, as consensus realities, they were negotiated by him with each group to identify him in the right light for that group—the essence of his negotiated identity and its polyvalent meaning in his Rinascimento series of discourses of identity.[15]

If we look at Nastagio in this light, as a fictional character in a short novella, obviously we have less information for imagining how he might have negotiated his identity with the groups that surrounded him in society. But Filomena makes one thing clear, for she has immediately informed us that for many of the groups around him in Ravenna, he was seen as an honorable, rich, and dedicated lover of the daughter of Paolo Traversaro, who suggestively goes unnamed throughout the tale.[16] The tale, then, quickly sketches how Nastagio negotiated with those around him his identity as an ideal youthful lover and, in turn, how completely and cruelly his beloved rejected his courtship and that identity. In doing so, she destroyed his attempt to fashion his consensus reality as an ideal young lover, as surely as Bruno and Buffalmacco destroyed the hoped for, but never realized, consensus reality that Master Simone had attempted to construct for himself as a powerful lawyer and true aristocrat in Florence.

Nastagio was not dumped privately in shit; rather, and much worse, he was denied harshly and disdainfully before the groups with whom he negotiated his consensus reality, his identity as an aristocratic young lover. Not simply, then, as a lover but in his self-presentation as someone suitable to be seen as a noble young suitor and a worthy courtier, he was heartlessly and violently dumped in the shit of his beloved's highly public *disdegno*. In a way, undeservedly, he had been made into Calandrino—Calandrinized, we might say—by the cruel woman he loved. Faced with Calandrino's attempts at being a noble lover, given his lower-class status and well-laid-out foolishness, a contemporary audience could laugh; faced with Nastagio's much more public destruction, upper-class lovers would certainly find things no longer such a laughing matter: his very identity as an honorable noble lover had been publicly and repeatedly ruined before the very groups who determined his identity. And Boccaccio-writer has carefully structured the tale to lead us and his readers through this demeaning and allow us to feel the impact of its violence.

Significantly, however, Nastagio does not take this destruction of himself lying down. In fact, he fights it with behaviors that once again at first might strike a modern reader as odd. For, at the behest of his friends and relatives, who suggest that he leave Ravenna because he is destroying himself and his wealth in attempting to court this hard-hearted woman who so cruelly rejects him, he finally realizes that indeed he must leave or be ruined for the consensus realities that make him who he is. But, tellingly, rather than fleeing to France or a distant city, the tale has him opt instead to move merely to the nearby island of Classe, again with echoes of Dante's coming to Classe in the *Divine Comedy*, where his own tale of personal discovery and reform begins. Underlining the apparent strangeness of this quite short flight is the fact that he prepares for the trip to the nearby rural island as if he is preparing a major trip to a distant land, sparing no expense to make his departure as noble and impressive as possible. In turn, once there in the countryside, he spares no expense to maintain his social life with his friends and peers from the city, offering frequent dinners and parties for them in his exile. All of this might seem hardly appropriate for someone fleeing the cruelty of the woman who has dishonored him by rejecting his courtship and him as a lover.

But it makes a great deal more sense from the perspective of consensus realities. For although he has given in to the pressures of those around him, who worry about what his unhappy love has done to him, he evidently was anxious to rebuild his consensus realities with those who gave him his identity in Ravenna. Thus, to renegotiate himself, he had to remain in contact with those groups in his city who gave him and his life identity and meaning. Classe was perfect for this. It spared him the ongoing dishonor and disdain that his failure as a lover encouraged daily in the intimate streets of Ravenna. There was no contact with his beloved, no interaction, no deeds to undermine him on that score. Rather, leaving with all the pomp and ceremony and display of wealth required to demonstrate his identity as an important young noble, he put before the groups that surrounded him in society the self that he would renegotiate—a rich, elegant, aristocratic young noble. And at Classe, rather than hiding in his grief, he invited his friends, family, and acquaintances to join him in his splendid aristocratic lifestyle. With his dinners and beautiful pavilions and all the accoutrements of urban civility, he virtually remade the countryside into a replica of the civil world of Ravenna, and, most significantly, he remade himself there as well. In the process, he turned what might well have been a fleeing negation of self and a form of social suicide into a renegotiation of his identity that minimized his destruction at the hands of a woman's cruel disdain.

How a Scholar Cleverly Punished Yet Another Woman Who Found Cruel Pleasure in Disdaining His Courtship and Love

This understanding of the tale gains greater weight in the context of the *Decameron* and Boccaccio's strategy as a writer, if we look at a story that is the longest and in some ways the strangest told: the tale of the violent revenge of a young upper-class Florentine scholar, Rinieri, on Elena, in turn a young Florentine widow of aristocratic lineage and a rather free life. She, much like Nastagio's love, had also cruelly rejected Rinieri's suit, but in this case with a humiliating and injurious *beffa* that almost caused his death in fact, not just metaphorically.[17] Told by Pampinea, at first reading the story seems quite similar to Nastagio's tale, as it also involves the punishment of a cruel woman for her mistreatment of a would-be lover. And both, rather atypically for the novella genre, stop the action of the tale frequently to explain and defend the rationale for the violence of the punishment involved. Yet their dissimilarities are as revealing as their similarities. Perhaps most significantly, in the tale of Rinieri, his mistreatment by the woman he is courting is largely private, whereas in the story of Nastagio, as we have seen, his rejection was widely known and even prompted those who befriended him in Ravenna to interfere to try to help him survive its worst effects.

For Rinieri, however, as the tale unfolds, his demise remains unknown or at least unrecognized as such by those who would have formed his consensus realities. This does not mean that consensus realities were not involved. Indeed, Rinieri was careful to keep his suffering at the hands of the woman he courted secret in part to limit its dishonoring impact on his reputation for those around him who judged his identity as a young lover. But, more centrally for the plot, he kept his victimization secret as part of a clever strategy—a *virtù*-ous strategy—to not arouse suspicions about his plans for revenge upon the woman who had treated him so cruelly. Cruelty, in fact, rather understates the case, as his beloved's *beffa* is portrayed as actually bringing him to the brink of the grave, in this case not via suicide but as a direct result of her physical mistreatment of her would-be lover.

The tale explains that this Elena had noticed Rinieri's attentiveness at a party, and, as a woman who is described as enjoying attracting the attention of vulnerable men, she encouraged it perversely, even though she already had a lover. The negative valence of this behavior was made clear, as she was depicted as a predatory and vain woman who did not demurely lower her eyes like other women but rather boldly looked over the men present to pick out those men "who were attracted to her."[18] Evidently, she was being presented as being far from the ideal retiring widow that Florentines would be expected to see as having a positive consensus reality in this tale or in everyday life in their city.

And, if there was any doubt about that, the narrative rapidly confirmed for contemporaries her stereotypically negative characteristics as a widow who was an amoral sexual predator, freely cultivating her sexual pleasures and perverse sense of self at the expense of the men who fell victim of her wiles. Noting Rinieri's interest, she said to herself, "I have not come here [to this party] today in vain, for if I am not mistaken I have sunk my hooks into a little bird who I can lead by the nose."[19] And she began to give him little glances and flash her good looks in order to encourage his interest. Rinieri, as the designated victim, fell immediately into her trap and began to court her with all the youthful enthusiasm of a young lover, much like Nastagio, but always handicapped in the tale by the fact that he was a scholar and perhaps too much of a thinker to be the passionate lover he wished to be. Moreover, curiously, while at this point in the tale he is portrayed as a young scholar, later in the narrative, although only a few months have passed, he will lose his youth to become a more mature lover. Why Rinieri becomes more mature as the tale progresses will be considered later, but, for the moment, what is abundantly clear is that Elena is not only cruel to Rinieri, she quite enjoys her cruelty and takes pleasure in mistreating a man who loves her.

This pleasure that a few women find in making male suitors suffer their love in the tales told in the *Decameron* might be seen as an emotion associated with love and sexual desire that merits being considered more carefully for its deeper meaning. For it is another theme that weaves through tales and appears to be, in its own right, a relatively unrecognized emotion associated with love at the time. Clearly, in the depiction of evil women finding pleasure in playing with would-be lovers and cruelly rejecting their love, there is a Rinascimento misogyny involved for contemporary readers as well as for modern ones. Yet, reading against the grain, if we think in terms of the way young women were socialized to protect their virginity and chastity and the traditions—supported by prescriptive literature, family, peers, and aggressive preachers—that placed such a high value on women rejecting love and the advances of lovers, it is not hard to see that women who acted as they were supposed to act might well have felt a certain pleasure and pride in doing so. Simply put, there was a legitimate reason for women to feel pleasure and self-worth rejecting love in such a social world of courting.

Doing so, moreover, could be and was, I would suggest, an important aspect of constructing positive consensus realities for young women, at least with some of the groups that surrounded them in society, such as family, neighbors, and friends. In addition, in a society that was particularly patriarchal, the pleasure to be had in saying no to a man in love surely had its attractions. In this context, we might argue that Elena's pleasure in playing and denying Rinieri should perhaps be seen as the particularly negative pole of yet another range of emotions associated with love, a negative pole associated with the Italian verb "*schernire*" in this tale and at times with "*disdegnare*" in others. Both verbs might be translated in a straightforward way as "to scorn," but in this case (and others in the *Decameron*), they have the force of a violent but pleasurable mocking, an emotion associated with the rejection of the value, and virtually the identity, of another—a pleasurable if negative emotion that we seem to have largely lost or at least no longer recognize as such.

In a society where the negotiation of consensus realities played a major role in creating personal identity, the pleasure of mockery, *schernire* or *disdegnare* (encountered earlier in the tale of Nastagio), was a powerful and dangerous emotion that could undermine and at times even destroy. For both Nastagio and Rinieri, that was the case, even if in Rinieri's tale its power was blunted by the more private nature of Elena's mockery. Of course, a refusal of love could also be more kind and gentle, or even sad, as we see in a few *Decameron* stories, where young women who are loved deny those who court them sadly, but high-mindedly, to protect not only themselves but also their would-be lovers from misplaced passions.[20]

Returning to Elena's cruelty, her pleasure in mocking and mistreating Rinieri is made abundantly clear, and its negative, violent dimension places it dramatically at the negative pole of such emotions. After stringing him along for a while, she decides to "cool" the "heat" of his love—the courtship that leads up to this plays frequently on his claims of the "heat" of his passionate love—with a heartless *beffa* at his expense. Thus she invites him to come secretly to her house for dinner and the pleasures that will follow to finally cool his passion one particularly cold and snowy night. When he is safely locked in her courtyard, anxiously awaiting entry to her home and her arms, she has a female servant, who is in on the joke, inform him that she is entertaining one of her brothers who has arrived for dinner unexpectedly and thus he must wait quietly to keep their impending tryst secret. The servant, however, promises that as soon as the brother leaves, Elena will come to let him in so that they can enjoy their promised evening of passion. Unfortunately for Rinieri, however, the lover she planned to enjoy that evening with was not him. For rather than her brother arriving unexpectedly, she had actually invited her young lover to spend the evening with her and mockingly watch her *beffa* unfold, enjoying with her her cruel cooling of Rinieri's ardor.

Still, the tale makes it clear that pleasing her lover was not the central motive for her *beffa*. Rather, it was the pleasure she took *(schernire)* in making the scholar she had encouraged in his passion suffer at her hands—she had become the cruel widow par excellence that haunted patriarchal nightmares and those of young would-be lovers as well. This is highlighted by the fact that, throughout the *beffa*, Elena and her lover watch and delight in Rinieri's suffering in the cold, while they in cruel contrast enjoy their night of love safely and warmly ensconced in her bed. With the snow continuing to fall and Rinieri growing colder and colder waiting locked in her garden, finally, around midnight, Elena says to her lover while "playing" with him in her warm bed, "Beh, let's get up and go down to see if the fire is indeed spent that my silly lover is constantly writing me about."[21] What they find spying on him secretly, not surprisingly, is a freezing Rinieri pacing back and forth in the newly fallen snow, trying to keep warm.

Doubling down, Elena then opens the window to coldly play him for her pleasure and that of her watching lover. As Rinieri pleads to be let in from the cold until her brother leaves, she denies him with the weak excuse that her brother would hear the opening of the door and investigate. Then, mockingly evoking his days as a scholar, she reminds him that he must have experienced far greater cold in Paris, implying that in the name of seeking knowledge, he had once been more willing to suffer the cold than he is now in seeking her love. The give and take continues for a while, with Rinieri lamenting the cold, until she cuts off the conversation with a cleverly cruel, "I don't see how that could possibly be true, if what you have written me so many times is true; that is that the love you feel for me is burning you up, so I am confident that you are just joking at my expense *(che tu mi beffi).*"[22] Of course, we know that the *beffa* was actually on Rinieri. And, adding to the irony of her remark, as he remained freezing in the snow, Elena and her lover returned to her warm bed, where they slept "very little" for the rest of the night, "enjoying themselves" and "the *beffa* at the expense of the scholar."[23]

Only with the morning was Rinieri let out, nearly frozen to death, by the same servant who had locked him in, with profuse false apologies and a false promise that the next time he came things would work out better. The wiser for his suffering, he replied with equal falsity, proclaiming his ongoing love, and hurried home to thaw out. But the cold of the night had been so devastating that, well beyond cooling his ardor, Elena's *beffa* had left him on death's door. In fact, the doctors called in to treat him concluded that "if it were not for the fact that he was young ... he would have had too much [cold] to survive."[24] Significantly, however, he kept to himself what had happened, and, once he recovered, keeping secret the "hate" that had replaced his former love, he returned to wooing Elena. Unlike Nastagio, clearly, he wished to maintain the consensus realities of himself as her would-be lover for those around him in society and more importantly for his plans of revenge.

The tale cuts quickly to those plans. For soon thereafter Elena's fickle young lover deserts her, leaving her desolate. Her female servant, trying to help her overcome her loss, suggests foolishly *(uno sciocco pensiero)* that perhaps Rinieri in his student days in Paris had learned some magic "that might be able to force [her lover] to return by some type of necromancy."[25] Overcome by love, and thus equally foolishly, Elena agrees to try the ploy and contacts Rinieri, who is still pretending to court her, to ask for his help in the matter. Obviously, it is all downhill for her from this point on, as the *beff*-ess becomes the *beff*-ee. Rinieri plays Elena and her maid, confirming his ability as a necromancer and promising that no matter where her former lover has gone, he has the magical ability to bring him back. He does admit, however, that his magic will require the active cooperation of Elena and a bit of discomfort for her as well—with an honesty whose cruel irony is soon revealed.

She accepts, as much a victim of her love as Rinieri had once been of his. So he explains to his anxious victim that one night, when the moon is on the wane, she must go alone to an isolated spot in the countryside with a magical figure prepared by him at the hour of first sleep and plunge herself naked in a stream seven times. Then, still naked, she must climb a tree or a high building and, facing north, repeat the words that he will give her. Shortly thereafter there will appear two beautiful women who will ask her what she wants, and all she has to do is request the return of her lover and he will come back to her before the middle of the next night. Elena responds enthusiastically, noting that she knows just the spot to do this and explains where it is to Rinieri. Although he knows the spot as well, and appreciates how perfectly its isolation will suit his plot, he claims to have never heard of the place, falsely again.

Thus, with the knowledge of when and where Elena will attempt his magic, Rinieri is ready to enjoy his revenge. On the chosen night, he and a servant are safely hidden in the bushes when Elena arrives with the magic figure that he has supplied her; and they watch—as do we—voyeuristically as she undresses and bathes herself seven times in the nearby Arno River just as he had instructed her. Indeed, Pampinea slows the tale down to describe her naked beauties as she passes the hidden Rinieri and portrays him as both aroused by the sight and feeling a little pity for what his counter-*beffa* is about to do to her and her beautiful body.

Again, following his instructions, the naked Elena climbed the isolated tower she had described to Rinieri and began reciting the incantations that he had given her.[26] While she was occupied in this, Rinieri and his servant quietly removed the ladder that she had used to scale the tower, leaving her stranded naked in the chill of the night. Unaware, Elena waited until dawn for the three maidens to appear, but, with the first light, it finally dawned on her that she had been tricked and that Rinieri had claimed his vengeance. Nevertheless, in the economy of vendetta and vengeance, she still felt some pleasure in the knowledge that she had come out on top because she had mistreated a man who loved and courted her, mocking him *(schernire)* and nearly freezing him to death, while she had merely spent a chilly summer night naked on top of the tower with no one any the wiser, her consensus realities apparently safe.

That momentary sense of superiority and victory, however, was short-lived, for, when she went to climb down from the tower, she found that the ladder had been removed and she was trapped. At first she was worried about what would happen to her reputation in Florence when she was found naked on top of a tower in the countryside and how her neighbors and brothers would respond—her consensus realities suddenly were not so safe. But then, catching sight of Rinieri just as he, waking up from his sleep, caught sight of her, she pleaded with him to help her down for the love he felt for her and to protect her good name. She even offered to become his lover in return for his helping her down. But, as his love had turned to hate following her nearly lethal *beffa* and blossomed into a very fourteenth-century Florentine desire for vengeance, once again the violence associated with love and sex was moving her future in another direction.

Rinieri laid out in several long speeches his grievances and the suffering she had caused him to make it clear to her and to the readers of the tale why the violence to follow was merited. In fact, the give and take between them brings the action of the story once again to an uncharacteristic halt for the action-oriented genre of the novella. And the reader is treated to an extended, and at times suggestively personal, discussion by Boccaccio-writer of the way the cruelty of Elena's mocking *beffa* affected a scholar and a writer, who now in the tale has suddenly become no longer a *giovane* but rather a mature and sensitive adult male. It might be suggested that the strangely personal nature of this discussion explains the sudden strange aging of Rinieri, who, as noted earlier in the tale, had been described as a young man *(giovane)* but now suddenly has become a more mature scholar.

Indeed, one wonders if the pain felt by a more mature man at the cruel treatment of a young thoughtless woman has a bit of the bitterness of a personal recollection. Has Rinieri, the scholar and writer, for a moment become an alter-ego of Boccaccio and thus gained his years, wisdom, and bitterness? Be that as it may, recollecting angrily the total disregard for his very survival in her *beffa*, Rinieri claims, "[My] life is still able to be always one hundred thousand times more useful than one of your type. So I will teach you with this suffering what it means to mock *(schernire)* men who have feelings and what it means to mock *(schernire)* scholars. And I will give you good reason to never again engage in such folly, if you survive."[27]

Still, it should be noted that Rinieri not only lays out in detail the justification for what is to follow, he also feels pity for what Elena will suffer. Critics have often noted that this tale features a reversal of the cruel treatment of a lover, with Rinieri's treatment of Elena reversing her treatment of him. Yet the reversal, although evident, is less symmetrical from an emotional perspective than usually recognized, as her *schernire* (pleasure in mocking) of Rinieri was carefully portrayed as without any feeling of pity—she actually richly enjoyed it with never a thought to his suffering, aside from the mocking pleasure that it brought her and her lover. Rinieri, the scholar and the thinker, will enjoy his revenge as well, but it is consistently tempered by the emotion of pity *(compassione)*, and, suggestively, Pampinea, the narrator of the tale, and presumably Boccaccio, also express pity even as they support the justice of Elena's demise. With both pity and pleasure, then, Rinieri rejects her pleas to be helped down.

The negative implications of that began to become clearer when the sun started to turn hot and Elena could find no place to hide from its burning rays. To make matters worse, her tower—as per Rinieri's instructions, a high point in the countryside far from any dwellings—was so isolated that there was no one around to help her down aside from Rinieri. To make the long and unlovingly detailed account of her suffering under the burning summer sun and the summer insects that feasted on her naked flesh short, she spent the day there in agony with Rinieri returning once to continue a long discourse on the cruelty of her *beffa*, which not just denied his love but showed disdain for him and love itself. As he lays out his case in detail, he notes that as a scholar and a writer, if all else failed, he could have gotten his revenge by writing about her "in such a way that when you learned of them [those writings] you would have wished a thousand times a day that you had never been born."[28]

And he concludes with the virtually proverbial "the powers of the pen are far greater" than many realize who have not felt their weight—a claim that again seems to evoke a writer and self-identified lover like Boccaccio himself. Significantly, there follows a defense of older, more mature men, as Rinieri has now become, where he points out with clever wordplay that as lovers they understand better how to sexually please women, even if they may not be as "hard-riding" as younger men:

> More mature men . . . also know things that younger men
> still have to learn. . . . You believe that younger men are
> better knights and able to do more miles in a day's ride than
> more mature men. And I will admit, of course, that they can
> stroke your pussy with greater energy, but mature men, like
> experts [that they are] know better those places where the
> fleas hide. . . . Hard riding will break and tire anyone . . . but
> a sweet slow ride, although it may get you home a little later,
> at least will get you there [finally] satisfied.[29]

Whether this is an echo of Boccaccio's vision of himself or merely a fairly typical, if graphic, defense of scholars and older men as sexual partners against the mockery of young women, it remains an extremely violent expression of the emotion of a rejected lover and from a modern perspective an undoubtedly misogynistic one.

But from a fourteenth-century perspective, for all its violence and accusations against a specific type of woman—one who took pleasure in the pitiless violence of disdaining and rejecting a would-be lover—and thus not all women, it could be read as a familiar type of vendetta vengeance that essentially undid an original misdeed by virtually reversing it. In this vision, the victim of the crime, Rinieri, became the punishing judge and undid the crime by subjecting the culprit to the same suffering he had suffered. If the balance of the retribution was perfect—obviously a big if—the matter would have been settled and life could return to normal. In fact, the same vendetta / vengeance dynamic can be seen in the actual physical punishments for crimes in contemporary

Florence, in chronicle accounts of vendetta / vengeance, and in prescriptive literature of the time pointing out the dangers of such private
forms of justice.[30] Still, there is no doubt that Rinieri's punishment of
Elena was extreme and described with troubling detail that once again
evokes Dante's *Inferno,* even if the tale adds Rinieri's pity to soften a
bit its violence. But the point is that for all its violence associated with
love, it was carefully portrayed as integral to a deserved punishment
that reversed and undid earlier cruel deeds and disdainful pleasures
that were virtually violent crimes in their own right associated with love
and courtship.

Where in Contrast a Woman's Honest Rejection of a Suitor, Heroic Love, and a Falcon's Death Win a Happy Ending

Another *Decameron* story where a woman rejects a suitor's attentions
without intentional cruelty or the pleasure of *disdegno* makes perfectly
clear the distinction between the ideal of correct behavior in courtship
and love and its negative possibilities. And, as it follows immediately on
the fifth day the violent novella of Nastagio, I would suggest its placement there is not by accident.[31] In that famous story told by Fiammetta,
Federigo degli Alberighi sacrifices all that he has in courting a noble
woman, Monna Giovanna, who first loyal to her husband, and later as a
widow loyal to her chastity and widow's honor, politely but firmly re-
fuses his love. And although he has been financially ruined by the cost
of his courtship and love and apparently much like Nastagio retired to
the countryside, losing his civil identity and status as a young lover as a
result, Monna Giovanna significantly is not portrayed as particularly
cruel or evil in her refusal.

She simply did not return his love or recognize his true merit when
he was trying to win her favor with jousts and parties that he paid for
himself, eating up his inherited wealth like many a foolish young man
in love. And from a contemporary Florentine perspective, one might
well ask why should she have responded to his courtship. She was married and loyal to her husband, not a predatory widow like Elena or a
vain disdainful noble like Nastagio's love. More importantly, she had
no interest in encouraging Federigo and certainly no interest in taking

pleasure in refusing his suit or worse yet disdaining his courtship or dishonoring him because he loved her.

That this was a normal part of courtship, the tale's narrator, Fiammetta, suggests and Boccaccio-writer underlines by paying virtually no attention in the telling of the tale to Monna Giovanna's lack of interest in his suit. Indeed, while the story details all the things that Federigo did to win Giovanna's love, Fiammetta merely briefly describes her response as "she, no less honest than beautiful, paid no attention to the things that he did to win her, nor to him."[32] The contrast with both Nastagio's beloved and Rinieri's Elena is clear, even if quickly sketched. Giovanna is an "honest" woman, and, as befit an honest married woman, she paid no attention to Federigo's courtship. No more need be said. In contrast, Nastagio's beloved's disdain and cruel public rejection and Elena's even crueler *beffa* both require a much more complete and painful detailing of their rejection that demonstrates their perfidy and the dangerous violence that they bring to courtship and love.

And, in fact, that is the motive that Fiammetta gives for telling her tale immediately following Nastagio's. She explains, as she begins her narration, "I most dear ladies will willingly tell you a tale somewhat similar to the previous one, so that in part you may understand how much your attractiveness can influence the gentle / mannered heart [of male lovers], but also so that when necessary you can judge when to be the awarders of your favors without leaving this always to fortune."[33] Giovanna, in sum, is not the victim of fortune or of an unwanted suitor; she is an example of an honest wife who, as a wise woman in control of her emotions and her life, decides who she will and will not give her love and sexual favors. And although it is not spelled out in the tale that follows, Fiammetta suggests that Giovanna does so with an awareness of the power that her attractiveness has on the heart of a gentle / mannered lover. Implied is the fact that this requires a discretion and understanding—a *virtù* in courtship—totally lacking in the behavior of Nastagio's beloved or Rinieri's Elena.

In the end, of course, Giovanna's discretion and understanding pay off, as after great suffering on her part (losing first her husband and then her beloved son) and on Federigo's part (losing all his possessions and even his most prized falcon)[34]—Giovanna as a rich widow, and pressed by her brothers to remarry, finally recognizes the true depth

of Federigo's *virtù* and love and marries him. And in accordance with
the typical ending of such correctly ordered tales of love in the *Decameron,* they live happily ever after. Which brings us back to the troubling
and much-discussed ending of Nastagio's tale, for there too Nastagio
and his beloved marry in the end. Many, however, have wondered if it
was to live happily ever after despite the narrator's claim that that was
the case.

Where Thanks to Divine Justice the "Happy" Ending of Nastagio's Tale and Its Many Shades of Violence Are Reconsidered

Nastagio, considering with a mixture of "pity and fear" the violent punishment that he had just witnessed of the "arrogant and cruel" woman
who had harshly rejected her lover, realized that the lesson of that retribution should not be lost. Thus, as he knew that the scene was repeated
every Friday, with her cruelly rejected lover running her down with his
hunting dogs and ripping out her heart, Nastagio decided to invite all
the groups with whom he negotiated his consensus reality—his friends,
family, and his own cruel beloved and her family—to Classe to dine
with him the very next Friday. To make the invitation more inviting, he
promised to all that, if they came, he would give up his courtship for
the woman he now recognized as "his enemy." So it was that the next
Friday they all joined him, including his beloved (who came only "reluctantly"), for a magnificent feast at precisely the spot where Nastagio
knew that the violent punishment would be reenacted.

Just as the guests were finishing their meal, right on schedule, there
appeared the crying young woman pursued by the hunting dogs and
her rejected lover. As the violence unfolded, the guests, much like Nastagio earlier, tried to interfere to save the girl. But they were warned off
by her lover, who explained to them the reason for the gruesome penalty
that they were witnessing. With everyone overcome by fear and tears, he
carried out the sentence decreed by divine justice in all its brutality. Afterward, everyone began discussing what they had witnessed, "but . . .
the most troubled was the *cruel* young woman loved by Nastagio, who
had clearly seen and heard everything and understood that more than
any other person there it applied to her, remembering the *cruelty* with

which she had always treated Nastagio."[35] In fact, it is pointed out that "it seemed to her that she was already fleeing before him [Nastagio] and the dogs at her flanks."[36]

So great was her fear that that very evening, "her hate having turned into *love*," she sent a servant to Nastagio to ask him to come to her, promising to give him all that he desired. Nastagio, however, refused her offer because, as was pointed out by Filomena, even if he greatly desired her love and sexual favors, he would not accept them at the expense of her "honor." Thus, he asked that she marry him so that he could enjoy her love while preserving her honor—with her honor preserved by marriage, they both could enjoy the sexual pleasures of their love. "The girl knowing that she alone was the reason that they were not already married replied that she would be pleased *(le piacea)* [to marry him]." She then requested her parents' permission to marry Nastagio. They consented, and the very next Sunday they married, "and together they lived happily for a long time,"[37] the imperatives of family, honor, and apparently even love and sexual pleasure in marriage finally observed in line with the *Decameron*'s favorable vision of marriages founded on love.

There is much to unpack in this quick and apparently happy ending of the tale. Almost lost in the apparent violence of the moment is the care that Filomena takes to point out the cruelty of Nastagio's beloved, not once but twice in the same sentence: first labeling her "the cruel young woman" *(la crudel giovane)* and then labeling her treatment of him "the cruelty with which she had always treated Nastagio *(crudeltà sempre da lei usata verso Nastagio)*.[38] And although it might seem unlikely to a modern eye, the narrator also claims that the woman's fear before the violent scene and its poor victim, a victim whose cruel behavior she identified with immediately, quickly transformed the hate that she felt for Nastagio previously into love. Yet the *Decameron* and life at the time, I would suggest, was rife with just such rapid transformations when strongly felt emotions were involved, like fear, hate, and love. And love itself was often seen as literally exploding when the moment was ripe and youthful emotions were strong, whether driven by fear, desire, or merely a glance or a telling word or gesture.

To the modern eye, of course, a love evoked by fear does not seem one destined to last. Yet in the context of the day, marriages, if well matched, were expected to have the best possibility of reinforcing sudden love with an enduring form of affection, actually more likely to survive than the quick passions of young lovers. And Nastagio and his beloved, the tale has been careful to point out, were indeed well matched, even if she was from a more aristocratic family than his. Moreover, the young woman's parents agreed quickly to their marriage, an apparent reflection again on the appropriateness of the match. In addition, this was a confirmation that they had judged the match as acceptable with a mature and unemotional eye that heretofore his love had clearly lacked. In sum, while it might be argued, and it makes sense to argue from a modern perspective, that the violence she witnessed essentially blackmailed her into accepting Nastagio as her husband, the tale is constructed by Boccaccio-writer with considerable care to present a different picture: her marriage, because it was finally based on the shared emotion of love, promised that it would be a success and bring them both a happy ending to a courtship that had begun badly.

Well-founded modern doubts about that happy ending aside, that seems clearly the way the tale was told. Nastagio's beloved was a cruel young woman who treated a suitor with disdain and without the manners or kindness that courtship required for both men *and* women. Her atypicality is portrayed carefully and paralleled with the divinely and justly punished cruel woman Nastagio and his fellow citizens of Ravenna witness on Classe. The result is a violent lesson on correct courting behavior. And as Monna Giovanna demonstrates clearly in the next tale told, that lesson does not mean that women must accept any man who, courting her correctly, proffers his love, becoming a victim of fortune and masculine desire. Rather, in the well-ordered play of civilized courtship, both men and women must behave with manners and a sensitivity to its complex emotional dimensions and the very exposed public scrutiny that it invited.

In sum, both men and women courting in the intimate world of Rinascimento cities put their consensus realities up for vigilant and often judgmental examination by those who surrounded them, with potentially devastating results. Death and suicide, even the ripping out of hearts and throwing them to the dogs, were the nightmare negative pole of a range of emotions that could and did swing from pleasure to disdain, fear, hate, and deadly rage. Taking pleasure in disdaining or mocking *(schernire)* a would-be lover required punishment to undo the violence involved, and it seems that Boccaccio expected his readers, male and female, to accept that reality, even if there is a subtle undertow in the tale as told that suggests even his own lack of comfort with the violence involved. But why should one expect anything different—even justified punishment and violence could and did evoke pity in those who witnessed it, as the tales themselves make perfectly clear. Pious pity *(pietà)* is what the tale requires, as Filomena alerts us from the first.

Still, the very last line of Nastagio's tale adds to the discomfort of a modern reader, for Filomena concludes that not only did the fear that led his beloved to accept him in marriage bring them pleasure, it also led "all the other women of Ravenna" out of fear to become "much more open to men's *pleasures* than they had been in the past."[39] Again, the fear evoked by the violent scene witnessed on Classe seems suddenly to re-enter the tale as a form of blackmail that made the women of Ravenna more open to the advances of the men of the city and consenting to give them their "pleasures." Yet, the vagueness of what those pleasures would be makes the import of what is implied unclear. Are we speaking of the wide range of pleasures associated with a mannered and gentle court-ship, or are we speaking of the illicit sexual pleasures that less honorable men desire without true love and honorable marriage? Nastagio's be-havior and emphasis on honor preserved via marriage and Fiammetta's emphasis on making choices in courtship that are reasoned rather than based on fortune in her introduction to the very next tale of Monna Giovanna would suggest the former over the latter. But, in the end, per-haps it is best to embrace the vagueness of the ending and the violence of the tales discussed here as well, for the emotions that associate love, sex, and violence are the most difficult to parse in any society. And the most troubling.

3

Sorrow

Tears, Mourning, and Self in the Time of the Plague

How Lisabetta Gets the Head of Her Lover, Grows Basil in It, and, Watering It with Her Tears, Dies Mourning

In a dark wood not far from the Sicilian city of Messina, Lisabetta and her servant went searching through the undergrowth for his body. Finding a spot where the soil seemed freshly disturbed, she brushed aside the dried leaves and began to dig. It did not take long before she began to unearth his corpse; the corpse still virtually uncorrupted of her lover, Lorenzo, who had been murdered by her brothers. Even though the sight of his dead body in the cold, dark earth was devastating, she knew that this was not the time or the place for tears. And although she would have liked to carry the body back for a proper burial, realizing that her brothers would not allow it, she showed her moral fiber, her lover's courage, by fearlessly cutting off her beloved's head as a memento of her lost love—more than a memento *mori*, it might be styled a memento *d'amore*.

Back in her room, alone with her head, she cried over it for hours, the tears washing it clean. After lavishing it with a "thousand kisses," she took a largish pot *(un testo)* and put the head *(la testa)* in it, then covered it with soil and planted there several Salernitan basil plants, a variety noted for its reddish color and rich odor. Day after day, she lovingly tended her *testo / testa* memento *d'amore,* never watering it with anything but rose water, water from orange flowers, or more often her own free-flowing tears. So lovingly cared for, the basil flourished, giving off an intense odor, a fresh odor of life aided by the richness of the soil and, of course, her dead lover's decaying head. Yet, it seemed that as her tears made the basil flourish, she in contrast waned, becoming ever more pale, thin, and hollow-eyed.

Her neighbors and her brothers, noting her decline and her strange attachment to the plant, began to worry that there was something amiss and that in some way the flourishing herb was involved. Hoping to reverse her rapid emotional and physical decline, one day they took away the *testo* and unwittingly her lover's *testa.* Her insistent demands for its return and her continuing tears led them to investigate what was in the pot, discovering Lorenzo's decaying head—for them a dangerously incriminating memento. Realizing their danger, they secretly buried the *testa,* discarded the basil, and, in an unbrotherly fashion, abandoned their sister, fleeing Messina for less perilous climes.[1] Left alone, poor Lisabetta had only her tears and her laments about her lost memento as she continued to decline and shortly thereafter died. No one knew the reason for her death, and as she died without family or friends, apparently no one mourned her passing—there was not even a report of a funeral.

Although this all sounds like a gothic romance with its tragic love and grisly decomposing head growing basil, most will recognize this story as yet another well-known novella from the *Decameron.*[2] As we have seen, one of the primary goals of the *brigata* who retreated to the idyllic series of gardens in the hills above Florence was to lift the group's spirits with their stories as an antidote to the terrible mortality of the plague. Yet, as a merry tale to lift the spirits of its listeners, Lisabetta's tragic death seems to fall rather short of the mark. In fact, much like the humor of Calandrino's *beffa* or the violence of Rinieri's violent revenge, which no longer today seem self-evidently uplifting tales and thus call for a closer analysis to understand how they worked in their time and culture, this tale in its tears and tragedy seems to call for a closer analysis.

Once again, those familiar with the *Decameron* might well suggest a quick, easy answer, for Lisabetta's tale with her memento *d'amore* stands as the fifth tale told on the fourth day of stories and might seem simply another that fit the day's theme: lovers whose love had an unhappy ending, emphasizing the sorrow that love and sex could often entail. Certainly, the deaths of Lisabetta and her lover, Lorenzo, at first glance appear a perfect fit. Yet, in many ways, their tale seems out of place in the context of the other sad stories of the day, especially as the fifth and central tale. Perhaps most notably, most of the other lovers in the tales of that day are ennobled by their tragic loves, and when they die their deaths are heroic—judged and celebrated as such publicly. Not so much publicly in the sense of the public sphere of Habermas but rather in the sense of the groups—family, neighbors, friends, peers, fellow workers, fellow confraternity members, and broader communities and solidarities—who evaluated each person and negotiated with them a Rinascimento sense of identity. As discussed earlier, these groups formulated, nourished, and sustained consensus realities about their fellows, who in turn negotiated these imagined shared understandings of who a person was and thus their identity.[3]

In this context, the deaths, funerals, and public mourning of the various groups that formulated and nourished consensus realities that figure so prominently in the tales of the fourth day were crucial moments in the economy of the tales that revealed a final evaluation of who a person was and had been.[4] And, read in terms of both consensus realities and *virtù*, many of the stories of the *Decameron* offer a rich perspective on such measuring of identity within the tales themselves and in the frame story. Indeed, in both there are multiple moments of such evaluations, regularly explained and commented on. Thus, significantly, the characters in both the frame and the tales repeatedly make group judgments of others in terms of key fourteenth-century values that measure an individual's identity in ways that are critical for understanding how the tales and characters within them would have been understood at the time and add suggestive historical texture and nuance to their reading today.

In the tragic tales of the fourth day, this is regularly underlined by a stress on the heroic deaths or lack of same for the lovers who are the focus of stories.[5] And one of the best examples of such evaluation that provides a telling contrast with the tale of Lisabetta is the novella that opens the stories told on day four, another case of cut-out hearts briefly discussed in Chapter 2. Like many other tales, this novella relates a story of illicit but true love, in this case between a young widow, Ghismonda, and a young man of lower-class origins named Guiscardo, who served her father, Tancredi, the prince of Salerno. Another love, however, drove the violence of the tale: the love of Tancredi as a father for his daughter. For Tancredi, because of his love for his daughter, had been reluctant to marry her at all. And with a possessiveness that seems to cry out for a modern psychoanalytical reading, after the death of her first husband, he had kept this young, vivacious daughter virtually locked away, refusing all offers for her hand.[6]

But without Freud or Lacan, it is clear that Tancredi was portrayed as enjoying, actually virtually cherishing, his close relationship with his daughter. And rather than remarry her as befitted a young widow, he was evidently anxious to maintain his own close relationship with her. That love, however, was not without its serious problems and the potential for violence encountered in Chapter 2, as Boccaccio notes that Ghismonda, "living with her doting father . . . and realizing that because of his love he showed little interest in marrying her again, she, not having the courage to ask him to do the honest thing [and marry her] decided to secretly find if possible a worthy lover."[7] Young love and its accompanying sexual desires against the power and love of old men—a classic literary conflict and a very familiar one in the everyday life of the Rinascimento and in the *Decameron* as well.

Where with *Virtù* Ghismonda Dies for True Love, Becomes a Hero, and Overcomes the Violence of Honor as Her Father Cries Like a Baby

As one might expect in a novella where young love and sexual desire were in play, Ghismonda had little trouble finding a suitable lover, even if her choice might seem a little off the mark for the daughter of a prince. For the man she decided on, Guiscardo, was a mere page in her father's service. Here, I would suggest, Boccaccio found himself in a bit of a bind, or, to be more accurate, the story he was retelling had put him in a bit of a bind; for given the traditional values and consensus realities

of his Rinascimento audience, Ghismonda was striking out in directions decidedly dangerous and unlikely to win a reader's sympathy. In
deciding to love and make love with Guiscardo, she was going against
the loving wishes of her father (but, of course, fathers were supposed to
rule in the Rinascimento), she was entering a sexual relationship outside of marriage (a form of sex condemned by the Church), she was indulging her own desires and sexual appetites (once again, a feared pro-
clivity of widows, especially young ones), and one could go on.

Worst of all, however, she was ignoring and breaking across major
social and class divides for this love, much like Calandrino, but without
the comic turn to ease the weight of her deeds. Hers, as we shall see,
was a serious love, and no one was laughing. In sum, she was breaking
a host of the most traditional and deeply held values of her day with
dangerous ramifications for how those around her would evaluate
her honor and that of her father. At this point, one might well expect
that a fourteenth-century reader would find an ending that violently
punished her love and her sexual exploits with a commoner a positive
one and, rather than tears, expect cheers from patriarchal readers. It
may well be that Boccaccio, faced with this situation, would have appreciated the postmodern death of the author, for he would have been
spared a difficult problem in telling the tale of Ghismonda's love: how
to retain the sympathy of his readers, winning their hearts for her, her
lower-class lover, and their highly problematic sexual relationship at
the expense of her loving father.

Enter *virtù*—the magic key discussed earlier that in the Rinascimento opened all doors and hearts and served as a major disciplining
concept.[8] But, to briefly reprise that earlier discussion, the term had
virtually revolutionary potential, especially in the fourteenth century,
as it was used regularly to distinguish the social values of a new elite,
the *popolo grosso*, from the traditional values of an older nobility. Merchants, bankers, lawyers, and a smattering of rich, powerful artisan
masters of the most important guilds, who by then had already won
power in many of the major cities of northern Italy, found in *virtù* a
rich disciplining ideal that, if captured and colonized with their values,
could make their political power, often conquered with violence, a social power defended by the most basic values of society. *Virtù*, if it incorporated their values and rejected traditional noble values, built this

new elite's dominance into the very ideological underpinning of society, virtually into the DNA of its social organization and culture.

It should come as no surprise, then, given the authoritative status of the ancient world, that the search for classical roots for the contemporary ideal of *virtù* should have attracted the attention of scholars and the support and patronage of early Rinascimento regimes and elites or that a form of civic *virtù* emerged at the heart of civic ideals and the self-presentation of contemporary governments, especially republican ones dominated by the *popolo grosso*. In fact, this vision of civic *virtù* had a long life, living on in republican ideology, as one can see clearly in Machiavelli and the early modern republican thinkers more generally, and even having some impact on more aristocratic and courtly contexts.[9] But, clearly, for the urban elites of northern Italy, *"virtù"* was a crucial and, in turn, a contested term. Readers of Boccaccio could hardly avoid its siren call, for the appeal and power of many of his *novelle* in the *Decameron* turn on the workings of *virtù* and its challenge to older values.

Boccaccio-author, in retelling this tale, early on plays the *virtù* card when he describes this young noblewoman's decision to take a lower-class lover: "And observing many of the men who were at her father's court, both noble and non-noble . . . and considering their ways and manners . . . among them there was one, a young page of her father called Guiscardo of very humble family, but still she found him attractive *more than anything else because of his noble manners and virtù*."[10] Simply put, his *virtù* made Guiscardo a superior man and a suitable choice for Ghismonda's illicit love and sexual pleasures.

Luckily for Ghismonda—as if luck was needed in literary love affairs, in their happy moments at least—Guiscardo returned Ghismonda's love and all that was required was the means to bring the young lovers together. With the cleverness and cunning that often typified Rinascimento *virtù* and the behavior of youths inspired by love and its sexual desires in Boccaccio's tales, Ghismonda closely watched her man and, when the moment was right, passed him a note that explained to him how they could meet secretly in her room. In turn, Guiscardo carried out her instructions perfectly and also used considerable ingenuity and prowess—again *virtù*—to overcome the numerous physical obstacles that made using the secret entrance to her bedroom difficult. Once more, we find formally questionable behavior elevated to a higher level by young love and *virtù*.

Sadly, as in all of the tales of the fourth day, however, young love and its shared sexual pleasures, even if it endured for many happy days and nights, was not to have a happy end largely because evil Fortuna and another love, that of Tancredi for his daughter, were to violently intervene. As Boccaccio notes, switching the tone of his tale from the happy pleasures of love to tragedy, "But Fortuna, jealous of such long and great pleasure, with sad deeds changed the happiness of the two lovers into sad tears."[11] So it came to pass that one day, unnoticed by Ghismonda or her servants, her loving father came to her room to chat with her as he often did, but, not finding her there, he laid down to wait for her in a little hidden nook and fell asleep. Ghismonda, unfortunately, had arranged to have her lover visit her that same afternoon and, thus, as the young couple in bed "played and enjoyed themselves as usual Tancredi woke up and heard and saw what Guiscardo and his daughter were doing. Overwhelmed by pain, at first he wanted to cry out, but then he realized it was better to keep quiet and keep hidden . . . so that he could do what he had already made up his mind to do with the minimum of shame *(vergogna)* for himself."[12] Honor and shame had reared their dangerous emotions, emotions also often associated with love, and would soon claim their due.

As soon as was discretely possible, Tancredi had Guiscardo secretly arrested and brought before him. And when he saw the youth "he said *almost crying*: 'Guiscardo, my kindness to you doesn't merit the offense and the shame *(vergogna)* you have given me."[13] As one might expect of a lover full of *virtù,* Guiscardo was not the least bit passive in the face of Tancredi's anger and, as a youthful lover, based his defense of his sexual relationship with his lord's daughter on young love: "Love is capable of much more than either you or I."[14] But, of course, young love was not capable of overcoming Tancredi's rage. And the irony is that, in the end, the love that Guiscardo was invoking was also adding (in the different form of Tancredi's love for his daughter) to the latter's outraged honor and driving his fury and the violent deeds to follow.

The next day, Tancredi went to Ghismonda's room, and, locking himself in with her, with tears (again) in his eyes, he reproached her for her affair. Not surprisingly, his reproaches began by calling on her *virtù:* "Ghismonda, I thought I knew your *virtù* and your chastity; thus, I would have never thought . . . if I had not seen it with my own eyes that you would give yourself [sexually] to any man who was not your husband."[15] He quickly moved on, however, to what upset him even more than her sexual relations with a man she was not married to. For Christian morality and the ideal of sex only in marriage were obviously important to him, but Ghismonda's affair with Guiscardo was upsetting for a deeper and more significant reason: "And in God's name I wish that if you had decided to fall to so great dishonor *(disonestà)* that you would have taken a man more in line with your nobility. But among all the men of my court, you picked Guiscardo, a youth of the most vile birth."[16]

Low birth abasing nobility and destroying honor—an old story eliciting violent emotions and tragedy in many societies. By contemporary standards, his audience might well have empathized with this wronged father. Indeed, what upper-class man or woman for that matter would feel sympathy for a beloved noble daughter who had broken across class lines to satisfy her illicit sexual desires! Even young, natural love and sexual attraction could hardly defend before the judging consensus realities of contemporaries such literally revolutionary desires and deeds—in fact, such passions were feared precisely because they could lead to revolution in the form of misalliances, overthrowing the very family structure that was seen as the basis of a divinely ordered hierarchical society.

Yet, as noted earlier, in the tradition of the Italian novella, where action and plot line are paramount, the action is usually quick and tight with minimal concern for describing the thoughts or the background to a character's deeds. And to repeat, significantly, there are virtually no Hamlets in the Italian novella tradition. What there is of deeper development of character is either conveyed by a few evocative words, references to stereotypes—the beautiful woman to be loved, the anxious lover, the jealous husband or wife—or by the action itself.[17] As a result, when the fast pace of a novella slows and characters begin long, set speeches, a reader does well to pay attention, because usually the author is taking the time to explain something not only important but so necessary to say that it warrants breaking the conventions of the genre and the flow of the narrative, as we have seen in the case of Rinieri's long defenses of his violent punishment of Elena. And here, faced with defending his young lovers against Tancredi's telling accusations of dishonorable behavior, Boccaccio's tale slams to a halt to play the trump card that he had been making allusions to all through the earlier action—*virtù*.

Although he does not use the term immediately, he presents a Ghismonda full of *virtù* in the face of her father's bitter recriminations. She does not break down in tears, the ubiquitous renaissance feminine emotion so prevalent in the tale of Lisabetta; indeed, her tears are totally absent. The only person crying, tellingly, is her father, who has given into his emotions. In contrast, she remains calm and cool. And, clearly, she understands her situation under fire, knowing exactly what her fate will be and what she has to do. It may be that her love for Guiscardo has given her these strengths and the ability to face without fear the tragedy that is upon her, but her actions are a perfect example of a woman's fourteenth-century *virtù* in the face of the violence that love and sex could invoke. And with her cool, calm, reasoned understanding, she has already begun to win not only our sympathy but also, more significantly, that of a Rinascimento audience and their sense of who Ghismonda really was via their judging consensus realities.

Indeed, the contrast with her father is instructive, for his righteous indignation and suffering is undermined by his own emotional behavior that clearly lacks that same *virtù* that his daughter displays so impressively. As noted earlier, Tancredi began his recriminations with tears in his eyes, and although what he said was quite reasonable, his tearful lack of self-control was telling and would be critical for the tale. And, as he finishes his reproaches, Boccaccio takes a moment to describe the prince and supposed patriarch: "having said this he hung his head crying as hard as a well-beaten child."[18] The contrast is striking: the *virtù*-uous lover Ghismonda in control of her emotions and dealing impressively with a difficult situation and the un*virtù*-uous loving father Tancredi, the victim of his emotions, totally out of control and crying like a "well-beaten child." It does not take a great leap of empathy to imagine who a Rinascimento audience was supposed to have sympathized with at that moment.

If anyone had missed the contrast, with perfect timing the action of the novella stops for another long explanatory speech: a truly revolutionary disquisition by Ghismonda that turns on a critical aspect of the early Rinascimento reign of *virtù*. She began, 'Tancredi, I have no desire to deny [anything] or beg for [mercy]. . . . But rather to confess the truth, first in order *to defend my reputation* with honest reasons and then *with deeds be most strongly true to the greatness of my soul*." No wilting woman, but steeled by a *virtù* that fortified her very soul, Ghismonda could hardly demonstrate a more attractive alternative to the sobbing and violently vengeful love of her father. "It's true," she continued ("with dry eyes"), "that I have loved and love Guiscardo and as long as I live—which will not be for long—I will love him. And if after death one loves, I will not cease to love him. This, however, is not a result of my feminine weakness, but rather your lack of readiness to marry me and to Guiscardo's *virtù*."[19]

Although Ghismonda has played the *virtù* card, she lets it lay on the table for a moment to defend the deeply related theme central to Boccaccio's tales, the imperatives of young love championed throughout the *Decameron:* love and sex as natural human passions that young people follow as the law of youth against the dictates of formal morality (and even at times, it must be admitted, even against the dictates of *virtù*). "It ought to be clear to you, Tancredi, as you are made of flesh that you fathered a daughter made of flesh and not of stone or iron; thus you should remember, even if you are now old, how powerful the laws of youth *(le leggi della giovanezza)* are. . . . I remain as you fathered me, of the flesh . . . and still young *(giovane)* and for both reasons I am full of sexual desire *(concupiscibile disiderio),* whose most wonderful powers I have already enjoyed as I was once married. . . . Certainly against this [desire] I used all my power *(virtù)* because as much as I could, I didn't want the attractions of this natural sin *(natural peccato)* to bring shame *(vergogna)* on you or me."[20]

The sins of the flesh are sins certainly, but for young people in love they are "natural sins," hard to avoid and best handled with understanding for what they are: very human and rather mild faults in and of themselves, even if their potential social danger was great in terms of shame, lost honor, and, more tellingly, disruptions in the marriage alliance plans of families and clans. Nakedly stated, and positively presented, young love and young sex go together naturally: the one entails the other, and while marriage might be the ideal and goal, shared sexual pleasures outside of matrimony remain small and very natural sins for young lovers, even if society frowned on them.

Suggestively, Ghismonda concludes this section of her discourse with the explanation that, aided by love and fortune, she found a way to keep her affair secret so that the social dangers involved were minimized and no one's honor or reputation was endangered. But now that the affair had been discovered by her father, she confessed freely what she had done; in sum, her hiding of the affair was not dishonesty so much as a thoughtful and clever strategy to protect their consensus realities: *virtù* once again—the wise mastery of events that controlled them for the best. And once that wise secret no longer served its purpose of protecting honor, she freely admitted what she had done. In fact, throughout the *Decameron,* the secret "natural sins" of young love are not a problem as long as they remain secret—in other words, not performed in a social setting that would make them the grist for the broader community evaluations of consensus realities. With sins and faults kept hidden, *virtù* still ruled, for it was essentially a demonstrated force, an outward quality evaluated by others, and, when unnoted by others, un*virtù*-ous deeds simply did not exist.

Leaving the laws of youth and natural sins behind, however, Ghismonda returns to the real heart of her loving father's outraged feelings and despair—her love for and sexual relations with a lower-class man, a mere page of her father. "I did not take Guiscardo, as many do, for some minor attraction, but rather with *deliberate consideration* I chose him over all the others and *with careful thought* I introduced myself to him and both he and I with *wise perseverance* have long enjoyed the fulfillment of my desires."[21] *Virtù, virtù, virtù.* Again, Ghismonda is asserting the *virtù* at the heart of her choosing Guiscardo: she relied on reason not emotion, and the relation went ahead with "careful thought" and "wise perseverance" to avoid negative ramifications in the consensus realities of the groups that surrounded and evaluated them. Still, she realizes that the question of her *virtù,* as far as her father is concerned, turns on that deeper issue in her choice of Guiscardo, the dishonor inherent in his lack of status, and she continues her counterattack by pointing out that this was not so much caused by some sin of hers as by fortune, which often places the most worthy at lower social levels and raises the unworthy to the heights. A troubling idea for a Rinascimento reader at first sight, but Boccaccio's Ghismonda presses ahead to express a crucial idea of the early Rinascimento most attractive to the new merchant-banker elites (the *popolo grosso*), who, as we have seen, were claiming superior social status against the older nobilities of northern Italy to go with their by now fairly well-established political and economic power. Status, she claimed, should not be based on the traditional standards of nobility—birth and blood given by fortune—but on newer behavioral models that turned on reason, manners, and the ability to get things done—in sum, the familiar attributes of upper-class *virtù*.

Ghismonda lectures her father and Boccaccio's audience,

> But let's move on [from the question of fortune], to consider a bit the origins of this situation. You will note that we are all made from the same flesh and created by the same Creator with souls of equal strength and potential and equal *virtù*. *Virtù* was what first created distinctions among us, who all were born and are born equal; and those who had the most *virtù and demonstrated it the most were named nobles* and the rest non-nobles. And even if later contrary practices have hidden this law, it has not been eliminated, or overturned by nature or good manners; for this reason, the person who *demonstrates virtù* reveals to all his nobility and those who call him otherwise are in the wrong. . . . Look carefully at all your nobles and examine their lives, their manners, and their ways, then consider Guiscardo in the same way. *If you judge them honestly you will admit that he is most noble and that all your nobles are peasants.*[22]

Virtù makes commoners noble and nobles peasants!

Here, starkly stated by a young woman in love and about to die, is the ultimate power of *virtù*: the person who displays *virtù* is superior, superior to the merely noble in name, to the merely rich in wealth, to the merely powerful in terms of position. And it is worth reflecting on the fact that here love and sex have revealed yet another level of their violent potential, for they had the violent, nay virtually revolutionary, potential to literally overthrow the social order of society—and indeed it at least appeared to be doing so in this tale as well as in the quotidian world of fourteenth-century social turmoil beyond Ghismonda's revolutionary claims. Now, of course, no one would deny that family status, great wealth, or powerful positions could and did regularly overwhelm *virtù* in the Rinascimento. In fact, the tragedy of the love of Ghismonda and Guiscardo is that the power of Tancredi as a prince, patriarch, and noble seemed to win easily over their love and their *virtù*.

Still, one of the most satisfying things about literature is that in that imaginary, but no less real for that, realm of life, often what is true and beautiful wins out—what regularly does happen in everyday life is replaced by what should happen because it is true and beautiful. And aside from all the significant things that that ability to replace the "does happen" with the "should happen" implies, for readers it means that literature offers a fascinating insight on how people felt things should be. Tancredi, nonetheless, in his loving but un*virtù*-uous rage—not so much immoral but emotional and unreasonable and blinded by his violent love—that very night had the two men who were guarding Guiscardo strangle him and cut out his heart. And the next day, he had the heart delivered to Ghismonda in a golden chalice with the words, "Your father sends you this to console you with the thing that you love the most, just as you have consoled him with that which he most loved."[23] Here, brutally, we are slapped in the face by the contrast between love governed by *virtù*, Ghismonda's for Guiscardo, and love so violently felt that it destroyed *virtù*, Tancredi's for his daughter. And, once again, a heart is cut out in the name of love.

Ghismonda, when she was shown the golden cup and heard her father's words, again with true *virtù*, turned his violent deeds and words immediately on their head—making of his tragedy of vengeance her triumph of love and once more winning a Rinascimento reader's approval and sympathy. "There is no more fitting tomb," she pointed out sagely, "than gold for a heart of the quality of this one: in this (at least) my father has acted with good judgment."[24] And again the contrast is clear, especially with Ghismonda's last ironic comment, that at least in placing her lover's heart in a golden chalice her father had finally shown some *virtù*; for throughout he had been blinded by his fatherly love and emotions, while the young lovers had lived up to and suffered true to their *virtù*-ous love. Now, sadly, it was Ghismonda's turn to meet her tragic fate, and, with perfect symmetry, she mixed with the tears *that she now finally shed* in the golden chalice a poison that she had brewed herself as she pronounced yet another soliloquy on love and the fine qualities of Guiscardo and his heart. Then she drank it down and lay down

"modestly" on her bed to await death and the reuniting of her heart and
soul with her lover.

Yet even poison conspired with *virtù* and Boccaccio's literary hand
to reveal the lessons of this tale, for Ghismonda lived on long enough
to confront her father's emotions and lack of *virtù* one last time. Called
by her servants, who realized too late what was happening, Tancredi arrived in tears and Ghismonda chastised him: "Tancredi, save those tears
for a less desired fortune than this, and don't waste them on me as I
don't want them. Who has ever heard of anyone aside from you, who
cried when he got what he wanted."[25] This prince was brought down by
his uncontrolled love and the violent emotions it evoked and as a result
lost, because of his lack of *virtù,* what was most dear to him—in this,
in a curious way, Boccaccio pre-echoes the warnings of Machiavelli. Indeed, Tancredi is a perfect anti-Machiavellian prince—and as we will see
in Chapter 5, he is not the only one in Boccaccio's apparently apolitical
tales. Lacking *virtù* and overwhelmed by uncontrolled emotions and
outdated notions of personal honor, he loses all that he holds most dear.

Ghismonda caps her father's fall, however, with a last request that
reveals one last time her own *virtù:* "But if there still is alive in you any
of that love which you once felt for me, as a last gift—even if you were
unhappy with the fact that I lived *secretly and quietly* with Guiscardo—
grant me that my body be buried with his where you have thrown it
in such a way that all may know [of our love]."[26] Here, in the virtually
eternal romantic *topos* of tragic lovers buried together, it is easy to miss
a significant detail: Ghismonda wanted their carefully hidden love and
shared sexual pleasures, in death, to be publicly acknowledged by the
consensus realities of their world, what had been hidden to become
seen through a public ceremony of burial in a common grave, and she
wanted it in the name of her father's love for her.

In this, her request for an honorable burial for her and her beloved
as *virtù*-ous lovers, lies the potential for a deeper reading of this story,
for it might be suggested that throughout it there is a conflict between
the disciplining dynamic of honor / shame and that of *virtù,* which
might be labeled the regime of *virtù.*[27] Tancredi was clearly driven by
a vision of honor and shame that was negatively associated at the time
with a traditional and violent nobility that the governments of early
Rinascimento city-states like Florence and Venice were anxious to limit

or eliminate. In that context, his vengeance on those who shamed him was to be expected and virtually required by his noble status and the "just" emotions that a noble should feel in the face of dishonor. Ghismonda and Guiscardo, however, followed the imperatives of a dramatically different regime of *virtù*—imperatives that, at least in the *Decameron*, Boccaccio seemed to place over and over again ahead of honor. The lesson is clear: the honor / shame dynamic could unleash dangerously destructive passions both socially and personally, even as it could serve to discipline—and this same point will be echoed tragically in Lisabetta's tale, as we shall see. Forced to decide between the two, the regime of *virtù* may well have seemed for Boccaccio the better choice for civil society, as it did much later for Machiavelli. Of course, in the best of Rinascimento worlds, honor sheared of its negative violent passions and *virtù* might overlap, reinforcing each other to create not tragedies but the best of all possible societies. And in the fictional world of Boccaccio, Ghismonda's tale ends with the young lovers' honorable burial—in the end, finally, honor and *virtù* work together.

What makes this hard to parse is the fact that honor often was closely interwoven with *virtù* in the Rinascimento: both were terms used to evaluate behavior and social position, both were largely evaluated by a broader community, both were frequently performative, and both were central for the disciplining of society, as we have seen. Moreover, often the terms were even used interchangeably. But I would suggest that honor was generally a narrower concept more focused on social station and the virtually ontological status of a person—what a person was at a deep level, whereas *virtù*, while also deeply concerned with status, was more concerned with what a person did and thus focused on an evaluation of one's abilities, prowess, and comportment in general.

Also, in part, because *"virtù"* was a term deeply associated with the power or active nature of things, when the term was applied to evaluating people, it tended to stress the active force of a person, the ability to accomplish things, more than honor did. Herbs healed by *virtù* of their healing powers; stones fell toward the center of the earth by *virtù* of their nature; prayers worked by *virtù* of God's grace. In this context, virtually everything had its *virtù*, its active principle, and thus, it was relatively easy and logical to use the term when evaluating a person with this strong sense of action. It may well be as well that the association of the active and action with the superior male and the passive with the less positive aspects of the female also strengthened the positive valence of the term.

In the Rinascimento, in large part because of this active principle of *virtù,* one could accomplish something with *virtù* that was not necessarily honorable or morally correct but nonetheless judged as socially or politically positive. This is something that has troubled modern commentators on Machiavelli but that can be seen more generally in representations of *virtù* across the period. Our young lovers' affair provides a perfect example: as noted earlier, it was not honorable on many levels, not so much because it was hidden but because it crossed class lines in ways that caused loss of honor; yet, as retold by Boccaccio, it was essentially a parable of *virtù,* and, in terms of *virtù,* it was a positive affair that demonstrated the best of both characters. In turn, people could be honorable without necessarily demonstrating *virtù,* as Tancredi poignantly reveals. Killing Guiscardo and having his heart cut out and presented to his daughter certainly could be seen as having redressed his lost honor and subsequent shame—a legitimate and even necessary vendetta in the face of the dishonoring affair that his daughter had had with a commoner. And here, significantly, the emotions associated with honor enter into the evaluation, for Tancredi's deeds were not so much based on a reasoned consideration of what his honor required but, as his tears and rage starkly underline, on strong emotions that caused him to lose the rational control a prince and a patriarch needed to maintain in the regime of *virtù* of the cities of fourteenth-century Italy.

In a more traditional telling of this violent and tragic tale, Tancredi could well have been presented as the hero / victim, an epitome of honor, regretfully exacting a just and rather poetically brutal vengeance on the dishonoring behavior of a wayward daughter and a disloyal servant—dishonoring shame requiring a symbolic retribution that reestablished the correct balance of honor with shame in the community and in the relationships of the protagonists. Ghismonda was dishonored and shamed—symbolically underlined by the brutal gesture of being given her lover's heart in a golden chalice—and that, in the end, ideally balanced the dishonor and shame of her father. One could even imagine the honorable conclusion of the tale with her being shipped off to a convent to leave Tancredi to live honorably ever after, respected by his subjects and Boccaccio's readers for his stern but just management of his own family.

Indeed, from this perspective, the real tragedy of this tale turns on a classic ethical double bind created by these systems of discipline that did not overlap perfectly. In the early Rinascimento, as the everyday conception of *virtù* shifted from values of an older aristocracy based on blood, warfare, and rural ideals to those of a newer urban elite (the *popolo grosso*) whose vision of *virtù*, as we have seen, tended to stress reason, self-control, and a planning, even cunning, mastery of the future, there developed a troubling disjunction between the disciplining drive of a more traditional honor / shame dynamic and the newer values of the regime of *virtù*. Although honor and *virtù* could often work effectively together to discipline society, when one or the other was taken to its logical conclusion, things became more problematic. For honor was a discipline that turned ultimately on shame and violence, often dangerous emotions from the perspective of *virtù*. In contrast, *virtù* turned more on reason and self-control—leaving little room for violence and violent passions associated with vendetta and the redress of lost honor—at least in the fourteenth century. From this perspective, Tancredi reflected the older values of traditional honor / shame, while Ghismonda and Guiscardo represented the values of a newer vision of *virtù*, and it is clear in this story, as it is clear throughout the *Decameron*, where Boccaccio's sympathy fell.[28]

If Tancredi had followed the dictates of *virtù*, as outlined by his daughter, he would have recognized Guiscardo's *virtù*-induced nobility, elevated his status at court, and married her to her lover quietly. With no one aware of his dishonor (as honor was also socially evaluated), it simply would not have existed for their consensus realities, and all three would have lived happily ever after: *virtù*-ous daughter, *virtù*-ous son-in-law, and *virtù*-ous prince. But the tragedy in all of this was that Tancredi was following a disciplining system that still worked, that was still believed in, and that even Boccaccio could see the value of (when it worked in conjunction with *virtù*). The ultimate disjunction between honor and *virtù* driven by the violent emotions associated with honor, which is at the heart of the tale, resulted in tragedy. But, actually, whether consciously or not, that tragic disjuncture was overcome at the conclusion of the tale, for at the last Tancredi repented and accepted his daughter's request to be buried together with her lover publicly and honorably.

Thus, as noted earlier, the lovers' *virtù* was recognized by the broader community and granted an honorable status with an "honorable" burial as the tale concludes. For hidden *virtù*—which was hardly *virtù* at all in a world where *virtù* and self were largely performative and social—with public recognition would finally gain its due. In this way, the lovers' tragedy was turned via the consensus realities of their community into triumph, and Boccaccio ended his tragically violent novella positively: "So the love of Ghismonda and Guiscardo ended in tragedy as you have heard. Repenting his cruelty when it was too late and after many tears, that Tancredi with the widespread mourning of the people of Salerno, had the two buried together in one tomb, *honorably*."[29] Beyond death, beyond the power of fathers, patriarchs, and princes, *virtù* ruled, and when it did, even the violent tragedies of love became virtually revolutionary triumphs—at least in the imaginative world of the Rinascimento—and occasionally beyond, I would suggest.

How Lisabetta's Death Does Not Fit the Tales of the Fourth Day, Where Tragedy Highlights the Heroic Nature of True Love

As the first tale of day four, the heroic deaths of the young lovers Guiscardo and Ghismonda set the theme for the day, giving many of the tragic stories a positive dimension that transcends their tragedy. In fact, celebrations of the true love and the happy sex involved along with the honorable burials of lovers with the implied support of the consensus realities that surrounded them are ubiquitous in the tales of the day. But strangely, Lisabetta's novella, as the fifth tale of the day, is merely tragic, lacking in heroic deeds, honoring burials, or even *virtù*, as we shall see. Still, not all the tales of the day involve heroic deaths. The third tale of the day explores how a strong emotion like love can itself be tragically warped by other strong emotions, in this case jealousy and wrath, which lead to terrible deeds, including murder. Needless to say, in it, the violence of jealousy and wrath are not presented as positively exemplary, and the novella seems to serve more as a warning of the dangerous ancillary passions that a strong emotion like love can evoke, much in line with the tales discussed in Chapter 2.

The fourth tale takes the danger of love yet further, exploring how love can become literally a mad passion, destroying a young man completely, making no crime too great to commit. This tale concludes with the young lover Gerbino having his head cut off, rather like Lisabetta's Lorenzo. But in this case, his own grandfather, the king of Sicily, had ordered this done as a public execution to demonstrate his own honor and commitment to his word. Gerbino's crime was that he broke his word to his grandfather and in that context caused the king's most solemn promise to the king of Tunisia to be broken. Even though he had only heard about the beauty and exceptional qualities of the daughter of that king, and she had only heard the similar praises of him, they had fallen deeply in love via word of mouth or reputation and were working on finding a way to act on their passion when her father, the king of Tunisia, decided to marry her to the king of Granada. Having heard of Gerbino's love for his daughter, he also asked Gerbino's grandfather, the king of Sicily, for his solemn word that there would be no interference with her voyage to join her betrothed, a promise that the king of Sicily sealed by sending him his glove, a sign of a most solemn promise. In turn, the king of Sicily demanded that Gerbino promise not to interfere. And he reluctantly complied.

As a result, Gerbino was placed in a classic double bind when his beloved asked him to prove his love and save her from an unwanted marriage to the king of Granada. Would he keep his word to his grandfather or prove his love? Gerbino chose love, and his love to this point could be seen as heroic. But what followed undercut his heroic commitment to his love and did so in the grips of uncontrolled emotions that went well beyond what love demanded or the wisdom of *virtù* required even of lovers moved by strong emotions. First then, to prove his love and win her hand against his grandfather's wishes and pledge, he outfitted a boat and, taking to the seas, intercepted the ship carrying his beloved. Seeing her for the first time on the fleeing ship, tellingly, he was more enflamed with love than ever. But, in the ensuing battle, the sailors on her ship, fearing that they were going to be taken or killed, threw her overboard to her death in the hopes of escaping their attackers. Totally losing control of his emotions in a blind rage that overwhelmed any *virtù* that he might have demonstrated to that point— once again, the dangerous violent potential of love—Gerbino continued his assault, boarded the boat, killed all the sailors, and sank it; thus, in the end, he lost his love and soon after his head as well due to his tragic, uncontrolled love and the violent rage it enflamed that went well beyond what love required.

In a way, Gerbino's demise seems at first sight to contradict the honor dynamic discussed earlier in the tale of Ghismonda. Gerbino's grandfather is presented as acting justly in executing him to redress his own lost honor when his grandson broke his royal pledge to the king of Tunis and, in turn, when Gerbino broke his word to him. Those broken oaths and the accompanying lost honor required Gerbino's head, and his grandfather became the righteous patriarch and prince. In the end, however, what changes the valence of the tale is Gerbino's transition from a heroic lover to an emotionally out-of-control one who has totally lost his reason and *virtù* in the passion of the moment. Love with *virtù*, even violent true love driven by reason, can be positive and heroic, but without the careful measure of *virtù*, it becomes dangerous and at times deadly, as Gerbino's princess and his own head tragically reveal. Ghismonda died a heroic lover with an honorable burial thanks to her *virtù;* Gerbino died a violent criminal in dishonor because his passionate love overwhelmed his *virtù*.

The other two tales of the day that do not end in *virtù*-ous deaths are far less tragic. The second tale of the day warns about the dangers of self-love. In this tale, as discussed earlier, an extremely vain Venetian noblewoman is convinced by a corrupt friar that the angel Gabriel has fallen in love with her, unable to resist her celestial beauty. As the poor angel lacked a physical body and thus the means to consummate his love, the friar kindly offered his own body to the angel to use in making love to her. In this unique example of Rinascimento gift exchange, the angel Gabriel repays the favor by allowing the spirit of the friar freed from his body to spend the same time visiting heaven and enjoying the pleasures of paradise. Thus, nicely, the friar's clever lie is virtually true, for the friar as Gabriel in the bed of his foolishly vain victim is in the more worldly paradise that Boccaccio often laughingly celebrates in his tales. Unfortunately for this hypocritical, but admittedly clever, friar, his paradise ended when the young woman's brothers arrived after hearing reports that the angel Gabriel had become her lover and decided to investigate that strange proposition. Caught in the act, the

not-quite-angelic lover saved himself, as noted earlier, by taking wing
from her window, but, lacking the necessary attributes for that form
of flight at least, instead of flying back to heaven, he plummeted into
the canal below and swam to apparent safety. But as word of the fallen
angel spread through the city, he was captured and eventually tarred
and feathered by an irate populace—hardly the stuff of real tragedy, as
long as one was not the friar or perhaps the angel Gabriel.

The last tale of the day, told by Dioneo, the most irreverent of Boccaccio's storytellers, takes advantage of the special dispensation that
allowed him to not follow the theme of the day. Noting that the whole
brigata had become depressed after hearing so many sad tales and tragic
deaths, he tells the tale of a certain Ruggieri who, while waiting for the
wife of an old doctor to join him in her bedroom for a night of love,
falls afoul of Fortuna. As he waits, he inadvertently drinks a powerful
sleeping potion left by the doctor, thinking it was water, and falls into
such a deep sleep that he appears to be dead. This kicks off a series of
dangerous adventures that Fortuna uses to try to thwart Ruggieri's
adulterous love, but when he finally awakes and regains the *virtù* that
love offers a young lover, he overcomes all obstacles and manages to re-
join his mistress in their adulterous affair. Thus, the tales of the fourth
day end with the *brigata* laughing once again and with love and shared
sexual pleasure triumphing over both Fortuna and, in this case, even
what appeared to be death—a salutary happy ending for a tragic day of
sad tales that frequently ended with the death of lovers.

But in the majority of the rest of the tales of the fourth day, the
endings focus not just on the noble and ennobling suffering of tragic
lovers but on the public mourning that invariably positively evaluated
both the life and love of the couples. In this way, from the perspective
of Rinascimento consensus realities, the tragic loves of the fourth day
became uplifting triumphs of true love and sexual desire and more
suited to a set of tales supposedly committed to raising the spirits of
their tellers in the time of the plague. Moreover, from this perspective,
the happy and lusty sexual play of many of Boccaccio's tales dedicated
to love finds love on this day often a deeper and more noble passion that
uplifts and ennobles, belying the claim often made that his characters
are moved more by lust than love.[30] And, certainly, at times the only

uplift in the tales seems to be in the form of the famous "resurrection of the flesh" of Rustico before the naked Alibech found in the tenth tale of the third day to be considered in Chapter 4. But it is also true that the narrators of his tales often stop to explain that love has the virtually miraculous power to make people capable of great deeds, deeds that transcend their normal capabilities and lift them to higher social and moral levels.[31]

Yet, tellingly, from this perspective Lisabetta's tale seems to stand even more alone in the fourth day, for while her love is evident, her *virtù* appears to be largely absent. In fact, it seems that evil Fortuna wins over a passionate, sad, and mourning love that is never judged by the con- sensus realities of those around her as ennobling or *virtù*-ous. Even her potentially ennobling tears over her lover's head are narrated without positive comment and apparently without positive results of any sort beyond the flourishing growth of her basil. Actually, sad, uncontrolled tears are virtually always a sign of lack of *virtù* in the *Decameron*. More- over, heroic burials, public acclaim of noble love by the groups that might have evaluated Lisabetta's consensus reality, or even positive comments about her mourning are totally absent. Unlike many of the other tales of the day, Lisabetta's burial is not even mentioned and, to add insult to injury, even her lover's corpse and his head went equally unremarked and were disposed of separately in ways that could be hardly characterized as burials; thus, that critical moment of evalua- tion and a final consensus reality was lacking in her case. Clearly, her love did not triumph over Fortuna or anything else for that matter, and in the end even love itself was hardly mentioned, forgotten or at least washed away by her tears and suffering. But, for all that, her bizarre head in a pot and her devotion to it make her tale seem like one that is trying to tell its fourteenth-century readers something.

Where Lisabetta's Growing Basil in the Head of Her Beloved Is Considered

What that was, however, today is clearly unclear. Of course, that very lack of clarity has attracted the attention of many who have suggested a host of possible readings. Yet virtually no one has looked more closely at the strange potted head growing basil as a memento and that, along with the way Rinascimento mementos worked in the context of consensus realities and notions of *virtù,* may offer a reading that not only makes sense of the tale and its central placement in the tales of the fourth day but at the same time offers a deeper appreciation of Boccaccio's vision of the powerful emotions of love and desire at the time of the plague.[32]

Although the word "memento" is rarely used in the Italian of the day, if a memento is considered as a material object with metaphoric quality that attempts to capture and reevoke a past emotional or spiritual state, it seems to fit well with the Rinascimento understanding of material *ricordi* or remembrances—a term with deep significance in a society that liked to think of itself as built on memory and the renewal or rebirth of ancient societies and cultures. Perhaps the most powerful material *ricordi* of the day were based on body parts, like Lorenzo's head—the holy body parts of saints and martyrs. These relics, upon which the Catholic Church was in a deep sense founded, were material metaphors of remembrance—mementoes, that is—that recalled superior spiritual lives or states of existence.

As material metaphors with a spiritual dimension, however, these mementoes did not merely recall, they *re*-called or reiterated a profound connection. For true metaphors, or in this case true relics, worked because their metaphoric quality was real: a relic did not simply commemorate a special spiritual state; its materiality actually participated directly in that special spiritual state across time. Thus, under the altar of virtually every church in fourteenth-century Europe, and of foundational importance, were the relics of saints and martyrs, which conjoined the material and spiritual space of those churches to the founding material and spiritual spaces of the ongoing Ecclesia. As material metaphors of the eternal and ongoing Church, they helped empower the very special spiritual space where the miracle of the mass could be repeated until the end of time and the reuniting of the saved in paradise. At a humbler level, the miracles and healing properties of such body part mementoes were widely recognized and celebrated by everyday people, touted by preachers and church leaders, and even promoted by civic authorities, perhaps most notably with processions and festivals that acclaimed and, indeed, often called upon their powerful transtemporal connections.[33]

The language of material life and language itself, of course, were also alive with metaphor / mementoes that still evoked real living connections with the past. In fact, there was a wide range of magic that drew on this quality of Rinascimento language itself. Take, for example, the fascinating case of Giulia, the daughter of Lodovico da Verona, who when testifying before inquisitors of the Venetian Holy Office in 1584 admitted that to command the love of a man, she wrapped up a lizard in swaddling bought in the name of the Great Devil *(Gran Diavolo)* and boiled it alive in a new pot, saying, "I do not bind this lizard, rather I bind the heart of him [the lover sought] in the name of the Great Devil who rules and governs." At its most simple, the metaphor turns on: as the lizard is bound and perhaps dies painfully for this love, so too will a lover's heart be bound in the name of the devil who rules, presumably, this world. In the end, the case reveals a much deeper sense of the metaphorical quality of the world, the binding powers that control it, and the way in which the underlying metaphorical quality of words and things command love and action. But that cannot detain us here; the point is simply that this underlying metaphorical quality of language was widely seen as offering great power, and examples of such use of metaphor could be easily multiplied from both literary and archival texts.[34]

Less openly diabolic magic often had similar metaphoric dimensions. Sticking needles in animal hearts or in the genitals of wax figures to punish a reluctant lover or make him impotent until he succumbed to love are only the most pointed examples[35]—material metaphors that the archival record portray as often being extremely effective. In a rich and rather troubling case that suggests the impact of a rather different form of heart magic, Elena Zamberto testified before the Venetian Holy Office that, unaware that magic aimed at punishing her heart had been placed under her door, she was suddenly struck down ill one day: "the first day of this year at night [the day the magic was placed under her door, according to the testimony of others] I came down with a very serious stomach ache and heart palpitations. . . . It was so bad that I thought I was close to death. After that there continued certain pains in my heart that felt as if I were being cut into."[36] These symptoms passed when, again unbeknownst to her, the magic was removed. And troublingly, the case establishes that she did not know, and could not have known, the woman who was attacking her with the magic or her motivation or, more telling yet, when it was removed, making it hard to see how this magic actually worked with modern explanations.

Where the Magical Uses of Severed Heads Are Considered

In fact, it was accounts of just such love magic, and especially the use of the bones of criminals and occasionally heads, that drew me first to the tale of Lisabetta. Court records offer cases of cunning women seeking the bones of executed men including their heads and that, along with the many relics of saints' and martyrs' heads to be found in the churches of northern Italy, seemed to suggest that there might be something magical about Lisabetta's head. That hypothesis was reinforced by the fact that in more learned texts on magic from the period the claim was occasionally made that a sure way to become invisible was to plant beans in a skull.[37] The beans that were produced, it was promised, would make the person who ate them invisible when the correct words and rituals were done. Thus, it seemed probable that there might be some magic associated with growing basil in skulls as well.

To make a long, unfruitful story short, to date I have found none. Moreover, as I searched for such magic, this hypothesis began to seem less and less likely, for rereading the *Decameron* with this in mind, what should have been clear from the first became evermore evident—Boccaccio does not treat magic or even relics with much sympathy, tending to dismiss both as things that were used to fool the gullible, even if he is well aware and makes regular reference to their attraction for many in his day. In fact, in the context of consensus realities, Boccaccio's tales seem often to aim to elicit laughter at those who foolishly believe in magic and relics and show how they are victimized or made the butt of jokes by clever people who understand that such beliefs are foolish and play on those ignorant enough to believe in them. One of the best examples of this is tale three of day eight, where the perennial butt of many clever *beffe*, our Calandrino, collects supposedly magical stones from a local river (the Mugello) after being convinced by his friends Bruno and Buffalmacco that they would make him invisible—it seems clear that their consensus reality of him was that he was so lacking in *virtù* that he would fall for even this scam, and the tale confirms their judgment.[38]

Moving beyond magic, however, the basil of Lisabetta's memento did seem to have explanatory potential, especially in the context of her cutting off her lover's head, for perhaps the most famous tale of a woman acquiring the severed head of a man in the Christian tradition—Salome asking for and obtaining the head of John the Baptist—in many accounts involved basil. In several versions of the tale, John's head was eventually placed in a vase and buried, and basil was found growing there afterward.[39] Also intriguing is the fact that John's mother was named Elizabeth, like the Lisabetta of Boccaccio's tale. But perhaps most suggestively, John the Baptist was one of the patron saints of Florence, and thus the association of a severed head in a vase with flourishing basil might seem to recall images of that patron saint, especially in a period after the plague, when the loyalty and support of patron saints might have seemed particularly important to invoke.

A still stronger connection is suggested by the fact that in fourteenth-century Florence, John the Baptist was often seen as closely associated with the Guelph party and the strong traditional ties of the city to the Guelph cause. Writing his work in a period when that party was trying to reassert a leadership role in the city and beginning to label new men who had entered the city after the plague non-Guelphs to eliminate them from Florentine political and social life, Boccaccio might be seen as using a clever metaphor that associated John's martyrdom, Lisabetta's love for her martyred lover, and the Guelph love of the city to support their program.[40] But Boccaccio's narration of the tale provides no suggestion of any such associations, metaphoric or otherwise. At best, the lovers, although living in Messina, had Tuscan roots. Her family was a merchant family from San Gimignano, and he was from Pisa, and thus neither was a suffering Florentine Guelph. Moreover, the head merely rots passively as the basil grows and Lisabetta dies—a not very encouraging metaphor for the power of the Guelph party to eliminate new men or even its love of Florence.

It almost seems as if a negative vision of the Guelphs' strategy might make a better reading, with the party's rejection of new men being paralleled with the beheading of John the Baptist, both cutting off his special positive relationship with the city. Once again, however, this reading seems a long and unlikely jump from a tale set in Messina without any hint of politics there or in Florence. One other possible political message might be very well hidden in the tale. For when the memento is destroyed with the head reburied and the basil thrown away, Lisabetta dies in short order—all of which might serve as a warning that if Florence denied their patron saint and their Guelph party, a similar civic death might be their fate. But, unfortunately for that unlikely explanation, Lisabetta was already dying even before the head and the basil were thrown away, when in fact she was literally worshipping them, as the tale makes abundantly clear.

Basil offered another possible spiritual connection via Helen, the mother of the first Christian emperor, Constantine, who in a number of medieval tales about the herb was reputed to have been the first to discover it growing wild under the spot where Christ was crucified. In this context, a significant strain of magic discussed in archival sources was based on using the earth from places of execution bathed with the blood of criminals for magical purposes, usually punishing magic based on calling up the wandering souls of criminals to aid in hammering enemies. For example, in the case of Isabella Bellocchio discussed earlier, she was accused of concocting the mixture designed to hammer a rival in love that included ground taken from between the Columns of Justice in Venice (where criminals were executed) and bones of the dead taken from various graveyards around the city. The mixture, which also contained "water of San Alberto, feces of dogs . . . wolf fat and other things," was reported to have been highly effective when applied secretly to her rival's door.[41] Such magic also from time to time involved planting herbs or beans in such soil, which when grown were then fed to victims, with devastating effect.

Christ, of course, was convicted as a criminal and allowed himself to die for his love of humanity, much as Lisabetta apparently died for her love of Lorenzo. Could the basil, then, be the sign that this and Lorenzo's head were a memento and a material metaphor of a deeper love between Christ and humanity associated with his crucifixion and the basil found by Helen growing on the spot where he was executed? As tempting as that suggestive reading might be, there is virtually nothing in the tale to sustain such a connection. The deaths of the lovers, as noted, are singularly unheroic. More telling yet, they are otherwise unremarkable, totally isolated from any religious context or hint of deeper spiritual meaning. In the end, aside from the fact that the basil's flourishing greenness may suggest life, a connection that will be considered shortly, its significance may be merely the mundane fact that that specific type of basil carefully pointed out in the tale—Salernitan basil—was well known at the time for its powerful odor that would have been capable of covering the smell of a rotting head. As reluctant as one is to admit it, sometimes a pipe is merely a pipe or, in this case, a basil plant noted for its strong odor is merely an odorous basil plant.[42]

Where Lisabetta's Head Growing Basil Is Considered in Terms of Ideals of Honor and Revenge

Another reading of our memento suggested by a number of critics sees it as part of a broader attack by Boccaccio on southern Italian superstition and the macabre vision of magic and life typical of southern culture. There is one major flaw with this interpretation, for although the novella is often referred to as the tale of Lisabetta da Messina or Lisabetta from Messina, it is not clear that Lisabetta was from Messina or the south. It seems that she, like Boccaccio and his storytellers, was from Tuscany and merely living in the south. Some who hold that the protagonists were southerners, however, argue that Lisabetta and her brothers were born and raised in Messina because the tale laconically reports merely that their father was from San Gimignano. Yet, even in that case, as Tuscan merchants working in Messina, they would have most likely remained outsiders.

Significantly, if they were born and raised there—something never mentioned—Boccaccio is equally silent about their acculturation to the life of Messina, something that would be expected if this was in some way a commentary on the differences between Tuscan values and southern ones. In fact, as will become clear, Lisabetta's brothers' actions reflect perfectly Tuscan notions of *virtù* seen throughout the *Decameron* and actually do not match up very well with the honor / vendetta ethic often portrayed as southern. In sum, it requires quite a stretch to attribute her macabre memento to her "southernism" or as an attack on the backward ways of the region. In fact, the only southerners who play a role in the story are her neighbors, who find her crying over her basil neither superstitious nor particularly southern, merely strange. In sum, this seems an unpromising interpretation that may say more about some modern critics' stereotypical vision of southern Italy than about the tale itself.[43]

The main characters' northern background also creates problems for those who see the story as an indictment of a southern Italian code of honor and vendetta. Certainly, the tale clearly states that her brothers killed her lover because they felt their family honor was threatened by her affair with him. Brothers in the absence of a father were generally held responsible for a sister's behavior, especially sexual, which had great potential to put at risk not only a woman's honor but that of the whole family. Contemporary criminal records often refer to brothers setting right with violence and vendetta similar cases of family dishonor caused by a sister's sexual activity. Indeed, many examples of a form of the honor / shame / vendetta dynamic that modern critics often associate with southern Italy can also be found in archival accounts of crimes driven by family honor and illicit sexual relationships also in the north, albeit with some important local twists.[44]

More pertinently, a focus on the honor / shame / vendetta dynamic misses the complexity of the story and the complexity of Boccaccio's vision of the role of honor in the early Rinascimento, something discussed earlier in the tale of Ghismonda and Guiscardo. But in Lisabetta's tale, it is noteworthy that her brothers' murder of her lover did not actually follow an honor / shame / vendetta paradigm. Rather, her brothers behaved much more in the context of consensus realities and the regime of *virtù*, even if the term *"virtù"* is never applied to their murder. Perhaps most significantly, they never made their vendetta / revenge, if it was that, public as a true vendetta would require. In fact, calculating correctly, with a sense of *virtù* very typical of the *Decameron,* they realized that if her affair was never revealed, their dishonor would not be known by those who judged their consensus realities, and as a result it simply would not exist. Thus, they secretly murdered Lorenzo so that no one was aware of the deed and, more importantly, so that their sister's sexual affair remained unknown. Murder obviously was an extreme response, but the violence associated with sexual honor and "misplaced" love was one that government and courts in northern Italy were well aware of, not just a southern problem and one at least that they attempted to limit by providing other options.[45]

In Lisabetta's fictional case in Messina, her brothers' more straight-forward violence kept questions of her virginity out of the public eye. And as a result of their reasoned and carefully planned behavior, for all their consensus realities she remained an honorable virgin and they her honest and honorable brothers.[46] Such a strategy, of course, was to-tally wrong for an honor / vendetta dynamic, which required a public evaluation of the justice of their violent revenge, yet it was perfect for the regime of *virtù*—in fact, their murder is portrayed as a cool, dispas-sionate deed based on an accurate evaluation of the issues at hand and a rational and effective, albeit illegal and immoral, plan. Thus, after their murder, they told their sister and their neighbors, their various judging publics, that they had sent Lorenzo on a business trip, a reason-able cover to keep their deed secret. That could have been the end of the matter. Without government, without litigation, public disruption, or vendetta, their carefully reasoned secret murder had the potential to settle things once and for all, protecting their honor and their sis-ter's chance for a marriage that they would find more suitable to their station.

How Lisabetta's Head Evokes Tears, Destroys *Virtù*, and Results in a Death That Is Not Heroic and a Warning for Readers, Rinascimento and Modern

Lisabetta's discovery of her lover's body ruined their best-laid plans, however, and in the end, alarmed by her strange compulsive attention to her basil plant, they secretly stole it from her. Then, finding the damning head in the pot, they quietly buried it and discarded the basil. Moreover, realizing that their sister was aware of their murder and might make public their crime at any moment, they quietly departed to distant parts, leaving her to die alone in her grief—hardly honorable or brotherly behavior.[47] Although this behavior was not virtuous in any modern sense, it comes much closer to a sense of *virtù* typical of the day and Boccaccio's way of representing it given their careful and calculated evaluation of their deed and what was required to control a potentially dangerous future if it should become known. Clearly, it also served to retain a head of one's own after committing murder.

Even Lisabetta exhibited what might be considered a certain *virtù* early in the tale when she recovered her lover's head. For when she found her lover's body, rather than collapsing in tears—giving in entirely to strong emotions—she managed to marshal the strength to cut off Lorenzo's head, clean it as best she could, and send it home, all done secretly so that neither her brothers nor any larger public were aware. Continuing her momentary *virtù*-ous behavior, she again secretly hid the head in a vase and planted basil over it so that the smell of the plant covered the odor of decomposition. Whatever deeper implications these deeds might have had, a contemporary reader would have seen in them that way of acting that was associated with *virtù* and realized that she was capable of *virtù*-ous deeds spurred by love, like many of the women of the fourth day. But from that point on, a different dynamic took hold in her developing relationship with her memento, and her emotional tears signal that she had lost that *virtù* that was necessary to make her love and her story heroic (much like Gerbino's uncontrolled emotions had destroyed his lover's *virtù*) and would eventually destroy her.

Many have argued that her mourning over her head and basil was what kept her alive and, from that perspective, when her brothers took it away, they inadvertently caused her death. It might seem, in fact, that her memento serves as a perfect example of the Bakhtinian analysis of the medieval grotesque body where life and death are a continuum, with life springing from death and death from life.[48] Lisabetta's lover's head in death gave birth to a flourishing basil plant, which in turn gave life to Lisabetta as long as she worshipped it. Unfortunately, however, for this attractive hypothesis, Lisabetta's memento did not give her life. In fact, the tale makes it perfectly clear that, rather like a vampire, it sucked the life out of her. As she cried over it, she actually became weaker and sicker. It was her decline virtually worshiping her memento that attracted the attention of her neighbors and her brothers. And they took it from her in part in the hope that doing so would stop her decline toward death, for "her beauty [was] destroyed and . . . her eyes seemed to have receded into her head."[49]

The contrast with another woman's response to a part of her lover's body is instructive. In the ninth tale of the fourth day, as discussed in Chapter 2, the wife of Guiglielmo Rossiglione was served the heart of her lover for dinner disguised as a gourmet dish. Her husband, after murdering her lover, had cut out his heart and given it to his cook, asking him to make it the best-tasting dish possible. A perfect fictional cook, he created a wonderful dish, much to the satisfaction of Guiglielmo's wife, who, unaware, ate it with relish. But when her husband, to gain his desired revenge, announced that the dish that she had just enjoyed so much was the heart of her lover, she did not give in to tears or mourning like Lisabetta. Rather, she declared nobly, "As God would not wish that anything be placed on top of so noble a dish like this heart of so valiant and courtly a knight . . . no other dish will ever pass [these lips]."[50] And she promptly jumped out the window to her death. Strong *virtù*-ous words followed by strong *virtù*-ous deeds in the face of another body metaphor—her lover's heart—that evoked her deep love and made her death truly noble and heroic. Tellingly, the tale ends noting that with "the greatest sadness and tears the two bodies [of the lovers] were brought together [by the public] and . . . they were buried in the same tomb inscribed with verses that explained who was buried there and the manner and reason for their death."[51]

Lisabetta, however, followed a different path. Rather than a heroic deed like the wife of Guiglielmo Rossiglione or the *virtù* of Ghismonda in the face of her lover's heart in a golden chalice and her crying father, Lisabetta demonstrated in the end neither *virtù* nor heroism. Instead, she gave in to tears, mourning over what was a memento that recalled merely death and tragedy. The key to reading the tale with a contemporary eye is that her *testa* in the *testo* memento was literally a dead metaphor, a metaphor of death. As a material recall of a past passion, it worked all too well. For Lisabetta was trapped by it in her state of mourning. Her strong emotions and tears turned inward and in continuously re-creating the emotions associated with a lost love, she was overwhelmed by her passions and lost to *virtù*. Tears once more were a potent sign for Boccaccio's audience. It is noteworthy that earlier when she acted with *virtù*, cutting off her lover's head, it was carefully pointed out that she did not cry, controlling her tears in order to be strong enough to carry out the deed. But once home she gave in to tears, much like the prince of Salerno, Tancredi, who was also destroyed by tears. And Lisabetta followed the same negative and tragic path once she potted her head and planted basil in it.

Unlike Tancredi, however, Lisabetta then had her memento, which ultimately separated her from her consensus realities and actually made it impossible to escape her fate. Early in the story, at least three consensus realities are presented that shaped her identity as a young woman in Messina—three groups with which she negotiated her sense of self: first, her brothers; second, her neighbors; and third, of course, her lover, Lorenzo. All three apparently viewed her positively. But progressively the tale cut away these sustaining groups, and her memento was key to her growing isolation. Her brothers, of course, when they discovered her affair, judged her negatively, and, as the tale relates, they began to treat her in threatening ways. In the end, however, they withdrew entirely, fleeing for their own safety and leaving her without family when they discovered the reality of her memento.[52]

The murder of her lover eliminated another measure of self in the *Decameron* and in life, leaving her only with a sad memory of that relationship, once again her tragic memento. And finally she cut away her neighbors and all other possible contacts as well to focus entirely on crying over and then lamenting her lost memento. In the end, then, Lisabetta had no publics with which to interact, no consensus realities to negotiate with to reformulate a sense of self and a life after the death of her lover. All she had was a truly dead metaphor: a memento *mori*. And her negotiation with that lifeless head in a vase, for all the flowering of the basil, was completely unidirectional, for it offered no consensus realities to re-found her identity—Lisabetta's isolated tears and uncontrolled mourning had only one exit: a slow decline and a sure death. Its destruction only sealed a fate already clear to the *Decameron*'s readers and fully confirmed by her unremarked death and unnoted burial.

In sum, her memento offered her only death. Smothered in tears that were meaningless to all but Lisabetta, and thus ultimately meaningless in a world where both *virtù* and honor were measured publicly by consensus realities, it ensured an anonymous, meaningless, and tragic final oblivion—a salutary warning for Boccaccio's youthful group of storytellers and their vision of love and passion in the time of the plague. For they had fled the mourning and suffering of that great mortality to create with their friends in their sweetly ordered gardens a safe haven of new consensus realities with their tales of love, sex, and *virtù*.

Reading Boccaccio's tale in the context of archival records and consensus realities recovers a different view of Lisabetta's tragic death. Her worshipping of her head and mourning over its loss isolated her from

the groups that were capable of forming her consensus reality and literally her sense of self and thus slowly transformed her isolation into the
ultimate isolation for the fourteenth century, a death alone and unremarked by society. In the end, getting ahead or actually getting a head,
as Boccaccio and his readers were well aware, required not just love and
passion but, crucially, also action and *virtù* in an ongoing negotiation
of self with the groups that formed a person's consensus realities in
the world of Rinascimento, as Lisabetta negatively demonstrated to all
with her tragic death that concluded the central tale of the fourth day
of tragic tales. Mourning the tragedies of life was not the answer and
definitely not the answer to the devastating mortality of the plague—
rather, sexual pleasure and love enjoyed and suffered with *virtù* were
then. And now?

4

Transcendence

Love, Sexual Pleasure, and a Woman as Savior

Where Neifile Brings the *Decameron*'s Storytellers to a
Very Special Garden to Hear Tales That Strangely
Do Not Seem to Fit Its Spiritual Promise

As love's promises seem to always whisper in the first warm breezes of
spring in the Rinascimento as well as today, I would like to begin this
imaginative foray into love's promise of sexual transcendence in the
Decameron by quoting from the frame story a short description of a
springtime garden discovered in the hills above Florence in the fourteenth century, which served as the setting for the third day of tales:
"Looking at that garden, its beautiful order, its plants and fountain
with the little streams that flowed from it, so pleased each of the young
women and the three young men that they all began to proclaim that if
paradise was to be created on earth they could not imagine it taking a
different form."[1]

Often overlooked is the fact that after the second day of tales on
a Thursday, the queen of the third day, Neifile, actually stops the daily
round of ten tales told by the *brigata* for two days of rest and spiritual

reflection—reflection on the sufferings of Christ on the Cross (on Friday) and the Virgin Mary (on Saturday)—and on the third day, Sunday, the day of Christ's resurrection and metaphorically a day of general rebirth, she moved the youthful band of storytellers to a new special garden before the storytelling resumed—a garden that seemed a paradise on earth reborn.

For, as the short excerpt quoted above from that much more elaborate description claims, it was a garden that, for its order, peace, and beauty, was deemed by the whole group to be virtually paradise. There, not only was nature perfectly ordered but wild animals lived peacefully together with each other, and even the air was perfumed with the odor of flowers and fruits—in sum, it seemed almost as if that Sunday Neifile had returned her charges to the earthly paradise, the Garden of Eden itself. And, in a way, that was fitting for a woman whose name, Neifile, evoked youthful love or new love or even a new order of life,[2] for the original Garden of Eden was also a place of new order and new love: the very first and ultimately the only true love, where God's creatures existed in perfect loving order and harmony loving Him.[3]

Yet, for all its Eden-like echoes and for all Neifile's explicit spiritual exhortations, never mind the preliminary two days of spiritual meditations, the stories told during her Sunday seem at variance with the apparently deep religious symbolism of that garden and her call for religious reflections, as commentators have often noted. In fact, the day starts out quite badly for things religious with the famous tale of the woodcutter, Masetto da Lamporecchio, who, pretending to be mute, manages to seduce all the nuns of the convent he served, including the abbess; father a number of "nunlettes"; and, after he reached a ripe old age when he was no longer capable of serving his mistresses, retired to live happily ever after. And outrageously the tale ends with its narrator concluding that "this was the way that Christ repaid one who gave him horns."[4] With that witty comment, Boccaccio seemed to go beyond the anticlericalism that is a recurring trope of the *Decameron* to evoke a deeper sexual and apparently blasphemous humor at the expense of Christ himself.

Yet perhaps most telling for a day that starts out with such rich religious symbolism, the declared theme of the day—gaining something much desired by dint of great labor—seems in every tale to be gained not via piety or high moral standards but rather via sex, often highly illicit sex at that. In fact, the sexual relationships gained in eight of the ten tales are adulterous and in four cases with people in holy orders bound by a vow of chastity. This apparent contradiction at a deep level has led some to argue that the stories of the third day are actually meant to be read as an indictment by Boccaccio of the sexual immorality of his own day following the plague. Perhaps. But the stories told are too funny, the characters too positive, the punishments for their behavior virtually nonexistent, and Boccaccio's evident sympathy for young love, young lovers, and, as he describes them, the "small," "natural" sins of youthful sexual desire too pervasive to make convincing even the most brilliant attempts to refashion the day and Boccaccio's vision as negative.[5] In fact, one is tempted to argue that the real theme of the day is the way love and the pleasures of sex together with the *virtù* of lovers can overcome any hardship and implicitly the horrors of the plague and perhaps even the wrath of God the Father with the sinners He created.

How Dom Felice Took Monna Isabetta to Paradise While Her Husband, Fra Puccio, Repented and Suffered with Enthusiasm

The well-known tale of Dom Felice and monna Isabetta, the wife of Fra Puccio, also told on the third day as tale four, demonstrates this erotic humor well. And with its conclusion featuring Felice and Isabetta's claimed return to "paradise," it seems to echo the paradise and religious promise of Neifile's new paradise-like garden, albeit mockingly. For, as those who remember the story will recall, their paradise bloomed in the bed they shared cuckolding her husband daily, not in the hills above Florence and not only on Sunday.[6] Panfilo, the narrator of the tale, begins his account by pointing out that while many people work hard to gain paradise, "sometimes unaware [of what they are doing] they send others there."[7] That smiling, but potentially blasphemous, claim sets the tone for the tale.

Dom Felice is described as the typical clerical predator of the *Decameron*; thus, like most, he is "quite young and handsome," with "acute intelligence and deep knowledge," and anxious "to relieve Fra Puccio of his fatigue."[8] In turn, Fra Puccio is depicted as the perfect victim of the plot: "a man good and rich called Puccio di Rinieri, who, being totally taken by things spiritual, made himself a friar in the third order of the Franciscans . . . And because he was extremely ignorant and thick headed," he did nothing but practice his extreme forms of devotion at the expense of everything else.[9] In turn, his wife, monna Isabetta, again evoking the virtually required excuse for female adultery in the *Decameron,* and making her the perfect companion for Dom Felice's lechery, was described as "a young woman still of twenty eight to thirty years, fresh, pretty, and nicely plump who seemed a perfect apple [ripe for picking], who because of the holiness of her husband, and perhaps because of his age, usually spent more time than she might wish dieting [from sex]; and when she would have liked to sleep or perhaps play around with him, he recited to her the life of Christ and the preaching of Friar Nastagio or the lament of Magdalena or similar things."[10]

Evidently, with these descriptions of the characters of the tale, things did not appear to be setting up well for most of the imaginable religious themes for the day. Moreover, thinking in the context of tales told to overcome the horrors of the plague, one wonders how this tale with its happy depiction of clerical sexual misconduct would have played with those who feared the role that the wrath of God over just such deeds and the general corruption of humanity played in the devastating plague, especially the *brigata* attempting to escape that wrath in their paradise-like garden.

But Panfilo's tale rolled on with the helpful Dom Felice (Friar Happy) living up to his name, trying to bring happiness to everyone by befriending Fra Puccio and his unhappily "dieting" (in a sexual sense) wife. Recognizing the type of meals that would make her happy, he let her know that he would like to end her fasting and feed her well. She, quickly understanding what the meals he promised offered, expressed her willingness to be served by the kindly friar and his charitable impulse. Although no mention is made of it, one cannot help thinking of this as implying a rather different Christian charity than normally preached given the theme of the day. Still for the would-be feasters, the problem remained Fra Puccio, as he seldom left home for any extended period of time, preferring it and his local religious enthusiasms. Making matters more difficult yet, Isabetta feared to leave home to meet with Felice, presumably concerned correctly about what impact being observed leaving the house unaccompanied would have on the consensus realities her neighbors had of her as a virtuous wife.

Once again, however, the Christian charity of the goodly friar, Dom Felice, brings succor and happiness to all, even to his intended victim, with a nice irony. For realizing that Fra Puccio's greatest desire was to live a pious and saintly life, he promised him that he knew a way for him to become virtually a saint—a strategy, in fact, used by popes and major church figures as a "shortcut" when presumably they did not have time to do all the things that Fra Puccio was doing daily in order to live a life of extreme piety. Dom Felice volunteered, "I have already many times thought that your desire Fra Puccio is to become a saint; but it seems to me that you are taking the long road, while there is one that is far shorter, which the Pope and his other high prelates know and use, but do not wish to become known."[11] Their motives for their secrecy returns the tale to the typical anticlericalism of the *Decameron,* for Dom Felice points out that the Church lives from the donations garnered in response to the reputation for exceptional holiness of its leaders, but if people knew that their holiness was easy and involved little spiritual effort, donations would dry up with the implication that the Church would wither away.

Ironically, as a tertiary of the Franciscan order, this claim should have rung true to Fra Puccio, as the Franciscans, following their founder, Saint Francis, and his emulation of what he saw as Christ's life of poverty, were deeply suspicious of the negative impact of wealth and property on the Church; thus, the idea that they were keeping this path to sainthood secret for material gain would have made sense, especially to this overly spiritual and rather foolish soon-to-be victim. So, it would not have been surprising to those hearing the tale that Puccio took the bait of Dom Felice's offer of help to follow the shorter path to sainthood.

After securing Puccio's promise not to tell anyone, he spelled out the secret penance that the "Holy Doctors" of the Church used to gain saintliness. First, then, he instructed Fra Puccio to carefully confess all his sins so that he could begin his penitential program sin free. Second, for forty days he was to abstain from even touching any woman, including his wife. Her fasting with her husband evidently would continue. And finally he was to construct in his own house a platform that was exposed to the heavens large enough that he could stand on it for a long period of time with a bit of support if necessary. Once that platform was built, as the sun went down, he was to mount it and lean back so that he could focus on the heavens, opening out his arms in the form of the Cross. Holding that position, he was to remain until daybreak.

And because he was illiterate,[12] the good monk decided not to ask him to read the normal special prayers used, substituting especially for him instead the recitation of "three hundred 'Our Fathers' with three hundred 'Ave Marias' as a form of reverence for the Trinity." But he did insist that all the time he should be "looking at the heavens, keeping constantly in mind that God was the creator of the heavens and earth, and the passion of Christ, standing in the same position as He had on the Cross." Then, when morning came, he could go to bed and sleep a bit, but, later in the morning, he had to go to church and hear at least three masses and say at least fifty "Our Fathers" and "Ave Marias." Moreover, after dinner he had to return to church, say new prayers, and, once they were completed, return home and begin his nightly vigil all over again.[13]

Given his foolish and excessive piety, Fra Puccio found the program a small price to pay for saintliness (and his unwitting cuckolding). So he was ready to begin that very Sunday and returned home to happily inform his wife of his impending saintliness. She, aware of what the program actually meant, supported him with enthusiasm, even promising to do her own penance along with him: "so that God would make his penitence profitable, she wanted to fast along with him, but not the rest."[14] Cleverly, even in her promise, the tale plays on the association of food and sex and her earlier unhappiness with her enforced dieting at the hands of her old husband and his religious obsessions.

And the association of food and sex continued right into the lovemaking that rewarded Fra Puccio's religiously following Dom Felice's program of penitence. For the very first night that Puccio climbed onto his platform and stood in the shape of the crucified Christ looking at the heavens and contemplating Christ's passion on the Cross, his mentor, Dom Felice, came to his house to dine with Isabetta—"eating well and drinking well"—and "then playing [giaceva: play, implying shared enjoyable sexual intercourse] with her until the morning."[15] Indeed, the final quip of the tale also turns on food, sexual play, and religious enthusiasm.

For, one night when the couple were playing (again, *giaceva*) too vigor-
ously, the platform on which Fra Puccio was pursuing his saintliness
(having already "said one hundred of his 'Our Fathers'") began to shake
because it was right outside the window of the bedroom where his wife
and Dom Felice were pursuing their own pleasures. Concerned by the
shaking, he called out to his wife, asking what all the shaking was about.
She, "who had a quick wit, perhaps riding on the beast of San Benedetto
or indeed that of San Giovanni Gualberto, replied 'Damn it, husband of
mine, I shake / agitate *(dimeno)* as much as I can.'"[16]

Her good husband, concerned for her, asked why and, while we
can imagine why, she retorted that he had warned her that people who
fasted in the evening often tossed and turned in their sleep and thus her
fasting was the cause. The irony, of course, was that thanks to the kindness of Dom Felice, she was no longer fasting but rather feasting. And
that is drawn out using the Rinascimento sense of the interchange-
ability of eating and sexual pleasure: for when her husband insists that
he had warned her that fasting was not good for her, she replies, "Don't
worry. No, I understand perfectly well what I am doing; you do [what
you are doing] well, and I will do as well as I can."[17] In terms of both
food and sex, she was no longer fasting, and, indeed, it seems she was
making the most of her meal.

The tale leaves no doubt about that with its final blasphemous ode
to Dom Felice and Isabetta's rather different penance. For the narrator,
Panfilo, laughingly concluded that Isabetta "often remarked to him
[Dom Felice] 'You make the friar do penance and thanks to that we have
gained paradise.'"[18] Such an outrageous quip deserves a moment of reflection, for she seems to be claiming that pleasurable sex happily enjoyed by a couple intent on giving each other pleasure *(diletto)* wins them
paradise, while misplaced religious enthusiasm leaves one a fool at best
and a cuckolded fool at that in this case. It is noteworthy, nonetheless,
that even Fra Puccio is happy with his penance and his foolish sense that
the kindly Dom Felice has given him the shortcut to sainthood. Indeed,
the tale ends with yet another telling compliment for the monk and illicit lovemaking: "thus it came to pass that while Fra Puccio doing his
penance believed he arrived in Paradise, he actually sent there the monk
. . . and his wife, who lived with him in the greatest need of that which
the monk, as a kind / charitable person, gave her copiously."[19]

In the end, then, as Panfilo promised, some people working hard and suffering to get to paradise inadvertently send others there; and Dom Felice's cleverly successful strategy reveals this in a way that seems to give the lie to the holy theme that appeared to be promised for the day. Or does it? For, suggestively, the paradise that he and Isabetta gained through clever, if not particularly hard, work was a paradise of pleasure where the hard fasting of Isabetta was with "charity" and "kindness" replaced with happy riding of various saintly nags and much shaking. Perhaps not quite the paradise garden of pleasure that Neifile had selected as the new site for the day's tales but at least a paradise recognized as such and much appreciated, as paradise should be, by both Dom Felice and Isabetta.

Indeed, in light of our earlier discussions of *virtù,* this tale might be read as perfect for the theme of the day—focused on much-desired things gained with great industry—for Dom Felice in his cleverness and cunning seems a perfect example of the effectiveness of *virtù* in gaining a much-desired end for all. And, in fact, Isabetta with her clever quips and quick understanding of how the monk's plan will benefit her shows a goodly dose of *virtù* as well. Clearly, of course, in neither case are their deeds virtuous in the traditional moral sense, but I would argue they were attractively *virtù*-ous in the manner of the *beffe* so popular with Florentines that we have encountered frequently in Boccaccio's tales. We laugh also at the couple's return to paradise, but fourteenth-century Florentines would have laughed more deeply, appreciating the cleverness of the ploy—for them this was a novella at its most novel and enjoyable. Perhaps so much so that it puts paradise and religious enthusiasm in play in the day in some rather unsuspected ways, as we shall see.

Where with *Virtù* and Love the "She Doctor" Giletta of Narbonne Wins a Noble Husband, Overcoming Social Barriers and Seemingly Impossible Trials Along the Way

Yet the *virtù* of the tale is dominated by Dom Felice, even if Isabetta shows some flashes of the same, for, of course, as pointed out earlier, *virtù* was not limited to men. Indeed, women are presented over and over again as particularly powerful and effective when they are aided in love by *virtù;* in fact, they are capable of truly miraculous accomplishments.

One of the best examples of this is the ninth tale of the day, where Giletta of Narbonne with impressive *virtù* transcends virtually impassable
social divides in the name of love to marry the major French noble and
count of Roussillon, Beltramo di Rossiglione.[20] In fact, Giletta and her
love are portrayed by the narrator of the tale and queen of the day, Neifile, as literally transcendent in both a spiritual and a social sense.

Giletta's "infinite love" had begun in early childhood and was characterized as "more intense than was suitable given her young age."[21] No
ordinary love then, and making it even more extraordinary was the fact
that Beltramo was the only son of the powerful lord Isnardo, the count
of Rossiglione (Roussillon), while Giletta was merely the daughter of
Gerardo, the count's favored doctor. Doctors, of course, were a highly
respected social group in Florence, and in France as well, but they fell
far below the social level of a French count. And although they almost
always were well educated with a university degree, they worked for
their living, and even in some cases with their hands, which seriously
hindered their claims of status.[22] Actually, in Florence, with its suspicion of old noble families, as we have seen, the most important families claimed instead a place in the *popolo grosso* and were decidedly not
noble.[23] In France, if anything, a love between a doctor's daughter and
a count's son was definitely not "suitable" and not just because of Giletta's young age. Actually, given the social distance involved, for the
story to make sense to a fourteenth-century Florentine reader, the tale
required an explanation about how the young Giletta would have had
the opportunity to see and fall in love with Beltramo; thus, it takes the
time to carefully explain that, as a child, the boy was allowed by his father to play with other youngsters of his age at his court, where Giletta's
father served as his doctor.

When, however, Beltramo's father died and he became the count
himself, he was separated from his youthful playmates and sent off to
Paris to be close to the king. Giletta, obviously, as a young girl, had no
way to follow her love, especially as she was then nearing "the age of
marriage." As one might expect in a tale of deep and pure love, she was
devastated. To make matters worse, her father also passed away, and,
as she was a rich and beautiful young woman, her relatives began to
suggest possible husbands for her—husbands more suited to her actual
social status, the *brigata* would have understood. She, however, turned

away every proposal, loyal to and demonstrating the deep love she felt for her Beltramo. At this point, a little unexpected good luck came to her rescue and drove the tale ahead on the highly unlikely path to realizing her virtually impossible love. For Giletta learned that the king of France was suffering from a painful fistula that none of his doctors had been able to cure; in fact, their treatments had just made it worse. Reflecting on the situation, she reasoned that if his fistula was what she thought it was, given what she had learned from her father, the famous doctor, she might well be able to cure him. And, if worse came to worst, going to Paris to treat him, at the least, gave her a legitimate reason to go to the city where her love lived, perhaps see him, and even somehow win his hand in marriage along with his love.

So it was that Giletta journeyed to Paris from the south of France to find her fortune and her love. And as was sometimes the case in the *Decameron* for young women (as well as young men) in love, in Paris, although she faced many doubts as a young woman offering to cure the king of France, *fortuna* worked together with her *virtù* to bring her an unlikely success—once again, the very stuff of happy tales. Thus, Giletta finally convinced the king that she could cure him where all others had failed. Of course, the king had serious doubts about a young girl from the provinces' ability to do so, and the tale gives him lines that many readers male and female may have found on point at the time. "That which the greatest doctors in the world could not and knew not how to cure," he wondered, "how could a young woman like you possibly understand [the treatment]."[24] Giletta replied with evident courage and *virtù*, "My lord you underestimate / disdain *(schifare)* my skill *(arte)* because I am young and a woman, but let me assure you that my healing does not rely on learning, but rather on God and the learning of my father, master Gerardo of Narbonne, who was a most famous doctor when he was alive."[25] This bold claim got the king thinking and even daring to hope that perhaps this young woman might actually be able to cure him.

But Giletta pressed her case and demonstrated her self-confidence by offering the king a courageous wager. "My lord," she proposed, "let me treat you and if within eight days I have not cured you, you can have me burned alive. But if I do cure you, what reward will you give me?"[26] Given the plot of the tale, obviously the king offered to give her a husband. And, equally predictably, Giletta countered with the requirement that she be allowed to choose her mate, diplomatically ruling out any son of his or member of the royal family. The king accepted the wager and indeed the successful outcome of her treatment was so required by the tale that little time is spent on it. Rather, it jumps quickly to the king's amazement and pleasure at being cured and Giletta naming the husband she wanted, none other than her longtime love Beltramo di Rossiglione. The tale might well have ended there with Giletta and Beltrame reunited in love, marrying with the blessing of the king of France and living happily ever after.

The tale, however, is about the transcendent quality of a pure, deep love and the *virtù* of a woman working together for the happy ending required by the theme of the day. Evidently, for that theme such an ending at this point would have been too quick and too easy. Thus, the great social divide that Giletta's love had to transcend is made manifest when Beltramo, faced with the king's request that he marry Giletta, violently rejects such a demeaning match: "Beltramo, who knew her and had seen her, notwithstanding that he found her very beautiful, realizing that she was not of the social standing which his nobility required, filled with disdain said, 'My Lord then do you wish to give me this woman doctor for a wife? God forbid that I should ever take such a woman for a wife.'"[27] The social gap that Giletta's love had to transcend could not have been more forcefully expressed, and, from a Florentine perspective, Beltramo's haughty rejection echoed all the city's negative stereotypes of their own rejected old nobility and their high-handed ways.

Still, the king had given his word to Giletta, so he pressed Beltramo to marry her; and in the end, as the king's man, he reluctantly knuckled under to his lord's demands. But even as he did so, he made it clear, "as far as this is concerned, I assure you that I will never be happy with this disgusting marriage *(maritaggio)*."[28] Thus, although he unwillingly *(mal volentieri)* went through with the great wedding organized by the king, immediately afterward he abandoned his bride to join the Florentines in their war against Siena, bringing the tale home to Boccaccio's Florentine audience.[29] Giletta, as the wife of the count of Roussillon, on the other hand, took up residence at his court in southern France and ran the count's household and territory with a sure hand, revealing again her wisdom and *virtù* and winning the hearts of his subjects.

Her success and her rule, not to mention her ongoing love, lacked just one thing: the count, her husband. Thus, she sent two knights to meet him in Florence and ask that he return to rule his lands either with her or, if he insisted, without her, as she was willing to go into exile in order to help those who had become their subjects and allow them to have their count back. But Beltramo rejected her plea and her as well one more time, saying "she could do as she pleased, but I will never return to be with her until she has on her finger this ring which I wear and a son that she has had by me in her arms."[30] Even if the tale had been returned to a familiar Florentine setting, this seems like a moment straight out of a medieval romance, replete with its apparently impossible hurdles to overcome in order to win one's love; notably, one of which—producing a son—implied sexual intercourse. But, of course, in this case it was not a knight errant who had to perform the impossible proving his *virtù*, it was a city woman of *virtù*, ideally much like those who made up the *popolo grosso* of Florence, demonstrating hers. And, as might be anticipated, this woman with the aid of her love and her *virtù* will, like the best medieval knight, win out in the end and (much like perhaps the best Florentine dreams of the *popolo grosso*) transcend the social divides of France to allow a woman doctor to marry a French count.

And, fittingly, she works the magic of her love and her *virtù* in Florence, which enjoyed seeing itself as the home of Rinascimento *virtù par excellence*. To meet Beltramo's seemingly impossible demands, Giletta journeys secretly to the city, leaving behind in Roussillon the impression that she is retiring from the active life to live a life of wandering and carrying out pious works. In Florence, well supplied with the money and jewels essential to carry out her plan, she took a room in a humble little lodging, posing as a pious wayfarer with a kindly widow. And as luck—the ubiquitous *fortuna* of young lovers—would have it, the very next day her husband passed by the inn on horseback with his companions. When she asked the widow who he was, she found, as was often reputed to be the case for widows, that the old woman was very well informed by local gossip.

Thus she learned that her husband was not only much loved in Florence, "he is the most in love man in the world with a neighbor of ours, who is a well-mannered, upper-class woman, but poor."[31] Bad news apparently, but good news followed quickly, as her host informed her that, although she was poor, the young woman's mother was a very honest woman who hoped to find a good mate for her daughter. That, in turn, meant that Beltramo had not been able to act on his love using the power of his wealth and status. In a nutshell, in this little moment of everyday gossip between women, one sees the weight of poverty on young women, even upper-class women; their bodies and their lives more normally were hardly their own in the face of wealth and power. It took an exceptionally good mother to protect her daughter from Beltramo's noble, ignoble sexual desires.

Still, in the economy of the tale, that reality opened the door for Giletta's *virtù*-ous plan in the fullest sense of the term: for her plan was wise, clever, and certainly not quite moral in many ways that Boccaccio's Florentine readers would have applauded. Realizing that the girl's mother was the key, one day she went to her house dressed as a pilgrim and pointed out that they were both victims of adverse *"fortuna"*; but, working together, there was a way they could both gain their ends. The mother, true to her character, expressed interest with the qualification that whatever they did would have to be done "honestly / honorably" *(onestamente)* and in reciprocal "trust" and good "faith."[32] Then, as a sign of that trust and good faith, Giletta honestly laid out her own dilemma, recounting her unhappy marriage and the double challenge her husband had set her for winning his hand. Wisely, she provided first the carrot to make her plan attractive to the mother, pointing out that her daughter was of marriageable age but needed a good dowry to marry at the social level that their station required, a dowry that she was prepared to provide if she and her daughter agreed to help her win her husband. When the widow agreed in principle, Giletta was ready to lay out her *virtù*-ous plan.

First, the widow was to let it be known to the count by someone she trusted to keep everything secret that her daughter was willing to "satisfy his every pleasure," but only if she could be sure that he loved her as he claimed—once more, sex and love going hand in hand. And the only thing that would convince her of that was if he gave her the ring that he wore and that "she had heard he loved greatly."[33] Once she received the ring, they were to arrange for him to come secretly to enjoy her daughter. But rather than her daughter, they would, of course, unbeknownst to him, substitute for her Giletta. The mother understandably was a bit worried that if the tryst became known it would reflect badly on her daughter and herself. Yet, as she considered the plan, she decided that for all its trickery and cunning, the plan was "honest / honorable" because it sought an "honest / honorable" end, to bring together a husband and a loving wife.[34]

So, secretly, "in the very first couplings that the count passionately enjoyed, *as was pleasing to God,* she (Giletta) became pregnant with twin boys."[35] Perhaps significantly here in this happy turn of fortune, the tale does not lay the credit at the feet of the always questionable pagan god Fortuna but rather in the hands of the Christian God; as if with all the trickery involved, even He smiled on true love and true *virtù,* giving them the ability to be truly transcendent at least as far as social distinctions and true love were concerned. Be that as it may, Giletta secretly and unbeknownst to her husband enjoyed his embraces, and he hers, leaving her "in the morning with numerous beautiful and expensive jewels, which she carefully guarded."[36]

Keeping her faith with the mother and daughter who had aided her in her plot, and having gained what had seemed impossible to gain, she gave them the jewels plus five hundred lire for the dowry of the young woman. In turn, the good woman sent her daughter off to the countryside to effectively end the supposed affair with Beltramo and avoid any problems with him. Then, having apparently satisfied his desire and his more mundane love / lust—ever the high-handed unattractive male noble—he finally responded to the calls of his subjects to return home to Roussillon and rule, persuaded by the fact that his unwanted wife had ostensibly left for good. Meanwhile, Giletta remained in Florence and quietly gave birth to twins. With his ring in hand and his twin sons in her arms, she was ready to return victorious to Roussillon, having accomplished the impossible and with her transcendent love and *virtù* to live happily ever after.

And so it came to pass. Giletta returned home and, after some initial resistance, deeply impressed by both her love and her *virtù,* much to the pleasure of his subjects and in the end to himself, she was accepted *and loved* by Beltramo, and the tale assures us that indeed they both lived happily ever after. Transcendent love, clever sex, and a woman of impressive *virtù* had overcome apparently impossible obstacles that echoed the heroism for love of medieval knights errant in a setting with social values that evoked more contemporary Florentine ones and would have won the special sympathies of a Florentine audience. They may have been slightly suspicious about a female doctor and her ability to cure the king of France, but with love, happy sex, and *virtù* working together all things were possible, as many of the stories of the day and the *Decameron* as a whole repeatedly proclaimed with a smile. And in the end they could even transform a haughty count into a loving husband and a disastrous marriage into a happy one.

That ability to transcend in the name of love, however, could go well beyond merely social transcendence, and that brings us back to the spiritual side of the tales of the day. For, for all the misbehaving monks, nuns, and priests of the day and all the anticlerical humor that sometimes seem to spill over into overt blasphemously, the religious themes of the day seem to fit well with the transcendent quality of love and sexual pleasure even as it concludes with one of the most apparently blasphemous tales of the *Decameron*. That smiling tale again takes us back to paradise-like gardens, corrupt monks who offer pleasure, and a special woman whose love promises great and literally transcendent religious happiness and perhaps more—the young innocent pagan Alibech, whose adventures end the day.

Where the Pagan Alibech Finds Transcendent Love in the Desert with the Christian Hermit Rustico, but Not Quite as One Might Expect

Nicely, this last tale of the day suggests all this and offers perhaps a rather unexpected way to view love, sex, and their springtime promise that allows readers and Boccaccio to have both their sexual desires and their religious aspirations—both the pleasures of the flesh and the pleasures of the spirit, both immediate "natural" little sins and ultimate salvation. For one of the most intriguing and humorous literary accounts of sexual play and pleasure from the Rinascimento is found in that famous tale of Rustico and Alibech told by the ever-irreverent Dioneo, the narrator who seems to be always pushing the sexual edge of the stories told. Dioneo begins his story with the "young," "beautiful," "courteous," and "rich" pagan Alibech, an innocent girl of about fourteen who lived in the city of Gafsa in Tunisia, deciding with youthful enthusiasm that she wanted to serve the Christian God, inspired by the highly positive things she had heard about such service from the Christians of her city. When she pressed those Christians about how this was done, she was told that He was best served by those who eschewed the distractions of this world and retired to the solitude of the desert to live as hermits.

So it came to pass that she fled the comforts of her home and her father's riches and journeyed to the nearby desert in search of the promised pleasures of serving the Christian God—as was perhaps fitting for a young girl whose name in colloquial Arabic has the ring of *Allah bik:* "God be with you."[37] And after a few days wandering there, she came upon a holy man at the door of his poor hut. Amazed to find such a young and beautiful girl there alone, he asked her what she was seeking, and she explained that she had come to the desert to learn how to serve the Christian God. Suitably impressed, but fearing the temptation of the Devil that her youthful beauty inspired, he provided her with the meager hospitality of his hovel, a quick meal of roots, dried dates, and water, then sped her on her way, suggesting that she find another hermit more capable of teaching her how to serve God and, although he did not admit it, less tempted by her beauty and the Devil.[38] But the next hermit she found, apparently troubled by similar concerns about her youthful beauty and his own devils, sent her on her way to yet another desert recluse. The tale might well have ended there, with Alibech wandering the desert unable to find a hermit to help her serve the Christian God—a humorous comment on the problems that even desert hermits in their barren self-denial had resisting sexual temptation that would have fit in well with the anticlerical tone of many of Boccaccio's tales, as noted earlier.

How Rustico Explains Christianity to Alibech, Much to Their Great Pleasure

But the tales of the third day were ones where people found what they were seeking by dint of their efforts; so Alibech was destined to find what she sought, yet, with a smile, not quite as she or Dioneo's audience might have imagined. Finally, she discovered a monk who was willing to take her in, one Rustico, "young, very holy and good." Alibech's dangerous beauty was not lost on him either, "but unlike the others in order to make a great trial of his *prowess* he did not send her away . . . but kept her with him in his cell."[39] Of course, true to Boccaccio's carefully constructed anticlerical humor, poor Rustico's "prowess" in self-denial failed almost immediately, to be followed rather quickly by a failure of his prowess in another area as well. But that is getting ahead of the story. First, with oblique questions, he confirmed his suspicion that this young girl was as innocent as she seemed and knew nothing about sex; and thus he decided that "she ought to give him his pleasures, under the pretense of serving God."[40] He began his conquest, then, with a short sermon on how the Devil was the enemy of the Christian God and how the best service to God was to help Him put the Devil back in Hell where God had damned him.

Quickly taking the bait, Alibech enthusiastically asked how one could provide this aid to God. And, of course, Rustico, more than willing to be her spiritual guide, instructed her to begin by undressing as he did so. Naked, and unwittingly returned to the original prelapsarian state of Adam and Eve in the Garden of Eden, "Rustico more than ever burning with desire now that he saw her so beautiful experienced *the resurrection of the flesh.*" Alibech, seeing his "resurrection" asked in her innocence the obvious question, "What is that thing that I see sticking out in front of you that I don't have?" "Oh my dear child," Rustico replied with perfect guile, but also with a ring of everyday poetic truth, "this is the Devil about whom I was telling you just now. And do you see that now he is giving me great tribulations, so much that I can hardly stand it."[41]

Without the slightest trace of pre-Freudian penis envy, Alibech exclaimed, "Oh thank God, for I see that I am better off than you for I don't have that Devil myself." But Rustico was ready to spring his neat little theological / sexual trap, pointing out that while she did not have the Devil, she had the other part of the holy equation, Hell: "You have Hell and I say that I believe that God sent you here for the good of my soul, given that this Devil gives me so much pain. For if you were willing to take pity on me and *let me put my Devil back in your Hell,* you would give me the greatest consolation and at the same time *give God the greatest service and pleasure.*"[42]

Thus it was that Alibech, after some original minor discomfort, quickly learned to her "great pleasure" how to serve the Christian God and put the Devil back in Hell. In fact, she was totally converted to serving the Christian God, confessing, "I see clearly the truth of what those good men told me in Gafsa, that serving God is such a sweet thing: certainly I don't know of any other thing that I have ever done that *gives me so much pleasure* as putting the Devil back in Hell."[43] For Alibech, putting the Devil back in Hell was the ultimate pleasure, and, with a humorous reversal of formal orthodoxy, it was so because it was the ultimate human way of serving God as well.

Where Rustico's Theology Is Taken Perhaps More Seriously Than It Merits and Alibech Is Saved by Foucault

But if we follow Boccaccio and Dioneo's lead and approach this tale of pleasure in the desert hovel of Rustico with a similar playful and perhaps irreverent attitude, I would like to suggest that not so much lurking behind it as perchance smiling behind it we may find a number of playfully serious ways of rethinking Christianity itself, ways that transform the innocent Alibech from the dupe of Rustico to an innocent Christ-like savior moved by her love in serving God. The first suggestion of this is to be found in the charming and clever, but clearly blasphemous, metaphors that underlay the humor of Boccaccio's prose. Naming what we would call today heterosexual intercourse as "putting the Devil back in Hell," as noted in the tale itself, was a reference to a contemporary euphemism for sex.[44] Nonetheless, for all its humor as it is used in this novella, it equates sexual intercourse explicitly with one of the central metahistorical goals of God: confining the fallen angel, Lucifer, to Hell. And this metaphor does so in a way that has deep and potentially dangerous resonances with many of the most traditional theological concerns about the dangers of sex, even if it does so in an apparently humorous and lighthearted manner, especially when faced with the ravages of the plague and a deity who could easily be seen as anything but lighthearted and forgiving in the face of decidedly questionable sexual behavior in His name.

For the Devil himself was often portrayed as highly phallic, a sexual and aggressively penetrating master. Moreover, as perhaps the most popular Church father during the Rinascimento, Saint Augustine, stressed in his *Confessions*, the primary danger of sex was that it made humans turn from the pleasure of God—the only real pleasure—to seek the false pleasures of the body—exactly what Alibech innocently did by putting the Devil back in Hell. This rejecting what does truly exist—the pleasure of seeking and finding God—for what ultimately is only a passing and hardly real thing at all—in this case, sexual pleasure—is the ultimate basis of all sin. Clearly, in this vision of turning away from God, as the ultimate source of all sin, the phallus could well be seen as a primary agent of the Devil, as it could easily be understood as a major deception that leads humans away from God. At a deeper level yet, what caused the fall of Lucifer himself was his own turning away from the truth of God, and thus one might see an even stronger connection between the Devil and the phallus—the phallus in its capacity to make one turn away from God might be seen as a personal Devil, exactly as Rustico portrayed it to the innocent Alibech.

Turning to Alibech's Hell, one also could find suggestive deeper theological resonances. The essence of Hell is absence—the absence of God. And, of course, a woman's genitals, for all their real physical presence, were often in the Rinascimento represented as an absence, a void. Paradoxically, an absence that had great power, like the absence that is sin; and again the parallel is intriguing. Putting the Devil back in Hell and finding pleasure in doing so, from this perspective, seems a bit more significant.

And the sense that there is a deeper theological core to the story is strengthened by the other famous metaphor of the tale, Rustico's "resurrection of the flesh." The outrageousness of the scene of Rustico's "resurrection" before the naked Alibech may so catch the modern imagination that one misses the simple fact that here we are faced with a sexual metaphor that turns on and seemingly mocks the central mystery of Christianity. Although the theological context has moved away from Old Testament teachings about the fall of Lucifer and the ultimate conflict between evil and good, nonbeing and being, Devil and God, we are still in the realm of Saint Augustine—since for him, and what had become the mainstream of Christian theology, the key to the message of the New Testament was that Christ had come to save humanity as both fully God and fully man as the Nicene Creed proclaimed. And Christ, in one of the deepest mysteries of the faith, was therefore resurrected *in the flesh* as a man as all humans who are saved will be resurrected thanks to His sacrifice.[45]

Yet, here in Boccaccio's tale, we have the resurrection of the flesh turned to a completely different end, to enjoying sexual intercourse with the innocent Alibech. Moreover, all this is done under the apparently false pretense and in the name of leading her to the Christian God and His service, when it is instead misleading her to her fall—again, from Saint Augustine's perspective, the ultimate evil. Evidently in the process she also loses her virginity, and, enjoying the pleasures of Rustico's Devil, she clearly forgets about any chastity that she may have had or valued before her trip to the desert. In fact, one might well be tempted to argue that Rustico's Devil was a real devil; for his Devil and the real one were both empty of God, literally false gods that led humans away from truth to their damnation.

But I am tempted by a rather different reading of the tale, and the thing that tempts me in that direction is once again the crucial metaphor of putting the Devil back in Hell. For Alibech does not fall as a result of her acceptance of and pleasure in Rustico's pornotheology; indeed, neither she nor Rustico are punished for their illicit and literally blasphemous pleasures. The judgment of a wrathful plague-sending God is totally absent—strangely, and thus intriguingly, absent in the time of the plague. And that changes the flavor of the metaphor itself. Indeed, there is no indication that she is a victim or even a sinner in any way. In the end, she returns to civilization, marries, and lives happily ever after putting the Devil back in Hell with her husband, who presumably is happily unaware of the full range of her earlier theological explorations. There is nothing in the story to indicate that she is any the worse off for her adventures or her service to God, which gave her only the greatest pleasure, just as she was promised by those who sent her off to the desert. Actually, there is only one blemish on her happy and pleasurable adventure, and that was the eventual failure of Rustico's prowess, the inability of Rustico's Devil to live up to the demands of her Hell; for, in a typically Rinascimento vision of female sexual desire, Boccaccio portrays her desire to put the Devil back in Hell as insatiable and thus her desire to serve God as well.

Yet, crucially, the comic failure of Rustico's Devil underlines the humor of this tale, a fact that is confirmed by the laughter of the entire *brigata* at its conclusion, from both the young men and the young women.[46] That laughter and the humorous tone of the narrative suggest that the story actually turns on a clever reversal of the accepted vision of things, so typical of Rinascimento humor, but with a deeply significant twist, because this reversal presents a playfully pseudo-Christian mythic rational for a vision of sex that seems to cleverly evoke the essence of Boccaccio's portrayal of sexual intercourse and the pleasures of the flesh presented throughout the *Decameron*.[47] For, in many ways, Alibech's search for the pleasures of serving the Christian God in putting the Devil back in Hell may also be reread as a wistful rewriting and reversal of the story of the Fall and the expulsion from the Garden of Eden with the triumph of a loving God of life over a wrathful God of plague and death.

In the traditional theological vision, with their first sin, Adam and Eve were thrown out of the terrestrial paradise, discovered shame and their nakedness, were burdened by sin, and knew all the negatives of the binary sexual division imposed upon them as punishment for their Fall from grace. This order of things marked the first age of human history described in the Old Testament, which endured until the *resurrection of the flesh* that was brought by Christ's suffering and death on the Cross, a death and resurrection that heralded the opening of a new era and a new order in the Christian vision of history: a second age, revealed in the New Testament. With the resurrection of Christ *in the flesh*, humanity's relationship with God changed in a fundamental way: punishment and alienation were replaced by love and the possibility of salvation—and all this turned crucially on the suffering of Christ and on the resurrection of the flesh.

If we can leave aside the blasphemy of the concept of Rustico's own resurrection of the flesh for a moment, it is interesting to note that his resurrection also provides a critical turning point in the couple's microhistory: it initiated the sexual intercourse that turned their desert into a new Garden of Eden, where the young Alibech willingly served God and not only enjoyed that service but found it the ultimate, virtually transcendent, pleasure that she innocently assumed Christianity as a superior religion should provide. While other desert hermits in contrast led a hard life of suffering and privation in search for their God—and the tale has taken us to their barren huts, which offered little Christian love and all too much fear of Alibech's God-given youthful innocence and beauty—Alibech, with a pure desire to serve God, found "great pleasure" in serving God, and for her the desert blossomed. For, to return to Alibech's happy proclamation as she learned to appreciate the pleasures of serving God, hers is an innocent claim of the ultimate pleasure: "I see clearly the truth of what those good men told me in Gafsa, that serving God is such a sweet thing: certainly I don't know of any other thing that I have ever done that gives me so much pleasure as putting the Devil back in Hell."[48]

Suggestively, this blossoming of the desert, this return to the Garden of Eden, is predicated also upon undoing the temptations of the Devil—Rustico's Devil is forced into serving God by going back to Hell. And while Rustico, in his clever misuse of the language of Christianity, was intentionally misleading Alibech to what might seem to be her personal Fall, in fact, such a reading appears self-evidently incorrect as the desert blossoms Eden-like for her in her service to God, and she concludes with a virtually beatific vision: "And because of this [pleasure to be found in the service of God] I hold that anyone who does anything else than serve God *is not human*."[49] In a striking fashion, she had indeed returned to the Garden of Eden and, as was the case for Adam and Eve, there she was perfectly content to only serve God—and even if clearly we must concede that her service was not quite what was portrayed in the Old Testament, it was a pleasurable service and literally outside the normal time and space of the post-Fall world.

In the Garden of Eden, Adam and Eve knew God as the source of their pleasure, and certainly the innocent Alibech did so as well. Yet it might well be objected that in the Garden of Eden there was no knowledge of sex and that that knowledge was one of the punishments inflicted upon humanity following the Fall. Nicely, however, as Foucault and his followers would point out, Alibech in her innocence did not know sex either in her new Garden of Eden—only the pleasure of her service to God. For her, sexual intercourse did not exist. Her pleasure with Rustico was simply the Christian pleasure that one dedicated to a loving God in the name of an ongoing metaquest to return the Devil to Hell. In fact, the point might be pressed further by noting that in the original biblical story of the Fall, it was the woman, Eve, who pressed Adam to eat the apple—and, of course, as portrayed in the Rinascimento, Eve was usually the one held responsible for the sin and ultimately the Fall itself. In this story, however, it was the man, Rustico, who pressed the woman, Alibech, to put the Devil back in Hell, and the innocent woman, then, who in accepting that request undid sin and regained admission to the Garden of Eden.[50]

Where Alibech's Pleasure in Serving the Christian God Is Taken Perhaps Too Seriously and Alibech Becomes a New Savior for Love

Yet, this suggests a still more apparently irreverent rereading of the tale. For, if instead of proposing a mere reversal of the Garden of Eden story, we posit a fundamental reversal of Christian theology itself, as suggested earlier, some additional elements of the novella fall intriguingly into place. Rustico, for example, might well be seen as the Antichrist who uses the central tenets of the Church in an ultimately evil way—the battle of God with the Devil and the resurrection of the flesh—to seduce a young woman away from the Church and destroy it. But in the process of seeking the ultimate evil, he inadvertently fulfills God's master plan and ushers in a new last age and a new last dispensation, just as the Antichrist was supposed to do.

 For in the Trinitarian vision of Christianity, where there were two ages, one dominated by God, the Father, and a second dominated by Christ, logic seemed to require a third to complete the trinity, dominated by the Holy Spirit. That last promised age, much like the age that preceded it ushered in by Christ, would change in fundamental ways humanity's relationship with God—certainly Alibech's approach to serving God was fundamentally different from that of the second age of human history, at least as interpreted by Saint Augustine and the Church. Sex in Alibech's new last age would no longer be in the service of procreation in pain and suffering as Genesis promised—tellingly, her service to God does not result in pregnancy—or to fulfill the needs of family continuity from a more traditional Rinascimento perspective. But rather it existed as the pure pleasure that came with serving a playful and pleasure-giving Holy Spirit, where that innocent bliss truly led to the negation of the Devil, the triumph of the spirit and love, and the last age of the Holy Spirit.

 Many expected a new last age and a new last dispensation in the fourteenth century, an age to be ushered in by an Antichrist who would destroy the Church, clearing the way for a third age of the Holy Spirit before the Last Judgment and the end of time. In fact, many expected it to begin in the north of Italy, perhaps even in Boccaccio's Florence, and for many the plague seemed to confirm its imminence. Yet, while there was considerable uncertainty about what that last age would be like, it must be admitted that virtually no one thought it would be an age of happy, playful, innocent sex in the service of a loving Holy Spirit in a new blossoming Garden of Eden—probably not even Boccaccio or his often irreverent storyteller Dioneo.

Still, preachers following in the footsteps of Saint Francis, most notably perhaps the Franciscan Spirituals, preached the imminent arrival of a third and last age of love led by the Holy Spirit, and Florence was a hotbed of their teaching in the second half of the fourteenth century. One of the central signs of this new age would be the conversion of the pagans, and, of course, Alibech was an enthusiastic pagan convert to serving the Christian God with love. Another sign would be the destruction of the old corrupt Church to be replaced by a new Christian community rapt in its love of God: and the tales of the third day confirmed the corruption of the Church while suggesting that the pleasures of sex were transformative and uplifting. Moreover, the whole project of the *Decameron* seems to reflect this Trinitarian view of human history, rejecting the vindictive and punishing Old Testament God, the Father, and emphasizing the contemporary corrupt Church of Christ, ready for destruction by the Antichrist. Along with the plague, perhaps foretelling the last days of an age, might one, then, imagine that new age as Alibech's new dispensation of loving service to the third person of the Christian God, an age of the Holy Spirit putting the Devil back in Hell in the name of love?

And, in this context, at a deeper level yet, one wonders why Dioneo told his tale of resurrections on Sunday in the frame story of the *Decameron*, as the last tale of the third day—the day of resurrections: resurrections of the flesh and of presumably new saviors and the beginning of new, last orders. And one wonders why on this day in that frame story, as we have seen, the band of storytellers is moved to a new beautiful garden, which is explicitly compared in its beauty, order, and loving pleasures to the Garden of Eden by Neifile (a name that evokes new love or perhaps even a new order). And, of course, one might also wonder a bit about Dioneo's name (literally, new god), as it conjures the image of a very different age and the Greek god of play, pleasure, and sex—Dionysius—just as his playful spirit throughout the *Decameron* suggests a rather different spiritual life that Christians might lead in a new last age.

Yet, for all this theological wondering, I fear many of you are probably wondering, did anyone at the time see a connection between this tale, putting the Devil back in Hell, the last age of the Spirit, and the various heresies that were abroad in Italy predicting its imminent arrival? Well, as unlikely as it may seem, the answer is a definite maybe.

In Franco Sacchetti's *Trecentonovelle*, a collection of *novelle* following closely in the tradition of Boccaccio, composed in the last decade of the century, there is a novella that turns on the metaphor of "putting the Devil back in Hell" that most critics have seen as harking back to the tale of Alibech and Rustico. In that tale, once again a monk, one Giovanni Apostoli, cleverly puts the Devil back in Hell, this time, however, not with just one innocent pagan girl anxious to serve God but rather with three innocent young nuns anxious to serve God. Supposedly bedding down with all three in one bed to avoid a cold winter night and with false claims of demonstrating his spiritual prowess again, Giovanni instead discovers bit by bit the first nun's body, lauding at each step the wonderful work of God as his hands move slowly down her flesh. Finally, she stays his hand, warning, "Giovanni don't go any farther down because you will come to hell." Following in Rustico's pornotheological footsteps, he immediately replies, "And I have here with me the devil, who I have been trying my whole life to put in hell."[51]

In the end, he follows the same course with each nun until all three have enjoyed serving God by putting the Devil back in Hell. But what is especially intriguing about Giovanni's use of this metaphor in Sacchetti's tale is the fact that this Giovanni was actually a fairly well-known historical figure earlier in the century, known primarily as a follower of the heretical sect of the Apostoli.[52] Significantly, the Apostoli were one of the many heretical sects who preached the imminent arrival of the last age of the Holy Spirit. So, to return to wondering, one wonders why Sacchetti associated this metaphor and Boccaccio's story with those who were predicting the imminent arrival of that promised last age. Perhaps even reception theory, then, suggests that the association of this metaphor with contemporary prophecies of the final age of the Holy Spirit is not as unlikely as it might at first seem.

And then, even at a simply spiritual mechanical level, Boccaccio's playful metaphor of putting the Devil back in Hell seems to promise an age where the Holy Spirit will be finally able to rule. For, of course, in the Trinitarian vision of Christianity, influenced perhaps by neo-Platonic understanding of the world-forming and ordering divine *pneus* or Spirit, the Holy Spirit was the ordering principle of creation, providing the meaning and the ontological foundation of this world behind its evident instability and chaos. From this perspective, of course, the Devil with his turning away from God and his constant injection of evil, chaos, and nonbeing into the world, could be seen as the ultimate foe of the Holy Spirit. As long as he was abroad in the world, the Holy Spirit could not fully order creation or rule it; instead, it would be constantly undermined by chaos, immorality, and ultimately tragedies like plagues. Thus, every putting the Devil back in Hell, at the microhistorical level, opened and opens the way for the Holy Spirit to rule more fully in this world, even the humble and very human way of putting the Devil back in Hell that we perhaps erroneously label sex, at least from Alibech's perspective.

One wonders if Boccaccio could have followed the logic of his metaphors to imagine that if everyone followed Alibech's advice and became "truly human," as she claimed, putting the Devil back in Hell, if that would simply and in itself be enough to give the Holy Spirit the opportunity to finally rule God's creation and end plagues and ultimately evil forever? Or if he could have ever realized that in the end for theology at its highest level or sex at its humblest level, with the resurrection of the flesh, both the Devil and Hell would once again worship and serve God with love and pleasure? And, thus, for a moment or forever might that pleasure transcend evil and time itself, as Alibech learned when she discovered the pleasure of serving the Christian God in the desert near Gafsa?

But, in the more imminent end of this chapter, mostly we may wonder about the innocent young woman who discovers in the time of the plague a new way to serve God and discovers the ultimate bliss and rapture in doing so. So let me just suggest with a Dioneian smile that we imagine a woman as savior—Alibech.[53] A simple, innocent woman, who in her pleasure in sex and her service to the Christian God, at least in Boccaccio's fiction / prophecy, promised to open a new, last age of love and the spiritual pleasures of the flesh: a last age where her followers would serve God, Christ, and the Holy Spirit in a new earthly paradise, putting the Devil back in Hell. For with Alibech as a savior, the pious promises of the frame story and its Sunday paradise setting make a deeply poetic sense of the third day and place the loving pleasures of the *Decameron* at the heart of its symphony of life.

5

Power

The Prince Who Refused to Love,
or Griselda Reconsidered

Where Agilulf, the King of the Lombards,
Demonstrates the Value of *Virtù*

Long ago one morning in the north of Italy, Agilulf, king of the Lombards, outraged by a truly grave affront to his honor, looked out over his assembled servants and staff, ready to have his revenge. He knew that one of the group had slept with his wife, the queen. And he knew how to identify him, even though it was the morning after the dishonoring deed. And the culprit, a mere groom from his stables, knew he knew. Yet, although he must have been able to imagine what punishments awaited him, the culprit was unafraid. And therein lies a story.

On the third day of the *Decameron,* Pampinea laughingly regales the *brigata* with this story, which is richly suggestive for its treatment of ideal princes and their honor. Indeed, it is a tale that might seem troubling for our understanding of both in the Rinascimento: the novella of the clever (*virtù*-ous) groom and his wise (*virtù*-ous) master, Agilulf, king of the Lombards. As Pampinea tells it as the second tale of that day, this humble but handsome and clever young groom was overwhelmed by love for his lord's wife, Teudelinga, at the same time that he recognized that "his love was completely impossible" given the great social gap that separated them. For although the courtly love ideal of the day and the *dolce stil nuovo* tradition often supported the notion of a humble young lover reaching up the social scale to love a woman of higher status, a groom who literally "smelled of the stables" becoming the lover of a queen was an unlikely gap to jump, even in the more contested and open social arena of fourteenth-century Italy or its world of literary imagination.[1]

And significantly, once again, this love was not depicted as only lust or a mere passing passion. For although winning Teudelinga's love was "without any hope," the groom spent his days trying to express his love by serving her in any way he could and felt "proud that his thoughts [of her] were of the highest order" even if in the end, as usual in the *Decameron,* they were coupled with sexual desire. Thus, Pampinea observed sagely that his unlikely but true love, "as we see frequently," increased in inverse measure as his hopes declined of satisfying it.[2] So it was that as the days passed and his love grew only stronger, the poor groom began to feel that he was going to die because of what in the Rinascimento was often perceived as love sickness, if his passion went unrequited.[3] Finally, he concluded that he had to do whatever was necessary to enjoy his love just one time, no matter how dangerous or violent it might be. And that enjoyment for him required that his sexual pleasure be shared with the woman he loved.

It would be easy to assume that, in the hands of a lowly groom, lofty love had become simply lust driven by his overwhelming desire. Pampinea, however, is careful once more to portray his love not as lustful or base but rather as heroic, in contrast to the love of Calandrino of Chapter 1, which was merely foolish and overreaching. In fact, realizing that his passion was impossible and that it endangered his beloved because he was having great trouble keeping it hidden, in the end he concluded that his only option was to end his life. By sacrificing himself, he would protect all involved (or actually not involved) from the many dangers his deep love entailed. Once he faced that martyrdom for love, however, he realized that it created the possibility of actually securing his desire at least one time before dying via a stratagem both clever and bold. It was a stratagem that at its heart was the essence once again of Rinascimento *virtù*—not quite honest, not quite correct, and certainly not without sin.

But, given its cleverness, it was potentially effective, and it offered the possibility of making his death serve his love and his desire.

Pampinea, then, proceeds to carefully lay out just how *virtù*-ous his stratagem was. For, tellingly, this humble lover did not decide to take by force his queen or die heroically, but foolishly, in the attempt. Rather, cleverness *(virtù)* inspired by love replaced the perhaps more typical violence of the period.[4] Thus, he thought over carefully the options his acceptance of death offered and ultimately devised an ingenious stratagem *(ingegno)*. Carefully observing the king's habits, he learned that he did not sleep with the queen but instead came to her chamber at night, knocking on her door two or three times with a rod. When the door was opened, the king entered his wife's dark room, often silently, and after a short stay returned to his own quarters. As the groom realized that he was about the same size as the king, he decided that he would attempt to take the king's place on a night when he saw that the king had decided not to visit the queen. Pampinea gives an extra, but telling, dose of verisimilitude to her tale for her listeners and contemporaries by noting that in order to carry off his switch, the groom had to take a hot bath so that he would smell like a prince and not like a stable hand, neatly underlining the audacity of the social leap the groom was attempting to make in the pursuit of love.

So it came to pass, as it must in such tales, that one night, well bathed, "when he knew that everyone was asleep, realizing it was time to either *gain his desire or nobly end his life* with a desired death,"[5] he went to her chamber and, using a rod, knocked two times and was let in by her chambermaid, who immediately withdrew. As he had observed that Agilulf seldom spoke when he was angry or disturbed, he pretended to be upset and, silently "full of desire," he took the queen in his arms and made love to her several times in succession.[6]

Afterward, not wanting to endanger transforming the pleasure of that lovemaking into sadness for his queen, he quietly left her and returned to his own bed in the servants' quarters. It may be reading too much into the text, but it is suggestive that Pampinea does not refer to the pleasures of that moment *(l'avuto diletto)* as his pleasures but instead simply as "the pleasure had," implying that the pleasures were shared.[7] Whether or not this is reading too much into the text, it seems clear that the queen was not displeased with his lovemaking, which was aimed at pleasing them both, even remarking later to the king that his attentions had been more passionate than normal that evening. And given her warm, familiar tone in doing so, it is suggested that she had enjoyed that passion and his love. The groom's lovemaking was certainly illicit, cunningly illicit in the way of *virtù*'s often nonvirtuous dimensions, but evidently it was pleasurable as well. Moreover, it was portrayed as both perilous and heroic—just as difficult to obtain true love often was, as we have seen in the trials of Cimone in tale one and Federigo degli Alberighi in tale nine, both told on day five.

Be that as it may, the groom had not only succeeded in making love to his beloved, he had done so for the moment with no harm to either himself or, more importantly, as a true lover for Teudelinga either; for as far as she and the consensus realities[8] of everyone else were concerned, aside from the groom, she had merely made love to her husband and apparently enjoyed it. In this way, what might be justly considered rape from a modern perspective, from a Rinascimento perspective became merely consensual pleasure. As far as consensus realities were concerned, Teudelinga was unaware of who made love to her as were the groups that evaluated her identity as a good wife and, thus, believing that she was making love to her husband rather than a victim of rape, she was a willing participant in the pleasures of marital sex. In turn, by keeping his secret even from the woman he loved, the groom heroically protected his love as he shared with her the pleasure of his love, as Pampinea is careful to note.

But that successful and happy ending for the groom, the queen, and Pampinea's listeners was far too easy to make a good story. And the one thing that endangered the tale's happy ending and the groom's cleverly conceived "small natural sin"[9] of young love and shared sexual pleasure was, of course, the prince. For, if Agilulf discovered what had happened to his wife, that happy moment had the potential to quickly turn to disaster and violence for all involved. If he learned that someone had imitated him in his wife's bed and cuckolded him, secret pleasures became rape and dishonor, and the listeners to the tale might well have expected him as a man to feel that his honor had been devastatingly besmirched and as a ruler to feel that his control of his court and land had been dangerously called into question—in this echoing the violent rage of Tancredi, the prince of Salerno (IV, 1), discussed earlier.

Moreover, readers would have been aware that the prince's wife's virtue might well have been seen as compromised, no matter how innocent she actually was. For much as was the case with Natalie Zemon Davis's tale of Martin Guerre, there would have been no lack of people who would have assumed that, as a wife, she should have been able to identify her husband in bed, especially his lovemaking. And, thus, they would have assumed that she was not actually the innocent wife that she was but rather a willing participant in the dishonoring of her husband. Indeed, the groom's moment of pure loving passion had the potential to spiral out of control and violently disrupt not only the prince's marriage but also his rule and virtually his whole world. In sum, the prince's discovery of what had happened had the potential to make Pampinea's story much more exciting and raise the emotions involved to much higher, violent, and ultimately tragic levels.

Such a storytelling opportunity was too rich to pass up; thus, not surprisingly, the tale continues to relate that that same evening, a little later than normal, Agilulf suddenly decided to visit his wife, arriving shortly after the groom left. And with this, obviously, the story entered new and extremely perilous territory. When the king seemed to return to her bedchamber, and in a good mood at that, Teudelinga could not help but innocently remark, "Oh my lord, what is this novelty *(novità)* tonight? You no sooner leave me after enjoying me more than usual and now so soon you return to start all over. Be careful for your health."[10] The queen's ingenuous concern, needless to say, had the potential to put the health of not just the king but all involved at risk. Yet, here the reality of Rinascimento consensus realities, and at a deeper level the complex of emotions associated with honor and *virtù*, gave Pampinea's story and the prince's dilemma a thoroughly contemporary twist that many a nonfictional medieval king of an earlier day and culture would not have felt. For, as we have seen, misdeeds not seen or judged by consensus realities to a large extent simply did not exist in the Rinascimento. And, in turn, if no one knew that one had been dishonored, then in the world of consensus realities, one simply had not been dishonored. Agilulf correctly judged from his wife's innocent comment that although someone else had just made love to her, she was unaware of the fact, *and thus from her perspective it had not happened.*

"He, being a wise man, immediately thought that as neither the queen nor anyone else was aware of what had happened, he would not tell her. . . . And moreover by keeping quiet he would suffer no shame (*vergogna*), whereas if he should speak he would have garnered great dishonor (*vitupero*)." Here the powerful Rinascimento disciplining discourse of honor and shame was significantly rephrased from the perspective of consensus realities and the regime of *virtù*. And critical for all of this was the prince's ability to control *virtù*-ously the emotions that honor seemed to call for him to feel and, more importantly, display. As Pampinea makes clear, "Many a fool would have acted differently instead crying, 'It was not me! Who was it! What happened? Who was here?'"[11]

Instead, Agilulf *virtù*-ously controlled the emotions associated with honor and shame. In fact, as Pampinea points out carefully, he controlled even his facial expressions to hide what he was feeling from his wife. For it was not that he did not feel the emotions that his honor required at the moment—his honor once again being presented as virtually an emotion.[12] Yet, as a wise and *virtù*-ous Rinascimento prince, rather than giving into that emotion, he realized that what had happened for everyone else had actually not happened. In a social world, where consensus realities ruled, despite whatever inner emotions he had experienced, what really mattered was that for those consensus realities that created his identity, essentially he had not been dishonored or shamed and his wife had not been compromised, as long as he did not display his emotions to make his betrayer's deed socially real. So, instead, he reassured his queen that everything was fine and that he had taken to heart her warning about endangering his health, and he quietly left.

At that moment, Agilulf demonstrated to Pampinea's listeners that he was an ideal husband and prince: his emotional control demonstrated his impressive wisdom and his, if anything, even more impressive *virtù*.[13] Yet, that did not mean that he did not feel the emotions that the cultural field of honor and shame encouraged him to feel. He still wanted revenge, but he wanted to satisfy that desire quietly and cleverly with *virtù*, again more like a contemporary Florentine member of the *popolo grosso* than perhaps a typical medieval prince. *Virtù* and cleverness did not negate the strong emotions that clustered around honor; they merely refocused them in the context of Rinascimento consensus realities.

Thus, both came to his aid, for as he rationally considered the situation, he realized that whoever had dishonored him had to have been a member of his household. And it was most likely that the traitor was still in the palace, probably sleeping in the nearby servants' quarters. Hurrying there, he found everyone apparently sleeping innocently. But, once again, he realized that if the culprit had been one of his servants, it was likely that that person would still be excited and have a heart that was beating strongly; therefore, he quietly walked among the beds, placing his hand on the chest of the sleepers, seeking someone whose heart would give him away—a perfect metaphor for the danger of this tale of love and sex driven by a lover's passionate heart. That lover, the groom, still awake, immediately understood what the king was up to, an understanding that did little to calm his already beating heart.

So, of course, as the tale required, it was only a matter of time before Agilulf found his man. Once again, however, the king's desire to keep what had happened secret led him to proceed cleverly, that is, with *"virtù."* Rather than waking the culprit and causing an uproar that would almost certainly have led to the whole matter becoming known once again to his dishonor and that of the queen, he instead made use of a pair of scissors that he had brought along on purpose and cut off a patch of the culprit's hair. With this clever ploy, he planned to identify the culprit in the morning, separate him from his comrades then, and quietly have his desired revenge served cold, without raising an uproar and with minimum impact on the consensus realities that judged him as a prince. There was, however, just one problem with this shrewd plan, and that turned on the moral of the tale, for although low born, the groom as a lover was also a true lover and, inspired by his great love, he was in his own right clever and quite capable of displaying a *virtù* as a lover that matched that of his prince.[14] *Virtù* and true love, once again, were powerful allies in the *Decameron* and once more together they transcended the social and moral boundaries of the day. Thus, after the king left, he got up and, taking a pair of grooming shears that were there used for shearing horses, proceeded to clip a similar patch of hair from all the other sleepers.

The next morning the king, expecting to identify the culprit, called his servants and staff together. And, of course, thanks to the groom's shrewd strategy, virtually all of them had the same cut to their hair.

Realizing that he had been outfoxed, the prince "thought to himself, 'this fellow that I am searching for, although he is of low condition demonstrates very well that he is of high intelligence.'"[15] Even if, perhaps to make the play on the contrast between "low condition" and "high intelligence" more parallel, the term *virtù* is not used, it is clear that in this case the groom's *virtù* trumped that of the king. And we are close to the happy ending that the story required—given the theme of the day, stories of love that end well (thanks usually to the *virtù* of the lovers involved)—but once again the prince had to control his emotions with his own *virtù* in the context of consensus realities for that to happen. "So seeing that he could not have what he wanted without creating an uproar, and not wanting to gain great shame *(gran vergogna)* in order to have his small revenge *(piccola vendetta)* ... Agilulf said to everyone, 'The person who did it, do not do it again and God be with you.'"[16]

Pampinea then celebrates the wisdom of the prince's *virtù*-ous control of his emotions: "Another [prince] would have wanted to string up, torture and examine [everyone] and in that way he might have discovered a thing that everyone is better off concealing and even if he had secured his full revenge [in this way] he would have greatly increased his shame and sullied the honor of his wife."[17] In sum, a truly *virtù*-ous prince had to control his emotions, especially those violent emotions that turned around honor and shame, shaping them in such a way that they worked in the context of the consensus realities of his day or, at least, the late fourteenth-century Italian urban world of Boccaccio's day. And in the end honor was saved, the prince demonstrated his wisdom *(virtù)* as a ruler, and the groom survived his love sickness thanks to his own cleverness *(virtù)*, and even the queen innocently enjoyed the pleasures of a heroic lover who she never knew she had and who, tellingly, goes unnamed throughout the tale.

How Gualtieri, the Marquis of Saluzzo, Decides Very Reluctantly to Take a Wife to Suit His Needs

That theme returns in many tales and, in fact, returns as a crucial theme in the famous last tale of the last day of the *Decameron*. For while that tale has been often read as the tale of Griselda and her virtually biblical acceptance of her own lord / husband's will, it can also be read as a tale about that husband, Gualtieri, the marquis of Saluzzo.[18] Gualtieri is presented throughout the novella as yet another prince moved by a strong sense of honor and shame, complex emotions that in his case were deeply colored by his rejection of love. A rejection that I would suggest meant that he was incapable of being a good sexual partner, a good husband, or a good ruler for the consensus realities of fourteenth-century Florentine readers at least. Thus, in a way that echoes the tale of the groom and his love for his queen, this tale is also deeply concerned with not just sex, love, and marriage but also, suggestively, with power and the rule of princes, in this case, however, negatively portrayed. Even the language of the day nicely sets up this theme: for the term *"signore"* (lord) had multiple meanings that could span the gamut of power relationships from the humble husband as *signore* / lord over his wife and household, to the local *signore* / lord / noble with power over those below him on the social scale, on to the *signore* / lord / ruler (either a prince or a tyrant, depending on one's perspective), and, of course, finally on to the ultimate *signore,* the *Signore* / God. As we shall see, all these meanings are at play in this tale of the *signore* Gualtieri.

The teller of this story of multiple *signori,* the irrepressible Dioneo, suggests the negative tone of the tale right from the start of his narrative. First, he immediately warns his listeners and readers that he finds Gualtieri's behavior in general and toward his wife to be "beastly"[19] and ultimately unacceptable, suggesting that they should respond in the same way. "I want to speak about a Marquis, not all that magnificent, but actually *an idiotic beast,* even if things turned out well for him in the end. In fact, I would not suggest that anyone follow his example, as it was a great sin that things worked out well for him."[20] He then more subtly attacks him as a ruler *(signore),* remarking that when the story begins, because he was a young man, he spent all his time "in hawking and hunting and in nothing else."[21] Here we have echoes of a tale discussed in Chapter 1 (II, 3) of spendthrift Florentine youths who threw away the riches left them by their noble father at the turn of the thirteenth century by living the thoughtless life of young Florentine nobles *(signori)* hunting, hawking, and living magnificently beyond their means.[22] And, tellingly, Gualtieri is also labeled by Dioneo immediately a youth *(giovane)* as well as a noble *(signore),* and we sense that both contributed to his "beastly" and "idiotic" behavior as the tale unfolds.

It will be recalled that those noble Florentine youths, after they lost their inherited fortune, significantly regained it by going to England and loaning money at interest to the apparently even more foolish English nobility—an unlikely event in the earlier period when the story was set but one that made eminent sense in the fourteenth-century banking city Florence had become.[23] Yet, sadly, they squandered it once again, because, as the story is at pains to stress, they returned to living like nobles *(signori),* eschewing the wiser ways of *popolo grosso virtù* with disastrous results. In the end, they were saved from their un-*virtù*-ous behavior by a *virtù*-ous nephew, Alessandro, who first reestablished their fortune via astute moneylending and then with his *virtù* (aided by that version of Lady Fortuna who often favors handsome young male lovers) won a bride that turned out to be the daughter of the king of England, effectively overcoming all the foolish deeds of his noble uncles.

Gualtieri, however, did have some excuse for his own noble behavior, for as a character in his tale, he was a medieval prince from Saluzzo, definitely not Florentine and never exposed to the profits and lifestyle of Florentine moneylenders, even imaginary ones and their quite different vision of *virtù.* Often the narrators of the *Decameron's* tales set untoward behavior in a safely distant past or place, making it easier for contemporaries to see and accept the lack of wisdom of those who were safely others. Nonetheless, the implication is clear that this *signore,* Gualtieri, not attending to anything else but his youthful pleasures, was not a good prince, ruling as he should with *virtù.* In fact, he was acting in a way that a contemporary Florentine would have easily associated with their fears about *signori,* not princes but tyrants in their present day; for such rulers, in contrast with the *virtù*-ous rule of the *popolo* in republican Florence, were seen by Florentines as ruling all too often merely to serve their own whims and pleasures (dangerous expressions of emotions both) at the expense of their subjects.

In fact, Florentines had recently had (in 1342) a brush with a tyrant of their own, and with a Gualtieri of their own at that. Walter (Gualtieri) of Brienne, the duke of Athens, had been appointed in that year of financial crisis to a one-year term as ruler of the city with the support apparently of both the old nobility and many members of the *popolo* as well, in the hopes of stabilizing the economic travails of the city. But, as was often the case with such short-term appointments in other cities, this Gualtieri attempted to transform his appointment to one for life, effectively becoming the *signore* of Florence. His increasingly unpopular rule, however, lasted only ten months. After he was driven out in July 1343, and following a brief period of transition, a popular government came to power that was very wary of lords / *signori* whether they were tyrants, neighboring lords, or local nobles.[24]

And the negative behaviors regularly associated with contemporary tyrants are immediately linked to the question of Gualtieri's marriage by Dioneo, who continues to note that not only did he not pay attention to anything else beyond his own personal pleasures, he "had no interest in either taking a wife or having children."[25] This, then, had created problems with his vassals. They, like all vassals, tied willingly or not to their *signore* (much like many a wife), wanted him to take on the responsibilities of a mature male and ruler by marrying, for marriage was the final sign of reaching full adulthood. And it implied taking on the sober responsibilities of an adult male and eschewing the freedoms and pleasures of the long masculine adolescence that often stretched for upper-class males from their early teens to their early thirties. Moreover, with marriage and its concomitant licit sex, a prince began to produce the heirs that would secure an ordered passage of power at his death, something that for vassals was highly important.[26] In Gualtieri's rejection of all this, in essence, Dioneo had presented his Rinascimento readers with a questionable *signore* / lord / ruler who refused to give up his youthful and irresponsible ways and pleasures, governed more by emotions than reason, to rule as a wise and mature adult. In fact, in the face of the reasonable requests of his subjects, he stubbornly resisted in the name of defending what must have seemed like his greatest weaknesses—and to top it all off, he sported a name that recalled Florence's still recent unhappy flirtation with a would-be tyrant.[27]

Thus, a fourteenth-century Florentine reader was set up to find Gualtieri a troubling figure at best. Even his attack on the idea of marrying, which might have been expected to win the support of quite a few contemporary males, was slightly off in a troubling way. For, instead of the typical misogynistic tropes against marriage that might have been expected, including fears of a young wife's lack of loyalty, predilections for dishonoring adultery, general sexual misbehavior, or even more prosaic attacks on vanity, nagging, or wastefulness, all were passed over in favor of once again his repeated desire to protect his pleasures and live the youthful carefree noble life he wanted to live: "My friends, you are pressing me to do something that I am completely against ever doing, considering what a difficult thing it is to find someone whose ways of behaving match up well [with mine]. . . . And how difficult is the life of the person who is stuck with someone unsuitable for him."[28] Those who saw love as the one true basis for a happy marriage, as Boccaccio's storytellers regularly did, could easily see the problems in Gualtieri's self-serving attack. Beyond wishing to maintain his unprincely personal pleasures at the expense of his subjects, he wished to marry, if marry he must, someone who would serve him and his pleasures unquestioningly, and neither love nor shared sexual pleasures entered his calculations.

Where Gualtieri Decides to Marry in His Own Way and Insists His Subjects Honor the Bride That He Will Pick

In the end, then, although he reluctantly gave in to his subjects' demands, he decided to do so in his own way. And, once again, the way he arranged his marriage would have troubled contemporaries. Actually, of course, arranged marriages were the norm in fourteenth-century Florence. But typically they were negotiated by parents or relatives to secure family alliances, whereas instead Gualtieri took his marriage personally in hand to secure his selfish desires with no concern for his family or his subjects. Beyond that troubling novelty, his motives for arranging his marriage also evoked the negative presentation in *Decameron* stories of arranged marriages more generally—that is, they overlooked love and thus led to unhappy matches, especially for young women. The *brigata* and their tales over and over again advocated avoiding such unhappy situations by advocating marrying for true love, exactly what Gualtieri aggressively rejected—a beastly character indeed. From his perspective, marrying for love and loving his wife in the shared emotional world of such a match would have endangered his solipsistic self-serving life, focused on his own personal and noble pleasures. Moreover, at the same time that such a marriage would undermine those pleasures, it would also signal the end of his freedom from his responsibilities as a ruler and declare that he had acquiesced in becoming the *signore* / prince he was supposed to be and that his subjects demanded he become.

Making his disgruntlement clear, when Gualtieri finally did knuckle under to his subjects' demands that he marry, he insisted, however, "But given that you *insist* in binding me in these chains and *given that I insist on being content*, in order to not hold anyone to blame but myself if worse comes to worst, I *insist* on choosing [my wife]."[29] He then continued to warn his followers that whoever he might chose, he expected and demanded that they honor the woman as their lady or feel his anger for having forced him to marry against his will. Evidently, with this warning, he was suggesting that the wife he might pick in some way might not match up to the ideal wife that his subjects expected of their prince.[30] The reality behind that warning was soon to be dramatically revealed. For Gualtieri, according to Dioneo, had for some time been observing a peasant girl who lived in a nearby village. She was beautiful, as required by such stories, even if she was a peasant. Yet, crucially, what made her most attractive to Gualtieri was the fact that "he considered that with her he could live very comfortably *(assai consolata)*."[31] In other words, he was confident that she would not interfere with his youthful noble pleasures that he was so anxious to protect and, in turn, neither love nor its accompanying sexual pleasures entered into his decision on a wife.

Following Gualtieri's misplaced desires, we are drawn ever deeper into the dark morass of arranged marriages as his matrimonial plans unfold. Having selected his bride without her even being aware of it, he informed his subjects, "My friends, you have wished that I take a wife, and I have decided to do so more to please you then from any desire of my own."[32] Needless to say, this was hardly an enthusiastic declaration of positive aspiration or a marriage to be based on love or even simple sexual desire. Nonetheless, he insisted that in a few days his subjects should come with him to join him in the celebration of his marriage to his unidentified bride. And so it was when the time came that they followed him to an unlikely nearby humble hamlet and the poor hut where the peasant girl Griselda lived in poverty with her father.

The scene is nicely set by Dioneo, as he describes how the richly attired relatives of Gualtieri and his most important subjects, ready for a sumptuous wedding ceremony, arrived on horseback at the tumbled-down hovel. Nobles, of course, traveled on horseback, peasants on foot. Drawing out the contrast, he details how the poor Griselda, dressed in rags, anxious like everyone else to see who their prince's new bride would be, rushes on foot onto the scene from the well, carrying water, as poor peasant women did as part of the daily routine of their humble life. No upper-class woman would have stooped to such a demeaning task that belonged to servants and those at the bottom of society and thus, clearly, even as she enters the scene, she should have been virtually invisible in it. But, of course, to everyone's surprise, and to no one's more so than Griselda, Gualtieri, while still on horseback, called down to her by name to ask where her father was. Suddenly actually visible, and now the focus of attention, she replied with the emotion that a modest lower-class young woman with good lower-class manners should have felt when replying to her *signore*—"shamefully" *(vergognosamente)*—that her father was inside.[33]

Gualtieri dismounted and, ordering everyone to wait, entered the "humble house" *(povera casa)* alone to talk with her father, Giannu-cole.[34] Even her father's name reeked of Griselda's humble status and lack of importance, for Giannucole is the diminutive for Giovanni. Using the diminutive for an adult male and a *pater familias* at that, even if his was a humble peasant family, essentially reduced him to the status of a boy and of no significance—as far from a prince as imaginable for those who heard Dioneo's tale. In a way, it literally obliterated any claim that Giannucole might have made to be a lord / *signore* even in his own humble little household. Indeed, Gualtieri did not waste any time with niceties on a person who, given his lack of status and apparent lack of honor, did not warrant them from a noble's perspective, and cut quickly to the heart of the matter. Yet, even in this, it should be noted that for those Florentines hearing the details of Gualtieri's high-handed ways, the distastefulness of this supposed prince's character and behavior was unmistakable.

It seemed almost as if his way of treating this humble man echoed what the citizens of Florence most disliked in the high-handed noble ways that they had rejected with their revered Ordinances of Justice, first passed at the end of the last century, ostensibly designed to punish mag-nates for just such high-handed ways and mistreatment of the *popolo*.[35] In fact, there had recently been an attempt to cancel the Ordinances, and the blame was often laid incorrectly at the feet of that other Gualt-ieri, Walter (Gualtieri) of Brienne, the would-be *signore* of Florence in the dark legend that grew up around his attempt to become the lord of the city permanently. Actually, after he was driven out in 1343, the Ordinances were momentarily repealed by a very narrow upper-class elite that briefly ruled the city, only to be reinstated by the popular government that quickly regained control of government. And they did so as a strong and celebrated reminder that the city would not allow lords *(signori)*, either magnate / nobles or tyrants, to interfere with their government.[36]

Continuing in the same high-handed manner, Gualtieri announced to poor Giannucole, "I have come to marry Griselda, but first I want to ask her some things in your presence." Then, turning to Griselda, he zeroed in on the heart of his concerns about marriage, demanding that if he took her for his wife, "would she always be committed to pleasing him and never do or say anything that would upset him." Once again the mantra of the evil, self-centered, unloving *signore* is evoked. Persisting in his aggressive questioning, he queried if "she would be obedient and many other things as well." To every lordly demand she answered, "My lord *(signor)*, yes."[37] Once again, the absence of love in Gualtieri's approach to his future bride is stunning, especially for the tales of the *Decameron*, at least the happy ones. Moreover, here the heavy-handed nature of this arranged marriage and of this unlikely match is hammered home with Gualtieri demonstrating unmistakably the personality of a rather crude would-be husband lacking in manners and refinement, virtually a tyrant in his arranged marriage with this humble peasant girl and implying similar tendencies as a ruler.

That perspective is underlined by the famous marriage scene that follows, for Gualtieri, with his demands met, takes Griselda by the hand and leads her from her hovel. And there in front of the whole group of his elegantly dressed subjects he orders her stripped naked—a telling moment played for his consensus reality both in the tale itself and for its readers.[38] He then has her redressed with the aristocratic clothing and the rich accoutrements that made up a noble's wardrobe. As often noted, this dramatic scene, in its undressing and redressing of his bride, essentially symbolized and perhaps contributed to the rebirth that Gualtieri was engineering, transforming Griselda from a humble peasant to a noble, using clothing as both a symbol and a tool. And there is much more that could be said and has been said about this symbolic moment and the importance that outward signs of inner worth like clothing played in formulating consensus realities in the Rinascimento.[39] In fact, the tale goes on to point out how quickly and successfully she impressed the gathering, appearing to take up easily the manner and bearing of a princess in her new noble clothing. That impression was confirmed in the days following, when, as Gualtieri's wife, she displayed once more for her consensus realities impressive noble manners and wifely virtues. In sum, redressed, she was capable of being transformed from a humble peasant to a noble princess—the very stuff of fairy tales and popular fantasy.

But it is also the very stuff of *popolo grosso* beliefs at the time, at least in terms of that group's ability to move up the social scale. Moreover, it was not just her clothing that made the transition a success. For, as the *popolo grosso* had moved up economically and politically to dominate society, they had also come to believe that there was nothing inherently superior about the old nobility and, in turn, to increasingly see themselves as not simply their equals but potentially superior to them socially and culturally as well. Thus, a humble peasant who gained the opportunity and the dress to move at the highest social levels was an attractive conceit, demonstrating that anyone with *virtù* could behave as well or better than the old nobility. From that perspective, Griselda had that delicious quality of fulfilling contemporary fantasies, even if many richer Florentines would have been comforted perhaps by the fact that such a leap for someone of her status was highly unlikely. And perhaps reassuringly in this tale, that leap was full of unpleasant pitfalls, again largely thanks to the beastly noble Gualtieri. Certainly a *virtù*-ous Florentine member of the *popolo grosso* could have imagined carrying off such a jump in status with greater aplomb and success, as the case of Alessandro, the young Florentine moneylender discussed earlier, who married the daughter of the king of England and easily flourished as her husband demonstrated (II, 3).

Yet, there is a way in which the dramatic stripping of Griselda—a theme that would have great popularity in the future, both in the retelling of the tale and in artistic re-creations of the moment—highlights another significant element of the marriage that would have resonated with contemporaries: the shame and honor involved. For, although she was a mere peasant, such a stripping would have been seen as shaming and confirming her lack of honor, at least until Gualtieri bestowed it on her by giving her his noble hand in matrimony. And, actually, as one looks back over the leadup to the troubling, loveless, arranged marriage of a peasant and a prince, it becomes clear that issues of honor had been there all along, lurking behind the action as a central element of the tale. Indeed, its Florentine audience would have been aware from the first that arranged marriages were virtually always ones where issues of honor and status were weighty. That was why fathers and families usually played such a significant role in arranging such affairs: they had, in theory at least, the mature judgment to evaluate the complex calculus of family honor involved in a marriage alliance without letting more unstable emotions like young love or sexual desire interfere.

Where the Role of Honor in Gualtieri's Marriage to Griselda and the Concomitant Lack of Love Are Considered

Unfortunately, from this perspective, the young, selfish, self-centered Gualtieri has already fallen far short of this ideal of building and sustaining honor by the time he arrives at the marriage scene, as the tale has made abundantly clear. Nonetheless, Gualtieri is portrayed as concerned about the honor of his marriage and is anxious to ensure it in his own high-handed way. Anticipating the resistance of his subjects to his marriage of a peasant and its implications for the honor of all involved, as we have seen, from the first he insisted that they accept his choice and "honor" it and him as their ruler in doing so. In an earlier day, with the story set in a feudal world, a prince's concern for his honor in marriage would have been viewed positively, but in this fourteenth-century novella, Gualtieri's concern for his honor becomes a strong negative theme running through the tale, significantly presented as a misplaced concern that makes him even less attractive as a prince and person, more a tyrant than a ruler.

At one level, of course, as long as honor is a driving force replacing love in his approach to marrying the humble Griselda, it cripples that relationship and his ability to be a good husband and suggests a similar situation vis-à-vis his subjects as a ruler where love is also lacking. Rather than being a model husband treating his wife with love, he is a tyrannical husband insisting on his pleasures and honor, and rather than being an ideal prince ruling his subjects with love, he is a tyrannical ruler once again insisting on his personal pleasures and honor.

In this way of seeing things, his behavior suggestively evokes strong echoes of other negatively portrayed husbands and princes in the tales of the *Decameron,* like Tancredi—husbands and princes whose lives are destroyed by their sense of honor. In turn, such behavior echoed Florentine fears about the dangers of a northern Italian world where it appeared—in many ways correctly—that the days of republics like theirs were a thing of the past, being rapidly replaced by the one-man rule of *signori* who claimed to be princes but more often than not seemed to Florentines to be self-serving tyrants like Gualtieri, once more, more concerned with their honor and pleasures than just rule.

It might seem a highly unlikely claim in light of Gualtieri's reasoned, if unseemly, arguments for insisting on his honor to argue once again here that, in the fourteenth century, honor could be seen as an emotion, and a dangerous one at that. Yet, in many ways, Gualtieri's selfish insistence seems to sum up the negative qualities of a number of male characters in the tales, who act in emotional ways that might in an earlier day have seemed reasonable and justified as honorable but who are in the *Decameron* portrayed as literally out of control. Over and over again, the behavior of such men, princes or husbands, is presented as lacking in *virtù,* out of control, and exhibiting a series of strong emotions that they cannot overcome or resist to their own detriment.

What I am suggesting, then, is that honor could be seen as such a deeply ingrained feeling that, if not an emotion in its own right, at least it could serve as a focus or focal point for a series of powerful feelings or emotions in the tales—what we might call once more a "complex emotion" associated with honor.[40] And, notably, as we have seen, emotions, especially complex emotions, in the *Decameron* were often portrayed as existing in a critical relationship with *virtù*—when *virtù* informed and disciplined such emotions things went well, but when its discipline was lacking or ignored they almost invariably led to disaster. In this honor was not all that unlike the complex emotion of love, although the group of feelings associated with love were usually rather different. In a way, then, honor in the Rinascimento could be seen as functioning much like a culturally constructed lens that focused and gave meaning to a range of emotions, giving them a social and personal sense that transformed them, if not disciplined by *virtù,* into powerful and, from the perspective of the *Decameron* at least, often dangerous elements of everyday life.

Significantly, then, when feelings of honor became virtually an emotion, they had the potential to escape or more accurately overwhelm the disciplining powers of consensus realities and their public evaluation of identity with devastating results. Thus, although set in a past time, as we have seen, Tancredi's emotional and uncontrolled tearful expressions of his outraged sense of honor led to the death of his beloved daughter, Ghismonda—in essence, his honor became an emotion that overwhelmed whatever *virtù* he had and his ability to negotiate with the groups around him in society who judged him and created his identity as a ruler. In contrast, Gerbino's grandfather, without emotion, as a wise ruler, sagely ordered that his grandson be executed for breaking both their words—and, in that case, honor without emotion became actually a demonstration of *virtù*.

But perhaps most telling is the case of Agilulf, the cuckolded prince discussed earlier. He was outraged by the fact that he and his wife had been dishonored by the unknown servant who had made love to her while impersonating him. His outrage is presented as a strong emotion associated with his sense of his honor—an internal sense, it should be noted, as well as one that the tale makes clear could also be judged by external consensus realities that he was very much aware of. But significantly, in the end, he did not give in to these emotions, and critical for his decision not to do so was his realization that if he controlled the feelings that he felt—the emotions that grouped around and were focused by his sense of honor, no one would know of his dishonor or the turmoil he was feeling. Shame, the traditional discipliner of honor, in fact, hardly entered his calculations. Once again, this turned on the fact that in a world of consensus realities, if no one was aware of his cuckolding, it virtually did not exist, and the shame that could accompany it was irrelevant. His emotions that gathered around his personal sense of honor were the only real danger he faced, for the fourteenth-century readers of his tale, then. And there, shame might lurk dangerously if his dishonor became public. But Agilulf controlled his emotions and, as a result, preserved his positive consensus realities as a husband and ruler, ideal prince and man that he was.

In turn, this suggests that in the Rinascimento honor had the potential to be a potent, complex emotion in its own right, gathering around itself a group of powerful and dangerous feelings. In that context, both *virtù* and consensus realities played a central disciplining role in the urban world of the day; both served to rein in emotions and their expression and, as a result, in a way civilize them—in the sense of making them serve a civil purpose. Thus, in a civil society where the regime of *virtù* ruled successfully, honor's emotional potential was controlled and evaluated by reason. But Gualtieri had demonstrated by this point in the tale that he was a person controlled neither by a strong sense of *virtù* nor any interest whatsoever in winning the support of the consensus realities of those he ruled.

And, in this context, Gualtieri's repeated insistence that both his subjects and his wife commit to honoring him without question takes on a deeper meaning, suggesting that the perilous emotions associated with honor were dangerously in play, as well as a deeper insecurity associated with those emotions. Unloved and incapable of loving because he was totally turned inward in defense of his immature personal pleasures, his defense was to demand that both his new bride and his unhappy subjects promise to accept a key aspect of the consensus reality that he needed to be a good ruler: his honor and his unquestioned honor at that. But consensus realities were *negotiated* with the various groups that surrounded one in society, and consensus realities that were demanded or ordered, especially for something like a ruler's honor, were dangerous chimeras sought by the insecure and, in this case, by a ruler who continued to demonstrate that he was more a tyrant than a prince.

Where Griselda's Successes as a Wife Are Brushed Aside by Gualtieri's Cruel Tests of Her Submission to His Will and the Demands of His Honor

For the moment, however, Gualtieri's insistence on his honor seemed to win out, aided significantly by Griselda's impressive transformation from a humble peasant girl into a beautiful, graceful, and mannerly lady. In fact, even Gualtieri's subjects began to hope that they had misjudged their *signore*. Rather than the tyrant that he seemed to be becoming with his high-handed, self-serving ways and his demands for honor, he might actually be a prince blessed with previously unperceived *virtù*. Dioneo, in fact, notes that they began to admit that while some had worried that "Gualtieri demonstrated little wisdom in taking such a wife," in light of her successful transformation, they began to think that maybe he was actually "the wisest and most perspicuous man in the world, because no one else . . . would have ever been able to recognize the great *virtù* hidden under that girl's [Griselda's] peasant garb."[41]

Things seemed to be looking up for Gualtieri's honor and his arranged marriage, as not only did Griselda win over his subjects, she soon became pregnant and produced a daughter. That auspicious event had even Gualtieri celebrating *(fece gran festa)*. But that apparent turn for the better was misleading for, not long after the happy birth, the flaws in his personality and his arranged marriage began to reveal a deeper, darker truth. Almost as if he feared to succumb to the success of his marriage and the dangerous feelings that might include love for his daughter and perhaps even Griselda, "a new *(nuovo)* thought entered his mind."[42] And once again the "new" of his thought reflects the negative valence of the term "new" at the time: for he decided on a series of troubling tests of his wife to assure himself that she was ready to honor all his wishes, no matter how cruel and tyrannical they might be.

Once more then, he defended his treatment of Griselda to her in terms of concern for his honor, complaining that his subjects were murmuring about her lowly peasant origins and the similar baseness of her daughter. Significantly, however, his claim was presented as untrue in the tale, for the question of his honor is never brought up by his subjects in this context; actually, they are portrayed as quite happy with his peasant bride, even as they are understandably surprised by her success as a lady. Nonetheless, Griselda is presented as accepting the weight of these false claims and as a result unhappily understands the claimed emotions of honor that are supposedly tormenting Gualtieri. Thus, she replies obediently as a subject to such a lord / husband must: "My lord *(signor mio)*, do with me what you will as whatever is best for your *honor or contentment* I will accept."[43] Once again, the feelings of honor and contentment played upon by her *signore* claim their due, and once again one wonders how this would have played for Florentine republican readers, who saw in such one-man rule and claims of honor the essence of tyranny—the greatest danger to their own republican values and way of life. And reinforced in the context of an unloving and unwisely arranged marriage across social lines with all its dangerous novelties, we are faced with a man and a relationship definitely gone wrong and a poor wife and subject doing her best to cope and perhaps just survive.[44]

Things quickly go from bad to worse, however, for Griselda. Evermore the tyrant, Gualtieri deceitfully uses his concerns about his feelings of honor to excuse his most outrageous demands on his wife / subject. First, he has a servant take her daughter away. And, making it clear that he is acting on the lord's orders, the servant implies that he has been instructed to kill the child. With great sadness, Griselda hands over her baby, even as she realizes that it will die, asking only that it not be left out in the wild to be torn apart by wild animals. Gualtieri is impressed by her obedience and strength *(costanzia)* in the face of his horrible demand. But, sticking to his testing of his wife, he allows her and his subjects to believe the child has been killed, while he secretly sends it off to relatives in Bologna to be raised.

Continuing his trying of her loyalty and commitment to defer to his alleged anxieties about his honor, when she shortly thereafter gives birth to a male child and heir, he once more claims the child's life, using again the excuse of fearing for his honor and his rule. "Woman, because you have made this male child, I cannot find any peace with my subjects as they complain insistently that a grandson of Giannucole will after me become their lord *(signore)*, so I have decided that if I do not want to be overthrown, I must do with him what I did to the other [child]. And given all this [I must also] leave you and take another wife."[45] Honor and its dangerous emotional component of fear, whether real or, as in this case, false, without the discipline of *virtù* lead to tragedy for all those subject to a lord's will.

Dioneo, however, shortly thereafter makes it clear to his listeners that this claim was again false, noting that Gualtieri's subjects were not complaining about the boy's humble background or the loss of honor it implied. In fact, he points out that in the face of the apparent murder of both children, those subjects "strongly damned him and held him to be a cruel man, while having great compassion for her [Griselda]."[46] Hardly the response of those anxious to see an unsuitable heir or wife eliminated. Still, as her lord and their tyrant, both she and they once again had no option but to bow down before his cruel will, yet another lesson about the honor of lords and their potential for heavy-handed tyranny that would not have been lost on republican Florence. Honor clearly had become a tool in the hands of a tyrant, whether it was a truly felt emotion or merely an excuse that could lead to appalling suffering for wives or subjects. Thus, the second child joined the first in apparent death—although, once again, he was sent off to Bologna to be brought up—while Griselda lived on sadly under the shadow of her husband's additional promise that sooner or later he would end the whole problem of her humble birth besmirching his honor and threatening his rule by putting her aside to take a more honorable bride.

The outrageousness of Gualtieri's behavior and the troubling acquiescence of Griselda has tended to cause many modern readers to pass over a telling detail offered by Dioneo that would have made Griselda's sacrifice have greater weight yet for contemporaries. For, tellingly, Dioneo notes that Gualtieri was impressed with how strongly Griselda had been attached to her children, describing her love as very intense and physical (carnalissima). Thus, her lord was confident that she was not accepting their deaths simply because she did not want "to have to take care of them" and was truly being tested in her loyalty to him.[47] This clarification was necessary for two reasons at the time. First, many upper-class women did not, in fact, raise their children for the first few years of their life, sending them off to wet nurses to be raised until they were weaned, usually at a fairly advanced age.[48] This was often depicted as being a practice that freed mothers, especially upper-class mothers, from the demeaning bother of having to breastfeed their children or care for them— a common practice regularly denounced by preachers and moralists as demonstrating a more general lack of concern by women for their children.[49] Second, many unwanted children were still being exposed in the Rinascimento, especially female children.

On this score, Griselda's earlier worry that her little daughter would be eaten by wild animals reflected her fear that her husband planned to have his servant expose the child, leaving it in the wilderness to die or be taken by wild beasts. The ideal behind this practice, if it can be called an ideal, was that much like Moses in the bulrushes, the child left out would be found and raised by someone more able or willing to care for it. The Rinascimento foundling home was a charitable response to this ongoing practice. Unwanted or unsupportable children could be left there, and it might be hoped that they would, in fact, survive without having to hope that if they were exposed someone would discover and decide to raise them. But this easily missed clarification suggests how widely exposure was still practiced and how easy it was to assume that a wife might more willingly accept the loss of her children.[50] For once, in having doubts about his wife's commitment to raising her children, Gualtieri was revealing a dark side of his thoughts about her and women more generally that may not have seemed that atypical or strange to Florentines, especially males, reading the tale.

With the passage of years—twelve to be exact—Gualtieri decided that his daughter had grown old enough to pass as a marriageable bride and that it was time for the last tests of his wife's acceptance of his desires and her willingness to sacrifice for his honor. Thus, finally, he acted on his earlier promise, informing Griselda that he was ready to return her to her father and her former humble state in order to take a more suitable wife. Claiming to have secured a dispensation from the pope to put her aside, he gathered his subjects together to make the announcement that he was returning her to her father and her humble position as a peasant. And, once again, we have consensus realities at play. For Gualtieri was not content to continue his cruel testing of his wife in the quiet of their domestic life; rather, his cruel deeds had to be displayed before his subjects. The power to rule and the honor it required were at play and perhaps also a desire to warn his subjects that he was their *signore* as well and capable of similar deeds to defend his honor and assert his control over them. But, considering what the Florentine readers of and listeners to the tale would have made of this new outrage is suggestive, for almost certainly they would have seen in this a cruel lord acting as a tyrant, mistreating his most loyal subject in a way that no right-thinking republican Florentine would ever accept. From the perspective of their consensus realities about Gualtieri, once again the dangers of a *signore* / tyrant were powerfully on display.

How Gualtieri Adds to His Cruel Tests a Promise
That Evokes a Yet Crueler Lord

Gualtieri, then, announced before his troubled subjects and the abject Griselda, "Woman [not even calling her by her name] in accordance with the concession made to me by the pope I may take another wife and leave you; and thus because in the past my ancestors were great

nobles and lords *(signori)* of these lands, where your ancestors were always laborers *(lavoratori)*, I wish that you will no longer be my wife, but
rather that you return to the house of Giannucole with the dowry that
you brought me, and I will take another wife that I have found that
pleases me and is befitting *(convenevole a me)*."[51] Although he does not
explicitly use the term "honor" in this speech, it is clear that that is
what he is using to make his behavior understandable. His ancestors
were nobles and rulers and Griselda's were humble laborers; therefore,
their marriage was a mismatch, and he was claiming that he was suffering the emotional dishonor of being a lord badly married.

The term *"lavoratori"* used to describe her ancestors, while it could
be used as a synonym for a peasant or a laborer on the land, may well
have suggested something more troubling yet for contemporaries. The
more normal terminology for Griselda's ancestors would have been *contadini, rustici,* or *villani,*[52] but by contrasting his nobility with her status
as descended from *lavoratori,* Gualtieri once again was asserting status
claims that would have ruffled Florentine feathers. For the *popolo* of
Florence, who had fought so hard across the thirteenth century to drive
out high-handed nobles like Gualtieri, had done so in the name of protecting the urban laborers *(lavoratori)* of the *popolo,* not rural peasants,
contadini, rustici, or *villani,* from just such high-handed and tyrannical
behavior. In fact, the Ordinances of Justice labeled such behavior as
typical of the magnates and nobles. And they were designed to discipline and punish them to protect the artisan *lavoratori* of the city and
make it a peaceful and prosperous republic. Once again, the recent re-
peal of the Ordinances following the short abortive attempt of Walter
(Gualtieri) of Brienne to rule the city as a *signore* in 1342 and the threat
that posed to the laborers of the city would have added weight to the
negative valence of this label for Griselda's ancestors.[53]

But there was a deeper cruelty in Gualtieri's proclamation: for poor
Griselda had not actually brought anything with her as a dowry to her
wedding. That meant that he was promising to return her to her father
just as he had taken her from him, naked. This, however, was not lost
on her. And she immediately pointed out the fact, admitting that she
had had no dowry. For once, however, Griselda went on to resist, albeit
humbly and in a way that underlined her powerlessness as a woman in
the face of a cruel husband / *signore,* asking only that in respect for her

virginity, which she had given him in marriage, that he grant her a shift
to return home in, with her nakedness covered.[54]

This stress on her nakedness, returned home defenseless and literally the poorest of the poor, while it highlights once more her lord's
beastly and uncivil ways, calls up echoes of another person often associated with Griselda and this tale, who had also suffered greatly under
his lord, but in his case it was the *Signore* / Lord, God—Job and his suffering in the Old Testament book named after him. In fact, commentators have often pointed to the parallels between Griselda's patient suffering at the hands of her *signore* / lord / husband and Job's suffering at
the hands of his *Signore* / Lord as a reason for seeing her as a hero and
loyal subject accepting her husband's just power.[55] Both were clearly
heroic in their suffering, but arguing that both were being held up as
ideals of correct comportment, Griselda as a wife and Job as a dedicated
worshipper of his Lord / God, however, is a little more problematic.[56]
And this is the case even if the tale has been often impressively read in
that way by excellent critics and scholars.

For, crucially and obviously, not all Rinascimento lords were always
the same, whether they were husbands, nobles, rulers, or gods. Even the
Christian God, for all the theological arguments for His oneness, appeared to display suggestive Trinitarian distinctions: distinctions between the Father, the Son, and the Holy Spirit that often created confusion and intense debate, not to mention a series of heresies that tended to
deny the unity of God. In fact, as we have seen earlier in the tale of Rustico
and Alibech (III, 10), distinctions based on the Trinitarian nature of the
Godhead had been and were a significant part of the complex religious
world of the day. As noted in that discussion, theologians, both orthodox
and heterodox, were much taken at the time by the idea that there was a
divine Trinitarian plan for history that mirrored and turned on the Trinitarian distinctions that distinguished the Christian Lord *(Il Signore)*.

Briefly recapping, many believed that the history of the world was
destined to move through three radically different ages, usually further
broken down into shorter periods. The first major age that came after
the Fall had been dominated by a vengeful God, often seen as dishonored by original sin (again, honor and emotion, this time seemingly felt
by God). In that age, humanity lived guided by the Old Testament and
its stern laws, which largely governed that unhappy fallen dispensation.

The second age arrived following the sacrifice of the second person of the Trinity, Christ, who out of love for humanity, and thanks to His willing self-sacrifice on the Cross, dramatically changed the very order of creation. This new age was dominated by the emotion of love, most notably between Christ and humanity overseen by the Catholic Church. A final age, many believed, would be the last age of the Spirit, led by the third person of the Trinity, the Holy Spirit, where a whole new order would obtain, dominated by an immediate loving spiritual relationship with God—the deepest, purist, and most spiritual form of love. And with that last age, the Trinitarian order of history would be fulfilled.

There was much debate in the Middle Ages and the Rinascimento about when that last age would arrive. The Franciscan Spirituals and their more radical offshoots, like the Fraticelli, preached that that age was nigh in the fourteenth century. In times of turmoil, such as during and after the plague, their vision gained many followers—followers who were especially taken by the idea that to prepare the way for the last age of the Holy Spirit, it was necessary to create a more spiritual Church, less involved with property and thus with secular matters. In fact, to many the Black Death seemed a sure sign that the last days of the second age had arrived, and in many ways the *Decameron,* with its opening focus on that epochal disaster, seemed to be responding to such ideas. Significantly, in Florence at the time, this message had particular power because the papacy, although apparently safely distant from the politics of Italy off in Avignon from the early years of the century, had begun to more aggressively seek to reestablish control of territory in central Italy and Tuscany that it claimed traditionally had been part of the Papal States. And in 1353, Pope Innocent VI ratcheted up those claims, appointing the warrior cardinal, Egidio Albornoz, to transform those claims from words to reality via military conquest.

Florentine resistance to this ongoing papal campaign after the Black Death, especially in the context of their own goals of territorial expansion in the center of Italy, gave the idea of three ages of humanity reflecting the three persons of the Trinity yet greater currency. For central in that vision was the anticipation that a more spiritual last age would be one where the Church would wither away and become progressively more spiritual by casting off its claims to property and land, living a purely spiritual existence—perhaps not quite like Alibech's approach but equally committed to serving the Christian God with love rather than with wealth and property. Needless to say, this ideal of a church unencumbered with property enjoyed wide support in Florence and could be traced back to both Joachim of Flora and Saint Francis and much further back to Christ's apparent poverty and the apostolic poverty of his followers depicted in the New Testament. Such ideas gained greater popularity, however, as tensions between the papacy over territorial claims in Tuscany escalated into a series of clashes over borders in the 1350s that would eventually lead to the War of Eight Saints (1375-1378) between Florence and the papacy.[57]

In turn, Florence became a city where even the officially heretical leaders of Franciscan offshoots, such as the Spirituals and the Fraticelli, preached and taught, openly calling for a more spiritual propertyless Church and promising the imminent arrival of the last age of the Holy Spirit. From this perspective, a more historical and Florentine reading of Gualtieri as a lord both in his marriage to Griselda and as a lord ruling over his subjects might be suggested, a reading that changes the feel of the tale and reframes the unlikely association of Gualtieri with godliness and God's treatment of Job. Indeed, there is a more immediate problem with that parallel, for Job's Lord did not actually deal out the setbacks that deeply wounded him. He merely withdrew His protection and left the door open for Satan to attempt to destroy Job's faith, ultimately without success. From that perspective, Gualtieri seems more to parallel and to evoke Satan than God; and Satan hardly seems the most defensible authority for how to treat wives in marriage, even for the most diehard patriarch.

Despite that often overlooked theological nicety, however, the God (*Signore*) of the Old Testament's treatment of Job does seem to parallel at a higher level the lord (*signore*) Gualtieri's treatment of Griselda and might well have seemed even more a parallel in fourteenth-century Florence. But, tellingly, in the Trinitarian view of time and history being preached aggressively in Florence after the plague, that first age of humanity and its difficult relationship with a vengeful God—whose honor, like Gualtieri's, was so important to Him—was widely seen as having been superseded by the coming of Christ. And that literal revolution in humanity's relationship to God had been motivated by Christ's *love and desire* to save humanity. Thus, even without the particular tensions of the historical moment, such a vision struck much deeper chords. And taken seriously, as it was by many, it changes significantly the valence of an association of Gualtieri with God; for the Lord that he seems most to parallel is the proud, vengeful God of the Old Testament moved by the dishonor of Adam and Eve's original sin.

Yet, significantly, that vengeful aspect of humanity's relationship with God had been superseded. Christ's love and His eschewing of His own honor to die as a common criminal to save humanity was the base of a new dispensation and order. And the godliness of that new age, Boccaccio's present, is totally alien to Gualtieri and totally alien to his relationship with his wife and his subjects—for he explicitly rejected love in favor of jealously protecting his honor, much like the vengeful Lord of the Old Testament and nothing like the God of love of the New Testament. In a work that over and over again stresses the importance of love, love in marriage and in the best relationships between men and women, Gualtieri becomes the cruel husband, the anti-prince, the tyrant par excellence, and a reflection of a relationship with God that no longer obtained following the loving sacrifice of Christ. And, of course, this last tale of the *Decameron* is told by Dioneo—*Dio neo:* literally, the new god (of love?) and evoking the Greek god of sexual pleasure, Dionysius—who makes it clear that he finds Gualtieri unsuitable as a husband, a ruler, and most certainly as any kind of a lover.

Returning to Griselda's being sent back to her father, naked as she had left him, Gualtieri grudgingly granted her request that she be given at least a shift to cover her nakedness in recompense for her having given him her virginity and producing two children for him. For once, it almost seemed that he felt uncomfortable about his testing of the poor woman, for we are told that even he almost began to cry at her humble plea for something to cover her nakedness as she returned to her poverty. But immediately Dioneo negates that moment of more sympathetic emotion in his villain, noting that Gualtieri resisted the feeling and replied curtly "with a hard face: 'And you can take a shift with you.'"[58]

So it was that Griselda, barefoot and wearing only a shift, having said her goodbyes to the courtly world that she had frequented for thirteen years with great success, as far as Gualtieri's subjects were concerned, walked home to become once again a peasant accompanied by the tears and laments of everyone except her *signore*. Clearly, Dioneo

intended those tears to evoke a deeper sympathy for Griselda in an audience that might have been tempted to dismiss her as a mere peasant
only receiving her due. And yet one might also read into those tears,
fears. For Gualtieri's fictional subjects had to fear that they too might
suffer Griselda's fate at the hands of their lord and actual Florentines at
the hands of their would-be lords. At home, she found that her father,
who, never believing that a lord would truly honor as a wife his humble
daughter for long, redressed her in the clothes that he had kept for years,
expecting her to be returned at any moment. In sum, the lord giveth and
the lord taketh away, at least the hard Lord of the Old Testament, the
cruel contemporary tyrants of Florentine fears, the unloving husbands
of arranged marriages, and Gualtieri.

But, of course, Gualtieri's outrageous behavior was not softened
in the face of Griselda's abject acceptance of his tyranny. And the last
act of his cruel testing came in the form of his humiliating demand
that she return to prepare and oversee his wedding to his new bride.
Claiming that Griselda, having been his wife for thirteen years, knew
his household better than anyone, he ordered her—apparently no longer
his wife—now as his subject to return to his palace and prepare his new
wedding. Once again, Griselda accepted this command but significantly
not simply as a subject. For while Gualtieri was acting as a lord, focused
on his honor and his tests of loyalty, Dioneo and Boccaccio-writer insist on making a critical clarification: they insist that Griselda accepted
not as a patient wife or loyal subject *but out of love for Gualtieri.* And in
this, at least, she seems heroic. As Dioneo explains, although Gualtieri's
request cut like "a knife stabbing her in the heart," still, because "she
had not been able to put aside the *love* she felt for him" as easily as she
had put aside her one-time good fortune, she agreed.[59] Thus, dressed
humbly, she returned to the palace where she had ruled, now as a servant to prepare the new wedding of her beloved to a new young bride.
Dioneo relates a number of humiliating moments in the preparations
and underlines once again their injustice by noting the deeply troubled
reactions of Gualtieri's subjects to her abuse and their repeated calls
for a more just treatment of his former wife—consensus realities again.

The humiliation comes to a head when Gualtieri has his young
bride brought to his palace for the wedding organized by Griselda.
Dioneo has already alerted his listeners that the bride is actually the

daughter that the tyrant supposedly had had killed. Tellingly, however, as we have been informed that that daughter was born twelve years earlier (the story tells us that Gualtieri and Griselda had been married thirteen years when he returned her to her father)—that meant that she was about twelve years old, a fairly typical age for arranged marriages in fourteenth-century Florence, as we have seen. Once again, the contrast between the humbly dressed servant Griselda, who must have been at least in her midtwenties and more likely nearing thirty, with the young, virtual child bride who was to replace her, called up images of more mature women cut out of the marriage market when they lost their first flower of youth in favor of child brides who often won out at least in obtaining a husband in the loveless arranged marriages of the day.[60] Needless to say, this practice was one that the tales of the *Decameron* often comment upon negatively, and that negativity here is underlined once more by the humiliation and mistreatment of Griselda before the child bride that is to replace her in yet another arranged marriage.

In the end, then, taking his testing to the final extreme, Gualtieri presents his soon-to-be bride to a humbly dressed Griselda—having denied his subjects' request that he at least dress her as a lady and not as a menial servant for the wedding—and asks her for her opinion of his new lady. Suggestively, Dioneo is careful to point out that he asked her opinion because he knew she was intelligent and that her calm demeanor masked the suffering that she had undergone, implying that he was fully aware of how cruelly he had treated her. And his cruelty was not disappointed. She answered, "My lord . . . she seems to me very good and if she is as intelligent as she is beautiful, as I believe, I am certain that you ought to live with her as the most content *(consolato)* lord *(signore)* in the world. But still I would pray that those wounds that you gave before to the earlier one [wife], you spare this one; because I doubt that she could resist them, for she has been raised with great gentleness [refinement], whereas the other was used to hardships from her childhood."[61]

How Griselda Finally Complains and Gualtieri Offers an Excuse for His Beastly Behavior

Yes, Griselda has suffered, and finally she has even complained. Albeit, subtly and without ever referring to herself by name. Accepting his final humiliation, she has pointed out at last the unjust nature of his rule over her and by implication his subjects. In doing so, she undercuts a bit her painful acceptance of Gualtieri's treatment that has always made her more a sad victim than a hero even of suffering, unless, of course, one argues that such acceptance of lordly cruelty is required of wives and subjects. Certainly, that is not the case in virtually all the other stories of the *Decameron*[62] or in the portrayal of Gualtieri as anything but an ideal ruler or husband. It may well be that even Griselda needs to finally stand up to her lord to hold the sympathy of her Florentine readers as the long tale of her mistreatment rushes to its surprising conclusion.

It would be satisfying to claim that Griselda's final demonstration of resistance caused Gualtieri to change his ways, but Dioneo has already informed us that she has passed all her lord's tests and that he has decided to change his ways even before she actually gives vent to her very subdued and subtle resistance. Thus, he hardly hears her comments and does what he already planned to do, declaring, "Griselda it is time that you finally hear the fruit of your long patience and that those who have held me to be cruel and unjust and bestial learn that it was all according to plan, wishing to teach you how to be a wife and to those others how to pick and keep a wife and to guarantee my peace as long as we would live together."[63] In the end, then, even Gualtieri admits that his lordly ways have been cruel, unjust, and bestial, but he defends them by claiming that in this way he has taught Griselda how to be a good wife.

Yet, crucially, *his cruelty did not teach her anything*, as the tale makes clear over and over again. She came to him, as she has just reminded us all, already accustomed to suffering and patiently accepting the hardships that life brought her as a non-noble peasant at the bottom of society. She was born into hardship and suffering. And she adapted quickly to her lord's mistreatment because of her own inherent peasant ability to suffer—the kind of *virtù* that was deemed natural to a peasant at the time. Indeed, one would be hard put to find a place where the tale or Dioneo suggest that she learned anything from Gualtieri. And while the fourteenth-century Florentine readers of this story were more usually urban dwellers than peasants and thus theoretically not as inured to hardship and suffering, they were proudly not nobles either, and it is hard to imagine them accepting at the hands of local nobles the treatment that Gualtieri, her noble lord, dished out. Moreover, it is hard to imagine that they would have felt sympathy for Gualtieri's defense of his bestial ways, as they too would have been unlikely to feel any need for such lessons from nobles or *signori* to learn the patience necessary to survive as subjects (as they had recently demonstrated, throwing out that other Gualtieri, the *Signore* Walter of Brienne) or even as wives.

Where Love Wins in the End as It Should in the *Decameron*

Actually, it might seem strange that, finally, after retaking Griselda as his wife and explaining his whole plan to his subjects and his victim, the couple are portrayed by Dioneo as living happily ever after. But, significantly, providing an explanation for that surprising happy ending is a startling admission by Gualtieri, for as unlikely as it might seem, all his cruel tests have led him at least and at last to one critical transformation—the decisive transformation of the novella. For he has discovered the emotion that he had always lacked, love, and has fallen finally in love with his victim, Griselda. He confesses at the end of the tale: "I am your husband, who loves you more than anything and believe me when I avow *(dar vanto)* that there is no man more content than I in his wife."[64]

Crucially, with that admission, and Griselda's ongoing love that survived his every cruelty, no longer is their marriage simply an arranged marriage with a wife subject to her husband, defending his honor and noble pleasures. Rather, now it is exactly the kind of marriage that the *Decameron* has advocated over and over again. With love as its emotional base, the happy ending that the story, and the *Decameron* itself, requires is possible, and Gualtieri, Griselda (his finally loved wife), and perhaps even his subjects can live happily ever after—not a divine comedy perhaps but a human one.[65] Indeed, in the face of Gualtieri's love, even his subjects forgive him—once more critical for his consensus reality—and hold him finally as most wise *(savissimo)*, even as they continued to question his treatment of his wife as "too harsh and intolerable." "But above all else they saw Griselda as most wise."[66] For, in the end, she survived a cruel lord, and with her willingness to suffer and peasant patience, she, not he, was the true teacher. In the end, she taught a *signore* who rejected love to love and to become a true lord—in this, she was perhaps more Christ-like than Job-like.[67]

Of course, not all were so forgiving of Gualtieri. And Dioneo offers the last words on the tale that seem nicely to reflect the rather irreverent contemporary Florentine vision of *signori* and their high-handed ways, whether they be husbands acting as lords, nobles acting as lords, or *signori* acting as tyrants: "What more needs to be said beyond the fact that even in the houses of the poor the divine spirits of heaven rain down, even as in the princely there are those who would be better employed as swineherds than as lords over men."[68] Clearly, here, we see the political dimension of the tale underlined. Gualtieri, from Dioneo's perspective, and I would suggest from that of most contemporary Florentines, was more fit to be a swineherd than a prince before he found love. And, significantly, this comment underlines the contemporary awareness widely shared that marriage was in a way merely rulership writ on a more personal micro level and thus Gualtieri's behavior was telling, not simply for the relationships of power within a family but for political ones as well. Moreover, we see that Gualtieri's approach to rule in Dioneo's narration of his tale, stressing as it did the former's personal pleasure and his feelings of honor, reflected everything that he and his contemporary Florentines would have found objectionable in lordship and noble pretensions.

Dioneo continues, however, offering one last famous comment on the marital and sexual dimension of his critique, for where there was a good marriage good sex could not be far behind in the *Decameron*: "Who else but Griselda would have been able without shedding a tear but almost smilingly to accept the stern and never before [thus once again negatively new] heard of trials of Gualtieri? Who would have acted incorrectly in the face of being thrown out of [her] house with just a shift, if she had found another to stroke her pussy *(scuotere il pillicione)*, winning herself in the process something positive *(una bella roba)*."[69] While there is room for doubt about just how earthy Dioneo meant to be with his *"bella roba,"* which is so vague that it could refer to anything from a pretty dress to something good or more metaphorically something positive, the broader context is clear. Most Florentine women of the day, in Dioneo's opinion, would not have accepted such treatment.[70] And if the reading of this essay is convincing, many Florentines of the second half of the fourteenth century would have agreed, albeit perhaps not so colorfully.

In the imaginary world of the *Decameron,* however, successful marriages were based on love and true sexual desire, and desires like those of Gualtieri that turned on an outdated and misplaced sense of honor were usually punished with adulterous wives or worse. Gualtieri, as long as he rejected love and insisted on protecting his personal pleasure and his outmoded and dangerous feelings of honor, was incapable of being a successful *signore* at any level—husband, noble, or lord—while being, in reality, an excellent lesson in the negative aspects of each. Florentine wives and Florentine citizens would never accept such lords and were quite capable of securing the pleasures of their world without such lordly lessons or bestial deceits. When the now true prince, Gualtieri, found love, the *Decameron* could end happily with a loving marriage and with Dioneo's laughing and irreverent, but always telling, quips. And perhaps those hearing this "new god's" laughter could imagine that love and sex in the time of plague might offer a path to a new age and the ultimate but most human transcendence of a very complex, dangerous, and beautiful group of emotions—serving the Christian God with pleasure along with Alibech?

Conclusion

A Decameron *Renaissance?*

$\mathcal{O}$ne hundred stories to save the unfortunate women of Florence overwhelmed by the plague? One hundred stories to save that city and its *civiltà* devastated by the plague? One hundred stories in Boccaccio's *Decameron* to even save the world from the wrath of an angry God manifested by the plague? Unlikely and hard to imagine.

Hard to imagine, especially when one considers that those stories were often of questionable morality focusing on questionable loves and even more questionable illicit sex. And what makes that even more unlikely, those one hundred stories were told explicitly in the face of God's damning wrath at humanity's sinning ways and corruption, a wrath exhibited with violent clarity in the form of the Black Death that carried off at least half the population of the day, made deserts of flourishing cities, and literally destroyed the social fabric of a Christian society, as Boccaccio-author worries in his introduction to the *Decameron*. All of this seemed to announce clearly and with devastating violence that the loving dispensation that the death of Christ on the Cross had brought humanity was over or at the least was coming to a definitive end. One hundred stories, often playful, often of doubtful rectitude, often troublingly irreverent or apparently simply irrelevant, seem more like attempting to deflect with a few humorous stories the tsunami of God's wrath than a realistic response to the moment. Indeed, even their power to save the unhappy women of Florence seems problematic.

Yet, even as I have tried in this book to demonstrate that those one hundred stories were indeed all that Boccaccio claimed in terms of salvation—and deserve to be read today as well for the simple pleasures of a good story well told and here hopefully retold in a way that re-evokes that pleasure—I have also tried to argue that the *Decameron*'s stories were much more and often more than Boccaccio claimed or realized. For following with wonder and respect in the footsteps of more than six centuries of commentaries that have explained the deeper meaning and ultimately serious purposes of the *Decameron*, I have attempted to show how those one hundred tales may be read as historical documents that at the time both proposed and, in their own way, created a *Decameron* renaissance for those who read or heard them in late fourteenth-century Florence, the cities of northern Italy, and more widely and, in turn, how they contributed in a foundational way ultimately to the birth of a more general European renaissance and perhaps to visions of marriage, love, and sexuality that still underpin Western notions that are central to our shared culture today.

In this way of imagining the *Decameron,* I may be as naïve as Boccaccio was in thinking that these one hundred little tales could have such an impact and such power. But my defense is a rather simple one. To claim the obvious, those stories, like most of the best tales, tell many stories. And although readers and listeners can be swept up in the storyline or trauma of a tale, that ability to capture the imagination of a reader is not all that simple. For a good story does many things beyond its storyline. In the case of the Italian novella tradition, as the name implies, it presents something novel or we might say newsworthy and new—not so much in the Rinascimento negative sense of the new, which saw change to the new as change away from the proven traditional ways, substituting for the obvious success of the past, dangerous innovation—but rather in the sense of the different, the unexpected, and / or the strange. In other words, novel in that the novella presents a tale that challenges the expected and givens of society and contemporary culture and in doing so offers an opening to the history of its day often at

its most conflicted and revealing. Certainly *virtù*-ous adulterers, young
lovers thwarting the values of their society and the goals of their families to enjoy formally illicit sex, and more particularly clever gardeners
giving Christ horns or nuns noting that their vows to God were just another easily broken oath, all fit well this sense of the novel. And tyrants
finding love and becoming princes or young pagans finding the true,
real pleasures of serving the loving Christian God press this novelty
even further, opening novel vistas on life and its possibilities, then and
perhaps now as well.

　　But the novelty of the novella offers insights to a deeper yet aspect
of these apparently simple tales, for in virtually every case the novelty of
the best turns on its ability to evoke deeper resonances in the imagination of its readers of their life as lived and the world as experienced at
the moment. Resonances that from a historical perspective can often be
seen as either virtually eternal concerns deeply tied to the very nature of
being human or, in contrast, turn on issues specific to the tensions of a
particular cultural moment or now and then tied critically to both the
eternal and the moment; and in each case they are richly revealing for
understanding the past. The presentation of the emotions that cluster
in the *Decameron*'s tales around the depiction of love and sex, I have suggested, provide particularly powerful examples of this historical potential of stories. We laughed or at least, I hope, smiled at Calandrino's
foolish love. Indeed, in asking you to imagine yourself as Calandrino,
my not-so-subtle goal was to insinuate that you, like me, had experienced and could not just identify with but perhaps momentarily feel his
sudden, foolish, and slightly mad infatuation.

　　Yet, of course, while at one level Calandrino's mistaken love and
sexual desire can be experienced as a virtually timeless verity, the tale
forces an attentive reader to become aware of the way even his foolish
love has historically specific qualities that make it also culturally specific.
Calandrino's perception of the adultery his love entailed and of his wife,
Tessa, both true to the moment and rather distant from modern perceptions of adultery and marriage, merely begin to reveal the culturally specific differences at play. In fact, the whole novella turns on the humor of
a highly popular form of contemporary Florentine humor, the *beffa*, that
his buddies Bruno and Buffalmacco used to play on Calandrino's foolishness. A *beffa* whose delicious conclusion with Calandrino—and you, if you

were still imagining yourself as him—being pummeled and having his face scratched by his irate wife and his supposed friends laughing at his disappointment and violent demise. Actually, from our modern perspective, this may have felt a bit too violent a conclusion for a laughing tale, a silly love, and a foolish sexual desire that in the end came to nothing. Nothing, that is, beyond your disappointment in your momentary desire for a wistfully refined love and the violent pummeling it engendered. So Calandrino's tale is compelling and novel both for its eliciting of apparently ahistorical feelings that we can share and for a range of historically specific and revealing ways its contemporary cultural frame subtly shifted the narrative in the process of making the novella truly novel for its day.

Yet, the violence of Calandrino's beating and the different ways it might be read today as well as in its day suggest another aspect of stories that gives them power both in their telling and in our rereading of them, because stories often speak to the deeper tensions of a society. And this is true whether the author of the story intentionally is evoking such tensions or is merely responding to them as a careful observer of a particular society and its culture. It is not by accident then, I would suggest, that violence frequently appears in the novella literature of the Rinascimento and is a frequent fellow traveler of stories that involve love and sex. For love and sex often dialed up emotions that called for violence. And, with a certain cruel irony, the institution that in theory transformed the dangerous emotions associated with love and sex into ideally safe and profitable domestic tranquility—marriage—often was itself at the heart of such violence, as the *Decameron* reveals with evident concern in tale after tale. Already in the first chapter we encountered Cimone's violent carrying off of his love, Efigenia, to marry her, an abduction that involved no shortage of tears and indeed several bloody murders. Here the narrative line has taken us to a deep tension that clearly troubled Boccaccio and many of his contemporaries, disturbed by the often unhappy matches that arranged marriages created. At its most simple level, matches that were formed by fathers, parents, or relatives for family goals often were not matches that worked well for the couples themselves.

The ideal was that mature adults, not young lovers, were more capable of evaluating what would make a good pairing and a marriage that would endure and that served all. This ideal had real merit in the contemporary imagination, as love was seen as quick, flighty, and often fickle, dominated by emotions too unstable to form a long-term and solid alliance like marriage. Much more reliable was the wisdom of patriarchs and mature adults in forming such lifelong pairings. But the reality often fell far short of the ideal—a theme that the tales of the *Decameron* return to and document over and over again. Thus, the *Decameron,* much like the literature of its day, both prescriptive and imaginative, as well as contemporary criminal records, often offer a different tale where young lovers thwart the more mature plans of patriarchs, running off together at times with considerable violence, much as was the case with Cimone. Indeed, although it is difficult for a modern reader to accept, his violence in the name of love might well have been viewed by the *Decameron*'s readers as a heroic proof of the extent of that love.

And, of course, the violence that went with truly unhappy marriages could be even worse—a reality and a deep tension in matrimony that the *Decameron*'s tales return to often. Unhappy sexual relations in marriage were frequently overcome with clever adultery (again, their cleverness implying *virtù*) at least in the smiling tales when mutual love was involved or even, tellingly, when merely mutual pleasure was enjoyed by both partners. Yet troublingly, that was not always the case, especially when contemporary passions associated with traditional male honor became involved. Indeed, those passions could be murderously violent, as the case discussed in Chapter 2 of Guiglielmo Rossiglione reveals troublingly. It will be remembered that he cut out the heart of his onetime best friend, Guiglielmo Guardastagno, and had it served to his wife after he learned of their adulterous love. And, once again, it illuminates the violent emotions involved with what might be considered a deeply troublingly, yet clever, *beffa;* for Rossiglione had his cook prepare the heart as a gourmet dish, which his wife enjoyed greatly, then he informed her that he was not surprised that she enjoyed it so much, because it was the heart of the lover who had given her such great pleasure in life. That violence and cruel *beffa* seem to suggest a deeper contemporary reality that is developed more fully in later chapters: that honor could be presented virtually as another dangerous emotion in its own right, often deeply intertwined with love.

Yet, tellingly, dishonor and its violent emotions at the time did not automatically involve or require violent deeds, as had once been the case. In fact, in the novella of Agilulf, king of the Lombards, discussed in Chapter 5, he *virtù*-ously controlled his feelings of outraged honor. His wife, Teudelinga, unbeknownst to her, had been made love to by his groom—more rape than adultery perhaps from a modern perspective. But that was not necessarily the case from a fourteenth-century one, the novella makes clear; thus, the king avoided all the unnecessary violence and dishonor that came with too quick and too emotional a response to his dishonor. And, rather than responding like Rossiglione with violence, with Agilulf's emotions controlled by his *virtù* / reason, he wisely brought the matter to a happy conclusion. At a deeper level, this was because he understood that in a society where consensus realities created identity and reputation, deeds like that of the groom, if unknown to those who judged and negotiated identity and reputation, simply did not exist. Thus, although he felt dishonored and outraged at the fact that someone had slept with his wife, he *virtù*-ously considered more deeply his feelings and accepted the fact that (from a contemporary perspective) there was nothing he could do about them that would not make the situation worse and sagely decided to close the matter with a warning to the unknown culprit to not try to repeat his crime. In sum, he was revealed as an ideal husband and an ideal ruler at least from the perspective of *virtù*, consensus realities, and the *Decameron*.

Yet, it is perhaps in the last chapter that the tyrant Gualtieri's misuse of honor reveals its most complex contemporary emotional dimensions. Playing on his peasant wife Griselda's love and loyalty to him as her husband and lord, he regularly evokes fears of dishonor that supposedly torment him because of his marriage with her, a peasant of no status. Once again, his deeds in the name of the feelings his honor evoked were not based on those feelings but rather actually calculated to test his wife's loyalty and commitment to satisfying him. Still, for Griselda, those lies about his feelings of honor work in the economy of the tale because she is portrayed as accepting this emotional component of honor. Significantly, then, the tale requires that the reader recognize honor as an emotion, even if Gualtieri's claims are presented as both calculated and false.

In the end, honor and its associated emotions permeate this tale, for even Griselda's quiet acceptance of Gualtieri's dishonoring treatment in putting her aside for a new more honorable wife turns on and evokes powerful emotions. When he informs her of his plans to put her aside— tellingly, in a public setting where all can judge via consensus realities her dishonor—he at first insists that she return home to her peasant hovel with only what she brought with her as her dowry. As she had no dowry, that means naked with all the dishonor that implied and, of course, that dishonor turns not only on her nakedness but yet another central honor issue associated with marriage in the tales and in life itself—the dowry. Griselda's lack of same was one more black mark on her honorable status, and by parading it before his subjects at this already vicious, demeaning moment, readers would have understood his cruelty and presumably felt her dishonor. Indeed, just in case anyone missed this, Gualtieri's subjects objected to this unfair treatment, revealing that they felt the dishonor and were uncomfortable enough about it to complain openly. And, finally, even Griselda showed a bit of emotion that might be associated with honor, asking that she be allowed to return home in at least her shift, pointing out that although she had brought no dowry to their marriage she had contributed her virginity.

Her logic (which would have been clear to contemporaries) was that the giving up of the honor of her virginity could be equated with the normally required sacrifice of a dowry in order to marry, a claim that was actually made in cases of broken promises of marriage in the courts. In such cases, women regularly claimed that they had given their virginity to their lovers in return for their promise of matrimony, as we saw in the tale of Alessandro winning the hand of the daughter of the king of England in marriage, thanks to his mannerly and *virtù*-ous ways (II, 3). There, although she admits her love for him, before consenting to give him her virginity, she demands that he promise to marry her. And, actually, that promise to marry him is played out in the tale in a way that suggests that, with the consent of both, they are actually married when they make love, even if the marriage is later approved and reenacted by the more powerful patriarchal figures that loom behind the action—literally patriarchal in the figure of the pope and in her father, the king of England.

But even Gualtieri was moved ultimately by Griselda's pleas for a modicum of honor and his subjects' demands that he treat the wife who had given birth to his two children with the honor that she deserved,

finally permitting her to return home in her shift, a concession so minimal that it reinforces the emotional weight of his cruelty. Doubling the
dose, he soon thereafter orders her to prepare his palace for his new bride
as a humble servant. All this playing on the emotions associated with
honor at the time leads to Dioneo's famous lines that sum up his sense
of how Griselda should have treated Gualtieri's multiple dishonors: "Who
else but Griselda would have been able without shedding a tear but almost
smilingly to accept the stern and never before [thus once again negatively
new] heard of trials of Gualtieri? Who would have acted incorrectly in the
face of being thrown out of [her] house with just a shift, if she had found
another to stroke her pussy *(scuotere il pillicione)*, winning herself in the
process something positive *(una bella roba)*." Honor and the emotions that
were its fellow travelers in love had the potential to be deeply dangerous
and destructive in the *Decameron.*

When we turn from honor to the violence that courting and courtship could evoke, a central focus of Chapter 2, the dangers of the feelings associated with love and sexual desire become, if anything, more
complex and troubling in the *Decameron.* The tale of Nastagio degli Onesti opens a vista on this theme that involves a more subtle and complex
violence. Indeed, with a certain modern justice, his tale has recently
been read as an example of the cruel violence that men at the time used
against women to obtain the sexual favors that a masculine view of
love and successful courtship seemed to require. The situation is made
more complicated by the fact that in many ways at the time the novella
evoked the literary tradition of courtly love still popular at midcentury
in the way love was imagined and idealized. In that tradition, a man
demonstrated his love by submitting to his beloved and demonstrating
through the many sacrifices of courtship a kind of heroic passion that
when successfully carried out seemed to virtually require that a woman
respond not just with love but with sexual favors to demonstrate that
she was indeed a fair and deserving object of masculine courtship. In
this vision, love and courtship formed the base of a complex "game"
where the players appeared to be locked into roles that required for all
sacrifice and for women the dangerous sacrifice of their highly prized
and often aggressively defended chastity and sexual honor. Obviously,
it is not clear how many actually accepted this extreme vision of courtship that seemed to lie at the heart of the courtly love ideal, especially

how many women. But for us the question remains: for the *Decameron*, was this extreme form of the game of courtship so binding, or were women offered in its tales other options—options that were intriguing, made for good stories, and in the process brought other emotions, admittedly still often violent, into play for them and for men.

In this context, Nastagio's tale offers plenty of violence and much to consider. What grabs the reader's attention most forcefully today perhaps is the bloody ripping out of the heart of a naked woman fleeing her lover and his hounds, witnessed in horror by Nastagio. Quickly, however, he learns that her lover had courted her assiduously in life and after death was condemned to repeat this vendetta vengeance over and over again on the island of Classe near Ravenna because of his own suicide for love. The scene clearly evokes Dante and the violent punishments that he encountered in the Hell he visited with Virgil as his guide, discovered, tellingly, while wandering lost in the middle of his life on Classe. But for Nastagio it evoked much more, because he was living there in exile from nearby Ravenna, because his own unsuccessful courtship of a disdainful young noblewoman had literally destroyed him in that city as a lover and, in turn, as a young man of worth in his own right. In essence, the consensus realities that created his identity as a young lover and aristocrat had been destroyed by that unnamed woman's disdain and scorn. The parallel between his own suffering and exile and the *Inferno*-esque punishment of the already dead lovers that he witnessed was not lost on him, as, of course, it was that violent vision that drove the tale toward its "happy" conclusion.

Realizing that that violent moment revealed the divinely ordained punishment of lovers who did not correctly master their emotions and play the game of courtship correctly with the required manners and mutual respect, Nastagio recognized that he could use that moment repeated regularly every Friday to convince his beloved that she had treated him cruelly and unfairly and thus win her understanding and her love. This at first might seem unlikely, but with a closer look at the emotions at play in both cases of courtship from a fourteenth-century point of view, the source of the violence in the tale is significantly shifted from the suffering male lovers involved to the women they courted. In both cases, the women had not just rejected the love offered them, as was ultimately their right; they had rejected that love disdainfully and with scorn. And they had done so repeatedly in the public arena where courtship was carried out—in the arena of consensus realities where one's very identity was on trial. In other tales, where women rejected male lovers gently and with the manners that courtship required, they were carefully presented as playing the game of courtship as it should be played. In those cases, as we have seen, they were portrayed as positive characters behaving correctly, even as they denied would-be lovers who courted them, often heroically, like Federigo degli Alberighi, whose courting of the chaste Monna Giovanna cost him virtually everything he had and prized.

But the emotions associated with a woman's disdain or scorn, especially publicly expressed in the course of a man's mannered and correct courtship, was a different matter, a giving in to or at times an enjoying of ugly emotions in courtship that even God punished—at least the God imagined in the tale of Nastagio, who justly ordered the eternally repeated gruesome penalty of the scornful beloved woman on Classe. Moreover, both rejected lovers, the living and the dead, the actual victims from the perspective of the tale, responded to this violent disdain with violent emotions as well but, significantly, against themselves. The dead lover condemned to carry out eternally the divinely ordained punishment of the woman he loved so much in life, of course, earned this punishment because he committed suicide in the face of his beloved's rejection, one might say an ultimate violence. Nastagio's violence is perhaps less clear at first, but his withdrawal from the civil world and from that central aspect of his identity that was as an aristocratic courting youth was a more metaphoric suicide but real nonetheless. Yet, still alive, of course, and in an exile, it was a violence at least more open to overcoming, which, of course, is required to make the story work.

The complexity of the violence and the emotions associated with Nastagio's mistreatment as a courting lover is further developed in the tale of Rinieri, the young scholar (who becomes suggestively older as the tale develops) who also courts unsuccessfully, in this case, Elena, a young widow who is presented as enjoying mistreating the men who fall in love with her and unwisely decide to court her. Once again, the tale's violence against a woman troublingly catches the modern eye. And there is no doubt that she is brutally treated, especially as her suffering is presented in particularly gruesome detail that seems to be spelled out with troubling cruelty and satisfaction. But her suffering, for all its extremes, is balanced by the earlier and equally detailed violence that Rinieri suffered at her behest. And, in fact, his earlier suffering came close to causing his death, while hers was "merely" extremely painful and momentarily disfiguring. Still, comparative levels of suffering or violence do not really capture the novella's import, as it is less about equality for different genders or equality in suffering and more about the reasons behind the emotions and deeds involved.

Once again, Rinieri suffered as a lover and a young man courting correctly the woman he had unwisely fallen in love with. In contrast, Elena enjoyed mistreating her would-be lover as he courted her. Although her scorn was less publicly expressed, it was actually more fully detailed with careful descriptions of the pleasure she felt in scorning and demeaning poor Rinieri—once again emphasizing the negatives of courting misused by a woman. Was this misogynist or a masculine fear of the power women could misuse in courting? Probably both to a degree, but at the same time, in her emotions expressed as she cruelly treats Rinieri, we see revealed what appears to be an emotion that the contemporary ideals of chastity and the ideals of correct female behavior could evoke: the pleasure of refusal in itself. Elena is presented first and foremost as richly enjoying her refusal and the power of her scorn, especially in its violence. And there is no question that in the economy of the tale she is presented, as a result, as the culprit, fully deserving her violent punishment. And, in turn, in the end, Rinieri demonstrates his *virtù* and deserved status as a man of worth, despite his foolish mistake in misjudging Elena and falling in love with her and afoul of her cruel pleasures at his expense.

Once again, behind all this, we hear a careful evaluation of the dangerous emotions that are entangled with love and courtship in the *Decameron*, in Boccaccio's fears, and at least in the imagination of those who read its tales in Florence at the end of the fourteenth century. Not surprisingly, that evaluation suggested rules for courtship in a public arena that protected with mannerly behavior both men and women from the emotions that courtship and love dangerously exposed. Men had to demonstrate their love via refined courtship—something that Calandrino or Master Simone, the eventual Count of the Cesspool, could not demonstrate—before they could hope for the rewards of courtship.

And, significantly, those rewards were not just sexual but at their best a happy long-desired marriage as is asserted in the tales of Nastagio or Federigo degli Alberighi. Women, in turn, had to demonstrate their correct behavior as lovers, at least in the *Decameron*, not by giving in to the sexual demands of their lovers but rather with a reciprocal refined and mannered behavior that indicated their interest in being loved (and the level of that interest) or their lack of same. Significantly, in this a woman's desires in courtship were presented as at once critical and, at times, more troublingly, as potentially dangerous and negative. And while this vision can be viewed as misogynistic, it should be noted that even in its most negative aspects, it stresses that women have real power and should have real power over their bodies and their loves. Even when a woman might seem to be pressed by courtship rules to succumb to male desire, as in the case of Nastagio's marriage to his beloved, the tale is careful to explain that his bride in the end loved him and did so because she realized that his courtship not only deserved but had won her love, once she recognized the incorrect emotions that had led her to disdain his true love. This is evidently a difficult reading to accept with modern sensibilities and values, but it functions in the economy of the tale and the contemporary ideals of courtship and marriage that are at the heart of the *Decameron*.

Of course, as these tales and others that detail the violent potentials of love in Chapter 2 suggest, such violence could and often did result in death. Chapter 3 follows that theme to a conclusion deeply related to the promised purpose of the *Decameron:* helping people and especially the women of Florence deal with the devastation of the plague. For, of course, for the survivors of the plague, mourning their lost loved ones was one of the most difficult emotions they faced. And in the tale of Lisabetta da Messina, mourning her dead lover, Lorenzo, that emotional suffering of loss had become so much a part of her life that it had become virtually her identity. Thus, although her lover's death was not a result of the plague but rather at the hands of her brothers, worried about their honor and hers in enjoying a secret premarital relationship with someone that they considered not worthy of their sister, that murder evoked many of the central themes of the *Decameron* as suited the central, fifth tale of the fourth day, dedicated to loves that ended tragically. For in addition to the central role of the concerns and emotions associated with mourning, love lost, and dishonor, once again consensus realities played a significant role not only in her brothers' decision to eliminate her lover but also in her slow but sure decline and death. For in the end, her mourning over her lover's head, first in its pot growing basil and ultimately in her refusal to put that memento of death away and move on with her life, isolated her from those around her in society and ultimately left her with no groups to help her rebuild her identity via their consensus realities of who she was. In a way, with her identity gone, lost to her mourning, she was already dead before she officially died.

And throughout this tragedy, *virtù*, the one thing that could have saved Lisabetta from death at the hands of her mourning, is significantly absent from her tale. And that is especially noteworthy in a day dedicated to tragic tales of love that turn out badly, for in most of the other tales told that day, the lovers are depicted as heroic, their tragedy elevated by their *virtù*-ous behavior carefully portrayed and identified as such. The contrast is clear. Lisabetta gave in to her passions and her mourning, never using *virtù* to moderate those emotions or to renegotiate the consensus realities that one needed for support and literally to exist and survive in the Rinascimento. Thus, unlike the other lovers of the day with their heroic loves that failed despite their impressive *virtù*, Lisabetta died unnoticed and clearly unhonored. Her tale was a morality tale that laid out starkly all the dangers that love offered when its emotions ruled unchecked by *virtù*, a moral particularly suited to the situation women found themselves in in Florence following the plague. In fact, this reading offers yet another reason for seeing the fourth day of tales as particularly significant, as Lisabetta's story pulls together all the themes that make the emotion of love dangerous and offers an answer that not only suits its historical moment but that also evokes the critical relationship between the emotions associated with love and sex and the power of *virtù* to mold those emotions into forms that offer the possibility of having a civic society, a *civiltà*, where love and sex could be enjoyed without death, violence, or even danger following the plague.

From this perspective, it is particularly significant that the *Decameron* ends after ten days of tales with the famous tale of Griselda's suffering at the hands of her cruel husband, Gualtieri, the marquise of Saluzzo. Often read as one of Boccaccio's most misogynist moments, with Gualtieri's harsh treatment of his humble peasant wife apparently defended as an ideal way to select and treat a wife, there is much in the telling of the tale by the *Decameron*'s most transgressive narrator, Dioneo, that undermines that traditional interpretation. Thus, in Chapter 5, drawing again on the crucial role of *virtù*, the story is re-framed as in a way Boccaccio's *The Prince*, anticipating Machiavelli and many of the political thinkers of the Cinquecento, who saw *virtù* as the answer to the perceived political and social crisis of that century. For, like many of those political thinkers, *virtù* becomes in this novella the key to successful political leadership as well as to successful citizenship and life in the urban world of the day. Suggestively, then, in this, the *Decameron*'s last tale, the cultural and social disciplining power of *virtù* and its ability to reform society after the plague becomes a key even in the political realm to a better future while providing a suitable ending to its tales.

This reading requires a healthy shift of perspective from the suf-fering of Griselda, which cannot be overlooked, obviously, to the per-spective of Gualtieri, who actually is carefully presented over and over again as lacking *virtù* not just in his relationship with Griselda but also in his relationship with his subjects as ruler of Saluzzo. For, in many ways, the tale plays on the many perceived parallels between the rule of a family by a husband and the rule of a prince over his subjects. And, once again, at the heart of that parallel lies *virtù*. For, in both areas, the tale offers one long account of untoward behavior that demonstrates its lack both in marriage and rule. And, tellingly but not surprisingly, in both cases this lack is reinforced by Gualtieri's lack of love in both areas as well; for regularly the reader is forced to witness his lack of interest in and love for his wife and his lack of interest in and love for his subjects. This central failure to love and to act with the *virtù* required of a hus-band or a prince literally opens the narrative of the tale and continues being more and more emphasized as it progresses.

Immediately, then, we learn that Gualtieri is upset with his sub-jects because they want him to marry and take up the reins of princely power, putting aside his youthful pleasures and undisciplined ways. For from the perspective of the day, marriage was the moment when men took up the mantle of mature males, leaving aside their earlier carefree ways and becoming responsible leaders of not only their families but, in this case, their realms. At least this was clearly what Gualtieri's subjects had in mind and expected of a prince who ruled them with the required love of a ruler. That love required the sacrifice of youthful pleasures and the taking up of the mantle of rule as a mature, *virtù*-ous adult male. But, as we have seen, this was not what Gualtieri wanted, and, unmoved by love for his subjects, he resisted their pleas in favor of his immature personal pleasures—evidently a fault of many rulers who were more tyrants than princes.

Finally, however, when he decided that he must marry to quiet the complaints of his subjects, he thwarted their expectations (and the expectations of the day), for, rather than arranging his marriage in consultation with his family and with the advice of his most important nobles, as was ideally the case in such important moments of matrimonial alliance, he chose unexpectedly to marry the humble peasant Griselda. She obviously offered none of the qualities that a prince truly interested in ruling well or serving his subjects would have opted for led by *virtù*. Poor, without connections, virtually without family, her only positive attribute when he married her was that she was so humble and poor that she would accept his every demand and not interfere with his youthful pleasures. And that was something that Gualtieri made clear from the first, asking her in their very first meeting if she was ready to accept his every request and not make any demands on him. This ultimatum he continued to make clear with test after test as the tale takes us deeper and deeper into its negative depiction of Gualtieri.

And, once again, that treatment of an unloved wife elicits the main themes of the *Decameron* now from a political / matrimonial perspective; for Gualtieri's treatment of Griselda, ultimately, because it lacked love, was dishonoring, cruel, and exactly "beastly," as Dioneo described him and ultimately as is displayed in full in his lack of *virtù*. And, of course, it was not a large jump to see that the same was true of his relationship to his subjects. Over and over again in the tale, Gualtieri comes across as the anti-prince or tyrant, just the type of tyrant that republican Florence, surrounded by aggressive tyrants at the time, feared and indeed just the type of tyrant that Florence had thrown out earlier in the century when they overthrew a Gualtieri of their own, Walter of Brienne. But without retelling once again Griselda's many trials at the hands of her tyrant / husband / lord, she does return at the end of the tale to finally play an exemplary role. Not as an ideally obedient wife but, rather, as fits the *Decameron* better, as an ideal loving wife despite all her mistreatment. In fact, Dioneo carefully specifies at the last that it was her love for Gualtieri, along with her peasant's ability to accept mistreatment, rather than the acceptance of her subservient status as wife, that led her to quietly acquiesce to her husband's every demand. And, in the end, her love triumphed. For with albeit hollow excuses for his mistreatment, Gualtieri finally admits that he has fallen in love with his wife, Griselda, and wishes to live with her happily ever after.

From a modern perspective, the triteness of this unlikely ending, which even Dioneo cannot resist making a few obscene comments about, tends to mask what a revolutionary ending it was when written. For, once again, as in the case of Cimone, love had literally exploded the potential of *virtù* in a character, Gualtieri, who had previously lacked both and been essentially incapable of either. And love did so in a marriage that was now transformed from a nightmare and a disaster into a success based on love, as unlikely as that would have seemed to many at the time. Moreover, discovering love thanks to Griselda, Gualtieri was now capable of loving his subjects, who, in turn, were ready to love and honor him because he had finally found love. Thus, the tyrant became the prince, with love and *virtù* winning in the end. Even Machiavelli would have been happy with that ending.

But, of course, that tale, while it was the last, was in many ways not the last word on the way love and *virtù* went together, because to a great extent it left out the last part of the trinity that drove the *Decameron*: sex. And it might be suggested that while politics clearly required their due in the symphony of life that its tales played, the driving line of its stories was the power that trinity had to change life following the plague at its most profound and personal levels. Perhaps the tales that reveal this best fall at the center of the work, the fifth day, where that vision is presented most positively, indeed, in the last tale of the day becoming virtually transcendent. That day is dedicated to lovers who by dint of their efforts—usually described as *virtù*—overcome great obstacles to gain their desires.

And it begins, not surprisingly given our discussion of the day's first tale in Chapter 1 with the adventures of Cimone, who was transformed apparently miraculously from a savage living in rural ignorance incapable of the manners or the *civiltà* that the social position of his family required to become an impressive youth, who flourished in the urban world as a refined upper-class aristocrat, not just with the manners and grace his status warranted but as essentially a philosopher. As noted above, the source of that miracle was perfectly true to the *Decameron*'s major themes, turning as it did on both love and *virtù*. And while some of his deeds as a heroic lover may justly trouble modern readers, they not only demonstrated the true depth of his love and the strength of the emotions it evoked in him; in the end, with love and *virtù*, he overcame all obstacles—as the day required, it will be remembered. Thus, finally, he married Efigenia, and once the dust settled, they lived happily ever after as married lovers, as the *Decameron* required for true love guided by *virtù*, even if at times that *virtù* required violence. As such, the tale of Cimone's winning of true love in the best form imaginable via marriage starts the day, evoking all its themes even as it suggestively complicates things with its troubling violence and clears the way for it to be truly heroic.

In fact, one of the most seductive examples of the complexity of these tales is the famous tale of Rustico and Alibech, which ends the fifth day and which in a way might be seen as the climax of the *Decameron*'s considerations of love and sex. Actually, however, I would suggest that it is not so much a summation as a tale that literally transcends the discourses on love and sex found in Boccaccio's tales, especially if one follows its imaginative and poetic implications to conclusions that the culture of the day would have allowed, even if it may be that those conclusions probably transcend even what Boccaccio might have seen in the tale. For, at one level, the tale is a simple story of a clever *beffa* cleverly carried off—again evoking the power of *virtù*—by a hermit who overestimates his moral resolve and ability to resist the temptations of a young, innocent pagan girl asking to be taught how to serve the Christian God that she has heard such good things about. Of course, as is the case in many of Boccaccio's anticlerical tales, this Rustico's noble resolve and moral standards are quickly overcome by the tempting beauties of the young woman, Alibech.

Thus, he appears to turn Christian theology at its most basic and profound level to his questionable purposes, cleverly and blasphemously explaining to her that the way to serve the Christian God is to put the Devil back in Hell where Christ condemned him in the beginning but from which he has escaped to create all the evil that troubles humanity in God's creation. And, of course, after instructing Alibech to strip naked as he does, she notices that he has something strange sticking out in front of him—described in the tale as the "resurrection of the flesh," adding blasphemy to blasphemy. When she innocently questions what that thing is, he helpfully, and in many ways in tune with the theological vision of the day, explains that it is his devil, a devil that is causing him great discomfort, which he then points out she can aid him with and in the process serve the Christian God by "putting that Devil back in Hell." A Hell that, in fact, she has for just that purpose. Thus it is that Alibech learns of the pleasures of serving the Christian God and humorously of the truth of the claims that those Christians had made that had led her to go in search of someone to teach her how to serve God. Satisfied with that Christianity and its pleasures, which she lauds enthusiastically, she stays on with Rustico until her increasing demands to serve God more often tire out her desert hermit, who finds that he was far too clever, given his meager diet of desert herbs and vegetables, to hold up his end of putting the Devil back in Hell. But he is saved, and in a way Christianity's reputation for offering the pleasures of serving God, by yet another deity, good old unreliable Fortuna. For just as things are falling apart in the suddenly blossoming desert paradise of Alibech, her father passes away, and she is called home to take up the fortune she has inherited and marry. All of which leaves Rustico to recover from his clever *beffa* and Alibech to live happily ever after, presumably serving the Christian God from time to time with her pagan husband putting the Devil back in Hell.

Yet, this rather simple and straightforward reading of the tale, while it highlights perhaps the highest form of love imaginable in the Rinascimento—the love of God—and the highest form of pleasure—the pleasure of serving Him—does so as the result of a doubly blasphemous pornotheological *beffa*: putting the Devil back in Hell and, more troubling yet, Rustico's "resurrection of the flesh." In contrast with Boccaccio's more typical critiques of clerical misbehavior, these much more questionable presentations of fundamental theological beliefs in a clearly carefully crafted story make this novella truly novel. The only other moment in the *Decameron* that might compare flashes by quickly at the end of the novella of Masetto da Lamporecchio (III, 1), where after a more typical tale involving the sexual exploits of nuns and the

children born in the process, referring to the relatively happy and contented retirement of their father, Masetto, from the convent where he
served so valiantly for years as the gardener plowing more than their
fields, Boccaccio-author comments that this is the reward that Christ
gives to those who put horns on his head. Clearly, however, the theological dimension is much more developed and much more imaginative in
Rustico and Alibech's tale and much more troubling for many readers
then and now.

First, of course, with its setting in the desert near Gafsa, where Alibech has gone to search out desert hermits to learn how to serve God,
the tale takes the reader to a virtually legendary holy site, where one
would expect that the serving of God was practiced at its best by men
who sacrificed their lives to live far from the pleasures of the city, fru-
gally surviving on herbs and wild roots, in humble hovels, totally committed to what they believe is the Christian life. Yet what Alibech finds
there is a series of barren hermits with all the negatives of their desert
life on display, literally and profoundly a desert after the Fall. And, despite their isolation, rather than being morally strong enough to accept
the beautiful young acolyte, they reject her, her divinely given beauty,
and her holy quest. Fearing the sexual temptation she represents—in
other words, fearing the emotions that she excites despite all their efforts at holiness—they fear to share their vision of Christianity with her
one after another until, of course, the foolishly overconfident Rustico
takes her in and fails rapidly in his own ability to resist.

Still, for all the blasphemy of his eventual and clever pornotheology
and his apparently false representation of Christianity, his failure to resist
the temptation of her beauty is presented humorously without distress or
even negative comments. Rather, having seen already the bleakness of the
desert and the life of the desert hermits, in contrast for Rustico and Alibech, the desert seems to bloom and come to life with Alibech's service
to the Christian God, putting the Devil back in Hell. With this sudden
blossoming of their desert, one is tempted to reconsider that new garden,
compared with the earthly paradise explicitly, that initiates the tales of
the fifth day. For, after a day of repose suitably dedicated to contemplating
Christ's loving sacrifice for humanity on the Cross, the *brigata* moves to
a new garden and initiates a series of tales that feature triumphant accounts of love overcoming all obstacles, the theme of the day. Thus, a

sudden blossoming of the desert into a virtual garden of Christian sexual pleasure in the name of the love for God in the last tale of the day suggests that we might consider that Alibech's service to God has re-created in their small lives a new earthly Garden of Eden.

If that is the case, and if one is willing to follow the theological implications of this vision a step further, it is interesting to note that Alibech in her innocence functions as a kind of anti-Eve in this tale. For Eve, of course, was widely believed at the time to have sinned by turning against God and eating the apple that caused the Fall, the exclusion of Adam and Eve from the Garden of Eden, and all the punishments of a wrathful God that her sin involved. Alibech, on the other hand, without sin—for she did not consider the pleasure she felt sexual but rather understood it and enjoyed it as service to God—undid that first sin in the name of a loving Christianity and returned the couple to a new Garden of Eden, suddenly blossoming in the desert near Gafsa. In a way, it might even be imagined that Rustico was the anti-Adam in this apparently cleverly imaginative reversal of the story from Genesis. For he, unlike Adam, was not the victim of an evil Eve (incidentally also seeking knowledge like Alibech) but instead the one who led her astray, thinking that he was sinning even as actually he was leading her back to the Garden of Eden. And, tellingly, in this love and sex, when pure and true, as was the case with Alibech, not only served God but together they provided the ultimate pleasure as she repeatedly and enthusiastically proclaims in her new Garden of Eden, serving God as Adam and Eve did before the Fall, even if that service was not quite what Genesis seemed to claim.

Already pushing the imaginative limits of the tale, a good historian might be wise to leave the theological reveries this tale evokes right there—a perfect ultimate and literally transcendental view of the positive possibilities of love and sex in a world in the process of reforming following the plague. But storytelling in a work like the *Decameron* as well as in the historical imagination it evokes creates a dangerous mix, especially when considering a truly novel novella, and thus I confess that in Chapter 4 I succumbed to the temptation to follow the pornotheological implications of Alibech's love and Rustico's sins not so much to their logical conclusion as to their poetic fruition. For the aesthetics and symmetry of the tale in the context of the religious controversies and visions that swirled about and deeply colored the life of early Rinascimento Florence (and northern Italy and Europe more generally), strengthened by the devastation of the plague, led many people to believe that a profound change was at hand. Some following in the classic line of biblical exegesis believed that the Last Judgment and the end of time had arrived with the plague being a powerful sign that, as long expected, the last days had come. Others, although less remembered today, however, were offering a different vision that was enjoying considerable support in Florence and northern Italy at the time. They, following in the footsteps of medieval prophets like Joachim of Flora and the logic of a Trinitarian vision of Christianity, argued that the plague and other signs revealed that the third and last age of human history was at hand, the age of the Holy Spirit.

In this vision, as we have seen, the first age of humanity had followed the Fall and exclusion of Adam and Eve from the Garden of Eden and was characterized by a troubled relationship with a wrathful God the Father; this difficult era or dispensation was overthrown with the incarnation of Christ and his loving death on the Cross to save humanity, inaugurating a new age characterized by a loving God, Christ, and his Church—the loving God Alibech sought to serve by putting the Devil back in Hell. But, in a Trinitarian view of human history, where there were two ages, there was bound to be a third led by the third person of the Trinity, the Holy Spirit. And theologians and prophets using the Bible to calculate the length of the first age were pointing out that if the ages were of parallel length, as logic seemed to require, the second age should be concluding (actually perhaps had already concluded), and the plague and the other strange changes of the day seemed to promise that this transition was nigh or even already underway.

Without repeating all the signs beyond the plague that seemed to indicate this, in a compelling way Alibech seemed to herald this change, for her approach to serving God did away with the Catholic Church—it was direct and immediate without the need of an intermediary, much as many assumed would be the case in the last age of the Holy Spirit. And while it might be objected that her service was actually just sex and not all that spiritual, a closer reading of her tale suggests quite the opposite. For as noted, preshadowing Foucault, she did not know her pleasure as sex. She was so young, so innocent, and so pure that she did not know what sex was. Rather, she knew it as the ultimate and direct pleasure given by God, and it is not hard to imagine from this perspective that it was the love of the Holy Spirit that would be typical of the last age dominated by the third person of the Trinity. In sum, just as Christ's sacrifice led to the second age, Alibech's pleasure opened the door to the last age—a last age and a new dispensation of loving direct spiritual pleasure in a purified flesh. Could such imaginative fantasies have been possible in the fourteenth century in Florence? Actually, for all their unlikelihood to modern eyes, the answer is yes; for indeed those who read the footnotes of Chapter 4 will recognize that this was almost exactly the message of more than one heretical sect that promised to lead its followers into the age of the Holy Spirit led by women holy figures. Alibech, as a new savior, however, is almost certainly too big a claim for even the centrally located last tale of the fifth day of the *Decameron* and the very high value that is given to the trinity of love, sex, and *virtù* in its tales. But it is a way of seeing the novella that is fun to imagine and adds to the pleasure of those one hundred tales dedicated to pleasure and to reimagining the world and a better life following the plague, for women, for men, and for us all.

NOTES

LISTENING TO THE *DECAMERON*

1. It is, then, a historical reading and as such, in the notes to this book, I will not attempt an extensive review of the massive critical literature on the *Decameron* or Boccaccio. Both would bury the discussion that follows in notes and threaten to make it unreadable. Rather, I will try to cite the most relevant works to the discussion in each chapter and focus on the historical world in which the tales of the *Decameron* were heard and read, in a way using it as the central focus for a microhistory or microstudy of its day and the emotions that swirled around love and sex at the time. See, however, Marilyn Migiel's review of the recent trends in the critical literature especially from the perspective of the reader's response, a perspective that I largely share in this book from a more historical perspective, in her *The Ethical Dimension of the Decameron* (Toronto: University of Toronto Press, 2015): 3–17, 161–63, even if many of her clever readings focusing on translation work less well from my historical perspective, as actually her critical approach anticipates would be the case. For the *Decameron,* I have relied on the authoritative edition of Vittore Branca: Giovanni Boccaccio, *Decameron,* ed. Vittore Branca (Turin: Einaudi, 1992) and its invaluable notes, which serve as an important starting point for any literary or historical discussion of the text. The English translations are mine throughout based on that edition. In addition, the publications of Branca on Boccaccio and the *Decameron* remain seminal: for a start, see his *Boccaccio medievale e nuovi studi sul Decameron* (Florence: Sansoni, 1996).

2. I use the term "Rinascimento" instead of the more common "Italian Renaissance" because in my major rethinking of the period in Italy, *The Renaissance in Italy: A Social and Cultural History of the Rinascimento* (New York: Cambridge University Press, 2015), I argued for a larger time span for the period when Italian society and culture were significantly different from the rest of Europe, essentially from c.1250 to c.1575. That work and the historical discussions that underpin the analysis there, and that follows here, have relied heavily on the path-breaking work of the last two generations of innovative Anglo-American scholars working on Florence

and the Rinascimento more generally from an archival perspective. Especially important have been the studies of Gene Brucker, Samuel K. Cohen, Lauro Martines, David Herlihy, and John Najemy listed in the bibliography. Also crucial have been the works of Robert Black, Peter Burke, William Caferro, Francesco Cardini, Philip Gavit, James Hankins, John Henderson, Philip J. Jones, Christiane Klapisch-Zuber, Catherine Kovesi, Thomas Kuehn, Carol Lansing, Edward Muir, Brian Pullan, Daniel Lord Smail, Sharon T. Strocchia, Nicholas Terpstra, Ronald Witt, and Andrea Zorzi, the most important of which are also listed in the bibliography. In many respects, the *Decameron* might be read, and often is read here, as an extension of their work and as a text that offers the base for a microhistory that exemplifies from the perspective of a literary text much of the discussion of the early Rinascimento presented in the first chapters of *The Renaissance in Italy*.

3. In a strange way, the tales were sung and translated widely in northern Europe as well, perhaps suggesting a sea change in the cultural world of the day that turned on and reflected the way in which the French leadership of the late Middle Ages was being replaced by an Italian leadership that would endure for two centuries at least. If that is too big a claim, at least the *Decameron* was a game changer for the genre of the novella / short story and the literary tradition of Europe more broadly. For this see now: *A Boccaccian Renaissance: Essays on the Early Modern Impact of Giovanni Boccaccio and His Works,* Martin Eisner and David Lummus, eds. (Notre Dame, IN: University of Notre Dame Press, 2019).

4. See note 2 above, as well as the bibliography and the notes throughout the text that indicate the most important studies.

5. That scholarship, needless to say, is immense and immensely erudite, but as my reading is concerned not with how Boccaccio may or may not have used the classic texts he studied but rather with how the *Decameron* and its tales would have been read and heard at the time by a broader public than a scholarly elite, it focuses more on the broader cultural world of his day. Still, the bibliography provides an overview of the studies that attempt to analyze the many classical and medieval influences on the tales discussed here. For this perspective, however, see the works listed in the bibliography by Guyda Armstrong, Albert Russell Ascoli, Vittore Branca, Martin Eisner, Tobias Foster Gittes, Michaela Pasche Grudin, Robert Grudin, James Hankins, Robert Hollander, Timothy Kircher, David Lumus, Simone Marchesi, Millicent Marcus, Ronald L. Martinez, F. Regina Psaki, Janet Levarie Smarr, Ronald Witt, and Gur Zak.

6. In sum, a historical reading of the *Decameron* as a source for the shared culture of its day. For a fuller discussion of the strengths and weaknesses of the concept of a shared primary culture and its implications for the cultural history of the Rinascimento, see Ruggiero, *The Renaissance in Italy,* 205–67.

7. For a brief but thoughtfully suggestive article on how scholars might re-think an elusive and multivoiced Boccaccio from an interdisciplinary perspective, see Guyda Armstrong, Rhiannon Daniels, and Stephen J. Milner, "Boccaccio as a Cultural Mediator," in *The Cambridge Companion to Boccaccio,* Guyda Armstrong, Rhiannon Daniels, and Stephen J. Milner, eds. (Cambridge: Cambridge University Press, 2015): 3–19, and throughout that volume, especially Stephen J. Milner's essay "Boccaccio's *Decameron* and the Semiotics of the Everyday," 83–100. An interesting example of the multiple approaches to reading Boccaccio's intent in the *Decameron* can be found in the recent series of three articles on the central role compassion plays in the *Decameron* published in *I Tatti Studies in the Italian Renaissance* (2019) 22.1 in a special forum titled "Boccaccio and Compassion": Gur Zak, "'Umana cosa è aver compassione': Boccaccio, Compassion, and the Ethics of Literature," 5–20; Olivia Holmes, "*Decameron* 5.8: From Compas-sion to Complacency," 21–36; and F. Regina Psaki, "Compassion in the *Decameron:* The Opening Sequence," 37–58. All three essays stress the poly-valent nature of the way compassion is presented in the tales, but each from an intriguingly different perspective and based on a different crit-ical approach. Needless to say, however, the immense critical literature on the *Decameron* is rife with examples of such multiple readings in the face of a text that clearly was not intended to present with its one hun-dred tales told by ten different narrators a univocal perspective on virtu-ally anything. The study that follows, by folding compassion back into the emotions that were seen as swirling around love at the time and in the *Decameron,* shifts the focus to love and sex but obviously, as will be-come clear, without forgetting the central role of pity and compassion in both.

8. *Decameron,* 14–15; italics mine.

9. Ibid., 20.

10. Ibid., 21.

11. Ibid.

12. At a much humbler level, but still all too significant, our current pan-demic seems to threaten the very civil society in which we live, and the disruption seems to be becoming a threatening reality with fears about the fate of democracy, capitalism, and simply a "new normal" in our future.

13. Boccaccio, as the narrator of the metafiction of the frame story, would have been thirty-four or thirty-five in 1348, by the standards of the time at the prime of his life. Later in the frame story, however, he refers to himself as an older man who has been criticized for his fascination with women, love, and desire and at the start of the fourth day of tales nar-rates in the frame story a story that he claims as his own about Filippo Balducci, who tried and failed to keep his son from being attracted to

women—the famous gosling story (*Decameron,* 459–70). Balducci, keeping his son isolated from women as he grew up, finally one day took him as a teenager to the city, where he saw his first women and was immediately smitten. When his father tried to discourage his enthusiastic interest in those "beautiful creatures" by telling him that they were merely goslings and implicitly of no value, his son, totally taken by them, immediately requested a gosling of his own. This allows Boccaccio as narrator to conclude in some detail that the love of women and the desire for them is God-given, natural, and really impossible to deny. Often read as a manifesto for Boccaccio's vision of love and sex as natural and, if sinful, merely small natural sins, it at least clearly presents this position, which will reappear frequently throughout the tales of the *Decameron,* as we shall see.

14. For this, see note 2 above and the bibliography more generally. For an overview, however, see Ruggiero, *The Renaissance in Italy,* 1–267.

15. For the more learned and philosophical view of *virtù* and virtue that sums up the extensive literature on the subject and offers a thoughtful new perspective now, see James Hankins, *Virtue Politics: Soulcraft and Statecraft in Renaissance Italy* (Cambridge, MA: Harvard University Press, 2019) and his briefer "Boccaccio and the Political Thought of Renaissance Humanism" in *A Boccaccian Renaissance,* 3–35, and for an earlier period Ronald Witt, *In the Footsteps of the Ancients: The Origins of Humanism from Lovato to Bruni* (Leiden: Brill, 2003). For works that focus more on the *Decameron,* see Teodolinda Barolini, Valerio C. Ferme, Victoria Kirkham, Giuseppe Mazzotta, Marilyn Migiel, Ada Novajra, and their studies listed in the bibliography. My own broader view of Rinascimento *virtù,* much influenced by my readings of the *Decameron,* are laid out more systematically in *Machiavelli in Love,* 163–211 as well as *The Renaissance in Italy,* where it forms one of the central themes of the underlying paradigm suggested for the Rinascimento (see especially, 217–34).

16. Stephen Greenblatt, *Renaissance Self-Fashioning from More to Shakespeare* (Chicago: University of Chicago Press, 1980); see also his reflections on the issue in the context of a broader methodological discussion of history and literature, "What Is the History of Literature?" *Critical Inquiry* 23 (1997): 460–81.

17. Guido Ruggiero, *Machiavelli in Love,* 8; for the broader discussion that ranges much beyond Machiavelli, see in that same work especially 100–36, 141–62, and *The Renaissance in Italy,* 108–115, 326–86. See also the more developed consideration of these issues in chapters 2 and 3.

18. William Reddy has been a pioneer both in the historical study of love as an emotion and emotions more generally, although his interdisciplinary approach with its emphasis on psychological theory has garnered criticism as well as plaudits. See his suggestive *The Making of Romantic Love: Longing*

and Sexuality in Europe, South Asia, and Japan, 900–1200 CE (Chicago: University of Chicago Press, 2012) and his earlier *The Navigation of Feelings: A Framework for the History of Emotions* (Cambridge: Cambridge University Press, 2001), especially the detailed discussion of the psychological issues involved in doing a historical analysis of emotions. For a more scientific discussion that attempts to incorporate a historical approach and offers some useful bibliography, see Jacob Dębiac, "The Matter of Emotions: Towards the Brain-Based Theory of Emotions" (2014) at researchgate.net/publications 264416715. But see also for a critique Ruth Leys, "The Turn to Affect: A Critique," *Critical Inquiry* 37, n. 3 (2011), 434–72. For a more literary approach, see the dedicated issue of the journal *PMLA (Publications of the Modern Language Association of America), Special Topic Emotions* 130, n. 5 (October, 2015). For a premodern philosophical perspective, see the edited volume *Emotions and the Cognitive Life in Medieval and Early Modern Philosophy,* Martin Pickavé and Lisa Shapiro, eds. (Oxford: Oxford University Press, 2012). Crucial for my approach to the history of emotions have been the works by Robb Boddice, Susan Broomhall, David Lynch, Martha C. Nussbaum, Barbara H. Rosenwein, Daniel Lord Smail, Peter N. Stearns, Carol Zisowita Stearns, and Anna Wierzbicka listed in the bibliography. See also in the bibliography the studies by Damien Boquet and Nagy Piroska, Carla Casagrande and Silvana Vecchio, Naama Cohen-Hanegbi, Samuel K. Cohen, Richard J. Davidson, Béatrice Delaurenti, Thomas Dixon, Seth Duncan and Lisa Feldmen Barrett, Carroll E. Izard, Peter King, Simo Knuuttila, Carol Lansing, Stephen J. Milner, Susan Broomhall, Sergio Paradisio and David Rudrauf, Dominik Perler, Luiz Pessoa, Jan Plamper, Fabrizio Ricciardelli, James A. Russell, and Andrea Zorzi for a quick overview of the issues involved and the current state of the literature.

19. Reddy, *Making of Romantic Love,* 15; he continues: "The claim is that neither such states nor their coordinated occurrences are the manifestations of a deeper, genetically programmed bodily 'appetite' that impels us towards sexual gratification." For an earlier and more complete review of the literature, see his *The Navigation of Feeling.* It should be noted, however, that Reddy seems to make his analysis yet more historical and culturally driven in his later book, *Making of Romantic Love.*

20. Reddy argues in his *Making of Romantic Love* that a distinctly Western linking of love with what was seen as a sexual drive was a product of the invention of courtly love in the twelfth century as a reaction against the Gregorian Reform movement and its attempts to discipline sex and marriage. See the impressive argument developed pp. 41–222 there. One wonders, however, if this association was so clearly a form of trickle-down cultural development among a small social elite or if that particular moment reflected broader changing attitudes toward both love and sex, as he notes as well. Demonstrating convincingly an elite origin for romantic love

clearly is undermined by the lack of documentation that would demonstrate such a broader sea change. And, in turn, with the more limited surviving documentation that focuses on elites, it is far easier to see their perspectives as the driving force in change.

21. This distinction is also useful for not falling into the teleological trap often associated with Nobert Elias's work on the civilization of manners and what he labeled the "civilizing process." Despite Elias's denials, many have seen his groundbreaking analysis as claiming a progressive linear development of controls via manners over emotions that is central for living together in a modern society and the key to the development of the modern. See for this Norbert Elias, *The Civilizing Process, I: The History of Manners; II: State Formation and Civilization* [1939], trans. Edmund Jephott (Oxford: Blackwell, 1994) and his added essay in this edition warning against reading his work as claiming a linear development of manners as the base for modernity. Here and elsewhere, by analyzing manners and emotions like love and sexual desire in fourteenth-century Italy as relating to a much more specific cultural and urban context focused on civic life at the time, I am avoiding making any claims about a broader linear development of manners and emotions in the Western tradition, claims that seem on their face highly unlikely.

22. Although clearly whether or not there has been a sexual revolution over the last two generations remains a controversial question, it is evident that love, sex, and marriage are no longer so tightly intertwined, at least in Western cultures. My own opinion, merely as one who has lived through the period, is that whether or not "revolution" is the right term, there has been a radical change in the way society in the West views and lives love, marriage, sexual relationships, and sexual practice that for all the ink (and unfortunately blood as well) that has been spilled still leaves much more to be explored.

1. LAUGHTER

1. As discussed in the introduction, in Florence as in other Italian cities, the names used to label the *popolo grosso* could vary; at times, for example, they were labelled the *popolo grasso* or *grande del popolo,* but in each case what the label denoted was a group of the most important members of the *popolo,* who from the late thirteenth century were progressively being recognized as socially and economically superior to the *popolo* as a whole. The classic works on the subject for Florence at least are by Lauro Martines, Gene Brucker, and John Najemy cited in the bibliography. For the central role the emergence of this social group played in my interpretation of the early Rinascimento, much influenced by Martines, Brucker,

and Najemy, see my *The Renaissance in Italy: A Social and Cultural History of the Rinascimento* (Cambridge: Cambridge University Press, 2015), 14–15, 72–89, 229–40 and throughout.

2. The richly complex and revealing meaning of this Italian term is briefly outlined in the introduction (for bibliography on the topic, see note 15 there).

3. Church doctrine held that, in order for sex not to be sinful, it must be practiced in the context of the "sexual debt" that partners in matrimony owed each other. Thus, ideally, this was without sinful pleasure and strictly for procreation. At its heart, the idea was that a marital partner practiced sexual intercourse not for pleasure but as an obligation meeting God's command to multiply and fill the world. Needless to say, this vision of sex in marriage did not contribute to advancing an ideal of loving sex in marriage. See on this in the *Decameron,* Grace Delmolino, "The Economics of Conjugal Debt from Gratians *Decretum* to *Decameron* 2,10," in *Reconsidering Boccaccio: Medieval Contexts and Global Interests,* Olivia Holmes and Dana E. Stewart, eds. (Toronto: University of Toronto Press, 2018), 133–67.

4. For an overview of some of the issues involved see the introduction and Ruggiero, *The Renaissance in Italy,* 212–20, 481–84.

5. Later inquisition records have documented a large number of *carte di voler bene,* also regularly attesting to their effectiveness in commanding love. In fact, the most impressive often made use of expensive *carta non nata* (velum) made from unborn lambs, which was what Bruno requested in this case. They were empowered by commanding or hammering prayers written on them that forced the victim to love the person who touched him or her with the *carta.* For example, in 1589, a *carta di voler bene* was found in the possession of a prostitute, Girolama, who used it to help in holding on to her clients / lovers. It began, "Oh Lord Jesus, oh you with great wisdom created the world and came into it where with great suffering you were prosecuted . . . and crucified, I ask you humbly in my great suffering, unhappiness, sadness and tribulations that you help me." But from a prayer-like call for help, the *carta* moves on to demand that Christ force "my lover to love me with good heart. . . . And moreover all those people who would get in the way or cause problems or annoy me are with your powers to be destroyed Lord as you punished Adam and Eve," Archivio di Stato, Venezia, Sant' Ufficio, Busta 64, Girolama di Venezia, 21 March 1589; hereafter cited as ASV, SU. For an extensive discussion of *carte di voler bene* and their use in Venice, see Guido Ruggiero, *Binding Passions: Tales of Magic, Marriage, and Power at the End of the Renaissance* (New York: Oxford University Press, 1993), 99–107.

6. *Beffe* (plural) were a favorite theme of the Rinascimento novella tradition, and many of Boccaccio's stories turn on these clever disciplining

jokes that often seem quite cruel to modern eyes. For the classic discussion of the subject, see Andrè Rochon, ed., *Formes et significations de la "Beffa" dans la littérature Italienne de la Renaissance* (Paris: Université de la Sorbonne Nouvelle, 1972) and for the *Decameron*, see Valerio C. Ferme, "*Ingegno* and Morality in the New Social Order: The Role of the *Beffa* in Boccaccio's *Decameron*," *Romance Languages Annual* 4 (1992), 248–53. A more extensive discussion of the *beffa* in a particularly troubling Florentine novella of the fifteenth century can be found in my "Mean Streets, Familiar Streets, or the Fat Woodcarver and the Masculine Spaces of Renaissance Florence," in *Renaissance Florence: A Social History*, Roger J. Crum and John T. Paoletti, eds. (Cambridge: Cambridge University Press, 2006), 295–311, especially 300 and note 10.

7. The tale is told in Giovanni Boccaccio, *Decameron*. Vittore Branca, ed. (Turin: Einaudi, 1992) IX, 5: 1061–72. Actually, it appears that Calandrino, along with his buddies Bruno and Buffalmacco, were real historical figures, artisan painters in Trecento Florence. Calandrino was the nickname of Nozzo or Giovannozzo di Perino; Buffalmacco, Buonamico di Cristofano; and Bruno, Bruno di Giovanni d'Olivieri. For more on Calandrino, see Norman Land, "Calandrino as Viewer," *Notes on History of Art* 23 (2004), 1–6, and the erudite article of Ronald L. Martinez, "Calandrino and the Powers of Stone: Rhetoric, Belief and the Progress of *Ingegno* in the *Decameron* VIII.3," *Heliotropia* 1 (2003), 1–32, which reviews with perceptive comments the four tales in which Calandrino features in the *Decameron* (and where, for example, the Dantean dimensions of Tessa's beating are discussed, 20). And finally, in this chapter, you are in a study first published in a shorter exploratory form as "Imagining Love, Lust, and *Virtù* in Boccaccio and the Italian Renaissance," in *Rituals of Politics and Culture in Early Modern Europe: Essays in Honour of Edward Muir*, Mark Jurdjevic and Rolf Strøm-Olsen, eds. (Toronto: Centre for Reformation and Renaissance Studies, 2016), 185–209, extensively revised and expanded here.

8. In 2012, Google labeled "what is love" the "most popular search on Google." See www.theguardian.com/commentisfree/2012/dec13/what-is -love-five-theories.

9. William Reddy has played a pivotal role in developing this area, although his interdisciplinary approach with its emphasis on psychological theory has garnered criticism as well as plaudits. See his suggestive *The Making of Romantic Love: Longing and Sexuality in Europe, South Asia, and Japan, 900–1200 CE* (Chicago: University of Chicago Press, 2012) and his earlier *The Navigation of Feelings: A Framework for the History of Emotions* (Cambridge: Cambridge University Press, 2001), especially the long discussion of the psychological issues involved in doing a historical analysis of emotions. See also the brief discussion in the introduction with bibliography in note 18 there and the

more extensive references in the bibliography. Here I am less interested in these questions or in Rinascimento learned theories of emotions or their traditions and more in how emotions were presented, understood, and lived in the shared culture of the day and in the *Decameron.*

10. "La Veniexiana," in *Five Comedies from the Italian Renaissance,* Laura Giannetti and Guido Ruggiero, trans. and eds. (Baltimore: Johns Hopkins University Press, 2003), 286.

11. See for a general discussion of the period and the role of *virtù* in it, *The Renaissance in Italy,* 16-17, 229-49, and throughout—a major theme of that book and its suggested new paradigm for understanding the period. See also note 15 in the "introduction" for additional studies on the term, especially in a more learned context and in the *Decameron.*

12. Ruggiero, *Machiavelli in Love,* in general and more particularly, 148-55.

13. *Decameron* V, 1: 593-608. Critics interested in Boccaccio's vision of love, who claim a more moralistic reading, have often seen the love portrayed as negative both morally and in terms of the violent passions it evoked. An impressive recent article that offers a more moralistic (and at times modern) reading and provides an overview of the literature on this tale is Julia Cozzarelli, "Love and Destruction in the *Decameron:* Cimone and Calandrino," *Forum Italicum: A Journal of Italian Studies,* 38 (2004), 338-63. Key to her reading, and that of others who see this as a negative tale about love, is the violent abduction that Cimone uses later in the tale to gain his love. A more historically grounded reading would point out that abduction, often violent, was frequently used in the period to found marriages based on love, when parents or other factors blocked the path of a deserving and often heroic lover. See my *Violence in Early Renaissance Venice* (New Brunswick, NJ: Rutgers University Press, 1980), 156-70, and *The Boundaries of Eros: Sex Crime and Sexuality in Renaissance Venice* (New York: Oxford University Press, 1985), 31-38, 89-109. See also the essays in the collection edited by Lauro Martines, *Violence and Civil Disorder in Italian Cities* (Berkeley: University of California Press, 1972). From this perspective, what is clearly excessive force to secure one's love from a modern perspective becomes in the Rinascimento far less negative, especially when it was seen as necessary to overcome adverse fortune. In that context, Cimone's violence would have seemed to contemporaries more heroic and another telling evidence of the danger that a true lover was prepared to face in order to prove love. For a classic reading of Cimone's violence that similarly stresses its historical specificity, see Aldo D. Scaglione, *Nature and Love in the Late Middle Ages* (Westport, CT: Greenwood Press, 1976), 80-81. (Originally: Berkeley: University of California Press, 1963). For a more traditional reading, see Antonio Toscano, "*Decameron:* Cimone's Metamorphosis," *Italian Quarterly* 29 (1988), 25-35, and for a

yet different perspective, Millicent Marcus, "The Sweet New Style Reconsidered: A Gloss on the Tale of Cimone (*Decameron* V, 1)," *Italian Quarterly* 81 (1980), 5–61.

14. *Decameron* V, I: 594.

15. Ibid. *Matto* might seem to imply mad, but the tale makes clear that he lacked the *virtù* to reason well and thus is depicted as more simple and lacking in refined manners than mad.

16. Ibid.

17. Cozzarelli sees his exile to the country in a different, and again a rather ahistorical light, yet not without its internal logic. Turning to the frame story and its apparently rural pleasures, she argues that his being sent to the countryside should be understood to reflect his "naturalistic role, and it also embodies his rejection of rational thinking." "Love and Destruction," 341. Cimone, however, did not reject rational thinking; he was incapable of it when he was sent to the countryside, because he lacked the *virtù* that made it possible, as the tale makes clear. Moreover, as the frame story is presented, its admittedly virtually utopian rural setting (and it was a highly organized, comfortable, and civil rural setting at that) was merely a stop-gap expedient made necessary by the devastation of the plague. Boccaccio's storytellers and his audience, in contrast, were decidedly urban, as the tales themselves underline with their familiar urban settings; thus, Cimone's being sent to the countryside for them would have been, as the story points out, a significant sign that he was incapable of *"cittadinesco piacere"* (urban / civil pleasure), the urban pleasure that was the key to a meaningful civil life in the city and a widely shared vision of the ideal civilized life itself in the Rinascimento.

18. Ibid., 595.

19. Ibid.

20. Ibid., 596.

21. Ibid.

22. Ibid. Noteworthy and significant here is the way in which the emotion of love and reason are so intimately intertwined.

23. Cozzarelli, stressing at this point Efigenia's fear of Cimone, reports that "after Efigenia wakes and fearing him, flees, Cimone returns to the city . . ." "Love and Destruction," 342. In fact, as noted, although she fears him, she allows him to accompany her home, "E quantunque la giovane sua compagnia rifiutasse, sempre di lui temendo, mai di sé partir nol poté infino a tanto che egli non 'ebbe infino alla casa di lei accompagnata. . . ." *Decameron*, 597.

24. Ibid., 598.

25. Ibid.

26. As noted earlier, the construction of the story would set the reader up to expect that lust would be what was driving the boorish Cimone, as he

encountered the lovely lightly clad body of Efigenia beside the pool. In fact, his first glance does note her body's beauties, rapidly enumerating them—even then, however, surmising that she was so beautiful that "she must be a god," not quite a lustful response. But if there was any doubt about his emotion being love not lust, the story then changes gears dramatically and to good effect, noting that when she woke up and he finally looked into her eyes, "he was filled with a pleasure he had never felt before." *Decameron,* 597. The eyes, of course, were classically the organs that aroused and communicated love, and it is Efigenia's eyes, not her godlike body, that bring out Cimone's true love. For an interpretation that rereads this moment as "more properly called lust," however, see again Cozzarelli, "Love and Destruction," 243.

27. *Decameron,* 598.

28. In fact, in Cimone's case, Fortuna is alternately described as blocking the successful winning of his love and favoring it. It is those vicissitudes that lead on to the violent climax of the novella and eventually its conclusion with the virtually required happy ending of tales of true love in the *Decameron:* marriage. One of the best examples of this envious Fortuna is the story of Ghismonda, *Decameron* IV, 1: 471–86, where Fortuna is described as "envious" of the young lovers' happiness and causes Ghismonda's father, Tancredi, to discover her affair. "Ma la fortuna, *invidiosa* di cosí lungo e di cosí gran diletto, con doloroso avvenimento la letizia de' due amanti rivolse in tristo pianto" (475, italics mine). This tale will be considered more fully in Chapters 2 and 3.

29. For an overview of the way love was portrayed by Boccaccio in other works before the *Decameron,* see *Boccaccio: A Critical Guide to the Complete Works,* Victoria Kirkham, Michael Sherbrg, Janet Levarie Smarr, eds. (Chicago: University of Chicago Press, 2013), and the *Cambridge Companion to Boccaccio,* Guyda Armstrong, Rhiannon Daniels, and Stephen J. Milner, eds. (Cambridge: Cambridge University Press, 2015), and for a brief summary see my *The Renaissance in Italy,* 216–19.

30. For this in Florence and more generally, see the classic works by Gene Brucker, Lauro Martines, and John Najemy cited in the bibliography and for a brief discussion of the Florentine *popolo grosso,* Ruggiero, *The Renaissance in Italy,* 77–82.

31. Although it may seem strange, as discussed in the introduction and as will become clear throughout our discussion of the *Decameron,* in its tales women and lower-class people are often portrayed as displaying *virtù,* and, in a way, that makes it clear that this was a widely accepted way of describing women who displayed *virtù*-ous behavior.

32. *Decameron* III, 3: 347.

33. Ibid.

34. Ibid., 347–48.

35. These social tensions were exacerbated at the time that Boccaccio was writing and revising the *Decameron* in Florence in the 1350s. See for this Samuel Cohn, *Creating the Florentine State: Peasants and Rebellion, 1343–1434* (Cambridge: Cambridge University Press, 2004) and Chapters 2 and 5 of this book. After the plague in Florence (and in many urban centers), social tensions were heightened by the arrival of what were perceived as large numbers of "new men" drawn from the countryside and other cities to replace workers lost in that great die-off. Such fears were not new and actually had a long tradition. But the rapid influx of new men (and women) following the plague added great weight to such fears and made them a major theme of political debates in Florence. Some of these new men were skilled artisans or more substantial people drawn by the incentives offered to attract them to replenish the population lost to the plague; others were quite humble peasants and day laborers. But virtually all were seen as endangering the social hierarchy and tranquility of the city. With this in play, more conservative visions of who among the *popolo grosso* deserved to be on top of society became more pressing; thus, some used distinctions like grace, manners, and love more aggressively to distinguish who really deserved elite status, as in the case of this more aristocratic woman unhappy with her rich husband. In fact, in Florence, the perhaps most noted "revolutionary" moment of the city's social conflict followed in the second half of the century in part driven by lower-class unrest but also significantly driven by more aristocratic members of the *popolo grosso:* the Ciompi Rising of 1378. See on this again the work of Brucker and Najemy cited above, and for a brief overview of this see also Ruggiero, *The Renaissance in Italy,* 154–61.

36. *Decameron* II, 3: 152–65; and for the quote, 154–55. Significantly, they were from a noted family associated with the Ghibelline party, which would have suggested more strongly yet that they were noble leaning and not particularly committed to the *popolo grosso* style of life—something that was more troubling yet to many Florentines following the plague when Boccaccio was writing and revising the *Decameron.* In traditionally Guelph Florence, negative noble behavior was frequently associated with Ghibelline leanings. And across those very years, the dominant accusations of traitorous loyalty to the Ghibelline party—in a way often quite typical of political labeling to eliminate perceived threats—were being used by both more aristocratic families favoring a more limited political participation and those who supported a more open political and social order. For this see Najemy, *A History of* Florence, 144–62, and also note 33.

37. *Decameron,* 157. Bank failures were a regular feature of Renaissance life, especially in Florence, as Boccaccio, who had once worked for the Bardi bank in their Naples branch, was undoubtedly well aware. In fact, this

tale may have evoked memories of the disastrous failures of the Florentine Bardi and Peruzzi banks in 1342, portrayed at the time as being a
result of the king of England reneging on his debts and causing a run on
these banks. The actual reason for their failures has recently been reconsidered, with unwise local land speculations and debts being seen as
more significant in their collapse.

38. Ibid., 159.
39. Ibid., 161.
40. Ibid., 160.
41. Ibid., 161. As noted earlier, it was not that unusual for people to share
beds when staying in inns.
42. Ibid. Interestingly, many translators transform this passage to make it
refer to heterosexual intercourse, when it actually refers to youthful
male / male sex and portrays it as lovemaking.
43. Ibid.
44. Ibid.
45. Ibid., 161–62.
46. Ibid., 162.
47. Ibid. It will be remembered that before the Council of Trent in the sixteenth century, all that was required for a marriage was the consent of
both parties. In this case, to make the matter more binding, the young
woman added a ring and a portrait of the Lord as their witness. Such additional gestures are also regularly referred to in the archival records created by litigation to determine whether or not couples were actually
married. As is well known, the simple requirement of consent to form a
marriage created many problems before the Council of Trent tried to set
more demanding standards; in that context before Trent, both criminal
and ecclesiastical records reveal that couples often added additional
markers to confirm their consent, such as rings or calling on God as
their witness. For another example of a quick wedding, this time following sexual intercourse, see the famous *Decameron* story of capturing
the nightingale V, 4.
48. Ibid., 165.
49. Ibid., IV, 2: 487–504. For an excellent description of the yearly ritual that
this tale seems to echo, see Edward Muir, *Civic Ritual in Renaissance Venice*
(Princeton, NJ: Princeton University Press, 1981), 160–62.
50. On this, see Lauro Martines's magisterial study *Lawyers and Statecraft in
Renaissance Florence* (Princeton, NJ: Princeton University Press, 1968),
and for Petrarch's negative vision of lawyers and physicians that may
well have influenced his friend Boccaccio, see George W. McClure's *The
Culture of Profession in Late Renaissance Italy* (Toronto: University of Toronto Press, 2004), 4–14.
51. *Decameron* VIII, 9: 983–1007; this quote is on 985.

52. Ibid., 985–86.

53. Ibid., 988.

54. Ibid., 990. Branca points out in a note to this speech by Bruno that Simone reveals his ignorance by hearing this negation as an affirmation that he would be able to command florins as well as women and that this misunderstanding adds to the humor of the moment.

55. Ibid., 999. Her name, as we shall see, refers to a small street in Florence known for being a place where feces were dumped; thus, she was literally the Countess of Cesspools.

56. Ibid., 1001.

57. Ibid.

58. Ibid., 1003–1004; italics mine.

59. Ibid., 1004.

60. Ibid., 1004–1005.

61. Douglas Biow discusses this case and draws a similar conclusion about the demeaning nature of Simone being thrown in the cesspool in his fascinating study, *The Culture of Cleanliness in Renaissance Italy* (Ithaca: Cornell University Press, 2006), 45–46. See also Victoria Kirkham, "Painters at Play on the Judgment Day (*Decameron,* VIII, 9)," *Studi sul Boccaccio* 14 (1983–84), 256–77, which compares Simone's fate to the punishment of flatterers in Dante's *Inferno.*

62. The translation here is perhaps too free in an attempt to convey the way his rough language reveals what an inept lover he is. The original Italian reads: "Gnaffé! tu sí le dirai in prima in prima che io le voglio mille moggia di quel buon bene da impregnare, e poscia che io son suo servigiale [instead of servidore or servente] e se ella vuol nulla: ha' mi bene inteso?" *Decameron,* 1065.

63. Ibid.

64. The Rebec, however, was traditionally seen as an instrument preferred by the lower classes. In fact, at the time it was often looked down on because of its lower-class connections.

65. One wonders if Boccaccio had another agenda as well that involved presenting painters as merely ordinary artisans. Could it be that the increasing enthusiasm for the artistic *virtù* of artisans such as Giotto and contemporary painters like Buffalmacco and Bruno were troublingly complicating the already conflicted world of social distinctions in fourteenth-century Florence that was such a concern in the tales of the *Decameron?* From this perspective, these characters with their laughable lower-class ways and ploys, even when they demonstrated *virtù,* remained safely lower class, and, tellingly, bad things followed if one treated them as peers or put too much trust in them. It should be noted also that in those few tales like that of the valet who nobly loved a prince's daughter Ghismonda (IV,1), to be discussed at length in Chapters 2 and 3 that seem to contradict this, Boccaccio's storytellers invest long speeches to

make it clear that in that very particular case, *virtù* did make the character a true noble, something literally confirmed by his *virtù*-ous deeds. The trouble taken to make that aspect of the tale work is a clear sign that that was a rarity not to be expected from the lower classes. Suggestive from this perspective is also the brief tale about Giotto (VI, 5) where, although Boccaccio lauds the painter with the highest praise for imitating nature and returning painting to its ancient glory—without, however, using the term *virtù* to describe his skill—he points out that he never wanted to demand a higher status and was perfectly happy to be just a highly respected artisan.

2. VIOLENCE

1. *Decameron*, V, 8: 677.
2. *Decameron* IV, 9: 565.
3. Ibid., 566.
4. Ibid., 567–68.
5. *Decameron* IV, 1: 483. This complex and richly revealing tale will be discussed in more detail in Chapter 3.
6. *Decameron* V, 8: 671. For a reading that sees this compassion as the central theme of the tale and that is suggestively different from the interpretation that follows in this chapter, see Olivia Holmes, *"Decameron 5.8: From Compassion to Complacency,"* *I Tatti Studies in the Italian Renaissance* 22 (2019), 21–36.
7. *Decameron* V, 8: 671.
8. For an excellent brief article on this that sums up the extensive scholarship on Dante's influence on Boccaccio in this tale, see Brittany Asaro, "Boccaccio's Francescas: Comparing Inferno V and the Tale of Nastagio degli Onesti (*Dec.* V. 8)," in *Women in Hell: Francesca da Rimini and Friends Between Sin, Virtue and Heroism/ Donne all'Inferno: Francesca da Rimini e Co. tra peccato, virtù ed eroismi. Giornate internazionali Francesca da Rimini. VI Edizione. Atti del convegno* (Romagna Arte e Storia, 2013). See also the classic work by Robert Hollander, *Boccaccio's Dante and the Shaping Force of Satire* (Ann Arbor: University of Michigan Press, 1997), and for a fascinating different perspective Kristina M. Olson, *Courtesy Lost: Dante, Boccaccio and the Literature of History* (Toronto: University of Toronto Press, 2014).
9. How they were perceived by those who viewed such penalties is more a matter of debate, but at least violent punishment was the order of the day and presented as both acceptable and positive. For a discussion of this and the nature of criminal punishment, see Andrea Zorzi, *L'amministrazione della giustizia nella Repubblica fiorentina. Aspetti e problemi* (Florence: Olschki, 1988); Fabrizio Riccardelli, "The Emotional Language of Justice in Late

Medieval Italy," in *Emotions, Passions and Power in Renaissance Italy*, Fabrizio Riccardelli and Andrea Zorzi, eds. (Amsterdam: Amsterdam University Press, 2015): 31-43; Guido Ruggiero, "Deconstructing the Body, Constructing the Body Politic: Ritual Execution in the Renaissance," in *Riti e rituali nelle società medievali*, Jacques Chiffoleau, Lauro Martines, and Agostino Paravicini Bagliani, eds. (Centro Italiano di Studi sull'Alto Medioevo, 1994), 175-90, and the other articles in the volume. See also Trevor Dean, *Crime and Justice in Late Medieval Italy* (Cambridge: Cambridge University Press, 2007), and for a different perspective, Daniel Lord Smail, *The Consumption of Justice: Emotions, Publicity and Legal Culture in Marseille, 1264–1423* (Ithaca: Cornell University Press, 2003), and Holmes, "*Decameron* 5.8," who sees this punishment as coming more from contemporary sermon literature.

10. See note 8.

11. *Decameron* V, 8: 671-72.

12. Ibid., 672. The use of the term "noble" may cause some confusion here. Both Nastagio and the woman he loves are portrayed as nobles, although he is presented as coming from a slightly less noble family. This attribution should not be too quickly associated with the nobility outside of Italy, for these were urban aristocrats claiming ancient family lines, but economically and socially they were quite distant from the rural nobility living beyond the Alps. And, once again here, the real measure of their status is their mannerly display of their *virtù* or their lack of same, in this case in their courting.

13. Ibid., 672.

14. It might well be argued that this may not have been adequate, given Nastagio's fervent love, but if she had behaved correctly and with gentleness, the misbehavior and social animus would have fallen on his shoulders and the many social mechanisms in place for restraining importuning lovers would have come into play, avoiding the violence of her disdainful and demeaning rejection.

15. Ruggiero, *Machiavelli in Love*, 100-36, 141-62, and for a more general discussion Ruggiero, *The Renaissance in Italy*, 326-86.

16. It is often argued that she goes unnamed because her desires in the tale are unimportant to the narrator or Boccaccio, but it might be suggested that actually her wishes are laid out clearly throughout and that they are so negative that providing her a name would have made her more identifiable, and, given her particularly objectionable behavior, that would have threatened to create a consensus identity unworthy of her noble family name. This tale has been considered often by scholars, particularly relevant to the interpretation to follow is Millicent Marcus's "Misogyny as Misreading: A Gloss on *Decameron* VIII, 7," *Stanford Italian Review* 4 (1984), 23-40.

17. *Decameron* VIII, 7: 944–75.
18. Ibid., 946.
19. Ibid., 946–47.
20. *Decameron* IV, 8; V, 9; X, 5 provide good examples.
21. *Decameron* VIII, 7: 950.
22. Ibid., 952.
23. Ibid.
24. Ibid., 953. At this point in the tale, he is still labeled *"giovane,"* although, as noted earlier, later he will be presented as an older lover. Why this change in age occurs will be discussed below.
25. Ibid., 954. Note that, as was the case with Calandrino's *carta di voler bene,* the tales of the *Decameron,* while recognizing that love magic was widely used and believed in by many, regularly poke fun at those who are gullible enough to believe in it.
26. In fact, for all the lies and foolishness of Rinieri's magic, much magic of the day actually was concerned with forcing lovers to return. On this see Ruggiero, *Binding Passions,* 88–129.
27. *Decameron,* 963. In a way, this seems to echo Boccaccio's famed defense of his love of women even as an older man in the *Decameron,* where he points out at the start of day four that although his hair is white he is still green below. And although trying to read Boccaccio's life into his stories must remain highly hypothetical, it is tempting to consider that Nastagio's suffering as the not quite noble and aristocratic lover might evoke echoes of Boccaccio's status as a young, not quite aristocratic enough, would-be lover during his own youthful days in Naples.
28. Ibid., 965. Needless to say, however, this tale was long popular with scholars, even the most misogynist who shared none of the pity that Rinieri felt. See, for example, Antonio Vignali's comment on the tale in *La Cazzaria,* "Ever since the world began, you will find that only one scholar has been torn to bits by women—the one Boccaccio mentions in the *Decameron*—and that one knew so well how to avenge himself that he has always been a terrifying warning to women against shaming scholars." Antonio Vignali, *La Cazzaria: The Book of the Prick,* Ian Frederick Moulton, ed. and trans. (New York: Routledge, 2003), 79.
29. Ibid., 966.
30. On this, see notes 8 and 9 above.
31. *Decameron* V, 9.
32. Ibid., 683.
33. Ibid., 682.
34. Although it would take us too far afield to recount the perhaps saddest moment in the tale, when the impoverished Federigo in his poverty serves his most prized possession, his falcon, to Giovanna when she arrives unexpectedly at his poor country home to ask for that very falcon

in the hopes that it will cheer up her dying son and perhaps save him; it is interesting to note the way this scene seems to echo the scenes of lovers' hearts discussed earlier. For on several levels Federigo's falcon might be seen as his heart. It is the thing he loves most, that keeps him alive in his poverty, and the tale focuses almost obsessively on its beauty. Moreover, birds, and especially soaring hunting birds, invoked at the time phallic associations—not quite the heart but perhaps the heart of a male lover's sense of self. In sum, Federigo sacrifices all this for his love, committing a metaphorical suicide not unlike Gismonda's real one, and in the process makes himself the heroic lover of a tale once again, as even Giovanna recognizes in the end.

35. *Decameron* V, 8: 679; italics mine.

36. Ibid. This "lesson" seems to echo at a more violent level a similar lesson experienced by a young lover in *The Art of Love* by Andreas Capellanus. There too a male lover is shown a vision where the King of Love leads a procession of dead lovers divided into three groups: one of women who were true lovers and their admirers; one of women who were too open in their love and their many, many admirers; and finally one of women who rejected love completely. The last group travel in rags and uncomfortable conditions and are forced to repose on briars and brambles as punishment for their cruelty. And, in this tale, the male witness of this punishment after death reports back to the living this vision to instruct and warn women. For this, see Andreas Capellanus, *The Art of Courtly Love,* John Jay Parry, trans. (New York: Columbia University Press, 1960), 71–83.

37. Ibid., 680; italics mine. Some critics have argued that Nastagio's insistence on marriage was a way of making his revenge last not just for a moment of pleasure but for a life, as the marriage put his "victim" in his hands and under his power for the rest of her life. This is a reading that makes sense from a modern perspective perhaps and might even have made some sense at the time as well; however, it needs to overlook the stereotypical nature of the ending of the tale. Nastagio, in holding out for marriage, is acting in a way that a traditional vision of honor and sexual practice required. Merely enjoying his beloved—especially after it is reported that her hate turned to love—would have involved dishonorable behavior and abased the love he had suffered so much to enjoy, perhaps even more so in a tale of divine justice. Rather, with both partners now in love, an honorable marriage was the required happy ending, as we see over and over again in the *Decameron*.

38. Ibid., 679.

39. Italics mine. Ibid., 680. For a sample of other less negative readings of the conclusion of this tale, see Branca's note 5 in *Decameron*, 680. But among the many other readings of this much read tale, see also Ray Fleming,

"Happy Endings? Resisting Women and the Economy of Love in Day Five of Boccaccio's *Decameron*," *Italica* 70 (1993), 30-45, and Cesare Segre, "La novella di Nastagio degli Onesti (*Dec.* V, 8): I due tempi della vision," in *In ricordo di Cesare Angelini: Studi di letteratura e filologia*, Franco Alessio and Angelo Stella, eds. (Milan: Saggiatore, 1979), 65-74; and now also Holmes, "*Decameron* 5.8."

3. SORROW

1. The tale leaves some room for uncertainty about whether her brothers left her behind or took her with them, as will be discussed below.

2. An earlier much shorter form of this essay with a slightly different perspective that emphasized its virtual detective story nature was published as "Getting a Head in the Renaissance: Mementos of Lost Love in Boccaccio and Beyond," in *Renaissance Quarterly* 57 (2015), 1165-90. The tale itself is *Decameron*, IV, 5: 526-33. Once again, I will focus on the most relevant scholarship to this reading of the tale of Lisabetta for this essay but make no claim to this being anything more than one reading based on the way a historian might read the tale from a historical and archival perspective, especially a historian wondering what this anomalous story about beans growing in a skull might be doing at the heart of the *Decameron*. For another reading by a medieval historian, see Franco Cardini, "Lisabetta e l'archetipo," in his *Le cento novelle contro la morte: Giovanni Boccaccio e la rifondazione cavalleresca del mondo* (Rome: Salerno, 2007), 127-42, a reading interesting especially for its rich tracing of the broader historical context of severed heads. But see also for a more class-oriented analysis of love in the tale Mario Baratto, "Struttura narrativa e messaggio ideologico," in *Il Testo moltiplicato: Lettura di una novella del "Decameron,"* Mario Lavagetto, Mario Baratto, Alessandro Serpiari, Cesare Segre, eds. (Parma: Pratiche, 1982), 29-42, and Vittorio Russo, "Perorazione d'amore da parte di donne e femmine nel *Decameron*," in his *Con le muse in Parnaso: Tre studi su Boccaccio* (Naples: Bibliopolis, 1983), 89-108. For her death as caused by love sickness, see Massimo Ciavolella, "La tradizione dell'*aegritudo amoris* nel *Decameron*," *Giornale storico della letteratura italiana* 147 (1970), 498-517.

3. See the discussion in Chapter 2 on consensus realities and identity.

4. For a fascinating study of the broader issues involved in responding to death in Florence, see Sharon Strocchia, *Death and Ritual in Renaissance Florence* (Baltimore: Johns Hopkins University Press, 1992), 1-29. See also Truus Van Bueren and Andrea van Leerden, eds., *Care for the Here and the Hereafter: Memoria, Art and Ritual in the Middle Ages* (Turnhout, Belgium: Brepols, 2005) and Marcel Tetel, Ronald G. Witt, and Valeria Finucci,

eds., *Life and Death in Fifteenth-Century Florence* (Durham, NC: Duke University Press, 1989), especially the essays by Alberto Tenenti, Sarah Blake McHam, and Sharon Strocchia.

5. Eight of the ten tales of the fourth day might be categorized as tragic tales of love that end with death and an evaluation of honor either positive or negative. Important overviews of the tales of the fourth day are provided by Roberto Fedi, "Il 'regno' di Filostrato. Natura e struttura della Giornata IV del *Decameron*," *Modern Language Notes* 102 (1987), 39–54; Giovanni Getto, "La novella di Ghismonda e la struttura della quarta giornata," in his *Vita di forme e forme di vita nel Decameron* (Turin: Petrini, 1958), 95–139; Giorgio Bàrberi Squarotti, "Amore e morte (non senza qualche vicenda di commedia)," in his edited volume, *Prospettive sul Decameron* (Turin: Tirrenia stampatori, 1989), 59–83; Victoria Kirkham, "Love's Labors Rewarded and Paradise Lost (*Dec.* III, 10)," *Romanic Review* 72 (1981), 83ff. See more recently Michelangelo Picone, "L' 'amoroso sangue': la quarta giornata," in *Introduzione al Decameron,* Michelangelo Picone and Margherita Mesirca, eds. (Florence: Franco Cesati, 2004), 115–39; and also by Picone, "La novella di Lisabetta da Messina di Giovanni Boccaccio (*Decameron IV.5*)," *Per Leggere* 19 (2010), 37–51; and Michael Sherberg, *The Governance of Friendship: Law and Gender in the Decameron* (Columbus: Ohio State University Press, 2011), 119–29.

6. I earlier essayed this tale in the context of a discussion of *virtù*, honor, and consensus realities in a longer discussion of Machiavelli's rather traditional vision of the relationship between *virtù* and honor in my *Machiavelli in Love,* 175–86, and returned to the issues involved in the tale in *The Renaissance in Italy,* 230–33, again in the context of a discussion of *virtù* in the Rinascimento. The discussion that follows builds on those early formulations to hopefully provide a fuller perspective on all three in the context of the *Decameron.*

7. *Decameron* IV, 1: 472.

8. As should be self-evident by now, in this chapter and throughout this book, I am primarily concerned with how the concept of *virtù* was used in the Rinascimento and its contemporary implications and much less in what the classical precedents were that may or may not have contributed to that usage. Needless to say, those classical precedents have been closely studied by intellectual historians and historians of humanism with great erudition. My goal is a humbler one here, merely to suggest how this complex concept actually worked and how it was perceived and lived at the time. It might be noted in this context that the search for origins can often cause problems for the project of understanding contemporary usage, as there is a tendency to assume that the original usage translated perfectly across time and social and cultural settings. That,

of course, was possible especially for works that were highly theoretical but much less likely, I would suggest, for works that attempted to comment on and have an impact on their contemporary society.

9. Again, the literature on this is immense, but the classic works remain John G. A. Pocock, *The Machiavellian Moment: Florentine Political Thought and the Atlantic Republican Tradition* (Princeton: Princeton University Press, 1975); William J. Bouwsma, *Venice and the Defense of Republican Liberty: Renaissance Values in the Age of the Counter Reformation* (Berkeley: University of California Press, 1968), Felix Gilbert, *Machiavelli and Guicciardini: Politics and History in Sixteenth-Century Florence* (Princeton: Princeton University Press, 1965); and now James Hankins, *Virtue Politics: Soulcraft and Statecraft in Renaissance Italy* (Cambridge, MA: Harvard University Press, 2019). For an overview of these themes in the Trecento, see once more Ruggiero, *The Renaissance in Italy,* especially 21–115.

10. *Decameron,* 472.

11. Ibid., 475. *Virtù,* of course, was frequently depicted as the one power that could overcome fortune in the Renaissance but often, in a typical Rinascimento reversal, fortune was seen as the nemesis of *virtù.*

12. Ibid., 476. Again *"vergogna"* or "shame" was a term closely related to *virtù;* people who publicly acted without *virtù* were often seen as having acted shamefully. Note also in light of this discussion the close association of play and pleasure in sex when the young lovers are described as enjoying themselves in bed.

13. Ibid.; italics mine. Actually, Tancredi says "given to my things *(cose),*" but here "my things" refers to his world and his life.

14. Ibid.

15. Ibid., 477.

16. Ibid.

17. See the discussion of the form of this genre and its relationship to historical analysis in Martines, *Sextet,* 11–14, and throughout.

18. *Decameron,* 477–78. For a discussion of the gender implication of tears and the prince of Salerno's lack of masculine emotional control, see Judith Steinhoff, "Weeping Women: Social Roles and Images in Fourteenth-Century Tuscany," in *Crying in the Middle Ages: Tears of History,* Elina Gertsman, ed. (New York: Routledge, 2012), 35–52.

19. Ibid., 478–79; italics in both quotes mine. Here *virtù* has, tellingly, both a social dimension via consensus realities and an internal dimension. Ghismonda wants to defend both her reputation (her consensus realities) and the greatness of her soul (her inner self).

20. Ibid., 479. For a similar vision, see also the discussion of Alibech and Rustico's natural sexual attraction and the way their pleasures made the desert bloom and their service to the Christian God a true pleasure in

Chapter 4. As noted earlier, we see youthful lovemaking and shared passions, even when formally illicit, described as small natural sins, virtually a *topos* of the *Decameron*.

21. Ibid., 480; italics mine. Note also that Ghismonda defends her affair as fulfilling "her desires." Clearly this is not simply a case of masculine desire and wish fulfilment; rather, over and over again in the *Decameron*, a woman's desires are recognized and presented as deserving to be taken seriously.

22. Ibid., 480-81; italics mine. Aldo D. Scaglione in his classic work, *Nature and Love in the Late Middle Ages* (Westport, CT: Greenwood Press, 1976; originally: Berkeley, CA: University of California Press, 1963), 17, points out that this was an idea already put forward in medieval courtly literature and provides the classic text from Andreas Capellanus, *De arte honeste amandi* or *De Amore*, Book I, Chapter 5: "For, since all of human beings are derived originally from the same stock and all naturally claim the same ancestor, it . . . was excellence of character alone which first made a distinction of nobility among men and led to the difference of class." In turn, such ideas can be traced back to the ancient world with classical authors like Seneca proclaiming similar ideals, ideals that were echoed in the Middle Ages as well by thinkers like Aquinas, even if they clearly went against the grain of social realities. But, crucially in the *Decameron*, with newer social realities in a very different urban world, similar sentiments played differently and significantly had greater weight. For a brief and perceptive vision of these issues that stresses their humanism and its classical base yet places major emphasis on virtue and thus reinforces and augments what is argued here from a much different perspective, see now James Hankins "Boccaccio and the Political Thought of Renaissance Humanism," in *A Boccaccian Renaissance: Essays on the Early Modern Impact of Giovanni Boccaccio and His Works*, Martin Eisner and David Lummus, eds. (Notre Dame, IN: University of Notre Dame Press, 2019), 3-35, especially 6-7.

23. Ibid., 483.

24. Ibid.

25. Ibid., 485.

26. Ibid., 485-86; italics mine. She closes her last request to her weeping father with a telling description of how the burial should be done: *"palese stea"*—in other words, "so that it will be known by all"—in clear contrast with the secrecy of the lovers' affair, which had been carefully kept hidden. It may be that the interpolation of "of our love" overstates what is implied, but the more neutral "our affair" or "our case" seems to undercut the clearly intended tragic, yet heroic, ending of the lovers.

27. For a fuller discussion of what I have labeled in earlier works the regime of *virtù* and its disciplining power in the Rinascimento, see Ruggiero, *Machiavelli in Love*, 17, 71-74, 86, 206-11.

28. Giuseppe Mazzotta, *The World at Play in Boccaccio's Decameron* (Princeton, NJ: Princeton University Press, 1986), 54-58, 146-50, follows this line of reasoning closely in his discussion of the tale, stressing the importance of *virtù* and Ghismonda's defense of her love and lover in terms of it, but then argues that she gives in to madness and a delusion based on the ideals of courtly love that in the end parallels the madness of her father committing suicide. Both, then, share a madness induced by love. Michael Sherberg, *The Governance of Friendship*, 120-24, is not as negative as Mazzotta about Ghismonda's suicide but is still ambivalent about how it and her love should be interpreted. Recently, Gur Zak also sees Ghismonda as in the end a negative figure because she lacks the required filial compassion for her father's suffering caused by her dishonorable affair and in her disdain for that suffering brings on her own death; see Gur Zak, "'Umana Cosa è aver compassione': Boccaccio, Compassion, and the Ethics of Literature," *I Tatti Studies in the Italian Renaissance* 22 (2019), 5-20, especially 16-20. All three provide compelling readings, but with their focus on literary and philosophical antecedents they tend to underestimate the interpretative valences that are added when one takes into account the contemporary shared culture of Boccaccio and his readers in fourteenth-century Florence. There and then terms such as *"virtù,"* "love," and "rule" had strong contemporary meanings and referred to crucial concerns of daily life not merely earlier literary or philosophical texts. Seeing Tancredi as an outdated prince operating with outdated visions of honor and *virtù* and Ghismonda defending a contemporary vision of love (with perhaps courtly love antecedents), as argued earlier, gives the tale a contemporary logic and force that make deeper sense of the honorable burial of the lovers and the crying tragedy of a prince lacking in *virtù*.

29. *Decameron*, 486; italics mine.

30. But, of course, as the tale of Gerbino suggests, it could also be a dangerous passion, literally a mad passion, with extremely negative results when love was not joined with *virtù*. For a suggestive classic discussion of this theme of the day, see Giuseppe Mazzotta, *Play*, 131-58.

31. A perfect example is the first tale of the fifth day, discussed earlier, where the hero Cimone was so boorish and ignorant that he seemed virtually a dumb animal, totally lacking in *virtù* and the civic graces necessary to live up to the aristocratic standards of his family. Yet, as we have seen, one day wandering through the forest, he came upon a young woman, Efigenia, asleep, and the sight of her beauty and the sudden love it engendered abruptly transformed him into a true lover. And that meant, as the tale makes clear, that his innate *virtù* that had once been blocked by evil fortune in a corner of his soul was suddenly released by love, and thus he rapidly became an intelligent and mannerly young lover; in the end,

then, he won the hand of his love, overcoming all the roadblocks that fortune threw in his way. In sum, when love and *virtù* worked together, young lovers were virtually unstoppable in the happy tales of the *Decameron* and even the nemesis of *virtù*, Fortuna, could be overcome.

32. Actually, the historian Franco Cardini did suggest that the head in the vase (the *testa* in the *testo*) served as a memento and considered the ramifications of that from a historical perspective without, however, using it as an interpretive tool for the tale itself. See Cardini, "Lisabetta," 131–38.

33. The classic study on relics remains Patrick J. Geary, *Furta Sacra: Theft of Relics in the Central Middle Ages* (Princeton, NJ: Princeton University Press, revised edition 1990); for a more global perspective, see Elizabeth Robertson and Jennifer Hahner, eds., *Medieval and Early Modern Devotional Objects in Global Perspective: Translations of the Sacred* (New York: Palgrave Macmillan, 2010), and for a good overview see the catalogue Marina Bagnoli, ed., *Treasures of Heaven: Saints Relics, and Devotion in Medieval Europe* (New Haven, CT: Yale University Press, 2010).

34. Archivio di Stato di Venezia (ASV), Sant'Ufficio, Busta 53, Giulia daughter of Lodovico da Verona, Testimony of same, 24 August 1584. Cited hereafter as ASV, SU. Giulia, however, was quite eclectic in her magic and relied on the holy as well as the diabolic for the power behind her metaphors. The cooking and domestic side of her magic also had a long tradition especially in women's lore. For more examples from Venice, see Ruggiero, *Binding Passions,* 99–107.

35. For example, see ASV, SU, Busta 61, Elena Cumano, Undated denunciation by Gian Battista Faceno (1588), where it is claimed that a witch supporting Elena in her effort to regain the love of a lost lover placed under the altar of the Cathedral Church in Feltre a wax statue of a nude man with "many needles stuck all over it, especially the eyes, temple, heart, and phallus."

36. ASV, SU, Busta 63, Isabella Bellocchio, testimony of Elena Zamberti, 4 May 1589.

37. A case involving beans grown in skulls in order to make one invisible involved the friars Costantino da Pesaro and Marc'Antonio Gandolfo, ASV, SU, Busta 54, 12 September 1584. For a discussion of learned texts that discuss various magical methods of producing invisibility including beans placed in a skull, see Richard Kiechefer, *Forbidden Rites: A Necromancer's Manual of the Fifteenth Century* (University Park, PA: The Pennsylvania State University Press, 1997), 42–68. Such practices are still circulating based on medieval and early modern texts. See for example "To Make Yourself Go Invisible," www.grimoire.org/spell/for-invisibility/.

38. *Decameron*, VIII, 3: 905–19. But see also II, 1: 132–40, where the inhabitants of Treviso, presumably less gullible than Calandrino, are nonetheless

duped by a witty Florentine and his friends into believing that the Florentine, faking that he is a cripple, is cured by contact with the miraculous body of a recently deceased holy man. The tale turns on the fact that the inhabitants of Treviso are more gullible about relics than at least some clever Florentines and make easy victims. In this case, however, the *beffa* goes wrong, the ruse is discovered, and the clever Florentine barely escapes Treviso with his life and his superior Florentine skepticism about relics and their magical properties.

39. As retold in the Bible, however, there is no mention of basil in either of the two texts that describe the event: Matthew 14:1–12 and Mark 6:16–8. For a study that briefly considers the relationship between John the Baptist and Lisabetta's tale, see Tatiana Crivelli, "Applicazioni ipertestuali e interpretazione critica: l'esempio di Lisabetta (*Decameron* IV, 5)," *Cuadernos de Filologia Italiana* (2001) n. extraordinario, 157–76. She also discusses the significance of the basil but does not associate it with John the Baptist's beheading. There is a rich tradition and popular lore that grew up about the Baptist's head and its burial, which still influences local religious practices today in Italy. For a more systematic discussion of the role of patron saints in Italian city-states, see Diana Webb, *Patrons and Defenders: Saints in Italian City-States* (London: I. B. Tauris, 1996). For the Florentine situation, see Heidi L. Chretien, *The Festival of San Giovanni: Imagery and Power in Renaissance Florence* (New York: Peter Lang, 1994) and more generally Marica Tacconi, *Cathedral and Civic Ritual in Late Medieval and Renaissance Florence* (Cambridge: Cambridge University Press, 2006).

40. Boccaccio probably wrote a first draft of the *Decameron* fairly quickly after the plague but continued revising it for years. Across these years, the Guelph party used the threat of being labeled a Ghibelline more and more aggressively, but the worst days of this practice fall a little too late to support this interpretation. See for this Najemy, *Florence,* 144–62. For a more general discussion of John the Baptist in Florence, see Webb, *Patrons,* 104 ff. Another severed head of significance in fourteenth-century Florence was the skull of the late third- and fourth-century saint and bishop of the city, Zanobio, which was dug up in 1331 and covered with a silver mask that reproduced his face. It was regularly carried in processions in the fourteenth century. For this see, Anna Benvenuti, "Le fonti agiografiche nella costruzione della memoria cronistica," in *Il pubblico dei santi: Forme e livelli di ricezione dei messaggi agiografici,* Paolo Golinelli, ed. (Rome: Viella, 2000), 98 n. 61.

41. ASV, SU, Busta 63, Isabella Bellocchio, testimony of Elena Zamberti, 4 May 1589. A year earlier, Regina Vassalin was accused of using earth from a new grave for similar magic, ASV, SU, Busta 61, Regina Vassalin, testimony of Polisena, wife of Giovanni Miola, 10 December 1588.

42. Of course, there are many excellent scholars ready with interesting hypotheses to save one from such naiveté. Jonathan Usher, "Narrative and Descriptive Sequences in the Novella of Lisabetta and the Pot of Basil (*Dec.* IV, 5)," *Italian Studies* 38 (1983), 56-69, uses a structural analysis to claim that her attention to the basil shows that she grows stronger as the basil grows, an argument that does not actually fit the tale as told, as will be considered later. See also Antonio Mazzarino, "Il basilico di Lisabetta da Messina (Boccaccio, *Decameron* IV. 5)," *Nuovi annali della Facoltà di Magistero dell'Università Messina* 2 (1984), 445-87; Daniel Devoto, "Quelques notes au sujet du Pot de Basilic," *Revue de littérature comparée* 37 (1963), 430-35; R. Glynn Faithfull, "Symbolism in Boccaccio," *Lingua e stile* 22 (1985), 247-57; Maria Teresa Maiorana, "Un Conte de Boccace: Repris par Keas et Anatole France," *Revue de littérature comparée* 37 (1963), 50-67, although primarily on the later writers. It has not been possible to consult Tommaso Cannizzaro, *Il Lamento di Lisabetta da Messina e la leggenda del vaso di basilico* (Catania: Battiato, 1902). For a rich bibliography on herbals, corpses, and death in the Rinascimento, see the dedicated issue of *Micrologus: Natura, scienze e società medievali* 7 (1999), especially 297-318.

43. There is, however, a southern connection that has been used to explain the source of the story, as the tale ends with the first lines of what appears to be a Sicilian popular ballad complaining "Who was that evil Christian,/ who stole my vase,/ etc." (*Decameron*, 532.), which Filomena reports was written in memory of Lisabetta's death. It is published in full in Natalino Sapegno, ed., *Poeti minori del Trecento*, in *La letteratura italiana*, vol. 10 (Milan, 1952), 557-58. It has little, however, that seems to relate to Boccaccio's tale as he tells it. Nonetheless, a thoughtful philological analysis of the ballad that argues that it is the source of the tale is provided by Michelangelo Picone, "La 'ballata' di Lisabetta (*Decameron* IV, 5)," *Cuadernos de Filologia Italiana* (2001) n. extraodinario, 177-91. However, Barbara Rossana Fenu in "La fonte delle lacrime di Elisabetta da Messina: *Decameron* 4:5," *Quaderni d'italianistica* 22 (2001), 103-20, argues strongly against his interpretation, suggesting instead as the source of the tale the *Legenda Aurea*. More recently, Ilaria Tufano, "'Qual esso fu lo malo cristiano': La canzone e la novella di Lisabetta (*Decameron, IV:5*)," *Critica del Testo* 10 (2007), 225-39, has also rejected the ballad as the source. See also for this, Jonathan Usher, "Narrative and Descriptive Sequences in the Novella of Lisabetta and the Pot of Basil (Dec. IV, 5)," *Italian Studies* 38 (1983), 69, who contends that the song reference reveals that her brothers' crime was discovered and that in the end she is honored by popular imagination, something, however, not included in the tale. The debate about the poem and the story's origins aside, it is this retelling of the tale and the way it would have been understood at the time that interests us here.

44. Although examples could easily be multiplied, the 1326 case of Caterina who was carried off from her home in Venice (perhaps willingly) is typical. Her brother brought the case to the Venetian authorities, complaining that his and his family's honor had been compromised by the deed. The authorities agreed and tried the deed as a crime that dishonored her brother and family even though they were lower class. ASV, Avogaria di Comun, Raspe, Reg. 3641, f. 23^r (1326). Cited hereafter as ASV, AC. For a more general discussion of the honor dynamic involved in such crimes, see, Ruggiero *Boundaries of Eros*, 17–23. The *Decameron* refers regularly to this duty of brothers; for example, see the tale of the vain Venetian woman and the angel Gabriel discussed above (IV, 2), which, tellingly, is set in Venice not the south.

45. In Venice, for example, the powerful Badoer family took the defense of their daughter's virginity when it became a public issue all the way to the famed Council of Ten, the secret policing council primarily concerned with matters that threatened the stability of the city. It seems that an illegitimate son of the also powerful Contarini clan was attempting to force the Badoer family to marry their daughter, another Elisabetta, to him by claiming publicly that he had slept with her and producing witnesses who supported his claim. By playing to noble consensus realities, he was undermining the Badoers' chance to marry their daughter to anyone but him, for if the consensus reality became that Elisabetta was no longer a virgin, she would be virtually unmarriageable and he would be their only option for a husband. In essence, Contarini was attempting to control this Elisabetta's marriage with a clever strategy that in Lisabetta's case her brothers had eliminated by eliminating her lover. After preliminary examination, the Council of Ten in Venice took the question to the larger and more representative Senate, where whatever Elisabetta's actual status as a virgin might have been, her consensus reality as one was confirmed. Moreover, to make sure there was no doubt on the matter (at least officially), they ordered that "Elisabetta [be] very secretly examined by most expert women of good fame in the presence of two noteworthy noble women appointed for the purpose." They reported that "Elisabetta was a virgin intact and immaculate." The Senate confirmed this as the official consensus reality by proclaiming Contarini a criminal, banishing him from the city, and sternly punishing his witnesses as well—not quite murder but close in its intended impact. ASV, Senato Terra, Register 4, f. 132^{r-v} and ASV, AC, Raspe, Register 3651, f. 80^{r-v} (1459).

46. In a case similar to that of Elisabetta Badoer discussed earlier, a lower-class woman was also examined by "women expert in such matters" to determine whether she was a virgin or not. After their examination, they declared her "pure as the day she was born." The results were ordered to

be proclaimed in her parish church, and the man who accused her of having had sexual relations with him was required to confirm that he had lied before the parishioners. Her neighbors were thus informed in their parish church what her correct consensus reality should be, and perhaps that offered her a realistic opportunity to marry someone else. For this case, see ASV, AC, Raspe, Register 3649, f. 54v (1408). In both cases, it seems that the Venetian authorities assumed that consensus realities were key for the young women's marital possibilities. For a different suggestive reading of the issue of honor involved, see Mary E. Leech, "Severed Silence: Social Boundaries and Family Honor in Boccaccio's 'Tale of Lisabetta,'" in *Heads Will Roll: Decapitation in the Medieval and Early Modern Imagination,* Larissa Tracy and Jeff Massey, eds. (Leiden: Brill, 2012), 115–36.

47. The account of the brothers' flight is so brief that it is possible to assume that they took along Lisabetta. All the text says, however, is that they wound up their affairs and fled to Naples. It might be argued that although the tale never states that they took their sister with them and never places her last suffering in a Neapolitan setting, their honor and sense of family would have required that they take her along. But the text is silent on this. Her brothers, realizing that she knew about their murder and could at any second reveal it given her complaints, grief, and apparent rapid decline (a likelihood that threatened not only their honor but their very lives), it seems more likely to assume that they considered their safest course would have been to flee, leaving the evidence of their dishonor and crime behind. Whether they took her with them or not, in the end, the tale's silence is suggestive. For, whether she was with them or not was irrelevant to the story as told, as the moral was that she was alone emotionally in her death; thus, it relates her death without mentioning her brothers or their response to it.

48. For the best known discussion of this vision, see Mikhail Bakhtin, *Rabelais and His World,* Hélène Iswolsky, trans. (Bloomington, IN: Indiana University Press, 1993). A brief overview of Bakhtin's theories can be found in Caryl Emerson and Gary Saul Morson, "Mikhail Bakhtin," in *The Johns Hopkins Guide to Literary Theory* (Baltimore: Johns Hopkins University Press, 2005). For another reading of the significance of Lisabetta's head, see Maria Antonietta Terzoli, "La testa di Lorenzo: Lettura di *Decameron* IV, 5," *Nuova rivista di letteratura italiana* 4 (2001), 207–26.

49. *Decameron,* 531.

50. Ibid., 568.

51. Ibid., 569. Once again in evidence here is the way Boccaccio provides his readers with a contemporary consensus reality judgment of his characters with their publicly supported honorable burial. Mazzotta provides a perceptive deeper reading of the role of the heart in this tale that stresses the significance of the broken friendship between the males involved, but interestingly, in this case he does not judge this heroic suicide negatively

as he does in the case of Ghismonda, discussed earlier, where he sees a similar suicide in the face of a lover's death as a sign of madness. Mazzotta, *Play*, 152–54. Once again, both seem examples of a lover's *virtù* (or lack thereof), a central theme of the tales of day four. See also for a more magical perspective on hearts and eating them reported in archival documents, Ruggiero, *Binding Passions*, 88–129, especially 110–13, 120–24.

52. Once again, considering the way consensus realities worked adds weight to this interpretation. She was a major threat to their consensus realities, and an uncontrollable one at that, with her very visible mourning and complaints—leaving her behind made eminent sense in this context. Moreover, as discussed earlier, if one were to assume that they did take her with them to Naples, there too she would have been isolated from them, as she knew they had murdered her lover and she could not count on them or rely on their support given the danger she posed for them. Significantly, as noted earlier, the tale makes no mention of any interaction with them as she declines and dies.

4. TRANSCENDENCE

1. *Decameron*, 326. This chapter is a much more developed exploration of a reading first more tentatively and briefly suggested in my *Machiavelli in Love*, 50–53, 59–65, and further developed in "A Woman as Savior: Alibech and the Last Age of the Flesh in Boccaccio's *Decameron*," in *Acta Histriae* XVII:1 / 2 (2009), 151–62. Actually, this began as a lecture in my first class taught on the Renaissance in 1972 and has been slowly evolving over the years since.

2. "Filo" was used in the sense of a new order, norm, or rule of life by both Dante and Boccaccio; see Dante, *Paradiso*, 24, 61–63: "Come 'l verace stilo/ ne scrisse padre, del tuo caro frate/ che mise teco Roma nel buon filo" and Boccaccio, "Io, giovinetta e lasciva, tirava semplice alli fermi anni le fila di Lachesis," in *L'Ameto di Giovanni Boccaccio*, I. Moutier, ed. (Florence: Nella Stamperia Magheri, 1834), 84, and quoted in Salvatore Battaglia, *Grande dizionario della lingua Italiana* (Turin: UTET, 1961) V, 1000.

3. It might be noted that in that perfect place, the emotions that surrounded love brought order and harmony—perfect order and harmony—without any of the dangers normally associated with those emotions. Indeed, suggestively in the Garden of Eden, as it was often viewed at the time, it was reason rather than emotion that threatened and eventually broke the perfect order of the earthly paradise with an original sin driven by dangerous reason and followed by the Fall with all that entailed.

4. *Decameron*, III, 1: 337. The humorous blasphemy of this comment turns on the fact that nuns were seen in the Rinascimento (as today) as the

brides of Christ; thus, sexual relations with them were seen as adultery where the cuckolded male was Christ (and thus his horns). For this vision of sexual intercourse with nuns as a crime against God, see Ruggiero, *Boundaries of Eros*, 70–88.

5. And one must admit that they have been brilliant. A particularly impressive reading is to be found in Victoria Kirkham's "Love's Labors Rewarded and Paradise Lost (*Dec.* III, 10)," *Romanic Review*, 72 (1981), 79–83, where she argues that day three begins in the Garden of Eden and descends through its stories to end with the tale of Rustico and Alibech in a garden of evil, which is a metaphoric hell. Day four, with its tales of love ending tragically, is seen as providing the counter moral message that love and sex outside of marriage are negative and rewarded with tragedy. In contrast, for an interesting discussion of Boccaccio's use of humor in the *Decameron* that suggests a similar vision to that of this chapter and takes it in some different suggestive directions, see the chapter, "'Such Tales Were Not To Be Told among Ladies,' Women's Wit and the Problem of Modesty in Boccaccio's *Decameron*," in Lisa Perfetti's volume *Women and Literature in Medieval Comic Literature* (Ann Arbor: University of Michigan Press, 2003), 63–99. For some other suggestive interpretations of this tale, see Diane Duyos Vacca, "Converting Alibech: 'Nunc spiritu copuleris,'" *Journal of Medieval and Renaissance Studies*, 25 (1995), 207–27; Marilyn Migiel, "Beyond Seduction: A Reading of the Tale of Alibech and Rustico (*Decameron*, III, 10), *Italica* (1998),161–77; Harry Wayne Storey, "Parodic Structure in 'Alibech and Rustico': Antecedents and Traditions," *Canadian Journal of Italian Studies*, 5 (1982), 163–76; Wiley Feinstein, "Twentieth Century Feminist Responses to Boccaccio's Alibech Story," *Romance Language Annual*, 1 (1989), 116–20; and Alfonso Paolella, "I livelli narrativi nella novella di Rustico ed Alibech 'romita' del *Decameron*," *Revue Romane* 13 (1987), 189–205, that argues that the story is based on the *Vita di Santa Maria Egiziana*. And for its Arab origins, Fabrizio A. Pennacchietti, "L'eventuale fonte araba della novella di Alibech e Rustico (*Decameron*, III, 10)," *Levia gravia: Quaderno annuale di letteratura italiana*, 8 (2006), 43–47. Recently, however, an important article by Martin Eisner has read the tales of the day as indeed offering an erotic theology, "Eroticizing Theology in Day Three and the Poetics of the *Decameron*," *Annali d'Italianistica* 31 (2013), 258–86. Although it reinforces my earlier theological vision of the day in *Machiavelli in Love* and to a degree my reading that follows in this chapter, it focuses on Boccaccio's poetics and sees the tales of the day and the work as a whole arguing for the theological importance of poetics, in this case erotic poetics in a more general sense and with less contemporary specificity than argued here.

6. *Decameron*, III, 4: 360–67.

7. Ibid., 360.

8. Ibid., 362. Not all clerical predators get off so easily as Dom Felice, but in this tale and in most where sinning clerics enjoy their sexual escapades without severe punishment, their victim is portrayed as deservingly so and the clerics' scheme is so clever and winning that their sinning seems to be forgivable. And, significantly, usually the sex is enjoyed by both parties, not just the clever cleric. Although the term is not used in this tale, this seems to draw on the very Florentine appreciation of the *beffa* as discussed in Chapter 1.

9. Ibid., 361. In the fourteenth century, it was not uncommon for deeply committed religious people to join lower religious orders. In this case, Puccio had joined the Third Order of the Franciscans or Franciscan Tertiaries, often referred to in Florence as the Bizzoti or Bigotti, and thus he was called Fra Puccio. In such lower orders, one could be married.

10. Ibid. In her late twenties, and given that women were usually married in their early to mid-teens in Florence, she would have been a mature and sexually experienced woman, still young enough to be attractive. And unhappy with her husband, she would have been a perfect choice for a cleric looking for a mistress to share the pleasures of lovemaking, as the tale makes clear.

11. Ibid., 363.

12. His illiterateness would have alerted Florentines to the fact that Fra Puccio was definitely lower class, if they needed any further indication, for the ability to read was unusually widespread in Florentine society and the major cities of northern Italy. For this, see Robert Black, *Education and Society in Florentine Tuscany: Teachers, Pupils and Schools* (Leiden: Brill, 2007), and the classic work of Paul Grendler, *Schooling in Renaissance Italy: Literacy and Learning, 1300–1600* (Baltimore: Johns Hopkins University Press, 1989).

13. *Decameron*, III, 4: 363–65.

14. Ibid., 365.

15. Ibid.

16. Ibid., 366.

17. Ibid., 366–67.

18. Ibid., 367.

19. Ibid.

20. *Decameron* III, 9: 429–42. In interesting ways, as we shall see, Giletta's love for her husband and its pairing with her impressive *virtù* offer a significant contrast with the apparently tragic cross-social-divides love of Griselda for her own noble, the Marquise of Saluzzo, which will be discussed in Chapter 5.

21. Ibid., 430.

22. Doctors, however, stood much higher on the social scale than surgeons because while they occasionally were forced to use their hands, they did

not engage in the messy and bloody manual labor of cutting or regularly working with their hands like surgeons.

23. In this lies an important distinction between how Giletta's love would have been viewed in France and in Florence. In the latter, as a member of the *popolo grosso* (who had at least ideally rejected the high-handed ways of nobles, actually eliminating them from government and to a great degree contesting their social standing), her love would have seemed less unlikely and if anything less socially acceptable because it aimed at a noble rather than a good solid member of the *popolo grosso*. In France, the tale would have played a bit differently with the son of a count being a highly desired catch for a doctor's daughter. Having said that, however, Boccaccio's tales often feature loves that involve such transcendent reaching across social divides, albeit often with problems created that drive the tale, as in this case.

24. *Decameron,* 431.

25. Ibid., 431–42. The fact that Giletta referred to her learning as an *"arte"* here and not just *scienza* (or learning), a term she also uses elsewhere, may have evoked positive resonances in a Florentine audience, where their *Arte*—the artisan guilds of the city—were what most agreed made the city rich and powerful.

26. Ibid., 432. The alternative of being burned alive if her healing did not work calls up images of women healers often associated with magic, who were treated at times as witches and could be burned alive for what was claimed was their witchery.

27. Ibid., 433.

28. Ibid. Branca suggests that "maritaggio" has a technical meaning in the *Decameron,* referring only to the marriage ceremony and not the actual consummation of the marriage. Given what follows, this makes sense, but the "aggio" ending also implies an extremely negative form of the noun that has "aggio" added on.

29. Ibid., 434. As this tale was apparently set in the thirteenth century, there were no shortages of wars between Florence and Siena that would have served. In fact, the same was true for the fourteenth century as well.

30. Ibid., 435.

31. Ibid., 436.

32. Ibid., 437.

33. Ibid., 438.

34. This seems to pre-echo Machiavelli's famous, and oft misunderstood, lines about ends and means and perhaps not by chance, for, as I argued in *Machiavelli in Love,* his vision of *virtù* and, in turn, its relationships to ends and means was much more embedded in earlier *popolo grosso* values than is usually seen by those more interested in classical sources than the shared everyday culture of the day. For this, see Ruggiero, *Machiavelli in Love,* 108–211, and especially 143, 249 n. 65.

35. Ibid., 439; italics mine. Perhaps it was "pleasing to God" as well that the count never realized that the woman he was making love to repeatedly was not the woman he thought but rather his wife. But even with God and the darkness of the room where they made love, his lack of awareness strains credulity and reminds readers that we must always be aware that we are dealing with fictions.

36. Ibid.

37. *Decameron*, III, 10: 443–50. I would like to thank Mario Casari for this reference and suggesting that Boccaccio could have heard this phrase as a youth in the streets of Naples frequented by Arab merchants used as a greeting and a parting salute. To his Italian ear *Allah bik* could well have had the ring of Alibech. Actually, the name has been little analyzed, but Fabrizio A. Pennacchietti has argued that it comes from the Turkish *Alî bek* meaning *Signor Ali* and refers to her important social status; for this, see his "L'eventuale fonte araba della novella di Alibech e Rustico (*Decamerone*, III, 10)," *Levia gravia: Quaderno annuale di letteratura italiana*, 8 (2006), 43–47 and 43, for this reading. Pennacchietti sees the story as coming from the Arabic tale "Susanna in the Desert," which also features a young girl seeking to serve God in the desert, but the rest of the tale is very different, as is the service rendered to God.

38. *Decameron*, 445.

39. Ibid. Vacca, "Converting Alibech," identifies this Rustico with a certain Rustico addressed in a letter of the Church Father Jerome, who had also failed to live up to a vow of chastity, but sees it as a clever reversal of that letter and critique of Jerome's negative attitude toward sex and pleasures of the body, 208–214. Although I discovered this article only after publishing an earlier much less developed version of the analysis to follow, it advances similar ideas about Boccaccio being humorously serious about Alibech serving God by putting the Devil back in Hell and uses a close analysis of Boccaccio's understanding of Aquinas to argue that for her, in her innocence, there is no sin in doing so, 216–220. There are also suggestions of a possible reading that would see Alibech as in a way reversing the Fall and returning to the Garden of Eden, 220–221, 227, as will be argued more fully below.

40. *Decameron*, 446.

41. Ibid.; italics mine.

42. Ibid., 446–47; italics mine.

43. Ibid., 448; italics mine.

44. Ibid., 450. Dioneo laughingly relates that Alibech innocently confessed that she had served God by putting the Devil back in Hell to the women who were preparing her for marriage after she returned to Gafsa. When they understood from her gestures what that service entailed, the phrase quickly became popular and spread rapidly from city to city, and Dioneo points out

that "the said way of speaking passed over the sea and is still used here [in Florence] today." While his etymology may be suspect, it is clear that he is referring to common usage in the Florence of Boccaccio's day.

45. For a classic analysis of this from the perspective of art, see Leo Steinberg, *The Sexuality of Christ in Renaissance Art and in Modern Oblivion* (New York: Random House, 1983).

46. Along with the laughter of the youths listening to Dioneo's tale and the humorous tone of the tale itself, contrasting the treatment of the theme of clerical seduction of a laywoman in this story with its treatment in IV, 2 is instructive. In that tale, as we have seen, Frate Alberto cunningly convinces a foolishly vain Venetian wife that the angel Gabriel has fallen in love with her and, as the angel has no physical body of his own, the friar cleverly has offered the use of his own body to the angel to make love to her. In her vanity, she is completely convinced by this scam and becomes his victim, believing that the angel Gabriel is making love to her. But her love is based on just that vanity, not service to God, and Frate Alberto is eventually savagely punished for his deed in the main square of Venice—a punishment portrayed as just and richly deserved. Clearly, he is depicted as misusing his clerical status like Rustico, but he is depicted as an ongoing fraud and sexual predator, whereas Rustico might be seen as cleverly innocent, overestimating his sexual prowess, as the tale ironically underlines. The difference and the humorous valence of the Alibech / Rustico story, however, I would suggest, turns on the fact that Alibech is the heroine of the tale, its real focus of interest, and not the least vain or crucially a sinner. This makes the story positive and also suggests a deeper theological meaning for her innocence and her way of serving God. Although some would see Alibech as a victim and a child victim at that, it is important to remember that that vision, thoroughly understandable from a modern perspective, works less well from a fourteenth-century perspective where fourteen was seen as a normal and ideal age for marriage for girls who were seen as no longer children but young women ready for marriage and sex. And although it may be argued that this was a masculine vision, it was one accepted by all and largely unquestioned. Finally, Alibech is not presented as a victim in any way; she is completely happy in her newfound religious enthusiasms, and the story turns on her repeated pleasure, not Rustico's, which quickly disappears. Thus, although from a modern perspective, the tale can be read as a cruel tricking of a young innocent girl and much worse, that would be a serious misreading of the tale as it would have been heard at the time, and Boccaccio's light humorous tone would have been completely out of place.

47. Vacca, "Converting Alibech," presents a similar argument that Boccaccio saw the pleasures of the body as small, natural sins that were unavoidable.

Her analysis stresses also the relationship between language and things, making the point that even renaming things does not change their underlying reality from Boccaccio's perspective, even as it reveals the innocence and naturalness of sexual attraction, 222–27. Eisner again focuses on the poetic use of language and its theological implications in "Eroticizing Theology," 205–7.

48. *Decameron,* 448.

49. Ibid.; italics mine. Literally "essere una bestia."

50. I say usually, because a few women writers did attack the notion of Eve's responsibility for the Fall. See for example Moderata Fonte (Modesta Pozzo, 1555–1592), *The Worth of Women: Wherein Is Clearly Revealed Their Nobility and Their Superiority to Men,* Virginia Cox, ed. and trans. (Chicago: University of Chicago Press, 1997), 93–94. Isotta Nogarola (1418–1466) a century earlier wrote *Questio utrum Adam vel Eva magis peccavit* as part of a literary exchange with the Venetian patrician Lodovico Foscarini, where she defended Eve against Foscarini's accusations; for a brief account, see Ruggiero, *The Renaissance in Italy,* 374–75; for more on Isotta, see Virginia Cox, *Women's Writing in Italy 1400–1650* (Baltimore: Johns Hopkins University Press, 2008), 4–12.

51. For the story, see Franco Sacchetti, *Il Trecentonovelle,* Valerio Marucci, ed. (Rome: Salerno Editrice, 1996) (novella 100), 304–10; text quoted 307; and editor's note 304, n. 1.

52. This sect was founded in 1260 in Parma by Gherardo Segarelli, who was executed for heresy in 1296. The historical Giovanni Apostoli, in fact, died in the prisons of the Inquisition in 1324.

53. It is noteworthy that at least two women in the thirteenth and fourteenth centuries were associated with prophecies of the last age: Guglielma and Prous Boneta. The followers of Guglielma preached after her death that as the Word had become incarnate in a man, Christ, so too the Holy Spirit would be incarnate in a woman, the resurrected Guglielma. With her resurrection, the Last Age of the Holy Spirit would begin. Boneta saw herself as the "abode of the Trinity and the giver of the Holy Spirit to the world." Just as Eve had been the cause of the Fall, she would be the path to salvation, ushering in the Last Age of the Spirit. For this, see the classic work by Majorie Reeves, *Joachim of Fiore and the Prophetic Future* (London: SPCK, 1976), 50–51; Marina Benedetti, *Di regine, sante e eretiche: Su Guglielma e sulla recente storiografia* (Florence: Firenze University Press, 2018); Nancy Mandeville Caciola, "A Guglielmite Trinity?" *California Italian Studies* 6 (2016), 1–20; Felice Tocco, "Guglielma Boema e i Guglielmiti," in *Atti della Reale Accademia dei Lincei, classe di scienze morali, storiche e filologiche,* 5 Serie. 8 (Rome, 1900), 1–32, and for the Inquisition trial of her followers Tocco's edition "Il processo dei Guglielmiti," in *Reale Accademia dei Lincei, memorie della classe di scienze morali,*

storiche e filologiche, Rendiconti, 5 Serie. 8 (Rome, 1899), 309-42, 351-84, 407-32, 437-69; and William H. May, "The Confession of Prous Boneta Heretic and Heresiarch," in *Essays in Medieval Life and Thought Presented in Honour of Austin Patterson Evans,* John Hine Mundy, ed. (New York, 1955), 3-30. Alibech, as a woman who undid the Fall, or might even lead the way to a new last age of the Holy Spirit, seems a little less fantastic in the context of these historical figures whose fame was widespread in northern Italy in the troubled times following the plague, especially among those expecting the imminent arrival of a last age of the Holy Spirit.

5. POWER

1. *Decameron,* III, 2: 338-45; and for the smell of the stables, 341.
2. Ibid., 339-40. Once again here, true love, sexual desire, and sexual intercourse in what is formally illicit sex are intertwined positively rather than being separated.
3. For the dangers of love sickness and its nature in the *Decameron,* see Massimo Ciavolella, "La tradizione *dell'aegritudo amoris* nel *Decameron,*" *Giornale storico della letteratura italiana* 147 (1970), 498-517, and more generally his *La malattia d'amore dall'antichità al medioevo* (Rome: Bulzoni, 1976), as well as the volume he edited with Donald Beecher with a slightly later focus, *Eros and Anteros: Medicine and the Literary Tradition of Love in the Renaissance* (Ottawa: Dovehouse Press, 1993).
4. In fact, violence was so common in courtship that the line between rape and courtship was a highly contested one, as argued earlier in the case of Cimone (V, 1) and in Chapter 2. The tale of Paganino of Monaco and the wife of Messer Ricciardo (II, 10) presents another good example of the way that violence was presented as relatively accepted on the path to eventual love.
5. *Decameron,* 341; italics mine.
6. Ibid., 342.
7. Ibid. Repeated bouts of lovemaking in an encounter between lovers in the *Decameron,* often dismissed by critics as merely masculine fantasies of prepotency, I would suggest also require that readers accept the premise that the sex involved was to be enjoyed by both partners and not just an issue of male pleasure, as is the case in this tale and often in the tales of the *Decameron* and more generally in the imaginative literature of the period. For a tale that expressed particularly well the idea that the mutual pleasure of both a woman and a man is an essential part of sex in loving relationships, see III, 7, where Tedaldo, in the context of a particularly virulent attack on friars, provides a long discourse on how loving sex should please both partners.

8. As discussed earlier, consensus realities were the varying understandings of a person's identity that were negotiated with the groups and solidarities that surrounded a person in the intimate urban spaces of Rinascimento life.

9. As we have seen, illicit sexual relations based on love are often referred to in the *Decameron* as "small natural sins" and virtually a *topos* in much of the earlier literature of courtly love. See, for example, the famous tale of the nightingale, where Riccardo Manardi happily makes love to the daughter of Messer Lizio da Valbona (V, 4), and their small natural sin is forgiven as such, albeit with a rather quick marriage of the lovers, or III, 7, where adultery based on love is similarly described.

10. *Decameron,* 342. Literally "be careful what you are doing," but the implication seems to be that too much sex and pleasure might have a negative effect on the king's health. In this case, obviously, it was too little sex for the king that actually presented the danger for all. As far as *"novità"* is concerned, labeling something as "new" implied that it was at best strange and more usually incorrect, as in this case; here it seems to have the sense of a strange innovation more than a mere novelty. See, for an extended discussion of this, Ruggiero, *The Renaissance in Italy,* 220-29.

11. *Decameron,* 342.

12. The representation of honor as a complex emotion in the *Decameron* discussed briefly earlier will be discussed more fully below.

13. The contrast with the behavior of a less *virtù*-ous prince, Tancredi (IV, 1), discussed earlier, is instructive. Learning of his beloved daughter's illicit affair with one of his servants (again), in tears and overcome by his emotions and a misplaced sense of honor, he makes the affair known to all and secures in the end the public airing of his shame and the loss of his daughter as well. In fact, as will be argued more fully in this chapter, along with love, *virtù* was crucial for Boccaccio in a true prince and its lack delegitimized one-man rule making would-be princes tyrants. For a rich discussion of this now, see James Hankins, "Boccaccio and the Political Thought of Renaissance Humanism," in *A Boccaccian Renaissance: Essays on the Early Modern Impact of Giovanni Boccaccio and His Works,* Martin Eisner and David Lummus, eds. (Notre Dame, IN: University of Notre Dame Press, 2019), 3-35. Hankins focuses on a later period in Boccaccio's life when he argues perceptively that Boccaccio was discouraged by his experiences with Florentine politics and corruption and places his views in a more classical tradition but also considers how Boccaccio's contemporary experiences played a role in his vision of virtue.

14. As story after story in the *Decameron* proclaims, true love makes lovers truly *virtù*-ous and capable of deeds that otherwise they would be incapable of; once again the story of Cimone (V, 1) discussed earlier in detail comes to mind.

15. *Decameron,* 345; and I use the term "outfoxed" intentionally as here the groom seems to be displaying virtually the same qualities that Machiavelli called for the prince to display as a fox and a lion in *The Prince.*

16. Ibid.

17. Ibid. The contrast is nicely suggested in a novella by Bandello that recounts a similar story of a would-be lover substituting himself for a lord and its very different results (Bandello II, 24). In that story, the victims are a Norman lord and his wife, and the lover is a corrupt Franciscan friar. And although the friar's love is also strongly felt—actually, virtually repeating some of the comments about the way unrequited love tends to grow dangerously—it is presented in a far less positive light, as is the friar himself. Once his deed is discovered with the wife's very similar innocent remarks about her earlier passionate lovemaking with what she thought was her husband, however, the tale takes a tellingly different turn. Bandello, noting that if this lord had behaved as Agilulf in the Boccaccio tale all would have turned out well, instead describes him as overcome by the strong, uncontrollable emotions associated with honor with devastating results. When the smoke clears, his wife is dead, having killed herself because of her husband's rage and the shame that would fall on her if she lived on; their son killed by accident in her passionate suicide; and her brother and the lord's much-loved brother-in-law dead at his hand in the confusion and because of the uncontrolled emotions unleashed. And, in the end, as Bandello notes with his usual dark vision, all this tragedy could have been avoided if the Norman noble had merely followed Agilulf's wise example and not been overcome by his feelings of honor in the face of a deed that no one had to know about—if he had merely kept quiet and not exposed what had happened to the consensus realities that surrounded them.

18. *Decameron* X, 10: 1232–48. An earlier, shorter version of this discussion of the tale was published as "The Lord Who Rejected Love, or the Griselda Story (X, 10)," in a festschrift for Konrad Eisenbichler, *Sex and Gender and Sexuality in Renaissance Italy,* Jacqueline Murray and Nicholas Terpstra, eds. (New York: Routledge, 2019), 21–34. Looking more closely at the Marquis of Saluzzo, I am following to a degree here the pathbreaking reading of Teodolinda Barolini in her impressive article, "The Marquis of Saluzzo, or the Griselda Story Before It Was Hijacked: Calculating Matrimonial Odds in the *Decameron* 10:10," 34 *Mediaevalia* (2013), 23–55, emphasizing even more a Florentine perspective and less her strategy of using modern game theory to explain what she labels the marquis's *beffa.* I suggest that Florentines would have focused more on the negative qualities of Gualtieri as a *signore,* while Barolini stresses his problems "as a man of power forced to marry against his will" (24): quite true, but too quick a conclusion to see all that is implied in the tale. For

a more recent similar reading, see Susanna Barsella's excellent article, "Tyranny and Obedience. A Political Reading of the Tale of Gualtieri (*Dec.*, X, 10)," *Italianistica* 42 (2013), 68-77. My account stresses more the marital as well as the political side of the tale and looks more closely at the Florentine political and social world of the day; she offers a more detailed analysis of the ancient and medieval theoretical literature on tyranny. In the end, however, we all agree that the tale is more about Gualtieri as a tyrant than about Griselda as a model wife. See also the important articles by Victoria Kirkham, "The Last Tale in the *Decameron*," *Mediaevalia* 12 (1989), 205-33; Shirley S. Allen, "The Griselda Tale and the Portrayal of Women in the *Decameron*," *Philological Quarterly* 56 (1977), 1-13; and Charles Haines, "Patient Griselda and *Matta Bestialitade*," *Quaderni d'Italianistica* 6 (1985), 233-40. For a brief introduction to the massive scholarly literature on this tale, see also this book's bibliography.

19. Ibid., 1233. "Beastly" often seems to serve as a code word or signal that the male so labelled has sexual appetites that are "unnatural" by Boccaccio's standards and hence like those of a beast. If "beastly" is being used in that sense here, it would add another dimension to the marquis's rejection of marriage and the love of women, one that Boccaccio regularly paints in a negative light. Barolini provides an interesting discussion of the term, drawing similar conclusions, but emphasizes its echoes of Dante's usage of the term along with its classical and Aristotelian dimension—a perspective that would undoubtedly have had its weight for learned readers and listeners but perhaps less for a broader audience at the time. Barolini, "Marquis of Saluzzo," 25-26.

20. Ibid.; italics mine.

21. Ibid., 1234.

22. *Decameron*, II, 3: 152-65. The three are described as the young sons of a noble knight named Tebaldo from either the Lamberti or the Agolanti families—both Ghibelline clans exiled from Florence in the late Middle Ages and thus immediately suspect in fourteenth-century Florence with its strong Guelf tradition.

23. It should be noted, however, that the prospects of profits from loaning money to the English had undoubtedly become less appetizing after the recent failure of Florentine banks in 1342, in part caused by the king of England's reneging on his debts to them. Actually, recent scholarship has argued that local bad loans in Tuscany and debts built up in the ongoing wars in the region were more responsible for the bank failures, but contemporary accounts tended to place a heavy emphasis on the king of England's actions—perhaps as a way to divert attention from the more local issues involved. Barsella notes also this connection in "Tyranny and Obedience," 74-75.

24. Walter (Gualtieri) of Brienne actually makes an appearance in the *Decameron* in his own right as one of the nine "lovers" of the sultan of Babylon's daughter, and a quite bloody "lover" at that (II, 7: 237-41 and 237, n. 7). Boccaccio also wrote a quite uncomplimentary account of his life and attempt to rule Florence in 1342 / 43 in his *De Casibus Virorum Illustrium*, Lib. IX, cap. 24. See now for a brief but perceptive account of Boccaccio's extremely negative vision of Walter's attempt to rule Florence as a tyrant with pertinent texts, Hankins, "Boccaccio and the Political Thought," 20-24, which stresses not just the lack of *virtù* of Walter but also of the Florentines who handed him the rule of their city.

25. Dioneo, however, does follow this comment with what appears to be a compliment for this lack of desire to marry, "for which he was reputed to be very wise." *Decameron*, 1234. "Reputed to be" but not necessarily very wise, and what follows undercuts further the force of this very traditional negative vision of marriage. More significantly, throughout the *Decameron*, we encounter regularly happy endings for tales of true love that feature marriage for the lovers, even as we rarely see what their "happily ever after" actually entailed.

26. For such age distinctions and the perceived long masculine adolescence of the day, see Laura Giannetti, *Lelia's Kiss: Imagining Gender, Sex, and Marriage in Italian Renaissance Comedy* (Toronto: University of Toronto Press, 2009), 18, 131-34, and the discussion in my *Machiavelli in Love*, 24-26, 172-73.

27. While the character Gualtieri had the same name as the recent Florentine would-be tyrant, this is not to argue that he was the only tyrant being referred to by the tale. In actuality, Florence was surrounded by dangerous and aggressive tyrants who were capable of instilling fear in the city even if they were not named Gualtieri. As often noted, the fourteenth century, following in the footsteps of the thirteenth, was a period where republics were losing out to tyrants everywhere, and Florence found itself surrounded by aggressive *signori* on virtually all sides. For a closer analysis of fear in this context in Florence, see the fascinating article of Andrea Zorzi, "The Anxiety of Republics: 'Timor' in Italy of the Communes during the 1330s," in *Emotions, Passions, and Powers in Renaissance Italy*, Fabrizio Ricciardelli and Andrea Zorzi, eds. (Amsterdam: Amsterdam University Press, 2015), 45-76.

28. *Decameron*, X, 10: 1234.

29. *Decameron*, 1234-35; italics mine. The lack of love in the marriage he sought, it might be suggested, also played a significant role in his lack of a positive relationship with his subjects, once again the micro level of life, in this case marriage, reflecting the macro level of life, in this case Gualtieri's rule. Both lacked love, and that stood literally at the heart of his negative consensus reality for his subjects and for the Florentine

readers of his tale. And, clearly, with the repetition of "insisting" and Gualtieri's will, the tale is playing on will as a dangerous source of sin when misplaced, as it is in this case. At this moment in the tale, with this willing misdeed, it might be argued Gualtieri confirms his fallen state.

30. Barolini, "Marquis of Saluzzo," 28–40, suggests that in these demands Gualtieri, unhappy with his subjects' calls for his marriage and limiting his freedom in this way, is setting up a *beffa* at their expense. The key to the *beffa*, for her interpretation, is his forcing them to accept the peasant wife that he will pick unbeknownst to them. Although there is a logic to this perspective, it seems more likely that the driving force the tale suggests is to be found in his decision to take a peasant as a wife is his realization that she will have to be totally subservient to him, something that Barolini also stresses.

31. *Decameron*, 1235. Tellingly, in the happy ending of the tale, it is remarked that when he finally does fall in love with Griselda, he is finally actually *consolata* with his wife and the match.

32. Ibid.

33. Ibid., 1237.

34. Ibid. Although the text is clear that Gualtieri entered the house alone (*solo*), the discussion between Gualtieri, the father, and Griselda requires that she has entered as well. Perhaps it is significant that she is so humble that her entering the house with Gualtieri does not require mention.

35. Obviously, neither Griselda nor her father as rural peasants would have been considered members of the *popolo* of an urban place like Florence, but in the past time of this tale set in a more rural and medieval world, both qualified as examples of members of a recognizable lower class (and by Florentine standards, an even lower class than their *popolo*) being mistreated in a high-handed and arrogant manner by someone who claimed to be their *signore*.

36. The Ordinances of Justice were first passed in Florence on January 18, 1293, and while their meaning at the time has been much debated, they soon became a kind of civic monument to the ideal of Florence as a republic ruled by the *popolo* without the interference of the traditional Tuscan rural nobility, labeled magnates (along with others deemed violent and high-handed in their treatment of the *popolo*), who had once dominated the city. For the debate and the more complex reality of the Ordinances and the magnates themselves, see my *The Renaissance in Italy*, 77–82 and 94–97, and the overview of Najemy in *Renaissance Florence*, 81–89, 92–95, 135–38, and for a more detailed study, see Carol Lansing, *The Florentine Magnates: Lineage and Faction in a Medieval Commune* (Princeton, NJ: Princeton University Press, 1991). Significantly, although it appears that Walter actually instituted policies that seemed to favor workers over the *popolo grosso*, after his fall most of his reforms were quickly forgotten,

replaced by a darker legend more suitable to the contemporary stereotypes of tyrants.

37. *Decameron*, 1237.

38. Ibid. Suggestively, Petrarch late in his life retold this tale in Latin,
claiming that in this way he was making it more broadly available for an
upper-class audience as it needed wider circulation to aid men to train a
wife to act correctly. In his rather different retelling of the tale, he tellingly softens this act of prepotency and cruel male power that in Boccaccio's tale powerfully presented Gualtieri's cruelty and lack of courtesy,
two negative attributes that undercut any real claim to true upper-class
status in its tales. In fact, Petrarch changes the incident to add the telling
detail that Gualtieri had Griselda surrounded by women of honor before
she was stripped. Here we see just one example of how the tale could be
changed to make it a hymn to a wise and careful husband anxious to arrange the right kind of marriage that would ensure a matrimony that
functioned as it should with the husband in command and the woman
subservient and obedient. But Dioneo's careful scripting of Gualtieri's
boorish and self-centered behavior in line with his high-handed ways
that evoke the psychological violence of the old nobility strongly suggest
a very different vision of Gualtieri and his marriage—a negative vision in
line with many of the tales about the injustices of arranged marriages in
the *Decameron* and men who seek marriages for motives other than love.

39. For a brief overview, see the chapter "Self" in my *The Renaissance in Italy,* especially 357–67. It might also be noted that this moment also suggests a
fear that underlay the explosion of sumptuary legislation after the plague.
Dressing like a member of the elite had the potential to allow clever lower-
class people to pass as superior; thus, dress and display had to be legally
controlled. See on sumptuary legislation, Catherine Kovesi, *Sumptuary
Laws in Italy, 1200–1500* (Oxford: Oxford University Press, 2004).

40. See this book's introduction and Chapter 1 for a fuller discussion of
complex emotions in contrast to simple emotions in the Rinascimento.

41. *Decameron*, 1238.

42. Ibid., 1239.

43. Ibid.

44. One might note here that although Griselda is clearly a victim, she is
hardly a heroine as often claimed at least at this point. There are, in fact,
numerous female heroines in the *Decameron* whose tales were constructed to show their *virtù* and ability to control their own lives in the
face of cruel males. Perhaps the best example of this, and a virtual anti-
Griselda tale, that gives the lie to later critics' vision of Griselda as a
model wife is the tale of Giletta of Narbonne (III, 9), discussed in Chapter
4, who, empowered by love, cures the king of France and overcomes a series of seemingly impossible trials (typical of the tales of lovers more

usually men in the literature of the day), and, thanks to her *virtù*, wins the love of the man she loves, her husband, Beltramo of Roussillon. Beltramo is also portrayed as a cruel lord, but Giletta is anything but passive and takes her life in her own hands to win out in the end—a model of what a woman can accomplish with *virtù* in the name of love. Similar *virtù*, overcoming a husband both cruel and foolish, is demonstrated in a tale (II, 9) where a Genoese woman, who takes the name Sigurano da Finale, passes as a male and flourishes in a series of adventures thanks to her *virtù* and in the end recovers the love of the husband she loves despite his murderous misdeeds.

45. *Decameron,* 1241.

46. Ibid.

47. Ibid.

48. Although this practice was often defended as saving a mother from the bother of raising and nursing a young child, it was also in reality largely controlled by husbands and a social necessity that demonstrated a family's status and wealth. For the complexity of this institution, see Christian Klapish Zuber's classic study, "Blood Parents and Milk Parents: Wet Nursing in Florence, 1300-1530," in her *Women, Family, and Ritual in Renaissance Italy* (Chicago: University of Chicago Press, 1985), 132-64.

49. For a thoughtful exploration of this vision of motherhood at the time and an excellent analysis of its inaccuracy, see Christian Klapisch Zuber, "The 'Cruel Mother': Maternity, Widowhood, and Dowry in Florence in the Fourteenth and Fifteenth Centuries," in her *Women, Family and Ritual,* 117-31.

50. For a powerful overview of the endurance of this practice, see John Boswell, *The Kindness of Strangers: Child Abandonment in Western Europe from Late Antiquity to the Renaissance* (Chicago: University of Chicago Press, 1988). A more focused and slightly later perspective is provided by Nicholas Terpstra, *Abandoned Children of the Italian Renaissance: Orphan Care in Florence and Bologna* (Baltimore: Johns Hopkins University Press, 2005), and Philip R. Gavitt, *Charity and Children in Renaissance Florence: The Ospedale degli Innocenti, 1410–1536* (Ann Arbor: University of Michigan Press, 1990).

51. *Decameron,* 1242-43.

52. In fact, this is the only use of the term *"lavoratori"* in the tale; usually she and her father are referred to as poor and it is noted that he is a peasant not a laborer. The title of the tale refers to her as *"una figliuola d'un villano"* and later when referring to her unexpected *virtù* in her dress and by inference her status, she is referred to as *"villesco": "l'alta vertù di costei nascosa sotto i poveri panni e sotto l'abito villesco."* Ibid., 1238.

53. For this, see Brucker, *Politics and Society,* 114-16; Najemy, *Florence,* 135-37. On the Ordinances, see note 36 above.

54. *Decameron*, 1243. Once again, this reference to the sacrifice of her virginity as a gift that in a way was like a dowry actually echoes a practice often seen in archival documents where women consented to sexual intercourse before marriage in return for a promise of marriage. This exchange of intercourse for a promise of marriage implied that virginity was a central element in the exchanges that surrounded marital practice. On the complex ways this did not always live up to the ideal, see my *Binding Passions*, 1-87, and the tale of the travails of Elena Cumano. See also the discussion of this in my *Boundaries of Eros*, 26-39, and for a later period Sandra Cavallo and Simona Cerutti, "Female Honor and Social Control of Reproduction in Piedmont between 1600 and 1800," in *Sex and Gender in Historical Perspective*, Guido Ruggiero and Edward Muir, eds. (Baltimore: Johns Hopkins University Press, 1990), 73-109.

55. Branca actually points out the textual parallels, noting that in the story of Job I:20, Job's *"Nudus egressus sum . . . nudus revertar"* seems to prefigure Griselda's *"ignuda m'aveste. . . . Io me n'andrò ignuda. . . ."* Ibid., 1243, n. 4. In the *New Oxford Annotated Bible*, the famous lament of Job is rendered, "Naked I came from my mother's womb, and naked I shall return; the Lord gave, and the Lord has taken away; blessed be the name of the Lord." Job I:20.

56. In fact, Petrarch's famous retelling of this tale, referred to in note 38 above, translates it into Latin and in doing so transforms it both in terms of language—his Latin rendition giving it a formally higher register as well as a masculine one, as women were generally held to be incapable of reading works written in Latin (this was actually one of Boccaccio's defenses for writing the *Decameron* in Italian)—and in terms of its moral message. In his retelling, as noted earlier, the tale focuses on Griselda as the perfectly obedient wife as well as on her as the perfect example of an obedient subject to a *signore*, drawing out more deeply and positively the parallel with the biblical Job. It should be noted that Petrarch, who lived much of his life supported by *signori*, often quite bloody tyrants like the Carrara lords of Padua and Visconti of Milan, was no friend of republics and, in fact, was taken to task by his otherwise friend Boccaccio for his antirepublican sentiments more than once. All this is to suggest along with a number of recent critics that Petrarch literally "hijacked" the tale and that his rewriting of it has deeply skewed many later commentators' reading of it. See on this, Barolini, "The Marquis of Saluzzo," 23-46 and especially 24.

57. For a brief overview of these developments, see Ruggiero, *The Renaissance in Italy*, 157-70.

58. *Decameron*, 1243.

59. Ibid., 1244-45; italics mine.

60. Although what those young women won could be highly problematic, as the *Decameron* frequently demonstrates. It should be noted as well that all the women of the *brigata* were actually quite a bit older than the normal age of women in Florence at their first marriages, with ages ranging between eighteen and twenty-eight. We are informed by Boccaccio of this when he describes them first gathering in Santa Maria Novella to plan their escape from plague-stricken Florence. The reality that they should have all been married by that date, given the standards of the day, might be explained by the fact that they were widows whose husbands had died in the plague. Indeed, this was an explanation that might well have made sense even without the plague, as many young women married to much older husbands were already widows at this age. But Boccaccio makes no references to their status as widows, nor for that matter to the fact that in their twenties they already qualified for the label "old maid" by the standards of the day. Perhaps the key to this anomalous situation turns on the implication that true love is unlikely at the normal age of marriage for women, especially arranged marriages. The older women of the *brigata*, in contrast, were capable of both feeling and understanding true love.

61. *Decameron*, 1246. Note that the term *"consolato"* here echoes the very thing that Gualtieri insisted that he must find in a wife if he was to take one early in the tale.

62. The one seemingly major exception is tale nine on day nine, told by Emilia. Indeed, although less studied, this troubling tale has been creatively reread to undercut its apparent acceptance of the beating of wives, even well-behaved wives, as an ideal and a way to keep them obedient and dedicated to the service of their husbands. Albert Ascoli, in the article "Solomon and Emilia, or the King and I: A Reading of Decameron 9.9," forthcoming in *Lectura Boccaccii, Day 9,* Susanna Barsella and Simone Marchesi, eds. (Toronto: University of Toronto Press, 2020), which he kindly shared with me, examines this tale with rare insight as he reviews the literature it has engendered with particular attention to the literature that seeks to reverse its apparent message. Ascoli argues impressively that there are multiple reasons for questioning the surface reading of the tale and makes a particular case for having suspicions about how seriously a reader is to take this story from Emilia, its narrator, as she is a character presented as one who is overly negative about the ability of women to govern themselves (expressed immediately in the introduction to the tales) and with the necessity of placing women under the rule of males, husbands, fathers, or brothers. There is much more to Ascoli's argument and in the literature that suggests that this novella should not be taken at face value. But for our argument here, perhaps it

is best to say merely that these tales are more a discourse that leans strongly in the direction of presenting such treatment of women negatively, often associated with lower-class males, even as this tale recognizes that such treatment was prevalent at the time and, indeed, widely defended. And, most significantly for the argument here, even as it is strongly criticized in Dioneo's last tale of the *Decameron*.

63. Ibid., 1247. Branca quotes in n. 2 to the text (p. 1247) that the late fourteenth-century copyist of the manuscript of the *Decameron*, Francesco di Amaretto Mannelli, commented in the margin of his transcription: "Piss in your hand Gualtieri! Who is going to give me back those twelve years? The *forche?*" *Forche* were the structures where criminals were hanged at the time in Florence and many other cities of northern Italy.

64. Ibid., 1247; *dar vanto* implies a formal pledge or declaration.

65. Critics have from time to time referred to the *Decameron* as "The Human Comedy," playing on an apparent contrast with Dante's *Divine Comedy*, but I would suggest that Boccaccio's comedy was more divine than it might at first seem and Dante's in turn more human.

66. *Decameron*, 1248.

67. Although I think it might be pushing the point too far, there is a way in which Griselda might be read as a parallel figure to Alibech, both as savior figures opening the way to a new age of love. And, suggestively, the tales of both women are narrated by Dioneo, perhaps the new god of a new age of love. From this perspective, it might be argued that Griselda is the humble and chaste Christ-like figure who leads into a new age of love with her passive suffering and the wounds from an evil Satan-like husband that are referred to as "puncturing" her in life much as Christ was punctured by the nails, spines, and lance on the Cross. Alibech, in contrast, does not suffer, leading the way into the new age of love, but does so happily and in a virtual holy ecstasy inspired by her "misunderstanding" or perhaps true understanding of the nature of making love in a new age of love. A number of critics have seen in Griselda a Christ figure; for a powerful reading, see Mazzotta, *The World at Play*, 120-30, which also focuses on Gualtieri's negative qualities.

68. *Decameron*, 1248.

69. Ibid.

70. In fact, here once again it might be suggestive to compare Dioneo's presentation of Alibech (III, 10) and Griselda and his claims about how contemporary women were more likely to respond to such treatment. Alibech humorously, but suggestively, elevates the pleasure sought in true love to the highest plane imaginable in the Rinascimento.

BIBLIOGRAPHY

Aberth, John. *From the Brink of the Apocalypse: Confronting Famine, War, Plague, and Death in the Later Middle Ages.* New York: Routledge, 2001.

Ahern, John. "Dioneo's Repertory: Performance and Writing in Boccaccio's *Decameron.*" In *Performing Medieval Narrative*, edited by Evelyyn Birge Vitz, Nancy Freeman Regalado, and Marilyn Lawrence, 45–58. Rochester, NY: D. S. Brewer, 2005.

Albanese, Giovanna. "Fortuna umanistica della Griselda." *Quaderni Petrarcheschi* 10 (1993): 571–627.

Albers, Irene. "The Passions of the Body in Boccaccio's *Decameron.*" *Modern Language Notes* 125 (2010): 26–53.

Alfano, Giancarlo, Teresa d'Urso, and Alessandra Perriccioli Saggese, eds. *Boccaccio angioino: Materiali per la storia culturale di Napoli nel Trecento.* Brussels: Peter Lang, 2012.

Alighieri, Dante. *"Il convivio" ridotto a miglior lezione e commentato.* Edited by G. Businelli and G. Vandelli. Vols. 4–5 of *Opere di Dante*, edited by M. Barbi. Florence, Italy: Le Monnier, 1934–1937.

——. *La Divina commedia.* Edited by Umberto Bosco and Giovanni Reggio. Florence, Italy: Le Monnier, 1979, 3 vols.

——. *The Divine Comedy.* Edited and translated by Charles S. Singleton. Princeton, NJ: Princeton University Press, 1970–1975, 6 vols.

Allen, Shirley S. "The Griselda Tale and the Portrayal of Women in the *Decameron.*" *Philological Quarterly* 56 (1977): 1–13.

Almansi, Guido. *The Writer as Liar: Narrative Techniques in the* Decameron. London: Routledge and Kegan Paul, 1975.

Amendolara, Rosaria. *Comunicare la realtà con la letteratura: Letture Decameroniane.* Bari, Italy: Adriatica Editrice, 2003.

Andrei, Filippo. *Boccaccio the Philosopher: An Epistemology of the Decameron.* Dallas: Palgrave Macmillan, 2017.

Anselmi, Gian Mario, Giovanni Baffetti, Carlo Delcorno, and Sebastiana Nobili, eds. *Boccaccio e i suoi lettori: Una lunga ricezione.* Bologna, Italy: Il Mulino, 2013.

Armstrong, Guyda. "Boccaccio and Dante." In *The Cambridge Companion to Boccaccio*, edited by Guyda Armstrong, Rhiannon Daniels, and Stephen J. Milner, 121–38. Cambridge: Cambridge University Press, 2015.

——. "Heavenly Bodies: The Presence of the Divine Female in Boccaccio." *Italian Studies* 60 (2005): 134–46.

Armstrong, Guyda, Rhiannon Daniels, and Stephen J. Milner. "Boccaccio as a Cultural Mediator." In *The Cambridge Companion to Boccaccio*, 3–19. Cambridge: Cambridge University Press, 2015.

——, eds. *The Cambridge Companion to Boccaccio*. Cambridge: Cambridge University Press, 2015.

Armstrong, Paul. *How Literature Plays with the Brain*. Baltimore: Johns Hopkins University Press, 2013.

Asaro, Brittany. "Boccaccio's Francescas: Comparing *Inferno* V and the Tale of Nastagio degli Onesti (*Dec.* V. 8)." In *Women in Hell: Francesca da Rimini and Friends between Sin, Virtue and Heroism / Donne all'Inferno: Francesca da Rimini e Co. tra peccato, virtù ed eroismi. Giornate internazionali Francesca da Rimini. VI Edizione. Atti del convegno*. Romagna, Italy: Arte e Storia, 2013.

Ascoli, Albert Russell. "Auerbach fra gli epicurei: dal canto X dell'*Inferno* alla VI giornata del *Decameron*." *Moderna* 11 (2009): 91–108.

——. "Boccaccio's Auerbach: Holding the Mirror up to Mimesis." *Studi sul Boccaccio* 20 (1991): 377–97.

——. *Dante and the Making of the Modern Author*. Cambridge: Cambridge University Press, 2010.

——. *A Local Habitation and a Name: Imagining Histories in the Italian Renaissance*. New York: Fordham University Press, 2011.

——. "Pyrrhus' Rules: Playing with Power from Boccaccio to Machiavelli." *Modern Language Notes* 114 (1999): 14–57.

——. "Solomon and Emilia, or the King and I: A Reading of *Decameron* 9.9." In *Lecturae Boccaccii, Day 9*, edited by Susanna Barsella and Simone Marchesi. Toronto: University of Toronto Press, forthcoming.

Bagnoli, Marina, ed. *Treasures of Heaven: Saints Relics, and Devotion in Medieval Europe*. New Haven, CT: Yale University Press, 2010.

Bakhtin, Mikhail. *Rabelais and His World*. Translated by Hélène Iswolsky. Bloomington: Indiana University Press, 1993.

Baldi, Andrea. "La retorica dell' '*exemplum*' nella novella di Nastagio (*Decameron*, V.8)." *Italian Quarterly* 32 (1995): 17–38.

Balestrero, Monica. *L'immaginario del sogno nel Decameron*. Rome: Aracne, 2009.

Barasch, Moshe. *Gestures of Despair in Medieval and Early Renaissance Art*. New York: New York University Press, 1976.

Baratto, Mario. *Realtà e stile nel Decameron*. Vicenza, Italy: Pozza, 1970.

——. "Struttura narrativa e messaggio ideologico." In *Il Testo moltiplicato: Lettura di una novella del "Decameron,"* edited by Mario Lavagetto, Mario Baratto, Alessandro Serpiari, and Cesare Segre, 29–42. Parma, Italy: Pratiche Editrice, 1982.

Bàrberi-Squarotti, Giorgio. *Il potere della parola: Studi sul Decameron*. Naples, Italy: Federico & Ardia, 1989; especially "La 'cornice' del 'Decameron' o il mito di Robinson," 5–63.

———. *Prospettive sul* Decameron. Turin, Italy: Einaudi, 1989.

Barbi, Michele. "Sul testo del *Decameron*." In *La nuova filologia e l'edizione dei nostri scrittori da Dante al Manzoni*. Florence, Italy: Sansone, 1973.

Barillari, Sonia Maura. "La testa nel testo: Per un'altra lettura di *Decameron* IV, 5." *L'immagine riflessa. Testi, società, culture* 5 (1996): 173–86.

Barolini, Teodolinda. "The Marquis of Saluzzo, or the Griselda Story Before It Was Hijacked: Calculating Matrimonial Odds in the *Decameron* 10:10." *Mediaevalia* 34 (2013): 23–55.

———. "'Le parole son femmine e i fatti son maschi': Towards a Sexual Poetics of the *Decameron* (*Decameron* II, 10)." *Studi sul Boccaccio* 21 (1993): 175–97.

———. "Sociology of the *Brigata*: Gendered Groups in Dante, Forese, Folgore, Boccaccio, From *'Guido, i' vorrei'* to Griselda." *Italian Studies* 67 (2012): 4–22.

———. "The Wheel of the *Decameron*." *Romance Philology* 36 (1983): 521–39.

Barsella, Susanna. "Boccaccio, i tiranni e la ragione naturale." *Heliotropia* 12–13 (2015–2016): 131–63.

———. "The Myth of Prometheus in Giovanni Boccaccio's *Decameron*." *Modern Language Notes* 119 (2004): S120–41.

———. "Travestimento autoriale e autorità narrativa nella cornice del *Decameron*." In *Vested Voices II. Creating with Transvestism: From Bertolucci to Boccaccio*, edited by Federica Pedriali and Rossella Riccobono, 131–44. Ravenna, Italy: Longo, 2007.

———. "Tyranny and Obedience. A Political Reading of the Tale of Gualtieri (*Dec.*, X, 10)." *Italianistica* 42 (2013): 68–77.

Bartels, H., and S. Zeki. "The Neural Correlates of Maternal and Romantic Love." *Neuroimage* 21 (2004): 1155–66.

Battaglia, Salvatore. *Giovanni Boccaccio e la riforma della narrativa*. Naples, Italy: Liguori, 1969.

———. *Grande dizionario della lingua Italiana*. Turin, Italy: UTET, 1961.

Battaglia Ricci, Lucia. *Ragionare nel giardino: Boccaccio e i cicli pittorici del "Trionfo della morte."* Rome: Salerno, 1987.

Bausi, Francesco. "Gli spiriti magni: Filigrane aristoteliche e tomistiche nella decima giornata del *Decameron*." *Studi sul Boccaccio* 27 (1999): 205–53.

Baxter, Catherine. "'Galeotto fu la metafora': Language and Sex in Boccaccio's *Decameron*." In *Sexualities, Textualities, Art and Music in Early Modern Italy*, edited by Melanie L. Marshall, Linda L. Carroll, and Katherine McIver, 23–39. Farnham, UK: Ashgate, 2014.

———. "Turpiloquium in Boccaccio's Tale of the Goslings (*Decameron*, Day IV, Introduction." *Modern Language Review* 108 (2013): 812–38.

Bec, Christian. "Sur le message du Décaméron." *Revue de études italiennes* 21 (1975): 284–303.

Becker, Marvin. "Church and State in Florence on the Eve of the Renaissance, 1343–82." *Speculum* 37 (1962): 509–27.

Bellosi, Luciano. *Buffalmacco e il Trionfo della Morte.* Turin, Italy: Einaudi, 1974.

Benedetti, Laura, Julia L. Hairston, and Silvia M. Ross, eds. *Gendered Contexts: New Perspectives in Italian Cultural Studies.* New York: Peter Lang, 1996.

Benedetti, Marina. *Io non sono Dio: Guglielma di Milano e i Figli dello Spirito Santo.* Milan, Italy: Edizioni Biblioteca Francescana, 1998.

———. *Di regine, sante e eretiche: Su Guglielma e sulla recente storiografia.* Florence, Italy: Firenze University Press, 2018; also in *Reti Medievali Rivista* 19 (2018): 1–20.

Benvenuti, Anna. "Le fonti agiografiche nella costruzione della memoria cronistica." In *Il pubblico dei santi: Forme e livelli di ricezione dei messaggi agiografici,* edited by Paolo Golinelli, 79–104. Rome: Viella, 2000.

Bernardo, Aldo S. "The Plague as Key to Meaning in Boccaccio's *Decameron*." In *The Black Death,* edited by Daniel Williman, 39–64. Binghamton, NY: Medieval and Renaissance Texts and Studies, 1982.

Besserman, Lawrence L. *The Legend of Job in the Middle Ages.* Cambridge, MA: Harvard University Press, 1979.

Best, Myra. "La peste e le papere: Textual Repression in Day Four of the *Decameron*." In *Boccaccio and Feminist Criticism,* edited by Thomas C. Stillinger and F. Regina Psaki, 157–68. Chapel Hill, NC: Annali d'Italianistica, 2006. (*Annali d'Italianistica, Studi e testi,* vol. 8.)

Biagini, Luca, Lia Lapini, and Maria Bianca Tortorizio. "Sulla giornata V del *Decameron*." In *Studi sul Boccaccio,* edited by Vittore Branca, 159–77. Florence, Italy: Sansoni, 1973.

Billanovich, Giuseppe. "La leggenda dantesca del Boccaccio." *Studi danteschi* 28 (1947): 45–144.

———. *Restauri boccacceschi.* Rome: Edizioni di storia e letteratura, 1947.

Biow, Douglas. *The Culture of Cleanliness in Renaissance Italy.* Ithaca, NY: Cornell University Press, 2006.

———. *Mirabili Dictu: Representations of the Marvelous in Medieval and Renaissance Epic.* Ann Arbor: University of Michigan Press, 1996.

Black, Robert. *Education and Society in Florentine Tuscany: Teachers, Pupils and Schools.* Leiden, Netherlands: Brill, 2007.

Boccaccio, Giovanni. *The Corbaccio.* Translated by Anthony K. Cassell. Urbana: University of Illinois Press, 1975.

———. *Il Corbaccio.* Edited by Giulia Natali. Milan: Mursia, 1992.

———. *Decameron.* Edited by Vittore Branca. Turin, Italy: Einaudi, 1992, 2 vols.

———. *Decameron.* Edited by Mario Marti. Milan: Rizzoli, 1974, 2 vols.

———. *The Decameron.* Edited by Mark Musa and Peter Bondanella. New York: Penguin, 1982.

——. "*Decameron*. Edizione critica secondo l'autografo Hamiltoniano." In *Scrittori Italiani e testi antichi pubblicati dall'Accademia della Crusca*, edited by Vittore Branca. Florence, Italy: Olschki, 1976.

——. "*Decameron, Filocolo, Ameto, Fiammetta*." In *La letteratura Italiana* vol. 8., edited by Enrico Bianchi, Carlo Salinari, and Natalino Sapegno. Milan: Riccardo Ricciardi, 1952.

——. *Tutte le opere di Giovanni Boccaccio*. Edited by Vittore Branca. Milan: Mondadori, 1967–1998, 10 vols.

Boddice, Rob. *The History of Emotions*. Manchester, England: Manchester University Press, 2018.

——. *A History of Feelings*. London: Reaktion Books, 2019.

Bologna, Corrado. *Tradizione e fortuna dei classici italiani*, vol. 1: *Dalle origini al Tasso*. Turin, Italy: Einaudi, 1993.

Bolongaro, Eugenio. "Positions and Presuppositions in the Tenth Tale of the Fifth Day of Boccaccio's *Decameron*." *Studies in Short Fiction* 27, no. 3 (1990): 399–404.

Bonadeo, Alfredo. "Marriage and Adultery in the *Decameron*." *Philological Quarterly* 60 (1981): 287–303.

——. "Some Aspects of Love and Nobility in the Society of the *Decameron*." *Philological Quarterly* 47 (1968): 513–25.

Bonavita, Lucilla. "Polyphonic Voices of the Mediterranean in Boccaccio's Sicilian Novellas." *Symposia Melitensia* 13 (2017): 1–7.

Bonino, Guido Davico, ed. *Così per gioco: Sette secoli di poesia giocosa, parodica e satirica*. Turin, Italy: Einaudi, 2000.

Boquet, Damien, and Nagy Piroska. "Medieval Sciences of Emotion in the 11th–13th Centuries: An Intellectual History." *Osiris* 31 (2016): 21–45.

——. *Sensible Moyen Âge: Une histoire des émotions dans l'Occident mèdièval*. Paris: Seuil, 2015.

Boswell, John. *The Kindness of Strangers: Child Abandonment in Western Europe from Late Antiquity to the Renaissance*. Chicago: University of Chicago Press, 1988.

Bouwsma, William J. *Venice and the Defense of Republican Liberty: Renaissance Values in the Age of the Counter Reformation*. Berkeley: University of California Press, 1968.

Boyde, Patrick. *Perception and Passion in Dante's "Comedy."* Cambridge: Cambridge University Press, 1993.

Bragantini, Renzo, and Pier Massimo Forni, eds. *Lessico critico decameroniano*. Turin, Italy: Bollati Boringhieri, 1995.

Branca, Vittore. *Boccaccio: The Man and His Works*. Edited by Dennis J. McAuliffe. Translated by Richard Monges and Dennis J. McAuliffe. New York: Harvester, 1976.

——. *Boccaccio medievale e nuovi studi sul* Decameron. Florence, Italy: Sansoni, 1996.

———. *Boccaccio visualizzato.* Turin, Italy: Einaudi, 1999.

———. *Giovanni Boccaccio,* Decameron: *Profilo biografico.* 2nd ed. Florence, Italy: Sansoni, 1992.

Broomhall, Susan, ed. *Ordering Emotions in Europe, 1100–1800.* Leiden, Netherlands: Brill, 2015.

Broomhall, Susan, Jane W. Davidson, and Andrew Lynch, eds. *A Cultural History of Emotions.* London: Bloomsbury, 2019, 6 vols.

Brown, Katherine A. "Splitting Pants and Pigs: The *Fabliau* 'Barat et Haimet' and Narrative Strategies in *Decameron* 8.5 and 8.6." In *Reconsidering Boccaccio,* edited by Olivia Holmes and Dana E. Stewart, 344–64. Toronto: University of Toronto Press, 2018.

Brownlee, Marina Scordilis. "Wolves and Sheep: Symmetrical Undermining in Day III of the *Decameron.*" *Romance Notes* 24 (1984): 262–66.

Brucker, Gene. *The Civic World of Early Renaissance Florence.* Princeton, NJ: Princeton University Press, 1977.

———. *Florentine Politics and Society 1343–1378.* Princeton, NJ: Princeton University Press, 1962.

———. *Giovanni and Lusanna: Love and Marriage in Renaissance Florence.* Berkeley: University of California Press, 1986.

Bruni, Francesco. *Boccaccio: L'invenzione della letteratura mezzana.* Bologna: Il Mulino, 1990.

———. *La città divina: Le parti e il bene comune da Dante a Guicciardini.* Bologna: Il Mulino, 2003.

Bruno Pagnamenta, Roberta. *Il 'Decameron': l'ambiguità come strategia narrativa.* Ravenna, Italy: Longo, 1990.

Burke, Peter. *The Historical Anthropology of Early Modern Italy: Essays on Perception and Communication.* Cambridge: Cambridge University Press, 1987.

———. *The Italian Renaissance: Culture and Society in Italy.* Princeton, NJ: Princeton University Press, 1986.

———. *Varieties of Cultural History.* Ithaca, NY: Cornell University Press, 1997.

Caciola, Nancy Mandeville. "A Guglielmite Trinity?" *California Italian Studies* 6 (2016): 1–20.

Caferro, William. *Contesting the Renaissance.* Oxford: Wiley Blackwell, 2011.

Calabrese, Michael A. "Feminism and the Packaging of Boccaccio's Fiammetta." *Italica* 74 (1997): 20–42.

———. "Male Piety and Sexuality in Boccaccio's *Decameron.*" *Philological Quarterly* 82 (2003): 257–76.

Camille, Michael. "The Corpse in the Garden: *Mumia* in Medieval Herbal Illustrations." *Micrologus: Natura, scienze e società medievali* 7 (1999): 297–318.

Campbell, Emma. "Sexual Politics and the Poetics of Translation in the Tale of Griselda." *Comparative Literature* 55 (2003): 191–216.

Candido, Igor. *Boccaccio umanista: Studi su Boccaccio e Apuleio.* Ravenna, Italy: Longo, 2014.

Cannizzaro, Tommaso. *Il lamento di Lisabetta da Messina e la leggenda del vaso di basilico.* Catania, Italy: Battiato, 1902.

Capellanus, Andrea. *Andreas Capellanus on Love.* Edited and translated by Patrick Gerard Walsh. London: Duckworth, 1982. (Latin and English edition.)

———. *The Art of Courtly Love.* Translated by John Jay Perry. New York: Columbia University Press, 1960.

Cardini, Franco. "Lisabetta e l'archetipo." In *Le cento novelle contro la morte: Boccaccio e la rifondazione cavalleresca del mondo,* 127–42. Rome: Salerno, 2007.

Carrera, Elena, ed. *Emotions and Health, 1200–1700.* Leiden, Netherlands: Brill, 2013.

Carruthers, Mary. *The Craft of Thought: Meditation, Rhetoric, and the Making of Images, 400–1200.* Cambridge: Cambridge University Press, 2000.

Casagrande, Carla, and Silvana Vecchio. *Passioni dell'anima: Teoria e usi degli affetti nella cultura medievale.* Florence, Italy: SISMEL, 2014.

Cavallo, Sandra, and Simona Cerutti. "Female Honor and Social Control of Reproduction in Piedmont between 1600 and 1800." In *Sex and Gender in Historical Perspective,* edited by Guido Ruggiero and Edward Muir, 73–109. Baltimore: Johns Hopkins University Press, 1990.

Cervigni, Dino S. "Making Amends and Behaving Magnificently: *Decameron* 10's Secular Redemption." *Annali d'Italianistica* 31 (2013): 416–58.

———. *From Divine to Human: Dante's Circle vs. Boccaccio's Parodic Centers.* Binghamton, NY: Center for Medieval and Renaissance Studies, 2009.

Cherchi, Paolo. *L'onestade e l'onesto raccontare del* Decameron. Fiesole, Italy: Cadmo, 2004.

Chiecchi, Giuseppe, and Luciano Troisio. *Il* Decameron *sequestrato. Le tre edizioni censurate nel Cinquecento.* Milan, Italy: Unicopli, 1984.

Chretien, Heidi L. *The Festival of San Giovanni: Imagery and Power in Renaissance Florence.* New York: Peter Lang, 1994.

Ciabattoni, Francesco, Elsa Filosa, and Kristina M. Olson, eds. *Boccaccio, 1313–2013.* Ravenna, Italy: Longo, 2015.

Ciabbatoni, Francesco, and Pier Massimo Forni, eds. *The* Decameron *Third Day in Perspective.* Toronto: University of Toronto Press, 2014.

Ciavolella, Massimo. *La malattia d'amore dall'antichità al medioevo.* Rome: Bulzone, 1976.

———. "La tradizione *dell'aegritudo amoris nel Decameron.*" *Giornale storico della letteratura italiana* 147 (1970): 498–517.

Ciavolella, Massimo, and Donald Beecher, eds. *Eros and Anteros: Medicine and the Literary Tradition of Love in the Renaissance.* Ottawa: Dovehouse Press, 1993.

Cioffari, Vincenzo. "The Concept of Fortune in the *Decameron.*" *Italica* 17 (1940): 129–37.

Cipollone, Annalisa. "Leggere e interpretare Petrarca: Griselda tra propizia e avversa fortuna." In *Per Petrarca Latino: Opere e traduzioni nel tempo,* edited by Natascia Tonelli, 223–41. Padua, Italy: Antenore, 2018.

Civitarese, Giuseppe. "Abjection and Aesthetic Conflict in Boccaccio's (L)Isabetta." *Journal of Romance Studies* 10 (2010): 11–25.

Clarke, K. P. "Text and (Inter)Face: The Catchwords in Boccaccio's Autograph of the *Decameron*." In *Reconsidering Boccaccio*, edited by Olivia Holmes and Dana E. Stewart, 27–47. Toronto: University of Toronto Press, 2018.

Clough, Patricia Ticineto, and Jean Halley, eds. *The Affective Turn: Theorizing the Social*. Durham, NC: Duke University Press, 2007.

Clubb, Louise George. "Boccaccio and the Boundaries of Love." *Italica* 37 (1960): 188–96.

Cocks, H. G. "Modernity and the Self in the History of Sexuality." *Historical Journal* 49 (2006): 1211–27.

Cohen, Elizabeth, and Thomas V. Cohen. *Daily Life in Renaissance Italy*. Westport, CT: Greenwood Press, 2001.

Cohen, Esther. *The Modulated Scream: Pain in Late Medieval Culture*. Chicago: University of Chicago Press, 2010.

Cohen, Thomas V. *Love and Death in Renaissance Italy*. Chicago: University of Chicago Press, 2004.

Cohen-Hanegbi, Naama. "A Moving Soul: Emotions in Late Medieval Medicine." *Osiris* 31 (2016): 165–92.

Cohn, Samuel K., Jr. *The Black Death Transformed: Disease and Culture in Early Renaissance Europe*. New York: Oxford University Press, 2002.

——. *Creating the Florentine State: Peasants and Rebellion, 1343–1434*. Cambridge: Cambridge University Press, 2004.

——. *The Cult of Remembrance and the Black Death: Six Renaissance Cities in Central Italy*. Baltimore: Johns Hopkins University Press, 1992.

——. *Cultures of Plague: Medical Thinking at the End of the Renaissance*. Oxford: Oxford University Press, 2010.

——. "Renaissance Emotions: Hate and Disease in European Perspective." In *Emotions, Passions and Power in Renaissance Italy: Proceedings of the International Conference Georgetown University at Villa Le Balze, 5–8 May 2012*, edited by Fabrizio Ricciardelli and Andrea Zorzi, 145–70. Amsterdam: Amsterdam University Press, 2015.

——. *Women in the Streets: Essays on Sex and Power in Renaissance Italy*. Baltimore: Johns Hopkins University Press, 1996.

Cohn, Samuel K., and Fabrizio Ricciardelli, eds. *The Culture of Violence in Renaissance Italy*. Florence, Italy: Le Lettere, 2012.

Cole, Howard C. "Interplay in the *Decameron*: Boccaccio, Neifile and Giletta di Narbona." *Modern Language Notes* 90 (1975): 38–57.

Corazzini, Francesco. *Le lettere edite e inedite di Giovanni Boccaccio*. Florence, Italy: Sansoni, 1877.

Cottino-Jones, Marga. "The City / Country Conflict in the *Decameron*." *Studi sul Boccaccio* 8 (1974): 147–84.

——. "Comic Modalities in the *Decameron*." In *Versions of Medieval Comedy*, edited by Paul D. Ruggiers, 151–71. Norman: Oklahoma University Press, 1977.

——. "Desire and the Fantastic in the *Decameron*: The Third Day." *Italica* 70 (1993): 1–18.

——. "Fabula vrs. Figura: Another Interpretation of the Griselda Story." *Italica* 50 (1970): 38–52.

——. "Magic and Superstition in Boccaccio's *Decameron*." *Italian Quarterly* 72 (1975): 5–32.

——. *Order from Chaos: Social and Aesthetic Harmonies in Boccaccio's* Decameron. Washington, DC: University Press of America, 1982.

——. "The Mode and Structure of Tragedy in Boccaccio's *Decameron* (III, 9)." *Italian Quarterly* 43 (1967): 63–88.

Cox, Virginia. *Women's Writing in Italy 1400–1650*. Baltimore: Johns Hopkins University Press, 2008.

Cozzarelli, Julia. "Love and Destruction in the *Decameron*: Cimone and Calandrino." *Forum Italicum: A Journal of Italian Studies* 38 (2004): 338–63.

Crivelli, Tatiana. "Applicazioni ipertestuali e interpretazione critica: l'esempio di Lisabetta (*Decameron* IV, 5)." *Cuadernos de Filologia Italiana* (2001): especially 157–76.

Crum, Roger J., and John T. Paoletti, eds. *Renaissance Florence: A Social History*. Cambridge: Cambridge University Press, 2006.

Cursi, Marco. *Il "Decameron": Scritture, scriventi, lettori; Storia di un testo*. Rome: Viella, 2007.

——. *La scrittura e i libri di Giovanni Boccaccio*. Rome: Viella, 2013.

D'Agostino, Alfonso. "Gli occhi di Lisabetta (*Decameron* IV, 5)." In *Dai Pochi ai molti: Studi in onore di Roberto Antonelli*, edited by Paolo Canettieri and Arianna Punzi, 703–20. Rome: Viella, 2014.

Dameron, George W. *Florence and Its Church in the Age of Dante*. Philadelphia: University of Pennsylvania Press, 2005.

Daniels, Rhiannon. *Boccaccio and the Book: Production and Reading in Italy, 1340–1520*. London: Legenda, 2009.

——. "Boccaccio's Narrators and Audiences." In *The Cambridge Companion to Boccaccio*, edited by Guyda Armstrong, Rhiannon Daniels, and Stephen J. Milner, 36–51. Cambridge: Cambridge University Press, 2015.

——. "Rethinking the Critical History of the *Decameron*: Boccaccio's Epistle XXII to Mainardo Cavalcanti." *Modern Language Review* 106 (2011): 453–77.

Darwin, Charles. *The Expression of Emotion in Man and Animals*. London: John Murray, 1872.

Davidson, Richard J. "Seven Sins in the Study of Emotion: Correctives from Affective Neuroscience." *Brains and Cognition* 52 (2003): 129–32.

Dean, Trevor. *Crime and Justice in Late Medieval Italy*. Cambridge: Cambridge University Press, 2007.

——. "Marriage and Mutilation: Vendetta in Late Medieval Italy." *Past and Present* 157 (1997): 3–36.

Dębiac, Jacob. "The Matter of Emotions: Towards the Brain-Based Theory of Emotions." 2014. www.researchgate.net/publication/264416715.

Delaurenti, Béatrice. *La contagion des émotions: Compassion, une énigma médiévale*. Paris: Classiques Garnier, 2016.

Delcorno, Carlo. "Boccaccio and the Literature of the Friars." In *Boccaccio 1313– 2013*, edited by Francesco Ciabattoni, Elsa Filosa, and Kristina M. Olson, 161–86. Ravenna, Italy: Longo, 2015.

——. "Ironia / parodia." In *Lessico critico decameroniano*, edited by Renzo Bragantini and Pier Massimo Forni, 162–91. Turin, Italy: Bollati Boringhieri, 1995.

Delmolino, Grace. "The Economics of Conjugal Debt from Gratian's *Decretum* to *Decameron* 2,10." In *Reconsidering Boccaccio: Medieval Contexts and Global Interests*, edited by Olivia Holmes and Dana E. Stewart, 133–67. Toronto: University of Toronto Press, 2018.

Dempsey, Charles. *The Portrayal of Love: Botticelli's "Primavera" and Humanist Culture at the Time of Lorenzo the Magnificent*. Princeton, NJ: Princeton University Press, 1992.

Devoto, Daniel. "Quelques notes au sujet du 'pot de basilic.'" *Revue de littérature comparée* 37 (1963): 430–36.

Díaz, Sara E. "Authority and Misogamy in Boccaccio's *Trattatello*." In *Reconsidering Boccaccio*, edited by Olivia Holmes and Dana E. Stewart, 164–88. Toronto: University of Toronto Press, 2018.

Dixon, Thomas. *From Passions to Emotions: The Creation of a Secular Psychological Category*. Cambridge: Cambridge University Press, 2003.

——. "'Emotion': The History of a Keyword in Crisis." *Emotions Review* 4 (2012): 338–44.

Dombroski, Robert S., ed. *Critical Perspectives on the* Decameron. London: Hodder, 1976.

Donaggio, Monica. "Il travestimento nel *Decameron:* Orizzonte e limiti di una rigenerazione." *Studi sul Boccaccio* 17 (1988): 203–14.

Dronke, Peter. *Medieval Latin and the Rise of European Love-Lyric*. 2nd ed. Oxford: Clarendon, 1968, 2 vols.

Duby, Georges. *The Knight, the Lady and the Priest: The Making of Modern Marriage in Medieval France*. Translated by Barbara Bray. New York: Pantheon, 1983.

Duncan, Seth, and Lisa Feldman Barrett. "Affect Is a Form of Cognition." *Cognition and Emotion* 21 (2007): 1184–211.

Durling, Robert M. "A Long Day in the Sun: *Decameron* 8.7." In *Shakespeare's "Rough Magic": Renaissance Essays in Honor of C. L. Barber*, edited by Cesar

Lombardi Barber, Peter Erickson, and Coppélia Kahn, 269-75. Newark, NJ: University of Delaware Press, 1985.

Eagleton, Terry. *Literary Theory: An Introduction*. Minneapolis: University of Minneapolis Press, 1983.

Eamon, William. *Science and the Secrets of Nature: Books of Secrets in Medieval and Early Modern Culture*. Princeton, NJ: Princeton University Press, 1994.

Edwards, Robert R. *The Flight from Desire: Augustine and Ovid to Chaucer*. New York: Palgrave Macmillan, 2006.

Eisner, Martin. *Boccaccio and the Invention of Italian Literature: Dante, Petrarch, Cavalcanti, and the Authority of the Vernacular*. New York: Cambridge University Press, 2013.

——. "Eroticizing Theology in Day Three and the Poetics of the *Decameron*." *Annali d'Italianistica* 31 (2013): 198-215.

——. "The Tale of Ferondo's Purgatory." In *The* Decameron *Third Day in Perspective*, edited by Francesco Ciabbatini and Pier Massimo Forni, 150-69. Toronto: University of Toronto Press, 2014.

Eisner, Martin, and David Lummus, eds. *A Boccaccian Renaissance: Essays on the Early Modern Impact of Giovanni Boccaccio and His Works*. Notre Dame, IN: University of Notre Dame Press, 2019.

Elias, Norbert. *The Civilizing Process*. Edited by Eric Dunning and Johan Goudsblom. Translated by Edmund Jephcott. Oxford: Blackwell, 2000.

Essary, Brandon K. "Between Two Sad Songs: The Trials and Tribulations of Marriage in *Decameron* 5." *Annali d'Italianistica* 31 (2013): 258-86.

——. "The Economy and Parody of Matrimony in Boccaccio's *Decameron*." PhD diss., Duke University, 2012.

Faithfull, R. Glynn. "Symbolism in Boccaccio." *Lingua e stile* 22 (1985): 247-57.

Fedi, Roberto. "Il 'regno' di Filostrato. Natura e struttura della Giornata IV del *Decameron*." *Modern Language Notes* 102 (1987): 39-54.

Feinstein, Wiley. "Twentieth-Century Feminist Responses to Boccaccio's Alibech Story." *Romance Languages Annual* 1 (1989): 116-20.

Fenu, Barbera Rossana. "La fonte delle lacrime di Elisabetta da Messina: *Decameron* 4:5." *Quaderni d'italianistica* 32 (2001): 103-20.

Ferme, Valerio C. "*Ingegno* and Morality in the New Social Order: The Role of the *Beffa* in Boccaccio's *Decameron*." *Romance Languages Annual* 4 (1992): 248-53.

——. *Women, Enjoyment, and the Defense of Virtue in Boccaccio's* Decameron. New York: Palgrave Macmillan, 2015.

Ferrante, Gennaro. "Control of Emotions and Comforting Practices before the Scaffold in Medieval and Early Modern Italy (with some Remarks on Lorenzetti's Fresco)." In *Emotions, Passions and Power in Renaissance Italy: Proceedings of the International Conference Georgetown University at Villa Le Balze, 5-8 May 2012*, edited by Fabrizio Ricciardelli and Andrea Zorzi, 209-36. Amsterdam: Amsterdam University Press, 2015.

Ferrante, Joan M. "The Frame Characters of the *Decameron*: A Progression of Virtues." *Romance Philology* 19 (1965): 212–26.

——. "Narrative Patterns in the *Decameron*." *Romance Philology* 31 (1978): 585–604.

——. "Politics, Finance and Feminism in *Decameron* II, 7." *Studi sul Boccaccio* 21 (1993): 151–74.

Ferrente, Serena. "Metaphor, Emotion and the Languages of Politics in Late Medieval Italy: A Genoese Lamento of 1473." In *Emotions, Passions and Power in Renaissance Italy: Proceedings of the International Conference Georgetown University at Villa Le Balze, 5–8 May 2012*, edited by Fabrizio Ricciardelli and Andrea Zorzi, 111–27. Amsterdam: Amsterdam University Press, 2015.

——. "Storia ed emozione." *Storica* 43–45 (2009): 371–92.

Ferrone, Giulio. "Eros e obliquità nella terza giornata del *Decameron*." In *Studi di filologia e letteratura italiana in onore di Gianvito Resta*, edited by Vitilio Masiello, 235–48. Rome: Salerno, 2000, vol. 1.

Fido, Franco. *Il regime delle simmetrie imperfette: Studi sul* Decameron. Milan: Franco Angeli, 1988.

——. "Rhetoric and Semantics in the *Decameron*: Tropes and Signs in a Narrative Function." *Yale Italian Studies* 2 (1978): 1–12.

Filosa, Elsa. "La condanna di Niccolò di Bartolo Del Buono, Pino de' Rossi, e gli altri congiurati del 1360." *Studi sul Boccaccio* 44 (2016): 235–50.

——. "Il 'mondo alla rovescia' nella 'Valle delle donne': Eros muliebre e trasgressione sociale nel *Decameron*." *Fusta: Journal of Italian Literature and Culture* 13 (2004–2005): 9–18.

Finucci, Valeria. *The Lady Vanishes: Subjectivity and Representation in Castiglione and Ariosto*. Stanford, CA: Stanford University Press, 1992.

Finucci, Valeria, and Regina Schwartz, eds. *Desire in the Renaissance*. Princeton, NJ: Princeton University Press, 1994.

Flasch, Kurt. *Poesia dopo la peste: Saggio su Boccaccio*. Translated by Tosa Taliani. Bari, Italy: Laterza, 1995.

Fleming, Ray. "Happy Endings? Resisting Women and the Economy of Love in Day Five of Boccaccio's *Decameron*." *Italica* 70 (1993): 30–45.

Fonte, Moderata (Modesta Pozzo). *The Worth of Women: Wherein Is Clearly Revealed Their Nobility and Their Superiority to Men*. Edited and translated by Virginia Cox. Chicago: University of Chicago Press, 1997.

Forni, Pier Massimo. *Adventures in Speech: Rhetoric and Narration in Boccaccio's* Decameron. Philadelphia: University of Pennsylvania Press, 1996.

——. "The *Decameron* and Narrative Form." In *The Cambridge Companion to Boccaccio*, edited by Guyda Armstrong, Rhiannon Daniels, and Stephen J. Milner, 55–64. Cambridge: Cambridge University Press, 2015.

Forno, Carla. "L'amaro riso della beffa: VIII giornata." In *Prospettive sul "Decameron,"* edited by Giorgio Bárberi Squarotti, 131–47. Turin, Italy: Tirrenia, 1989.

Franklin, Margaret. *Boccaccio's Heroines, Power and Virtue in Renaissance Society.* New York: Routledge, 2006.

Gabriele, Tommasina. "Aspects of Nudity in the *Decameron.*" In *Gendered Contexts: New Perspectives in Italian Cultural Studies,* edited by Laura Benedetti, Julia L. Hairston, and Silvia M. Ross, 31–38. New York: Peter Lang, 1996.

Gagliardi, Antonio. *Giovanni Boccaccio: Poeta, Filosofo, Averroista.* Catanzaro, Italy: Rubbettino Editore, 1999.

Gallagher, Catherine, and Stephen Greenblatt. *Practicing New Historicism.* Chicago: University of Chicago Press, 2000.

Gallagher, S., and D. Zahavi. *The Phenomenological Mind: An Introduction to Philosophy of Mind and Cognitive Science.* Abington, UK: Routledge, 2008.

Gavit, Philip. *Charity and Children in Renaissance Florence: The Ospedale degli Innocenti, 1410–1536.* Ann Arbor: University of Michigan Press, 1990.

Geary, Patrick J. *Furta Sacra: Theft of Relics in the Central Middle Ages.* Rev. ed. Princeton, NJ: Princeton University Press, 1990.

Gehl, Paul F. A. *Moral Art: Grammar, Society, and Culture in Trecento Florence.* Ithaca, NY: Cornell University Press, 1993.

Getto, Giovanni. "La peste del *Decameron* e il problema della fonte lucreziana." *Giornale storico della letteratura italiana* 135 (1958): 507–23.

———. "La novella di Ghismonda e la struttura della quarta giornata." In *Vita di forme e forme di vita nel* Decameron, 95–139. Turin, Italy: Petrini, 1958.

———. *Vita di forme e forme di vita nel 'Decameron.'* Turin, Italy: Petrini, 1958.

Giannetti, Laura. *Lelia's Kiss: Imagining Gender, Sex, and Marriage in Italian Renaissance Comedy.* Toronto: University of Toronto Press, 2009.

Giannetti, Laura, and Guido Ruggiero, eds. and trans. *Five Comedies from the Italian Renaissance.* Baltimore: Johns Hopkins University Press, 2003.

Giannetto, Nella. "Madonna Filippa tra 'casus' e 'controversia'. Lettura della Novella VI, 7 del *Decameron.*" *Studi sul Boccaccio* 32 (2004): 81–100.

———. "Parody in the *Decameron:* A 'Contented Captive' and Dioneo." *The Italianist* 1 (1981): 7–23.

Giardini, Maria Pia. *Tradizioni popolari nel* Decameron. Florence, Italy: Olschki, 1965.

Gibaldi, Joseph. "The *Decameron* Cornice and the Response to the Disintegration of Civilization." *Kentucky Romance Quarterly* 24 (1977): 349–57.

Giddens, Anthony. *The Transformation of Intimacy: Sexuality, Love, and Eroticism in Modern Societies.* Stanford, CA: Stanford University Press, 1992.

Gilbert, Felix. *Machiavelli and Guicciardini: Politics and History in Sixteenth-Century Florence.* Princeton, NJ: Princeton University Press, 1965.

Girardi, Raffaele. *Il tempo del mondo volto in novella: Per una lettura del 'Decameron.'* Rome: Bulzoni Editore, 2017.

Gittes, Tobias Foster. *Boccaccio's Naked Muse: Eros, Culture, and the Mythopoeic Imagination.* Toronto: University of Toronto Press, 2008.

——. "Boccaccio's 'Valley of Women': Fetishized Foreplay in Decameron VI." Italica 76 (1999): 147–74.

——. "St. Boccaccio: The Poet as Pander and Martyr." Studi sul Boccaccio 30 (2002): 133–57.

Giusti, Eugenio L. Dall'amore cortese alla comprensione: Il viaggio ideologico di Giovanni Boccaccio dalla 'Caccia di Diana' al 'Decameron.' Milan: LED, 1999.

——. "The Widow in Giovanni Boccaccio's Works." In Gendered Contexts: New Perspectives in Italian Cultural Studies, edited by Laura Benedetti, Julia L. Hairston, and Silvia M. Ross, 39–48. New York: Peter Lang, 1996.

Goldberg, Jonathan, ed. Queering the Renaissance. Durham, NC: Duke University Press, 1994.

Goldthwaite, Richard A. The Economy of Renaissance Florence. Baltimore: Johns Hopkins University Press, 2009.

——. Wealth and the Demand for Art in Italy, 1300–1600. Baltimore: Johns Hopkins University Press, 1993.

Gravadal, Kathryn. Ravishing Maidens: Writing Rape in Medieval French Literature and Law. Philadelphia: University of Pennsylvania Press, 1991.

Green, Louis. Chronicle into History: An Essay on the Interpretation of History in 14th-Century Chronicles. Cambridge: Cambridge University Press, 1972.

Greenblatt, Stephan. Renaissance Self-Fashioning: From More to Shakespeare. Chicago: University of Chicago Press, 1980.

——. "What Is the History of Literature?" Critical Inquiry 23 (1997): 460–81.

Greene, Thomas. "The Flexibility of the Self in Renaissance Literature." In The Discipline of Criticism. Essays in Literary Theory, Interpretation and History, edited by Peter Demetz, Thomas Greene, and Lowry Nelson, 241–64. New Haven, CT: Yale University Press, 1968.

——. "Forms of Accommodation in the Decameron." Italica 45 (1968): 297–313.

Gregg, Melissa, and Gregory J. Seigworth. The Affect Theory Reader. Durham, NC: Duke University Press, 2010.

Grendler, Paul. Schooling in Renaissance Italy: Literacy and Learning, 1300–1600. Baltimore: Johns Hopkins University Press, 1989.

Grimaldi, Emma. Il privilegio di Dioneo: L'eccezione e la regola nel sistema Decameron. Naples, Italy: Edizione Scientifiche Italiane, 1987.

Grimoire Encyclopædia. "To Make Yourself Go Invisible (Spell)." https://www.grimoire.org/spell/for-invisiblity/.

Gross, Daniel. The Secret History of Emotion: From Aristotle's Rhetoric to Modern Brain Science. Chicago: University of Chicago Press, 2007.

Grudin, Michaela Pasche, and Robert Grudin. Boccaccio's Decameron and the Ciceronian Renaissance. New York: Palgrave Macmillan, 2012.

Guardiani, Francesco. "Boccaccio dal Filocolo al Decameron: Variazione di poetica e di retorica dall'esame di due racconti." Carte Italiane: A Journal of Italian Studies 7 (1985–1986): 28–46.

Güntert, Georges. *Tre premesse e una dichiarazione d'amore: Vademecum per un let-tore del* Decameron. Modena, Italy: Mucchi, 1997.

Hagedorn, Suzanne C. *Abandoned Women: Rewriting the Classics in Dante, Boc-caccio, and Chaucer.* Ann Arbor: University of Michigan Press, 2007.

Haines, Charles. "Patient Griselda and *Matta Bestialitade.*" *Quaderni d'Italianistica* 6 (1985): 233–40.

Hairston, Julia L., and Walter Stephens, eds. *The Body in Early Modern Italy.* Bal-timore: Johns Hopkins University Press, 2010.

Hankins, James. "Boccaccio and the Political Thought of Renaissance Hu-manism." In *A Boccaccian Renaissance: Essays on the Early Modern Impact of Giovanni Boccaccio and His Works,* edited by Martin Eisner and David Lummus, 3–35. Notre Dame, IN: University of Notre Dame Press, 2019.

———. "Exclusivist Republicanism and the Non-Monarchical Republic." *Polit-ical Theory* 38 (2010): 452–82.

———. *Virtue Politics: Soulcraft and Statecraft in Renaissance Italy.* Cambridge, MA: Harvard University Press, 2019.

Harding, Jennifer, and E. Diedre Pribram, eds. *Emotions: A Cultural Studies Reader.* London: Routledge, 2009.

Hasting, R. *Nature and Reason in the* Decameron. Manchester, UK: Manchester University Press, 1975.

———. "To Teach or Not to Teach: The Moral Dimension of the *Decameron* Re-considered." *Italian Studies* 44 (1989): 19–40.

Henderson, John. *Piety and Charity in Late Medieval Florence.* Oxford: Clarendon, 1994.

Herlihy, David, and Christiane Klapisch-Zuber. *Tuscans and Their Families: A Study of the Florentine Catasto of 1427.* New Haven, CT: Yale University Press, 1985.

Hollander, Robert. "Boccaccio's Dante." *Italica* 63 (1986): 278–89.

———. *Boccaccio's Dante and the Shaping Force of Satire.* Ann Arbor: University of Michigan Press, 1997.

———. "Boccaccio's Dante: Imitative Distance (*Decameron* I.1 and VI.10)." *Studi sul Boccaccio* 13 (1981–1982): 169–98.

———. "The Struggle for Control among the *Novellatori* of the *Decameron* and the Reason for Their Return to Florence." *Studi sul Boccaccio* 39 (2011): 243–313.

———. "'*Utilità*' in Boccaccio's *Decameron.*" *Studi sul Boccaccio* 15 (1985–1986): 215–33.

Hollander, Robert, and Courtney Cahill. "Day Ten of the *Decameron:* The Myth of Order." *Studi sul Boccaccio* 23 (1995): 241–55.

Holmes, Olivia. "Beyond Exemplarity: Women's Wiles from the *Disciplina Clericalis* to the *Decameron.*" In *Boccaccio 1313–2013,* edited by Francesco Ciabattoni, Elsa Filosa, and Kristina M. Olson, 145–56. Ravenna, Italy: Longo, 2015.

——. "*Decameron* 5.8: From Compassion to Complacency." *I Tatti Studies in the Italian Renaissance* 22, no. 1 (2019): 21–36.

——. "'In forma della donna': In the Woman's Place (A Reading of *Decameron* lll.5)." In *Boccaccio and Feminist Criticism*, edited by Thomas C. Stillinger and F. Regina Psaki, 145–56. Chapel Hill, NC: Annali d'Italianistica, 2006. (*Annali d'Italianistica, Studi e testi*, vol. 8.)

——. "Trial by Beffa: Retributive Justice and In-Group Formation in Day 8." *Annali d'Italianistica* 31 (2013): 355–79.

Holmes, Olivia, and Dana E. Stewart, eds. *Reconsidering Boccaccio: Medieval Contexts and Global Interests*. Toronto: University of Toronto Press, 2018.

Horodowich, Elizabeth. *Language and Statecraft in Early Modern Venice*. Cambridge: Cambridge University Press, 2008.

Houston, Jason. "Boccaccio on Friendship (Theory and Practice)." In *Reconsidering Boccaccio*, edited by Olivia Holmes and Dana E. Stewart, 81–97. Toronto: University of Toronto Press, 2018.

Howes, David, ed. *Empire of the Senses: The Sensual Culture Reader*. Oxford: Bloomsbury Academic, 2005.

Hunt, Lynn, ed. *The New Cultural History*. Berkeley: University of California Press, 1989.

Izard, Carroll E. "The Many Meanings / Aspects of Emotion: Definitions, Functions, Activation, and Regulation." *Emotion Review* 2 (2010): 363–70.

Jaeger, Stephen. *The Origins of Courtliness: Civilizing Trends and the Formation of Courtly Ideals, 939–1210*. Philadelphia: University of Pennsylvania Press, 1985.

——. *Ennobling Love: In Search of a Lost Sensibility*. Philadelphia: University of Pennsylvania Press, 1999.

Jones, Philip J. "Florentine Families and Florentine Diaries in the Fourteenth Century." *Papers of the British School at Rome* 24 (1954): 183–205.

——. *The Italian City-State: From Commune to Signoria*. New York: Oxford University Press, 1997.

Jordan, Tracy. "'We Are All One Flesh': Structural Symmetry in Boccaccio's Tale of the Prince and the Princess of Salerno." *Studies in Short Fiction* 24 (1987): 103–10.

Karras, Ruth. *From Boys to Men: Formations of Masculinity in Late Medieval Europe*. Philadelphia: University of Pennsylvania Press, 2003.

——. *Sexuality in Medieval Europe: Doing unto Others*. New York: Routledge, 2005.

Kelly Wray, Shona. "Boccaccio and the Doctors: Medicine and Compassion in the Face of the Plague." *Journal of Medieval History* 30 (2004): 301–22.

Kent, Dale. *Friendship, Love, and Trust in Renaissance Florence*. Cambridge, MA: Harvard University Press, 2009.

Kern, Edith G. "The Gardens in the *Decameron* Cornice." *PMLA (Publications of the Modern Language Association of America)* 66 (1951): 505–23.

Kiechefer, Richard. *Forbidden Rites: A Necromancer's Manual of the Fifteenth Century.* University Park: The Pennsylvania State University Press, 1997.

King, Margaret. *The Death of the Child Valerio Marcello.* Chicago: University of Chicago Press, 1994.

King, Peter. "Dispassionate Passions." In *Emotions and Cognitive Life in Medieval and Early Modern Philosophy,* edited by Martin Pickavé and Lisa Shapiro, 1–28. Oxford: Oxford University Press, 2012.

———. "Emotions in Medieval Thought." In *The Oxford Handbook of the Emotions,* edited by Peter Goldie, 167–88. Oxford: Oxford University Press, 2010.

Kinoshita, Sharon, and Jason Jacobs. "Ports of Call: Boccaccio's Alatiel in the Medieval Mediterranean." *Journal of Medieval and Early Modern Studies* 37 (2007): 163–95.

Kircher, Timothy. "Boccaccio's Humanist *Brigata*: Reading the *Decameron* in the Quattrocento." In *A Boccaccian Renaissance: Essays on the Early Modern Impact of Giovanni Boccaccio and His Works,* edited by Martin Eisner and David Lummus, 36–55. Notre Dame, IN: University of Notre Dame Press, 2019.

———. "The Modality of Moral Communication in the *Decameron's* First Day in Contrast to the Mirror of the *Exemplum*." *Renaissance Quarterly* 54 (2001): 1035–73.

———. *The Poet's Wisdom: The Humanists, the Church, and the Formation of Philosophy in the Early Renaissance.* Leiden, Netherlands: Brill, 2006.

Kirkham, Victoria. "An Allegorically Tempered *Decameron*." *Italica* 62 (1985): 1–23.

———. "The Apocryphal Boccaccio." *Mediaevalia* 34 (2013): 169–220.

———. "The Last Tale in the *Decameron*." *Mediaevalia* 12 (1989): 205–33.

———. "Love's Labors Rewarded and Paradise Lost (*Dec.* III, 10)." *Romanic Review* 72 (1981): 79–93.

———. "Maria a.k.a. Fiammetta: The Men behind the Woman." In *Boccaccio and Feminist Criticism,* edited by Thomas C. Stillinger and F. Regina Psaki, 13–27. Chapel Hill, NC: Annali d'Italianistica, 2006. (*Annali d'Italianistica, Studi e testi,* vol. 8.)

———. "Morale." In *Lessico critico decameroniano,* edited by Renzo Bragantini and Pier Massimo Forni, 249–68. Turin, Italy: Bollati Boringhieri, 1995.

———. "Painters at Play on the Judgement Day (*Dec.* viii, 9)." *Studi sul Boccaccio* 14 (1983–1984): 256–77.

———. "Reckoning with Boccaccio's *Questioni d'amore*." *Modern Language Notes* 37 (1974): 47–59.

———. *The Sign of Reason in Boccaccio's* Decameron. Florence, Italy: Olschki, 1993.

———. "The Word, the Flesh, and the *Decameron*." *Romance Philology* 41 (1987): 127–49.

Kirkham, Victoria, Michael Sherberg, and Janet Levarie Smarr, eds. *Boccaccio: A Critical Guide to the Complete Works.* Chicago: University of Chicago Press, 2013.

Klapisch-Zuber, Christiane. "Blood Parents and Milk Parents: Wet Nursing in Florence, 1300–1530." In *Women, Family, and Ritual in Renaissance Italy*, 132–64. Chicago: University of Chicago Press, 1985.

———. "The 'Cruel Mother': Maternity, Widowhood, and Dowry in Florence in the Fourteenth and Fifteenth Centuries." In *Women, Family and Ritual in Renaissance Italy*, 117–31. Chicago: University of Chicago Press, 1985.

Kleinhenz, Christopher. "Texts, Naked and Thinly Veiled: Erotic Elements in Medieval Italian Literature." In *Sex in the Middle Ages: A Book of Essays*, edited by Joyce Salisbury. New York: Garland, 1991.

Knuuttila, Simo. *Emotions in Ancient and Medieval Philosophy*. Oxford: Oxford University Press, 2004.

Kodera, Sergius. *Disreputable Bodies: Magic, Medicine and Gender in Renaissance Natural Philosophy*. Toronto: Centre for Reformation and Renaissance Studies, 2010.

Konstan, David. *Sexual Symmetry: Love in the Ancient Novel and Related Genres*. Princeton, NJ: Princeton University Press, 1994.

Kovesi, Catherine. *Sumptuary Laws in Italy, 1200–1500*. Oxford: Oxford University Press, 2002.

Kriesel, James C. "Chastening the Corpus: Bembo and the Renaissance Reception of Boccaccio." *Italianist* 31 (2011): 367–91.

Kuehn, Thomas. *Law, Family and Women: Towards a Legal Anthropology of Renaissance Italy*. Chicago: University of Chicago Press, 1991.

Kuhns, Richard F. *Decameron and the Philosophy of Storytelling: Author as Midwife and Pimp*. New York: Columbia University Press, 2005.

Ladner, Gerhart B. *"Homo Viator*: Medieval Ideas on Alienation and Order." *Speculum* 42 (1967): 233–59.

———. *The Idea of Reform: Its Impact on Christian Thought and Action in the Age of the Fathers*. Cambridge, MA: Harvard University Press, 1959.

Land, Norman. "Calandrino as Viewer." *Source: Notes on the History of Art* 23 (2004): 1–6.

Lansing, Carol. *The Florentine Magnates: Lineage and Faction in a Medieval Commune*. Princeton, NJ: Princeton University Press, 1991.

———. "Humiliation and the Exercise of Power in the Florentine Contado in the Mid-Fourteenth Century." In *Emotions, Passions and Power in Renaissance Italy: Proceedings of the International Conference Georgetown University at Villa Le Balze, 5–8 May 2012*, edited by Fabrizio Ricciardelli and Andrea Zorzi, 77–90. Amsterdam: Amsterdam University Press, 2015.

———. *Passion and Order: Restraint of Grief in the Medieval Italian Communes*. Ithaca, NY: Cornell University Press, 2008.

Larner, John. "Chivalric Culture in the Age of Dante." *Renaissance Studies* 2 (1998): 117–30.

———. *Italy in the Age of Dante and Petrarch, 1216–1380*. London: Longman, 1980.

Lazzarini, Isabella. *Amicizia e potere. Reti politiche e sociali nell'Italia medievale.* Milan: Mondadori, 2011.

———. "The Words of Emotion: Political Language and Discursive Resources in Lorenzo de Medici's Lettere (1468–1492)." In *Emotions, Passions and Power in Renaissance Italy: Proceedings of the International Conference Georgetown University at Villa Le Balze, 5–8 May 2012,* edited by Fabrizio Ricciardelli and Andrea Zorzi, 91–110. Amsterdam: Amsterdam University Press, 2015.

Lee, A. Collingwood. *The Decameron: Its Sources and Analogues.* New York: Haskell House, 1966.

Leech, Mary E. "Severed Silence: Social Boundaries and Family Honor in Boccaccio's 'Tale of Lisabetta.'" In *Heads Will Roll: Decapitation in the Medieval and Early Modern Imagination,* edited by Larissa Tracy and Jeff Massey, 115–36. Leiden, Netherlands: Brill, 2012.

Lerner, Robert E. "The Black Death and Western Eschatological Mentalities." *American Historical Review* 86 (1981): 533–52.

Levenstein, Jessica. "Out of Bounds: Passion and the Plague in Boccaccio's *Decameron.*" *Italica* 73 (1996): 313–35.

Levy, Allison. "Augustine's Concessions and Other Failures: Mourning and Masculinity in Fifteenth-Century Tuscany." In *Grief and Gender: 700–1700,* edited by Jennifer C. Vaught, 81–94. New York: Palgrave Macmillan, 2003.

———. *Re-membering Masculinity in Early Modern Florence: Widowed Bodies, Mourning and Portraiture.* Aldershot, UK: Ashgate, 2006.

Lewis, C. W. *The Allegory of Love: A Study in Medieval Tradition.* Oxford: Clarendon, 1936.

Leys, Ruth. "The Turn to Affect: A Critique." *Critical Inquiry* 37 (2011): 434–72.

Lucente, Gregory. "The Fortunate Fall of Andreuccio da Perugia." *Forum Italicum* 10 (1976): 323–44.

Lummus, David. "Boccaccio's Hellenism and the Foundations of Modernity." *Mediaevalia* 33 (2012): 101–67.

———. "Boccaccio's Three Venuses: On the Convergence of Celestial and Transgressive Love in the *Genealogie Deorum Gentilium Libri.*" *Medievalia et Humanistica* 37 (2011): 65–88.

———. "The *Decameron* and Boccaccio's Poetics." In *The Cambridge Companion to Boccaccio,* edited by Guyda Armstrong, Rhiannon Daniels, and Stephen J. Milner, 65–82. Cambridge: Cambridge University Press, 2015.

Lynch, Andrew, and Susan Broomhall, eds. *The Routledge History of Emotions in Europe 1100–1700.* New York: Routledge, 2019.

Maclean, Ian. *The Renaissance Notion of Woman: A Study in the Fortunes of Scholasticism and Medical Science in European Intellectual Life.* Cambridge: Cambridge University Press, 1980.

Maiorana, Maria Teresa. "Un Conte de Boccace: Repris par Keas et Anatole France." *Revue de littérature comparée* 37 (1963): 50–67.

· Manetti, Giannozzo. *Biographical Writings*. Edited and translated by Stefano Ugo Baldassarri and Rolf Bagemihl. Cambridge, MA: Harvard University Press, 2003.

———. *Dialogus consolatorius*. Edited by Antonio de Petris. Rome: Edizioni di storia e letteratura, 1983.

Marafioti, Martin. "Boccaccio's Lauretta: The Brigata's Bearer of Bad News." *Italian Culture* 19 (2001): 7–18.

———. *Storytelling as Plague Prevention in Medieval and Early Modern Italy*. London: Routledge, 2018.

Marazziti, Donatella, and Domenico Canale. "Hormonal Changes When Falling in Love." *Psychoneuroendocrinology* 29 (2004): 931–36.

Marcelli, Nicoletta. "Appunti per l'edizione di un dittico umanistico: La latinizzazione del Tancredi boccaciano e la Novella di Seleuco di Leonardo Bruni." *Interpres* 19 (2000): 18–41.

Marchesi, Simone. "Intertextuality and Interdiscoursivity in the *Decameron*." *Heliotropia* 7 (2010): 31–50.

———. *Stratigrafie decameroniane*. Florence, Italy: Olschki, 2004.

Marcus, Millicent. "The Accommodating Frate Alberto: A Gloss on *Decameron* IV, 2." *Italica* 56 (1979): 3–21.

———. *An Allegory of Form: Literary Self Consciousness in the* Decameron. Stanford, CA: Anma Libri, 1979.

———. "Cross-Fertilizations: Folklore and Literature in *Decameron* IV, 5." *Italica* 66 (1989): 383–98.

———. "Misogyny as Misreading: A Gloss on *Decameron* VIII, 7." *Stanford Italian Review* 4 (1984): 23–40.

———. "Seduction by Silence: A Gloss on the Tales of Masetto (III, 1) and Alatiel (II, 7)." *Philological Quarterly* 58 (1979): 1–15.

———. "Ser Ciapelletto: A Reader's Guide to the *Decameron*." *The Humanities Association Review* 26 (1975): 275–88.

———. "The Sweet New Style Reconsidered: A Gloss on the Tale of Cimone (*Decameron* V, 1)." *Italian Quarterly* 81 (1980): 5–61.

Markulin, Joseph. "Emilia and the Case for Openness in the *Decameron*." *Stanford Italian Review* 3 (1983): 183–99.

Martin, John Jeffries. "Inventing Sincerity, Refashioning Prudence: The Discovery of the Individual in Renaissance Europe." *American Historical Review* 102 (1997): 1309–42.

———. *Myths of Renaissance Individualism*. New York: Palgrave Macmillan, 2014.

Martines, Lauro. *An Italian Renaissance Sextet: Six Tales in Historical Context*. Translated by Murtha Baca. New York: Marsilio, 1994.

———. *Lawyers and Statecraft in Renaissance Florence*. Princeton, NJ: Princeton University Press, 1968.

———. *Power and Imagination: City-States in Renaissance Italy*. New York: Knopf, 1979.

———. *The Social World of the Florentine Humanists: 1390–1460*. Princeton, NJ: Princeton University Press, 1963.

———. *Strong Words: Writing and Social Strain in the Italian Renaissance*. Baltimore: Johns Hopkins University Press, 2001.

———, ed. *Violence and Civil Disorder in Italian Cities, 1200–1500*. Los Angeles: University of California Press, 1972.

Martinez, Ronald L. "Also Known as Prencipe Galeotto *(Decameron)*." In *Boccaccio: A Critical Guide to the Complete Works*, edited by Victoria Kirkham, Michael Sherberg, and Janet Levarie Smarr, 23–40. Chicago: University of Chicago Press, 2013.

———. "Calandrino and the Powers of Stone: Rhetoric, Belief and the Progress of *Ingegno* in *Decameron* VIII.3." *Heliotropia* 1 (2003): 1–32.

Matt, Susan J., and Peter N. Stearns, eds. *Doing Emotions History*. Urbana: University of Illinois Press, 2014.

Matthews-Grieco, Sara F., ed. *Erotic Cultures of Renaissance Italy*. Burlington, VT: Ashgate, 2010.

May, William H. "The Confession of Prous Boneta Heretic and Heresiarch." In *Essays in Medieval Life and Thought Presented in Honor of Austin Patterson Evans*, edited by John Hine Mundy, 3–30. New York: Columbia University Press, 1955.

Mazzacurati, Giancarlo. *All'ombra di Dioneo: Tipologie e percorsi della novella da Boccaccio a Bandello*. Florence, Italy: La Nuova Italia, 1996.

Mazzamuto, Pietro. "La Meschinella siciliana." In *Le mani vuote: Scene e personaggi della cultura siciliana*, 7–16. Messina, Italy: Sicania, 1992.

Mazzarino, Antonio. "Il basilico di Lisabetta da Messina (Boccaccio, *Decameron* IV. 5)." *Nuovi annali della Facoltà di Magistero dell'Università Messina* 2 (1984): 445–87.

Mazzotta, Giuseppe. "The *Decameron*: The Literal and the Allegorical." *Italian Quarterly* 18 (1975): 59–60.

———. "Games of Laughter in the *Decameron*." *Romanic Review* 69 (1978): 115–31.

———. *The World at Play in Boccaccio's* Decameron. Princeton, NJ: Princeton University Press, 1986.

McClure, George W. *The Culture of Profession in Late Renaissance Italy*. Toronto: University of Toronto Press, 2004.

———. "A Little-Known Renaissance Manual of Consolation: Nicolaus Modrussiensis's *De consolation*, 1465–1466." In *Supplementum Festivum: Studies in Honor of Paul Oscar Kristeller*, edited by James Hankins, John Monfasani, and Frederick Purnell, Jr., 247–77. Binghamton, NY: Medieval and Renaissance Texts and Studies, 1987.

———. *Sorrow and Consolation in Italian Humanism*. Princeton, NJ: Princeton University Press, 1991.

McCracken, Peggy. *The Curse of Eve, the Wound of the Hero: Blood, Gender, and Medieval Literature*. Philadelphia: University of Pennsylvania Press, 2003.

McDaniel, June. *Offering Flowers, Feeding Skulls: Popular Goddess Worship in West Bengal*. Oxford: Oxford University Press, 2004.

McLaughlin, Martin. *Literary Imitation in the Italian Renaissance: The Theory and Practice of Literary Imitation in Italy from Dante to Bembo*. Oxford: Oxford University Press, 1996.

McLean, Paul D. *The Art of the Network: Strategic Interaction and Patronage in Renaissance Florence*. Durham, NC: Duke University Press, 2007.

McNamer, Sarah, *Affective Meditation and the Invention of Medieval Compassion*. Philadelphia: University of Pennsylvania Press, 2010.

Medin, Antonio. *Lamenti del sec. XIV*. Florence, Italy: Sansoni, 1883.

Medin, Antonio, and Ludovico Frati. *Lamenti storici dei secoli XIV, XV, XVI*. Bologna: Romagnoli-Dall'Acqua, 1887, 3 vols.

Mellyn, Elizabeth W. *Mad Tuscans and Their Families: A History of Mental Disorder in Early Modern Italy*. Philadelphia: University of Pennsylvania Press, 2014.

Migiel, Marilyn. "Beyond Seduction: A Reading of the Tale of Alibech and Rustico (*Decameron*, III, 10)." *Italica* 75 (1998): 161–77.

———. "Boccaccio and Women." In *The Cambridge Companion to Boccaccio*, edited by Guyda Armstrong, Rhiannon Daniels, and Stephen J. Milner, 171–84. Cambridge: Cambridge University Press, 2015.

———. "Encrypted Messages: Men, Women, and Figurative Language in *Decameron* V. 4." *Philological Quarterly* 77 (1998): 1–13.

———. *The Ethical Dimension of the* Decameron. Toronto: University of Toronto Press, 2015.

———. "Figurative Language and Sex Wars in the *Decameron*." *Heliotropia* 2 (2004): 1–12. https://scholarworks.umass.edu/heliotropia/vol2/iss2/1.

———. *A Rhetoric of the* Decameron. Toronto: University of Toronto Press, 2003.

———. "The Untidy Business of Gender Studies: Or Why It's Almost Useless to Ask if the *Decameron* Is Feminist." In *Boccaccio and Feminist Criticism*, edited by Thomas C. Stillinger and F. Regina Psaki, 217–33. Chapel Hill, NC: Annali d'Italianistica, 2006. (*Annali d'Italianistica, Studi e testi*, vol. 8.)

Miller, William I. *Humiliation and Other Essays on Honor, Social Discomfort and Violence*. Ithaca, NY: Cornell University Press, 1993.

Milligan, Gerry, and Jane Tylus, eds. *The Poetics of Masculinity in Early Modern Italy and Spain*. Toronto: Centre for Reformation and Renaissance Studies, 2010.

Milner, Stephen J. "'Bene Comune e Benessere': The Affective Economy of Communal Life." In *Conference Georgetown University at Villa Le Balze, 5–8 May 2012*, edited by Fabrizio Ricciardelli and Andrea Zorzi, 237–51. Amsterdam: Amsterdam University Press, 2015.

———. "Boccaccio's *Decameron* and the Semiotics of the Everyday." In *The Cambridge Companion to Boccaccio*, edited by Guyda Armstrong, Rhiannon

Daniels, and Stephen J. Milner, 83–100. Cambridge: Cambridge University Press, 2015.

———. "Coming Together: Consolation and the Rhetoric of Insinuation in Boccaccio's *Decameron*." In *The Erotics of Consolation: Desire and Distance in the Late Middle Ages*, edited by Catherine E. Léglu and Stephen J. Milner, 95–113. New York: Palgrave, 2008.

Molho, Anthony. *Marriage Alliance in Late Medieval Florence*. Cambridge, MA: Harvard University Press, 1994.

Monson, Don A. *Andreas Capellanus, Scholasticism, and the Courtly Tradition*. Washington, DC: Catholic University Press of America, 2005.

Muir, Edward. *Civic Ritual in Renaissance Venice*. Princeton, NJ: Princeton University Press, 1981.

———. "The Double Binds of Manly Revenge in Renaissance Italy." In *Gender Rhetorics: Postures of Dominance and Submission in History*, edited by Richard C. Trexler, 65–82. Binghamton, NY: Medieval and Renaissance Texts and Studies, 1994.

———. *Mad Blood Stirring: Vendetta and Factions in Friuli during the Renaissance*. Baltimore: Johns Hopkins University Press, 1993.

———. "The Virgin on the Street Corner: The Place of the Sacred in Italian Cities." In *Religion and Culture in the Renaissance and Reformation*, edited by Steven E. Ozment, 25–40. Kirksville, MO: Sixteenth Century Journal, 1989.

Muir, Edward, and Guido Ruggiero, eds. *History from Crime: Selections from Quaderni Storici*. Baltimore: Johns Hopkins University Press, 1994.

———. *Microhistory and the Lost Peoples of Europe: Selections from Quaderni Storici*. Baltimore: Johns Hopkins University Press, 1991.

———. *Sex and Gender in Historical Perspective: Selections from Quaderni Storici*. Baltimore: Johns Hopkins University Press, 1990.

Mulryan, John. "The Three Images of Venus: Boccaccio's Theory of Love in the *Genealogy of the Gods* and His Aesthetic Vision of Love in the *Decameron*." *Romance Notes* 19 (1979): 388–94.

Nagy, Piroska, and Damien Boquet, eds. *Le sujet des émotions au Moyen Âge*. Paris: Beauchesne, 2009.

Najemy, John M. *Between Friends: Discourses of Power and Desire in the Machiavelli-Vettori Letters of 1513–1515*. Princeton, NJ: Princeton University Press, 1993.

———. *Corporatism and Consensus in Florentine Electoral Politics, 1280–1400*. Chapel Hill: University of North Carolina Press, 1982.

———. *A History of Florence, 1200–1575*. Oxford: Blackwell, 2006.

Nelson, John Charles. "Love and Sex in the *Decameron*." In *Philosophy and Humanism: Renaissance Essays in Honor of Paul Oskar Kristeller*, edited by Edward P. Mahoney, 339–57. New York: Columbia University Press, 1976.

Niccoli, Ottavia. *Vedere con gli occhi del cuore: Alle origini del potere delle immagini*. Bari, Italy: Laterza, 2011.

Niebyl, Peter H. "The Non-Naturals." *Bulletin of the History of Medicine* 45 (1971): 486–92.

Novajra, Ada. "Dalla pratica della virtù all'esercizio del potere: X giornata." In *Prospettive sul* Decameron, edited by G. Bàrberi Squarotti, 165–82. Turin, Italy: Tirrenia Stampatori, 1989.

Nussbaum, Martha C. *Upheavals of Thought: The Intelligence of Emotions.* Cambridge: Cambridge University Press, 2001.

Ó Cuilleanáin, Cormac. "Man and Beast in the *Decameron*." *Modern Language Review* 75 (1983): 86–93.

———. *Religion and the Clergy in Boccaccio's* Decameron. Rome: Edizioni di Storia e Letteratura, 1984.

Olsen, Glending. *Literature as Recreation in the Later Middle Ages.* Ithaca, NY: Cornell University Press, 1982.

———. "Petrarch's View of the *Decameron*." *Modern Language Notes* 91 (1976): 69–79.

Olson, Kristina M. "'*Concivis meus*': Petrarch's *Rerum memorandum libri* 2.60, Boccaccio's *Decameron* 6.9 and the Specter of Dino del Garbo." *Annali d'Italianistica* 22 (2004): 375–80.

———. *Courtesy Lost: Dante, Boccaccio and the Literature of History.* Toronto: University of Toronto Press, 2014.

———. "The Language of Women as Written by Men: Boccaccio, Dante and Gendered Histories of the Vernacular." *Heliotropia* 8–9 (2011–2012): 51–79.

———. "Resurrecting Dante's Florence: Figural Realism in the *Decameron* and the *Esposizioni*." *Modern Language Notes* 124 (2009): 45–65.

Paden, Michael. "Elissa: La Ghibellina del *Decameron*." *Studi sul Boccaccio* 21 (1993): 139–50.

Padoan, Giorgio. *Il Boccaccio, le muse, il Parnaso e l'Arno.* Florence, Italy: Olschki, 1978.

———. "Mondo aristocratico e mondo comunale nell'ideologia e nell'arte di Giovanni Boccaccio." *Studi sul Boccaccio* 2 (1964): 81–216.

Palumbo, Matteo. "'I motti leggiadri' nella sesta giornata del *Decameron*." *Esperienze letterarie* 33 (2008): 3–23.

Panksepp, J. *The Archaeology of Mind: Neural Origins of Human Emotions.* New York: Norton, 2010.

Paolella, Alfonso. "I livelli narrativi nella novella di Rustico ed Alibech 'romita' del *Decameron*." *Revue Romane* 13 (1987): 189–205.

Papio, Michael. "'Non meno di compassion piena che dilettevole': Notes on Compassion in Boccaccio." *Italian Quarterly* 37 (2000): 107–25.

Paradisio, Sergio, and David Rudrauf. "Struggle for Life, Struggle for Love and Recognition: The Neglected Self in Social Cognitive Neuroscience." *Dialogues in Clinical Neuroscience* 14 (2012): 65–75.

Paredes, Raúl G., and Anders Ågmo. "Has Dopamine a Physiological Role in the Control of Sexual Behavior? A Critical Review of the Evidence." *Progress in Neurobiology* 73 (2004): 179–226.

Parma, Michela. "Fortuna spicciolata del *Decameron* tra Tre e Cinquecento: Per un catalogo delle traduzioni latine e delle riscritture italiane volgari." *Studi sul Boccaccio* 31 (2003), 203-70.

——. "Fortuna spicciolata del *Decameron* tra Tre e Cinquecento: Tendenze caratteristiche delle rielaborazioni." *Studi sul Boccaccio* 33 (2005): 299-364.

Pennacchietti, Fabrizio A. "L'eventuale fonte araba della novella di Alibech e Rustico (*Decamerone*, III, 10)." *Levia gravia: Quaderno annuale di letteratura italiana* 8 (2006): 43-47.

Perfetti, Lisa. *Women and Laughter in Medieval Comic Literature.* Ann Arbor: University of Michigan Press, 2003.

——. "'Such tales were not to be told among ladies,' Women's Wit and the Problem of Modesty in Boccaccio's *Decameron*." In *Women and Laughter in Medieval Comic Literature*, 63-99. Ann Arbor: University of Michigan Press, 2003.

Perler, Dominik. "Emotions and Cognitions: Fourteenth-Century Discussions on the Passions of the Soul." *Vivarium* 43 (2005): 250-74.

Pertile, Lino. "Dante, Boccaccio e l'intelligenza." *Italian Studies* 43 (1988): 60-74.

Pessoa, Luiz. "On the Relationship between Emotion and Cognition." *Nature Reviews Neuroscience* 9 (2008): 148-58.

Peterson, David. "The War of the Eight Saints in Florentine Memory and Oblivion." In *Society and Individual in Renaissance Florence*, edited by William J. Connell, 173-214. Berkeley: University of California Press, 2002.

Petrarch, Francesco. *Petrarch's Lyric Poems: The Rime Sparse and Other Lyrics.* Edited and translated by Robert M. Durling. Cambridge, MA: Harvard University Press, 1976.

Pickavé, Martin, and Lisa Shapiro, eds. *Emotions and the Cognitive Life in Medieval and Early Modern Philosophy.* Oxford: Oxford University Press, 2012.

Picone, Michelangelo. "L' 'amoroso sangue': La quarta giornata." In *Introduzione al Decameron*, edited by Michelangelo Picone and Margherita Mesirca, 115-39. Florence, Italy: Franco Cesati, 2004.

——. "L'Arte della beffa: L'Ottava giornata." In *Introduzione al Decameron*, edited by Michelangelo Picone and Margherita Mesirca, 203-25. Florence, Italy: Franco Cesati, 2004.

——. "L'autore allo specchio dell'opera: Una lettura di *Decameron* 1.7." *Studi sul Boccaccio* 19 (1991): 27-46.

——. *Boccaccio e la codificazione della novella. Letture del* Decameron. Ravenna, Italy: Longo, 2008.

——. "La 'ballata' di Lisabetta (*Decameron* IV, 5)." *Cuadernos de Filologia Italiana* (2001): 177-91.

——. "Dal lai alla novella: Il caso di Ghismonda (*Dec.* IV.1)." *Filologia e Critica* 16 (1991): 325-43.

——. "La novella di Lisabetta da Messina di Giovanni Boccaccio (*Decameron* IV.5).*" Per Leggere* 19 (2010): 37–51.

Picone, Michelangelo, and Claude Cazalé Bérard, eds. *Gli Zibaldoni di Boccaccio: Memoria, scrittura, riscrittura. Atti del Seminario internazionale di Firenze-Certaldo (26–28 Aprile, 1996).* Florence, Italy: Cesati, 1998.

Picone, Michelangelo, and Margherita Mesirca, eds. *Introduzione al Decameron.* Florence, Italy: Franco Cesati, 2004.

Plamper, Jan. *The History of Emotions: An Introduction.* Oxford: Oxford University Press, 2015.

PMLA (Publications of the Modern Language Association of America) Special Topic Emotions 130, no. 5 (October 2015).

Pocock, John G. A. *The Machiavellian Moment: Florentine Political Thought and the Atlantic Republican Tradition.* Princeton, NJ: Princeton University Press, 1975.

Potter, Joy Hambuechen. *Five Frames for the* Decameron: *Communication and Social Systems in the Cornice.* Princeton, NJ: Princeton University Press, 1982.

Psaki, F. Regina. "Boccaccio and Female Sexuality: Gendered and Eroticized Landscapes." In *The Flight of Ulysses: Studies in the Memory of Emmanuel Hatzantonis,* edited by Augustus A. Mastri, 125–34. Chapel Hill, NC: Annali d'Italianistica, 1997.

——. "Compassion in the *Decameron:* The Opening Sequence." *I Tatti Studies in the Italian Renaissance* 22, no. 1 (2019): 37–58.

——. "The One and the Many: The Tale of the Brigata and *Decameron* Day Four." *Annali d'Italianistica* 31 (2013): 217–56.

——. "Voicing Gender in the *Decameron.*" In *The Cambridge Companion to Boccaccio,* edited by Guyda Armstrong, Rhiannon Daniels, and Stephen J. Milner, 101–17. Cambridge: Cambridge University Press, 2015.

——. "'Women Make All Things Lose Their Power': Women's Knowledge, Men's Fear in the *Decameron* and the *Corbaccio.*" *Heliotropia* 1, no. 1 (2003): 33–48.

Pullan, Brian. *A History of Early Renaissance Italy: From the Mid-Thirteenth to the Mid-Fifteenth Century.* New York: Saint Martin's Press, 1973.

Quaglioni, Diego, and Silvana Seidel Menchi, eds. *Coniugi nemici. La separazione in Italia dal XII al XVIII secolo.* Bologna, Italy: Il Mulino, 2000.

——. *Matrimoni in dubbio. Unioni controverse e nozze clandestine in Italia dal XIV al XVIII secolo.* Bologna, Italy: Il Mulino, 2002.

——. *Trasgressioni: Seduzione, concubinato, adulterio, bigamia (secoli XIV–XVIII).* Bologna: Il Mulino, 2004.

Rabil, Albert. *Knowledge, Goodness and Power: The Debate over Nobility among Quattrocento Italian Humanists.* Binghamton, NY: Medieval and Renaissance Texts and Studies, 1991.

Raja, Maria Elisa. *Le muse in giardino: Il paesaggio ameno nelle opere di Giovanni Boccaccio.* Alessandria, Italy: Edizione dell'Orso, 2003.

Ray, Meredith K. *Writing Gender in Women's Letter Collections of the Italian Renaissance*. Toronto: University of Toronto Press, 2009.

Reddy, William M. "Against Constructionism: The Historical Ethnography of Emotions." *Current Anthropology* 38 (1997): 327–40.

———. "Emotional Styles and Modern Forms of Life." In *Sexualized Brains: Scientific Modeling of Emotional Intelligence from a Cultural Perspective*, edited by Nicole Krafyllis and Gotlind Ulshöfer, 81–100. Cambridge, MA: MIT Press, 2008.

———. *The Making of Romantic Love: Longing and Sexuality in Europe, South Asia and Japan, 900–1200 CE*. Chicago: University of Chicago Press, 2012.

———. *The Navigation of Feelings: A Framework for the History of Emotions*. Cambridge: Cambridge University Press, 2001.

Reeves, Majorie. *Joachim of Fiore and the Prophetic Future*. London: SPCK, 1976.

Ricci, Lucia Battaglia. *Scrivere un libro di novelle: Giovanni Boccaccio autore, lettore, editore*. Ravenna, Italy: Longo, 2013.

———. "'Una novella per esempio': Novellistica, omiletica e trattatistica nel primo Trecento." *Studi sul Boccaccio* 28 (2000): 105–24.

Ricci, Roberta Vera. "The Beautiful Woman in the Arms of Hypnos: *Maritalis Affectio* as Happy Ending? (*Decameron* V,1)." *Rivista di Studi Italiani* 23 (2005): 35–50.

———. "Sex? Love? No, Let Us Talk about Marriage: Back to Reality with Boccaccio's Brigata (X,10)." In *Misogynism in Literature*, edited by Britta Zangen, 15–38. Frankfurt: Peter Lang, 2004.

Ricciardelli, Fabrizio. "The Emotional Language of Justice in Late Medieval Italy." In *Emotions, Passions and Power in Renaissance Italy: Proceedings of the International Conference Georgetown University at Villa Le Balze, 5–8 May 2012*, edited by Fabrizio Ricciardelli and Andrea Zorzi, 31–43. Amsterdam: Amsterdam University Press, 2015.

Richardson, Brian. "Editing Boccaccio in the Cinquecento." *Italian Studies* 45 (1990): 13–31.

———. "'For Instruction and Benefit': The Renaissance Boccaccio as Model of Language and Life." In *A Boccaccian Renaissance: Essays on the Early Modern Impact of Giovanni Boccaccio and His Works*, edited by Martin Eisner and David Lummus, 202–21. Notre Dame, IN: University of Notre Dame Press, 2019.

———. "The 'Ghibelline' Narrator in the *Decameron*." *Italian Studies* 33 (1978): 20–28.

———. "The Textual History of the *Decameron*." In *Boccaccio: A Critical Guide*, edited by Victoria Kirkham, Michael Sherberg, and Janet Levarie Smarr, 44–45. Chicago: University of Chicago Press, 2013.

Robertson, Elizabeth, and Jennifer Hahner, eds. *Medieval and Early Modern Devotional Objects in Global Perspective: Translations of the Sacred*. New York: Palgrave Macmillan, 2010.

Rochon, Andrè, ed. *Formes et significations de la "beffa" dans la littérature Italienne de la Renaissance.* Paris: Université de la Sorbonne Nouvelle, 1972.

Rocke, Michael. *Forbidden Friendships: Homosexuality and Male Culture in Renaissance Florence.* New York: Oxford University Press, 1996.

Ronchetti, Alessia. "Between *Filocolo* and *Filostrato:* Boccaccio's Authorial Doubles and the Question of *amore per diletto.*" *Italianist* 35 (2015): 318-33.

Rosenwein, Barbara, ed. *Anger's Past: The Social Use of Emotion in the Middle Ages.* Ithaca, NY: Cornell University Press, 1998.

———. *Emotional Communities in the Early Middle Ages.* Ithaca, NY: Cornell University Press, 2006.

———. *Generations of Feeling: A History of Emotions, 600–1700.* Cambridge: Cambridge University Press, 2016.

———. "The Place of Renaissance Italy in the History of Emotions." In *Emotions, Passions and Power in Renaissance Italy: Proceedings of the International Conference Georgetown University at Villa Le Balze, 5–8 May 2012*, edited by Fabrizio Ricciardelli and Andrea Zorzi, 15-29. Amsterdam: Amsterdam University Press, 2015.

———. "Problems and Methods in the History of Emotions." *Passions in Context: Journal of the History and Philosophy of Emotions* 1 (2010): 12-24.

———. "Worrying about Emotions in History." *The American Historical Review* 107 (2002): 821-45.

Rossi, Luciano. "Il cuore, mistico pasto d'amore: Dal 'lai Guirun' al *Decameron.*" *Studi provenzali e francesi* 82 (1983): 28-128.

———. "In luogo di sollazzo: I fabliaux del *Decameron.*" In *Leggiadre donne: Novella e racconto breve in Italia*, edited by Francesco Bruni, 13-27. Venice, Italy: Marsilio, 2000.

———. "Presenze ovidiane nel *Decameron.*" *Studi sul Boccaccio* 21 (1993): 125-37.

Rotunda, Dominic P. *Motif-Index of the Italian Novella in Prose.* New York: Haskell, 1973.

Rougemont, Denis de. *Love in the Western World.* Translated by Montgomery Belgion. New York: Fawcett, 1958. Originally published as *L'amour et l'Occident.* Paris: Plon, 1939.

Ruggiero, Guido. *Binding Passions: Tales of Magic, Marriage and Power at the End of the Renaissance.* New York: Oxford University Press, 1993.

———. *The Boundaries of Eros: Sex Crime and Sexuality in the Italian Renaissance.* New York: Oxford University Press, 1985.

———. "Deconstructing the Body, Constructing the Body Politic: Ritual Execution in the Renaissance." In *Riti e rituali nelle società medievali*, edited by Jacques Chiffoleau, Lauro Martines, and Agostino Paravicini Bagliani, 175-90. Spoleto, Italy: Centro Italiano di Studi sull'Alto Medioevo, 1994.

———. "Getting a Head in the Italian Renaissance." *Renaissance Quarterly* 67 (2014): 1165-90.

———. "Imagining Love, Lust, and *Virtù* in Boccaccio and the Italian Renaissance." In *Rituals of Politics and Culture in Early Modern Europe: Essays in Honour of Edward Muir*, edited by Mark Jurdjevic and Rolf Strøm-Olsen, 185–209. Toronto: Centre for Reformation and Renaissance Studies, 2016.

———. "The Lord Who Rejected Love, or The Griselda Story (X, 10) Considered Yet Again." In *Sex, Gender and Sexuality in Renaissance Italy*, edited by Jacqueline Murray and Nicholas Terpstra, 21–34. London: Routledge, 2019.

———. *Machiavelli in Love: Sex, Self, and Society in the Italian Renaissance*. Baltimore: Johns Hopkins University Press, 2007.

———. "Marriage, Love, Sex and Renaissance Civic Morality." In *Sexuality and Gender in Early Modern Europe: Institutions, Texts and Images*, edited by James Grantham Turner, 10–30. New York: Cambridge University Press, 1993.

———. "Mean Streets, Familiar Streets, or the Fat Woodcarver and the Masculine Spaces of Renaissance Florence." In *Renaissance Florence: A Social History*, edited by Roger J. Crum and John T. Paoletti, 295–311. Cambridge: Cambridge University Press, 2006.

———. *The Renaissance in Italy: A Social and Cultural History of the Rinascimento*. New York: Cambridge University Press, 2015.

———. *Violence in Early Renaissance Venice*. New Brunswick, NJ: Rutgers University Press, 1980.

———. "A Woman as Savior: Alibech and the Last Age of the Flesh in Boccaccio's *Decameron*." *Acta Histriae* 17, no. 1/2 (2009): 151–62.

Russell, James A. "Emotion, Core Affect, and Psychological Construction." *Cognition and Emotion* 23 (2009): 1259–83.

Russell, Jeffrey B. "Courtly Love as Religious Dissent." *Catholic Historical Review* 51 (1965): 31–44.

Russell, Sara Elizabeth Christina. "Courtship, Violence and the Formation of Marriage in the Early Modern Italian Novella Tradition." PhD diss., University of California, Berkeley, 2010.

Russo, Vittorio. "Perorazione d'amore da parte di donne e femmine nel *Decameron*." In *Con le muse in Parnaso: Tre studi su Boccaccio*, 89–108. Naples, Italy: Bibliopolis, 1983.

Sacchetti, Franco. *Il Trecentonovelle*. Edited by Valerio Marucci. Rome: Salerno Editrice, 1996.

Sapegno, Natalino, ed. *Poeti minori del Trecento*. In *La letteratura Italiana*. Milan: Riccardo Ricciardi Editore, 1952, vol. 10.

Sasso, Luigi. "L' 'interpretatio nominis' in Boccaccio." *Studi sul Boccaccio* 12 (1980): 129–74.

Scaglione, Aldo D. *Nature and Love in the Late Middle Ages*. Westport, CT: Greenwood Press, 1976. (Originally: Berkeley, CA: University of California Press, 1963.)

Schultz, James A. *Courtly Love, Love of Courtliness, and the History of Sexuality*. Chicago: University of Chicago Press, 2006.

Scott, Anne, and Cynthia Kosso, eds. *Fear and Its Representations in the Middle Ages and Renaissance*. Turnhout, Belgium: Brepols, 2002.

Sebastiano, Leonardo. "I 'mirabilia amoris' nella quarta giornata del *Decameron*." In *Studi in onore di Michele dell'Aquila*, vol. 1, Special Issue of *La Nuova Ricerca* 11 (2002): 85–116.

Segre, Cesare. *Lingua, stile, e società. Studi sulla storia della prosa italiana*. Milan, Italy: Feltrinelli, 1974.

——. "La novella di Nastagio degli Onesti (*Dec.* V, 8): I due tempi della visione." In *In ricordo di Cesare Angelini: Studi di letteratura e filologia*, edited by Franco Alessio and Angelo Stella, 65–74. Milan: Il Saggiatore, 1979.

Serafini-Sauli, Judith. "The Pleasures of Reading Boccaccio's *Decameron* and Female Literacy." *Modern Language Notes* 126 (2011): 29–46.

Sère, Bénédicte, and Jörg Wettlaufer, eds. *Shame: Between Punishment and Penance: The Social Uses of Shame in the Middle Ages and Early Modern Times*. Florence, Italy: Sismel, 2013.

Shemek, Deanna. "Doing and Undoing: Boccaccio's Feminism *(De Claris mulieribus, On Famous Women)*." In *Boccaccio: A Critical Guide to the Complete Works*, edited by Victoria Kirkham, Michael Sherberg, and Janet Levarie Smarr, 195–204. Chicago: University of Chicago Press, 2013.

——. *Ladies Errant: Wayward Women and Social Order in Early Modern Italy*. Durham, NC: Duke University Press, 1998.

Sherberg, Michael. "Bembo, Boccaccio, and the *Prose*." In *A Boccaccian Renaissance: Essays on the Early Modern Impact of Giovanni Boccaccio and His Works*, edited by Martin Eisner and David Lummus, 185–201. Notre Dame, IN: University of Notre Dame Press, 2019.

——. *The Governance of Friendship: Law and Gender in the* Decameron. Columbus: Ohio State University Press, 2011.

——. "The Patriarch's Pleasure and the Frame Tale Crisis: *Decameron* IV-V." *Romance Quarterly* 38 (1991): 227–38.

Sherberg, Michael, and Marc Schachter. "*Libido Sciendi*: Boccaccio, Apuleius, and the Study of the History of Sexuality." *Publications of the Modern Language Association* 124 (2009): 817–37.

Sinicropi, Giovanni. "Chastity and Love in the *Decameron*." In *The Olde Daunce: Sex and Marriage in the Medieval World*, edited by Robert R. Edwards and Stephen Spector, 104–20. New York: SUNY Press, 1991.

Siraisi, Nancy C. *Medicine and the Italian Universities, 1200–1600*. Leiden, Netherlands: Brill, 2001.

Smail, Daniel Lord. *The Consumption of Justice: Emotions, Publicity and Legal Culture in Marseille, 1264–1423*. Ithaca, NY: Cornell University Press, 2003.

——. "Debt, Humiliation, and Stress in Fourteenth-Century Lucca and Marseille." In *Emotions, Passions and Power in Renaissance Italy: Proceedings of the*

International Conference Georgetown University at Villa Le Balze, 5–8 May 2012, edited by Fabrizio Ricciardelli and Andrea Zorzi, 129–44. Amsterdam: Amsterdam University Press, 2015.

———. "Hatred as a Social Institution in Late-Medieval Society." *Speculum* 76 (2001): 90–126.

———. *On Deep History and the Brain*. Berkeley: University of California Press, 2008.

———. "Violence and Predation in Late Medieval Mediterranean Europe." *Comparative Studies in Society and History* 54 (2012): 1–28.

Smarr, Janet Levarie. *Boccaccio and Fiammetta: The Narrator as Lover*. Urbana: University of Illinois University Press, 1986.

———. "Other Races, Other Spaces: Boccaccio's Representation of non-European and non-Christian People and Places in the *Decameron*." *Studi sul Boccaccio* 27 (1999): 113–36.

———. "Ovid and Boccaccio: A Note on Self-Defense." *Mediaevalia* 13 (1987): 247–55.

———. "Rewriting One's Precursors: Notes on the *Decameron*." *Mediaevalia* 5 (1979): 163–76.

———. "Regendering Griselda on the London Stage." In *A Boccaccian Renaissance: Essays on the Early Modern Impact of Giovanni Boccaccio and His Works*, edited by Martin Eisner and David Lummus, 293–310. Notre Dame, IN: University of Notre Dame Press, 2019.

———. "Speaking Women: Three Decades of Authoritative Females." In *Boccaccio and Feminist Criticism*, edited by Thomas C. Stillinger and F. Regina Psaki, 29–38. Chapel Hill, NC: Annali d'Italianistica, 2006.

———. "Symmetry and Balance in the *Decameron*." *Medievalia* 2 (1976): 159–87.

Spani, Giovanni. "Il vino di Boccaccio: Usi e abusi in alcune novelle del *Decameron*." *Heliotropia* 8–9 (2011–2012): 79–98.

Squarotti, Giorgio Bárberi. "Amore e morte (non senza qualche vicenda di commedia)." In *Prospettive sul* Decameron, 59–83. Turin, Italy: Tirrenia stampatori, 1989.

———. *Il potere della parola. Studi sul* Decameron. Naples, Italy: Federico & Ardia, 1993.

Stearns, Peter N., and Carol Zisowitz Stearns. *Anger: The Struggle for Emotional Control in American History*. Chicago: University of Chicago Press, 1986.

———. "Emotionology: Clarifying the History of Emotions and Emotional Standards." *American Historical Review* 90 (1985): 813–36.

Steinberg, Justin. "Mimesis on Trial: Legal and Literary Verisimilitude in Boccaccio's *Decameron*." *Representations* 139 (2017): 118–45.

Steinberg, Leo. *The Sexuality of Christ in Renaissance Art and in Modern Oblivion*. New York: Random House, 1983.

Steinhoff, Judith. "Weeping Women: Social Roles and Images in Fourteenth-Century Tuscany." In *Crying in the Middle Ages: Tears of History*, edited by Elina Gertsman, 35–52. New York: Routledge, 2012.

Stillinger, Thomas C. "The Language of Gardens: Boccaccio's 'Valle delle Donne.'" In *Boccaccio and Feminist Criticism*, edited by Thomas C. Stillinger and F. Regina Psaki, 105–27. Chapel Hill, NC: Annali d'Italianistica, 2006. (*Annali d'Italianistica, Studi e testi*, vol. 8.)

Stillinger, Thomas C., and F. Regina Psaki, eds. *Boccaccio and Feminist Criticism*. Chapel Hill, NC: Annali d'Italianistica, 2006. (*Annali d'Italianistica, Studi e testi*, vol. 8.)

Stone, Gregory B. *The Ethics of Nature in the Middle Ages: On Boccaccio's Poetaphysics*. New York: St. Martin's Press, 1998.

Stoppino, Eleanora. "Contamination, Contagion and the Animal Function in Boccaccio's *Decameron*." *Critica del Testo* 17 (2014): 93–114.

Storey, Harry Wayne. "Parodic Structure in 'Alibech and Rustico': Antecedents and Traditions." *Canadian Journal of Italian Studies* 5 (1982): 163–76.

Strocchia, Sharon T. *Death and Ritual in Renaissance Florence*. Baltimore: Johns Hopkins University Press, 1992.

Suzuki, Mihoko. "Gender, Power, and the Female Reader: Boccaccio's *Decameron* and Marguerite de Navarre's *Heptameron*." *Comparative Literature Studies* 30 (1993): 231–52.

Tacconi, Marica. *Cathedral and Civic Ritual in Late Medieval and Renaissance Florence*. Cambridge: Cambridge University Press, 2006.

Talvacchia, Bette, ed. *A Cultural History of Sexuality in the Renaissance*. Oxford: Berg, 2011.

Tambling, Jeremy. *Dante in Purgatory: States of Affect*. Turnhout, Belgium: Brepols, 2010.

Tateo, Francesco. *Boccaccio*. Rome-Bari, Italy: Laterza, 1998.

Tenenti, Alberto. "La rappresentazione della morte collettiva nel *Decameron*." *Intersezioni* 12 (1992): 235–46.

Terpstra, Nicholas. *Abandoned Children of the Italian Renaissance: Orphan Care in Florence and Bologna*. Baltimore: Johns Hopkins University Press, 2005.

——, ed. *The Art of Executing Well: Rituals of Execution in Renaissance Italy*. Kirksville, MO: Truman State University Press, 2008.

Terzoli, Maria Antonietta. "La testa di Lorenzo: Lettura di *Decameron* IV, 5." *Nuova rivista di letteratura italiana* 4 (2001): 207–26.

Tetel, Marcel, Ronald G. Witt, and Valeria Finucci, eds. *Life and Death in Fifteenth-Century Florence*. Durham, NC: Duke University Press, 1989.

Thompson, Nicholas S. *Chaucer, Boccaccio and the Debate of Love: A Comparative Study of the* Decameron *and the* Canterbury Tales. Oxford: Oxford University Press, 1996.

Thrift, Nigel. *Non-Representational Theory: Space, Politics, Affect*. London: Routledge, 2008.

Tocco, Felice. "Guglielma Boema e i Guglielmiti." *Atti della Reale Accademia dei Lincei, classe di scienze morali, storiche e filologiche*, 5 Serie. 8 (Rome, 1900): 1–32.

———. "Il processo dei Guglielmiti." *Reale Accademia dei Lincei, memorie della classe di scienze morali, storiche e filologiche, Rendiconti*, 5 Serie. 8 (Rome, 1899): 309–42, 351–84, 407–32, 437–69.

Toce, Alessandra. "Dalle novelle orientali al *Decameron*." *Levia gravia* 2 (2000): 165–80.

Todorov, Tzvetan. *Grammaire du* Décaméron. The Hague: Mouton, 1969.

Toscan, Jean. *Le Carnaval du langage: Le Lexique èrotique des poètes de l'équivoque de Burchiello à Marino*. Lille, France: Atelier de reproduction des theses, Université de Lille, 1981, 4 vols.

Toscano, Antonio. "*Decameron*: Cimone's Metamorphosis." *Italian Quarterly* 29 (1988): 25–35.

Trinkhaus, Charles Edward. *Adversity's Nobleman: The Italian Humanists on Happiness*. New York: Octagon Books, 1965.

———. *In Our Image and Likeness: Humanity and Divinity in Italian Humanist Thought*. London: Constable, 1970, 2 vols.

Tufano, Ilaria. "Boccaccio e la letteratura religiosa: La Prima e la Seconda Giornata del *Decameron*." *Critica del Testo* 16 (2013): 185–207.

———. "'Qual esso fu lo malo cristiano': La canzone e la novella di Lisabetta (*Decameron*, IV.5)." *Critica del testo* 10 (2007): 225–39.

Turnbull, G. H., and M. Solms. "Awareness, Desire, and False Beliefs: Freud in the Light of Modern Neuropsychology." *Cortex* 43 (2007): 1083–90.

Tylus, Jane. "Petrarch's Griselda and the Sense of an Ending." In *Inventing a Path: Studies in Medieval Rhetoric in Honor of Mary Carruthers*, edited by Laura Iseppi, 391–420. Nottingham, UK: Nottingham Medieval Studies, 2013.

Usher, Jonathan. "Boccaccio's *Ars Moriendi* in the *Decameron*." *Modern Language Review* 81 (1986): 621–32.

———. "Frame and Novella Gardens in the *Decameron*." *Medium Aevum* 58 (1989): 279–85.

———. "Industria e acquisto erotico: La terza giornata." In *Introduzione al* Decameron, edited by Michelangelo Picone and Margarita Mesirca, 99–114. Florence, Italy: Cesati, 2004.

———. "Narrative and Descriptive Sequences in the Novella of Lisabetta and the Pot of Basil (*Decameron* IV, 5)." *Italian Studies* 38 (1983): 56–69.

Vacca, Diane Duyos. "Carnal Readings: On Interpretation, Violence and *Decameron* V.8." In *Boccaccio and Feminist Criticism*, edited by Thomas C. Stillinger and F. Regina Psaki, 167–87. Chapel Hill, NC: Annali d'Italianistica, 2006. (*Annali d'Italianistica, Studi e testi*, vol. 8.)

———. "Converting Alibech: 'Nunc spiritu copuleris.'" *Journal of Medieval and Renaissance Studies* 25 (1995): 207–27.

Van Bueren, Truus, and Andrea van Leerden, eds. *Care for the Here and the Hereafter: Memoria, Art and Ritual in the Middle Ages*. Turnhout, Belgium: Brepols, 2005.

Vasvári, Louise. "'Buon cavallo e mal cavallo vuole sprone, e buona femina e mala femina vuol bastone': Medieval Cultural Fictions of Wife-Battering." In *Discourses on Love, Marriage, and Transgression in Medieval and Early Modern Literature*, edited by Albrecht Classen, 313–36. Tempe: Arizona Center for Medieval and Renaissance Studies, 2004.

———. "The Story of Griselda as Silenced Incest Narrative." *La Corónica: A Journal of Medieval Hispanic Languages, Literatures, and Cultures* 35 (2007): 139–56.

———. "*L'usignuolo in gabbia:* Popular Tradition and Pornographic Parody in the *Decameron.*" *Forum Italicum* 28 (1994): 224–51.

Veglia, Marco. "Boccaccio '*lector in-fabula*' e le novelle del *Decameron.*" *Italianistica* 46 (2017): 15–27.

———. "Messer Decameron Galeotto. Un titolo e una chiave di lettura." *Heliotropia* 8–9 (2011): 99–112.

———. "Il Petrarca, la genesi del *Decameron* e la teologia poetica del Boccaccio." *Humanistica* 4 (2010): 61–78.

———. *La strada più impervia: Boccaccio fra Dante e Petrarca.* Rome: Antenore, 2014.

———. "*La vita lieta*": *Una lettura del* Decameron. Ravenna, Italy: Longo, 2000.

Velli, Giuseppe. "Seneca nel *Decameron.*" *Giornale storico della letteratura italiana* 168 (1991): 321–34.

Weaver, Elissa, ed. *The* Decameron *First Day in Perspective: Volume One of the Lecturae Boccaccii.* Toronto: University of Toronto Press, 2004.

Webb, Diana. *Patrons and Defenders: Saints in Italian City-States.* London: I. B. Tauris, 1996.

Webb, Heather. *The Medieval Heart.* New Haven, CT: Yale University Press, 2010.

Weissman, Ronald F. E. "The Importance of Being Ambiguous: Social Relations, Individualism and Identity in Renaissance Florence." In *Urban Life in the Renaissance*, edited by Susan Zimmermann and Ronald F. E. Weissman, 269–80. Newark: University of Delaware Press, 1989.

Wessley, Stephen. "The Thirteenth-Century Guglielmites: Salvation through Women." In *Medieval Women*, edited by Derek Baker, 289–303. Oxford: Blackwell, 1978.

Wickham, Chris. "*Fama* and the Law in Twelfth-Century Tuscany." In *Fama: The Politics of Talk and Reputation in Medieval Europe*, edited by Thelma Fenster and Daniel Lord Smail, 15–26. Ithaca, NY: Cornell University Press, 2003.

Wierzbicka, Anna. *Emotions across Languages and Cultures: Diversity and Universals.* Cambridge: Cambridge University Press, 1999.

Wilkins, Ernest H. *Studies on Petrarch and Boccaccio.* Padua, Italy: Antenore, 1978.

Witt, Ronald. *In the Footsteps of the Ancients: The Origin of Humanism from Lovato to Bruni.* Leiden, Netherlands: Brill, 2000.

Wofford, Susanne L. "The Social Aesthetics of Rape: Closural Violence in Boccaccio and Botticelli." In *Creative Imitations: New Essays in Renaissance*

Literature in Honor of Thomas H. Greene, edited by Thomas H. Greene and David Quint, 189–238. Binghamton: State University of New York, 1992.

Zaccarello, Michelangelo. "Il 'lieto fine' come cardine strutturale: La quinta giornata." In *Introduzione al Decameron*, edited by Michelangelo Picone and Margarita Mesirca, 141–61. Florence, Italy: F. Cesati, 2004.

Zaccaria, Vittorio. *Boccaccio narratore, storico, moralista e mitografo*. Florence, Italy: Olschki, 2001.

Zak, Gur. "Boccaccio and Petrarch." In *The Cambridge Companion to Boccaccio*, edited by Guyda Armstrong, Rhiannon Daniels, and Stephen J. Milner, 139–54. Cambridge: Cambridge University Press, 2015.

——. "'Umana cosa è aver compassione,' Boccaccio, Compassion, and the Ethics of Literature." *I Tatti Studies in the Italian Renaissance* 22, no. 1 (2019): 5–20.

Zorzi, Andrea. "The Anxiety of the Republics: 'Timor' in Italy of the Communes during the 1330s." In *Emotions, Passions and Power in Renaissance Italy: Proceedings of the International Conference Georgetown University at Villa Le Balze, 5–8 May 2012*, edited by Fabrizio Ricciardelli and Andrea Zorzi, 45–75. Amsterdam: Amsterdam University Press, 2015.

——. *L'amministrazione della giustizia penale nella Repubblica fiorentina. Aspetti e problemi*. Florence, Italy: Olschki, 1988.

——. "Rituali di violenza, cerimoniali penali, rappresentazioni della giustizia nelle città italiane centro-settentrionali (secoli XIII–XV)." In *Le forme della propaganda politica nel Due e nel Trecento*, edited by Paolo Cammarosano, 395–426. Rome: École française de Rome, 1994.

ACKNOWLEDGMENTS

It seems only fitting that I finally decided to write this book in the spring of 2012 in the hills above Florence as I walked through the Renaissance gardens of Villa I Tatti, where at the time I was once again enjoying its idyllic setting and great library working on several projects as the Lehman Senior Visiting Professor. For Boccaccio, of course, placed his *brigata* of ten storytellers in much the same idyllic location and in similar gardens to escape the plague and tell their one hundred tales. It would be even more fitting if I could claim that that was the actual beginning of the project and that the book grew out of that moment of inspiration that reevoked the tales as I walked along the trickle-that the Mensola has become and the rich blossoming scents of an early spring day. But, ironically, rather like the *Decameron* again, the book actually had been brewing over a long career and owed a great deal to a much wider range of institutions and most importantly a much larger group of people than the happy *brigata* of *studiosi* and friendly staff who graced the villa that springtime under the leadership of a true *signore* and *signoressa* of our days, Lino Pertile, director of the villa, and his consort, Anna Bensted.

Actually, however, one of this book's first beginnings was in the very first class I taught in the early 1970s as a visiting assistant professor at the University of Cincinnati, when, despite the fact that I was buried with the typical new class preparations of that first position, I foolishly promised an enthusiastic group of ninety students after a lively discussion of the *Decameron* that concluded that there was far more lust than love in its stories that I would provide a lecture in the next class that showed that love was actually their central concern. There followed a sleepless night and a rushed day of lecture writing in an attempt to pull that rabbit out of the hat, which resulted in an early form of the central discussion of transcendent love in Chapter 4. And, indeed, the lecture was so successful (and so necessary) that it has been a staple of my Renaissance classes ever since. Although I should admit in these bleak days of contested news claims that the current president of the American Historical Association, Mary Lindemann, who was in that first class and survived to have a very successful career nonetheless, recently assured me that she remembers not a word of that lecture.

Still, that disappointing little factual detail does not detract from the mythic quality of that much earlier start. And, as I reflected on the many, many people who needed to be thanked in these acknowledgments, it was clear that pride of place really had to go to the students like Mary who over the years since that first class have discussed with me with enthusiasm what the *Decameron* had to say about the world in which it was written and read. Not only have they, in what seems like their thousands, helped me to refine my ideas in classes, seminars, and lively discussions in the halls or walking across campus, they have played a critical role in pressing me to rethink and learn from them in dialogues that were virtually always engaged and exciting. Consistently they showed me how stimulating the *Decameron* was as a work to think with historically, at the University of Cincinnati, the University of Tennessee, Syracuse University in Florence, the University of Connecticut, the Pennsylvania State University, and finally the University of Miami as a peripatetic scholar who began his career when there were no jobs and nonetheless survived in large part thanks to the kind help he received along the way.

At each of those universities, colleagues and staff also played a role in creating an academic environment—often under severe financial constraints caused by the underfunding of the humanities and universities more generally—where I could pursue the research that built the historical foundations of this book. The same was true at the archives in Italy where I worked, especially the State Archives of Venice and Florence and the local archives of the Veneto and Tuscany, and at the institutes and libraries that hosted me over the years, including the Princeton Institute for Advanced Study, the American Academy in Rome, and once again Villa I Tatti. Grants and fellowships over the years also provided the support and the freedom to pursue my fascination with the *Decameron* and the broader historical world in which it was written and existed. Thus, thanks are also in order to the Guggenheim Foundation for a John Simon Guggenheim Memorial Fellowship, and a series of Taft Foundation and Research Council Grants from the University of Cincinnati, Delmas Foundation Fellowships from the Gladys Kreible Delmas Foundation, as well as two NEH Fellowships, an American Philosophical Society Fellowship, several Research Council Grants at the University of Connecticut, a number of Orovitz Fellowships at the University of Miami along with a Humanities Center Fellowship and becoming a College of Arts and Sciences Cooper Fellow there. Finally, being named the Josephine Berry Weiss Chair in the Humanities at the Pennsylvania State University provided me with much-appreciated and generous research support, support that was continued at the University of Miami as I served as chair and then as a regular faculty member there. Without this highly valued backing, this book and the other books that built toward it would simply not have been possible.

But because this small book in a way really does sum up that long career and because over that timespan from the early 1970s to the present I have published widely aspects of the research that this book utilizes, rather than reproducing my CV here with all the places where early forays of that research were published in bits and pieces in books and exploratory articles, I have cited them in each case in the notes where pertinent and would like to thank all for their permission to republish them usually in much revised form here. In that context, the publishers of my earlier books—all of which are relied on for this study—warrant a special thanks for taking the chance to publish books hopefully innovative and significant but always controversial: Cambridge University Press, Rutgers University Press, Johns Hopkins University Press, Blackwell, and Oxford University Press, along with now Harvard University Press and the I Tatti Studies Series, edited by Nicholas Terpstra, who encouraged this book at every stage of the way.

Still, so many people contributed to this book that just a sample of the names of the people who really made this all come together must be cited, with apologies to the many who are left out but still deeply appreciated. Colleagues, friends, and more, they include mentors Boyd Hill, Gerhardt Ladner, and Lauro Martines; historians and friends who taught me so much, James Amelang, Gene Brucker, William Caferro, Julia Calvi, Chris Celenza, Gaetano Cozzi, Natalie Zemon Davis, Konrad Eisenblickler, Nick Epstein, Jim Farr, Joanne Ferraro, Felix Gilbert, Christiane Klapische-Zuber, Catherine Kovesi, Michele Laughran,

John Marino, John Martin, Silvia Mitchell, Ed Muir, John Najemy, Claudio Povolo, Michael Rocke, and Kenneth Setton; historians of literature and art, again special friends and critical mentors, Albert Ascoli, Karen Barzman, Douglas Biow, Valeria Finucci, Martin Elsky, Mary Frank, Jessica Goethals, Julia Hairston, Deborah Howard, Ann Rosalyn Jones, Denis Looney, Suzanne Magnanini, Gerry Milligan, Frank Palmieri, John Paoletti, Alina Payne, Courtney Quaintance, Margaret Rosenthal, Deanna Shemek, Peter Stallybrass, Mihoko Suzuki, Bette Talvacchia, Jane Tylus, Elissa Weaver, and Linda Woodbridge; and colleagues and once more prized friends, first all my colleagues in the special history department we built at the University of Miami (especially Eduardo Elena, Mary Lindemann, Michael Miller, Donald Spivey, Hugh Thomas, and Ashli White) and then Richard Brown, Ronnie Pochai Hsia, Karen Kupperman, Robert Proctor, Matthew Restall, Sophie De Schaepdrijver, and Londa Schiebinger. Albert Ascoli, Jim Farr, Laura Giannetti, Mary Lindemann, Ed Muir, and Nicholas Terpstra read all or parts of the book at various stages of its gestation, and their suggestions and critiques were invaluable. The readers for Harvard University Press offered much-appreciated support and a few crucial suggestions. And although I would like to blame them all for the many questionable readings that remain, sadly they remain mine. Laura Giannetti, colleague, friend, partner, and much more deserves more than thanks for her mentoring and calm support through the turbulent waters of the years this book took to write. Without her understanding and support, it would not have happened. In almost every way, she was the inspiration for this book and its savior along with a character from the *Decameron* who has been with me from those distant early days of the 1970s when I first wrote that lecture dedicated to Alibech and love over lust. Thus, this book is dedicated to them both and their inspiration.

INDEX

Action: in novella tradition, 7–8, 95–96; *virtù* associated with, 102–103

Adam (biblical figure), 138, 142–143, 177, 203

Adultery: Boccaccio's self-revelation of views on, 7; sex with nuns as, 123, 236n4; shared cultural views on, 5, 7, 125, 186, 188; social class differences as motivation for, 46–48; true love in, 3, 5, 26–28, 32, 48, 53, 243n9

Agilulf (character), 149–156; honor of, 152–154, 167, 189; *virtù* of, 149, 154–156, 189

Albornoz, Egidio, 175

Alessandro (character), 48–52, 158, 164, 190

Alibech (character), 136–148; Eve compared to, 138, 142–143, 203–204; Griselda compared to, 252n67, 252n70; as hero vs. victim of tale, 240n46; implications for Christianity of tale of, 139–148, 200–205; meaning of name, 137, 239n37; move to desert, 136–137, 202; on putting the Devil back in Hell, 138–148, 201, 239n44; Rustico's explanation of Christianity to, 137–139, 200–202; as savior, 139, 144–148, 205, 252n67

Alice in Wonderland (Carroll), 2

Amore (god), 41–42, 49, 60, 228n22

Antichrist, 144–145

Anticlericalism, 123, 126, 136, 138, 200

Apocalypse, 1, 8–9, 204

Apostoli sect, 146, 241n52

Arabic language, 137, 239n37

Aristippus (character), 39

Arranged marriages: age of women in, 38, 179; of Gualtieri for himself, 160–165, 169, 198, 246–247nn29–30; honor in, 165; love distorting judgment as reason for, 38, 165, 188; in lower classes, 32; negative presentations of, 2, 27, 160–161, 179, 187–188, 248n38, 251n60; shared cultural views on, 5, 179, 187–188

Artisans: guilds of, 15, 17; love and, 32, 44, 47, 57–59; status of, 4, 18, 22, 30–32, 54, 173; *virtù* of, 21, 59, 92, 220n65

Artists, in social order, 18, 30, 54, 58–59, 220n65

Ascoli, Albert, 251n62

Audience, of *Decameron*: northern European, 208n3; shared culture of, 4–11

Augustine (saint), 139–141, 144

Badoer, Elisabetta, 233n45

Badoer family, 233n45

Bandello, Matteo, 244n17

Banking: Boccaccio's work in, 21, 218n37; in England, 48–49, 158; in Florence, 15, 218n37, 245n23

Bardi bank, 218n37

Barolini, Teodolinda, 244n18, 245n19, 247n30

A
ROSE
BY ANY
OTHER
NAME

Praise for
THE BOOK OF GOTHEL

"Smart, swift, sure-footed, and fleet winged, *The Book of Gothel* launches its magic from a most reliable source: the troubled heart. Mary McMyne is a magician. Her take on the Rapunzel tale glows like a cloisonné gem set against a fist of dark soapstone."

—Gregory Maguire, *New York Times*
bestselling author of *Wicked*

"Both gently and fiercely told, *The Book of Gothel* is a sweeping, sharp story of how history twists into fairy tale and back again."

—Hannah Whitten, *New York Times*
bestselling author of *For the Wolf*

"*The Book of Gothel* is wonderfully rich with historical detail, and sparkles with the intermingled magic of gods and goddesses, seers and wisewomen. Haelewise is a memorable heroine, worthy of legend. Readers will see the story of Rapunzel in a new and refreshing light."

—Louisa Morgan, author of
A Secret History of Witches

"McMyne's shimmering debut gives a fresh, exciting backstory to one of the most famous villains in fairy tale lore: the witch who put Rapunzel in her tower....The result is a sprawling epic, full of magic, love, and heartbreak. Fans of *Circe* and *The Wolf and the Woodsman* will devour this taut, empowering fairy tale."

—*Publishers Weekly* (starred review)